This book is based on the three-part option studio
"Common Frameworks: Rethinking the Developmental
City" held at the Harvard University Graduate School of
Design in 2012, 2013, and 2014. City analysis and design
projects are the work of Harvard GSD graduate students.

HARVARD DESIGN STUDIES

**Harvard University
Graduate School of Design**

Common Frameworks

Christopher C. M. Lee (ed.)

Rethinking the Developmental City in China

The Megaplot

ESSAYS

ANALYSIS

PROJECTS

Cross-Border City

The Countryside as a City

Foreword

Cities in China are in a state of transition. An extreme increase in population has been matched by a rapid rate of urbanization, with increasing numbers of people moving from the countryside to cities, where there are greater opportunities for economic, social, and cultural development. The desire for progress and for a better quality of life is noticeable across the nation. And yet, it is not so clear that the means of achieving a better life are consistent with the creation of better environments.

We have learned from the typical developmental city in China the consequences of relentless, homogeneous developments that result in the extension of the city into larger and larger "ring roads." This type of development and its financial benefits have led to more cars, phenomenal traffic jams, and unprecedented levels of pollution. Our knowledge and capacities related to the procedures and methods of urbanization have been incapable of coping with such developments. Are developmental cities in China beyond saving, or is there something that can still be done? What can we learn from the current patterns of urban development that can contribute to those yet to be imagined in the future?

This book is a case study of three conditions in the context of three very different Chinese settings. The idea for this initiative grew out of a series of conversations between faculty members at the Harvard Graduate School of Design and Sean Chiao, currently the president of Asia Pacific at AECOM, and some of his colleagues. We decided at the beginning to consider a large number of locations, each with a set of specific challenges, and then through a process of analysis and deliberation chose Xiamen, Macau, and Taiqian. What was important in our investigation was not only the geographic, economic, and political context of each area but the opportunities it provided for design inquiry.

Professor Christopher C. M. Lee conducted this three-year cycle of research studios in collaboration with teaching associate Simon Whittle and with the participation of an exceptional group of graduate students. Their research and projects provide innovative concepts in response to the themes of the megaplot, the cross-border city, and the countryside as a city. For each theme and each site, the team identified and creatively revisited a prevalent urban condition. In the city of Xiamen, site of the first graduate studio, the selling of large plots of land to developers is a common practice. These developments produce "megascale" private projects sanctioned by public bodies. What are the alternatives to this tendency, and what shape might they take? How will the relationship between private and public development be reframed to best benefit the citizens of Xiamen? What role does landscape play in the formation of new types of public space? These are only some of the questions asked by the studio, which continued on to the border city of Macau and the new agricultural town of Taiqian.

What is critical about the outcome of this three-year cycle of investigations is the manner in which the GSD has utilized a set of specific, real-world conditions of practice as the basis for speculative design thinking. Equally important in this process is the question of method. Rather than using diverse representational techniques, the studio projects demonstrate the application of a consistent and visually coherent mode of addressing the three subject areas.

The systematic persistence of the approach together with the technical, local, and cultural knowledge and guidance of our colleagues at AECOM has made this body of work an exemplary contribution to the future practice of urban design.

Mohsen Mostafavi

Preface

It is not uncommon for practitioners and researchers who have encountered China after its market liberalization in the early 1980s to be mesmerized by its dazzling scale and the equally dazzling speed of its urbanization. The rapid pace of development renders any critical reflection or attempts to document and understand the transformation in a wider cultural and historical context impractical if not onerous. Perhaps it is not surprising that, in a symposium held in Shanghai in 2012 to inaugurate the Harvard GSD AECOM Project on China, a Chinese city planner declared that architecture is, at present, unable to shape the fate of the city. This reflected his frustration at the impotence of architecture but also offered an insight into the way cities in China are realized today. They are developmental cities—cities that are developed for excessive profit. Architecture arises from this demand and must conform to this regime. But four years is a long time for such a view to hold sway given the rate of change to which the city's politics, economy, and environment are subjected. Indeed as our engagement with China progressed, its economy slowed and the certainties of "build it and they'll come" or "design it and they'll buy" began to ring hollow. Calls for more balanced development emanated from on high.

This book documents the outcome of our three-year effort to understand, critique, and propose alternatives to the developmental city in China. The Project on China is a research and design project premised on two fundamental ambitions: to recuperate an idea of the city and to pursue alternative forms of urbanization in response to the challenges posed by the developmental city. The former treats the project of the city as a cultural, political, and aesthetic act; the latter views the city as a site for urbanization, articulated through architecture, landscape, and infrastructure. This endeavor is analytical and propositional in equal measure.

Each year, the Project on China focuses on a theoretical problem and practical challenge posed by the model of the developmental city in China, using a particular city as an exemplar. The first year centers on the problem of the megaplot, the basic planning unit for rapid and speculative urbanization, using Xiamen as a case study. The second year investigates the challenges faced by cities in city-regions and the effects of cross-border urbanization, with Macau as the paradigm. The third year examines the status of the countryside in the context of state-driven initiatives to urbanize rural areas, with a focus on existing villages and in-progress new agricultural towns in Zhongmu County. The choice of cities and themes is by necessity not definitive and not complete, for the developmental city poses many more challenges than can be addressed comprehensively here.

This book, presented in three independent but related parts, brings together design projects from three sixteen-week studios with research and writings on cultural, political, and historical aspects of the megaplot, the cross-border city, and the countryside. It presents a critical reflection on the developmental city, making no attempt to sustain the status quo. In proposing several alternatives for the future development of cities in China, the book is informed by a reading of the architecture of the city and articulated through an architecture envisioned as a common framework for the city. Its implicit ambition is to bring about a city that is plural and equitable.

This endeavor would not have been possible without the leadership and vision of Mohsen Mostafavi and the generous support of AECOM. I would like to express my gratitude to Sean Chiao, Nancy Liu, Hung-Chih Liu, Han Hsi Ho, Guy Perry, and Kamiena Wong for their enthusiasm and camaraderie and to Rahul Mehrotra, Peter G. Rowe, and Charles Waldheim for their intellectual generosity.

I offer my heartfelt thanks to colleagues and collaborators in the three cities we visited. In Xiamen, the Xiamen Planning Bureau, especially Director Zhao Yanjing, provided assistance and support. In Macau, Lao Long of the Land, Public Works, and Transport Bureau of Macau SAR assisted us in our research; Thomas Daniell, Rui Leão, and Nuno Soares hosted us; and Francisco Vizeu Pinheiro of the University of St. Joseph in Macau was an invaluable guide. The Macau Urban Planning Institute, especially Natalie Hon and Kamiena Wong, offered assistance and support. In the countryside, my deep appreciation to Li He and Dangfeng Zheng from Zhengzhou Architectural Design Institute for assisting us with our research, and to Qindong Liang, Sandy Wang, and Yi Lee for their generous insights. Gang Liu, Benju Bai, and Xia Chen from Yellow River Engineering Consulting Co. Ltd. scoured the vast area surrounding Zhengzhou for potential sites and partners.

A special thanks to Beth Kramer, Ben Prosky, Jennifer Sigler, and Meghan Sandberg at the Harvard GSD; Sam de Groot; and Rebecca McNamara. I am grateful to our consulting editor, Andrea Monfried, whose precision, rigor, and patience never cease to amaze me.

My deep appreciation and thanks to Ling Fan, Piper Gaubatz, Har Ye Kan, Dingliang Yang, Peter Rowe, Jianfei Zhu, and all the students for their contributions to the research. I have benefited much from the knowledge, intelligence, and wisdom of my colleagues at the Harvard GSD and invited external critics: Iñaki Ábalos, Leire Asensio-Villoria, Dana Behrman, Ben van Berkel, Eve Blau, Sean Chiao, Felipe Correa, Ling Fan, Eric Höweler, Florian Idenburg, Linxue Li, Nancy Lin, Jing Liu, David Mah, Rahul Mehrotra, Mohsen Mostafavi, Carles Muro, Joan Ockman, Guy Perry, Albert Pope, Charles Redmon, Moshe Safdie, Hashim Sarkis, Renata Sentkiewicz, Jorge Silvetti, Nick R. Smith, Spela Videcnik, Paola Viganò, Charles Waldheim, Bing Wang, Zhao Yanjing, and Tao Zhu. Last, my deep-felt thanks to Simon Whittle, my teaching associate, for his intelligence, tenacity, and artistry.

Christopher C. M. Lee

Introduction: Common Frameworks

At the heart of China's recent excess urbanization is the model of the developmental city. If the root of urbanization in the 19th century was the expansion of cities in the West in response to housing demands, the growth of the developmental city follows an imagined demand for real estate—an urbanization of pure speculation conjured by professional place makers including architects, urban designers, planners, developers, and advertisers. This model appeared to work well for China, especially with the market liberalization of the late 1970s. Because its industries and service sectors were poorly developed, the state put to use its most abundant asset—state-owned urban land. The land was divided into large plots and sold to developers, minimizing the burden of infrastructure provision by the state. Since the developmental city relies on market speculation as its modus operandi, it requires that planning strategies and parameters avoid restrictions or political resistance in order to attract developers and financiers; these strategies are often legitimized as "rational planning" or the "scientific method"—euphemisms for a resistance-free utilitarianism.

The architectural and spatial output of the developmental city has by now become evident—isolated, oversized plots surrounded by highways; monotonous, unrelenting, and cheaply built towers; colossal and impenetrable shopping podiums; lifeless, windswept ground planes. Overurbanization in China is also exerting environmental stresses, creating a burden for present and future generations. Many densely built new cities and townships remain underpopulated, with apartments and offices standing empty. This form of speculative urbanization squanders precious resources; taxpayers and savers, via state write-offs, bear the final brunt.

This phenomenon is not unique to cities and their immediate peri-urban areas. The same model, with the same political and economic logic, affects city centers, expanded urban territory, townships, and even villages. Farther afield, the same impulse is carried to the borders between administrative territories, taking an exacerbation of difference as a methodology for urbanization. Following the long reach and varied mutations of the developmental city model, the research and design propositions of the Harvard GSD AECOM Project on China address the territories of the center, the border, and the countryside. Framed by the specific challenges posed by the developmental city, the three studios are critical of its pervasive logic and strive for meaningful alternatives that nevertheless acknowledge that design and strategic urban propositions must be rooted in the realities of practice.

Of equal importance is the understanding and revalidation of the idea of the city itself. Cities are not exclusively engines of economic growth. The city at its most rarefied is an artifact of civilization made up of architecture, infrastructure, and landscape. It is the outcome of the cultural, political, social, and aesthetic achievements of its citizens. It reflects the moral and ethical values of the land, that is, the way its inhabitants live and the way they want to live. The city is a space of coexistence par excellence and, at its best, a space for the common good. Thus, the hyperspeculative and excessive nature of Chinese urbanization is not an inevitability, a fact beyond the influence of a discursive collective will.

The determination of sites and themes for the Project on China reflects these concerns. Each of the three choices identifies both a practical challenge and a theoretical problem, combining consideration of the pressures and processes that affect the production of contemporary urban developments and the potential of reconstituting the internal discourses of architecture and urbanism that are tied to these challenges. The three segments presented here reflect this endeavor. "The Megaplot" delves into the most common planning tool for urban developments in China. This oversized plot, an efficient planning apparatus that allows the government to urbanize quickly, varies between four hectares in urban areas and forty hectares in city peripheries. The outcome of this laissez-faire planning mechanism is the sea of enclave urbanization that carpets the cities of China. Megaplot developments do not constitute any idea of the city, either as a space of partnership or coexistence in the European tradition or as an administrative framework with a clear and legible deep structure in the Chinese sense.

From the city center we moved to the border. "Cross-Border City," using Macau as a case study, exposes the developmental city at its worst. Macau has made a Faustian bargain with the casinos. As Francisco Vizeu Pinheiro, my affable guide, once quipped, "Macau is not a city with casinos; it is a casino with a city." Of city planning, he says, the motto is "No plan is the best plan." His light-hearted remarks sum up the challenges that face Macau: the city is both addicted to and beholden to the gambling industry; a hands-off approach to planning sustains the developmental appetite of the city's largest economic generator. It appears that there are no lessons here, no salvation in this city.

But beyond the hypnotic lights of the casinos it quickly becomes apparent that these exaggerated developmental identities are the symptoms of a typical cross-border city, that is, one that defines itself against another. The tendency for cross-border cities is to exploit comparative differences to gain developmental advantages. The border that separates cities with opposing political and economic systems underpins the very nature of this developmental city. Spaces along the border and within the borderlands are urbanizing rapidly and intensively. This is apparent not only at the borders between China and its various special administrative regions but between the United States and Mexico and between Malaysia and Singapore. The plague of casinos is a specific indication of the more general problem of the border city.

From the city to the border and then from the border to the countryside. When we first embarked on the Project on China, the plan to end with the countryside appeared altogether counterintuitive. At the time, the action, so to say, was in first- and second-tier cities. It was unthinkable for architects and urban designers to ignore these areas, let alone challenge the trinity of speed, quantity, and density of China's unstoppable urbanization. But much has happened since 2012. Economic growth in the country has slowed from double digits to 7 percent, and China's cities are bloated with a glut of real estate. Shortly after assuming his position as China's president in 2012, Xi Jinping visited the small village of Liangjiahe—to which he had been banished as a fifteen-year-old during the Cultural Revolution—to cast himself as a man of the people. This is a stark contrast to Deng Xiaoping's famous southern tour of 1992. The leader visited Guangzhou, Shenzhen, Zhuhai, and Shanghai, cities that were to spearhead his promarket reforms. In 2014, strikingly, Xi declared an end to "weird" architecture in China, taking weirdness as a symptom of excess. Together with the sputtering economy, it is becoming apparent that hyperdense cities and their exotic architecture are no longer forgone conclusions; that they are less the outcome of need than of greed; and that their projections are mere speculations.

So it is an opportune time to end with the countryside in "The Countryside as a City." In addition to the efforts focused on the transformation of rural China and the improved standard of living for rural residents on the part of Premier Li Keqiang's administration, the Chinese countryside has always held a special political, cultural, and social place as the source of "Chineseness," the wellspring of renewal and revolution. Our efforts were twofold: first, to narrow, through design, the rural-urban divide in China, a divide precipitated in the era of Mao and maintained since; second, to conceptually dissolve the distinctions between rural and urban, city and countryside, and architecture and landscape by reinvigorating the Chinese philosophical concept of polarism. In other words, we made an audacious attempt to rethink the city *without* speed, quantity, and density.

The urban strategies and design propositions across the three themes and sites are based on a typological approach to the problem of the city. This is both an ontological and an epistemological endeavor, for the investigation into and redefinition of the city reveal its persistent architectures, or dominant types. Any attempt to define type is an attempt to define what is typical; what is most typical is common to all. Thus, type is an effective heuristic device through which to locate commonalities, both abstract and concrete. The goal of a search for what is common in architecture is not formal or tectonic likeness but instead commonly held ideas that invest architecture with a social and political role.

The renewed understanding of the concept of type and the idea of the city is, in part, a revalidation conducted through the traditions of city making and philosophical concepts of the ancient Chinese, cultural constructs that still persist today. This understanding offers a conception of an architecture of the city that embodies the qualities of the space of plural coexistence, that is, an architecture that allows true difference to exist yet maintains a legible, coherent, and recognizable whole. As a common framework, it accommodates the plurality of city life and is in constant alternation with the natural environment. A singular discursive idea, it is realized through addition and accumulation and at multiple scales.

Beyond its status as a potential urban artifact, emblematic of the collective life of the city, this framework of recognition is an important regulator of urban change. It owes this function to the pliability of its deep structure, or irreducible typological structure. The deep structure is weathered by use and time and bears the traces of both daily life and exceptional events. More important, it might organize new program while maintaining a precise spatial arrangement. For instance, the walled courtyard of Beijing can be used equally effectually as a family dwelling, a temple, or an imperial residence. What the courtyard lacks in programmatic specificity is com-pensated for by its organizational precision.

The deep structure, acting as a common framework, is thus not only an administrative tool for the management of the imperial city but also an embodiment of the collective culture that underwrites Chinese social relations. Transparent to function, the deep structure inherently becomes a projective element that can accommodate new uses and bear the potential for programmatic transformation. Seen in this way, the common framework is neither an inert artifact nor an architectural style. It is rather a grammar for architectural and urban transformation, adaptation, and accommodation. Additions and insertions within the city, at the border, and in the countryside are often met with resistance when their scale, typological structure, and speed of change are incongruous with the persistent structures of the city. Therefore, by drawing upon the deep structure of the typical elements of the city, the common framework forges a recognizable, and valuable, link to the immediate past. Establishing this continuity adjusts the rate of urban transformation to one that is more tolerable.

As a whole, the investigations and propositions of the Project on China do not pretend to bring immediate and complete change to the forces that drive the country's urbanization. What they hope to achieve, first, is to understand this form of urbanization, not in gawking awe or Orientalist condescension but in recognition that the developmental city model has roots deep in Chinese history and tradition. The inquiries then seek to offer plausible alternatives, not as blueprints for instant implementation but as typological and strategic ideas for adaptation and further alterations. Finally, the work assumes a position against, on one hand, a belief in the determinism and absolute authority of so-called scientific planning and economic development and, on the other, the defeatism of the profession when it adopts the role of disinterested architect and urbanist, of neutral observer and drive-by reporter who accepts everything and offers nothing. In sum, our efforts aim at conceiving a project for the city from an understanding of the city itself, from its shortcomings and its strengths, and always through its architecture. And when architecture can offer an alternative model, one that is not subservient to the status quo, that architecture can renew its cultural, political, and social relevance in the wider milieu of its operations.

Christopher C. M. Lee

The Megaplot

The City as a Common Framework

Rethinking the Developmental City in China

Christopher C. M. Lee

Fig. 1　Shanghai, the developmental city, c. 2012.

The contemporary Chinese city is a developmental city (fig. 1). In the developmental city, the political legitimacy of the governing party is sustained by, above all other considerations, its ability to initiate, promote, and administer economic growth. The developmental city relies on market speculation as its modus operandi; it requires that planning strategies and parameters have minimal developmental restriction or political resistance in order to attract developers and financiers; and it is often legitimized as "rational planning" or the "scientific method"—euphemisms for a resistance-free utilitarianism.

The developmental city uses the megaplot as a basic planning module. This oversized tract can vary greatly in size between urban areas and the peripheries of the city. It is an efficient planning apparatus that allows the government to urbanize rapidly by shifting to developers the investment required for infrastructure. The state is responsible only for widely spaced infrastructure; the developer must provide infrastructure and public goods within the plot.

The basic parcel of a master plan, the megaplot is represented by a colored patch indicating use. The lack of architectural and spatial attributes promotes efficiency in planning and land transactions. The megaplot is a tabula rasa, a condition that is favored by speculative developers for the speed and freedom of development it offers. Within the megaplots, buildings are regulated by planning parameters that result in either freestanding towers in large, unconsolidated open spaces or colossal superblock housing developments, gated luxury communities or, in the cheaper version, unrelenting rubber-stamped blocks. The urbanization of these megaplots results in the dissolution of the city as a legible artifact; the civic dimension and public sphere play no part. This sea of speculative enclaves does not constitute any idea of the city, either in the European tradition, as a space of coexistence, or in the Chinese sense, as an administrative framework with a clear and legible deep structure. What is lost is the idea of the city as a common space par excellence.

This essay argues that a critical reading of the history and tradition of city making in China has the potential to counter this imbalance in development. It does not aspire to a re-creation of the city form or urban fabric of ancient China. Rather, it proposes a recuperation of the cultural and philosophical ideas that have underpinned the political, artistic, and aesthetic production of the city as a total work of art—a collective artifact.

1

In 1992, Manuel Castells referred to Singapore as a developmental city-state. He claimed that "a state is developmental when it establishes as its principle of legitimacy its ability to promote and sustain development, understanding by development the combination of steady high rates of economic growth and structural change in the productive system, both domestically and in its relationship to the international economy."[1] Singapore, he argued, is achieving its impressive economic success because the government exercises tight control of society and also because the population accepts such measures. The developmental city-state is driven by two important ideas. First, the state prioritizes the transformation of economic conditions above everything else. Second, economic development is elevated to a high status both due to its larger goals and as an end in itself. Singapore is ruled by a one-party system with a highly centralized decision-making structure that micromanages all aspects of economic and social development. This structure takes the view that the city is an apparatus for development as well as a demonstration of the state's ability to deliver tangible improvements to the lives of its citizens. A city conceived through this ideology is always in a state of becoming; continually remolded according to a political agenda, the city is made suitable and adaptive for capital accumulation following the economic logic of neoliberalism. As Rem Koolhaas declared in 1995, this developmental model is being implemented in cities across China.[2]

J. C. Oi has argued that this concept of the developmental state was attractive to the Chinese government, but with one crucial difference: "The state responsible for much of this growth [in rural industry] is *local* governments that treat enterprises within their administrative

purview as one component of a larger corporate whole. Local officials act as the equivalent of a board of directors and sometimes more directly as the chief executive officers. At the helm of this corporate-like organization is the Communist Party secretary."[3] In China, the developmental state, or local government, was an outcome of the economic liberalization of 1979, in which the transformation and development of the city was central to China's transition from a planned to a more market-oriented economy. As noted by Fulong Wu, Jiang Xu, and Anthony Gar-On Yeh, this transition can be summarized as one "from state-led extensive industrialization to urban-based intensive urbanization."[4] Given that land is owned by the state or collectively and that the state is unable to address the infrastructural shortage, the government opted for extracting rent from state-owned land. With the land and housing reform that followed,[5] urban spaces were put to work, commodified through land-leasing that turned housing into real estate. This ideological flip did not diminish the power of the state but represented a shift from the state defending "proletariat ideology" to promoting "economic rationality."

Eager to attract foreign direct investment, local governments began adopting the methods of global-oriented production, thereby turning urbanization into a tool for economic growth. Urbanization was no longer reactive to demands for housing the proletariat, as in Britain and Europe in the mid-19th century. It was now predictive, in the form of speculative real estate. The Socialist city, which emphasized production in both function and symbolic representation, had been reconceptualized as the developmental city. To capture the flow of capital in the city, the state increased the level of urbanization and allowed rural-to-urban migration. Rural counties are subject to the leadership of the city; the city's resources are extracted for speculative profit.

An urbanization process that offers the least resistance to capital, encourages speed in its realization, and absolves the state from the provision of public goods found its physical model in the megaplot. The 1989 City Planning Act vested in local government the right to regulate development and authorized it to prepare tiered plans for development. At the apex of this process is the master plan, a document accompanied by a series of maps that outlines the designated functions of a city, its

1   Manuel Castells, "Four Asian Tigers with a Dragon Head: A Comparative Analysis of the State, Economy, and Society in the Asian Pacific Rim," in *States and Development in the Asian Pacific Rim*, ed. Richard P. Appelbaum and Jeffrey Henderson (Newbury Park, CA: Sage, 1992).

2   Rem Koolhaas, "Singapore Songlines," in *S,M,L,XL: Small, Medium, Large, Extra-Large* (New York: Monacelli Press, 1995), 1,009–89.

3   J. C. Oi, "The Role of the Local State in China's Transitional Economy," *China Quarterly* no. 144 (Dec. 1995), 1,132–49, quoted in Fulong Wu, Jiang Xu, and Anthony Gar-On Yeh, *Urban Development in Post-Reform China: State, Market, and Space* (London: Routledge, 2007), 11–12. Bracketed text and italics appeared in Wu et al.

4   Wu, Xu, and Yeh, *Urban Development*, 5.

5   There are two primary land markets in China—one used by the state to allocate urban land, one used by rural collectives to allocate collectively owned land. Land reform can generally be divided into three stages. From 1979 to 1986, coastal cities tested the paid use of urban land. From 1987 to 1997, land experiments were legalized in the constitution. From 1998 onward, the central government on numerous occasions restricted local governments from allocating land to cool down the overheated market. Wu, Xu, and Yeh, *Urban Development*, 28.

Fig. 4   Housing development on typical megaplot, c. 2011.

Fig. 2   Typical master plan, with colored patches indicating land use, c. 2008.

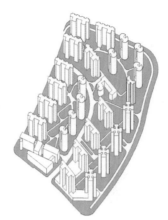

Fig. 3   Typical megaplot.

development goals, target size, and general land-use structure. Guiding the growth of a city over 20 years, it is essentially a general perspective of the prospective city.[6] Once approved, the master plan becomes a statutory plan. The document represents the city as patches of color, each one designating the land use for a developmental plot, or megaplot (fig. 2). These parcels are necessarily large, ranging from approximately 4 hectares in city centers to 40 hectares in its peripheries, and are surrounded by oversized arterial roads. The responsibility for secondary roads, along with other public goods, is transferred to the developer. These planning trade-offs are often negotiated between local government and developers rather than legislated; flexibility makes investment more attractive and development of the megaplots more likely. However, more often than not, the delivery of public goods is delayed (sometimes indefinitely) because it is an expense that generates no profit for the developer.

The architecture of the megaplot can be divided into two categories—the norm and the exception. The former is architecture at its most efficient, a product of pure real estate logic that maximizes the number of units or the amount of floor area allowable on a plot with the lowest construction cost alongside an image sufficiently tolerable for purchase. Buildings are usually monotonous residential towers or slab blocks with remedial landscape beautification inserted into the leftover spaces on the ground. The form of these high-rises results entirely from the extrusion of the plans of the most salable apartment. The uniformity and pervasiveness of this architecture are the outcome of the pure marketization of urbanization and its generic planning parameters and developmental controls (fig. 4).

The architecture on a typical megaplot (fig. 3) is generated by a procedure that starts with defining the plot boundaries. Regulations prescribe a 30-meter setback from major roads and a 15-meter setback from minor roads. Infrastructure within the megaplot, implemented by the developer, often incorporates a redundant perimeter road for local access, exacerbating the disconnection between the megaplot and its neighbors. Buildings are placed within the site according to spacing regulations.

6   The 1989 City Planning Act employs a five-tiered planning structure, involving the national people's congresses, State Council, Ministry of Construction, local people's congresses, and local government. The act stipulates the comprehensive function of urban planning: defining the size, economic orientation, and structure of the city; preparing a "rational" city plan; carrying out construction; determining size. See Wu, Xu, and Yeh, *Urban Development*, 164–65.

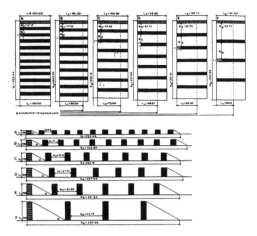

Fig. 5   Walter Gropius, diagrams illustrating parallel rows of tenement blocks of different heights on a rectangular site, 1925.

Fig. 6   HOK, Liang Ann Financial District, Xiamen, 2012: the architecture of exception in the megaplot.

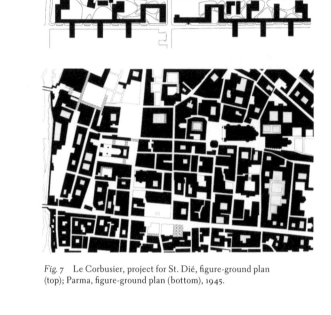

Fig. 7   Le Corbusier, project for St. Dié, figure-ground plan (top); Parma, figure-ground plan (bottom), 1945.

When the buildings are positioned in a north-south orientation, the spacing is equal to their height; the typical height limit for a residential tower is approximately 50 meters. Within this limit, height is dictated by parameters derived from the desired floor area ratio. The building footprint is further controlled by coverage and green area ratio. The implementation of the planning parameters and its regulations can lead to only one outcome: a Corbusian city of towers in a field.

The city of towers, a model developed in the 1920s, accepts standardization and utilitarianism as the sole architectural strategies that can be used to design new habitable spaces. A diagram prepared by Walter Gropius clearly shows the "scientific method" for solving housing problems, which is much like a mathematical puzzle; this formula can be implemented in any number of places (fig. 5). This method was discredited, mainly in the 1960s

and 1970s, for its indifference to the heterogeneity of urban life. Its most devastating critique came from Colin Rowe.[7] Rowe used figure-ground plans to emphasize the striking contrast between the building figure in typical modernist architecture and that in a historic European city (fig. 7). Comparing Le Corbusier's St. Dié and the Italian city of Parma, Rowe argued that in the former, the buildings are the figures, spaced apart as markers. In Parma, the void is the figure; tightly spaced buildings are space definers. Rowe believed that the Corbusian city laundered the ground plane of its textural richness while the urban spaces of Parma, defined by the city's architecture, expand and contract, creating friction and containment for the urban encounters so crucial to social intercourse.

In cases where the megaplot is utilized to serve up an alluring image of the city, the architecture is designed

7   Colin Rowe and Fred Koetter, *Collage City* (Cambridge, MA: MIT Press, 1978), 50–85.

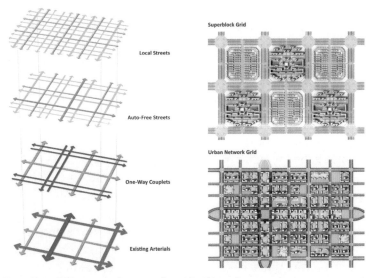

Fig. 8   Peter Calthorpe, transformation of arterial grid into urban network, 2012.

as the exception, not the norm. Local governments, usually the city planning bureaus, engage urban design consultants to make a development attractive and unique.[8] Once the designs have been accepted by the local government, the urban plan is subjected to the planning parameters and color patches of the master plan, but in a way that is calibrated to encourage the intended outcome. The central business district—an oxymoron—is the most common example of this exception in China. In a CBD, the form of an office tower is anything but the pure extrusion of a plan (fig. 6). Instead, the high-rise—never less than 30 stories—tapers, chamfers, folds, bends, twists, and contorts. Exterior form molds interior floor plates. The building announces, bombastically, the ability of the sponsor to accumulate the capital necessary to build the vast structure and to afford the cutting-edge building technology required. The spectacular image of the CBD conveys the promise of success and disguises speculation as certainty.

As a result, the architecture of both norm and exception serves up an urbanism of enclaves fragmented and closed off according to social class. They are fragmented by inflated and duplicated roadways, spaced-out towers, large building blocks, remedial decorative landscape, and lifeless ground planes. And they are closed off by fences, security gates, hoarded open spaces and luxury amenities, and roads so wide that they make walking onerous if not hazardous. This sea of urbanization is not what constitutes the true meaning of the city, the space of coexistence.

Practitioners of "new urbanism" and purveyors of "transport-oriented development" claim that the remedy to such ills is simple: narrower roads (but more of them); buildings that define the edges of streets; mixed programs; reasonably scaled blocks that promote walking and bicycling; public transport with dense transportation nodes (fig. 8).[9] While practical and commendable, these solutions neglect the fact that the city is not just the efficient management of spaces for work, living, and leisure with a functional and mechanistic inevitability that is outside a cultural and political will. A rethinking of the developmental city must challenge and offer an alternative to its ideological premise. It begins with a recuperation of the idea of the city.

2

Aristotle's definition and conception of the city remains one of the most enduring and profound. In the opening paragraph of his *Politics*, he defines the city as a partnership (*koinōnia*) or species of association:

Observation shows us, first, that every city [*polis*] is a species of association, and, secondly, that all associations come into being for the sake of some good—for all men do all their acts with a view to achieving something which is, in their view, a good (1252a1).

8   In recent years, foreign urban design and architectural practices have been engaged by city planning bureaus to design the megaplots. The preparation of master plans, in contrast, is closed to foreign consultants due to national security concerns.

9   Peter Calthorpe, "Low Carbon Cities: Principles and Practices for China's Next Generation of Growth," accessed January 30, 2013, http://www.calthorpe.com/files/China%20Design%20Manual%20Pamphlet.pdf.

For Aristotle, the purpose of the city is for the individual to live a fulfilled life.[10] The city-state, or *polis*, in Greece during Aristotle's time was not subordinate to a state or nation; it existed as a sovereign entity and controlled the surrounding agricultural territories. Aristotle defines the political community as a partnership pursuing a common good. The highest good is the virtue and happiness of the citizens, and the purpose of the city is to allow the attainment of this common good through education and law, that is, to be a rational and just society. For Aristotle, the city is essentially the shared and common pursuit of virtue.

Aristotle argues that the *polis* is a compound and a whole rather than an aggregation: "A city belongs to the order of 'compounds,' just like any other thing which forms a single 'whole,' while being composed, none the less, of a number of different parts" (1274b39). Additionally, the *polis* is neither a geographical location nor an aimless collection of human beings. Its identity consists in its organization (form) and structure (artifact). The concept of form is important in understanding both Aristotle's political philosophy and his definitions of the *polis*. For example, a sculptor conceives a form before he sets to work, and the sculpture that he produces has this form. The form is the final goal of the sculptor's effort. The same pattern of analysis applies to human beings, as well as to other living things. Thus, the *polis* is both a physical place to live and an abstract space for politics.

For Aristotle, the constitution comprises the form of the *polis*. The *polis* requires the constitution to exist. But the *polis* can also be an artifact, like a house (that is, the form of the house and the artifact of the house). This concept of form, as constitution or *nomos*, suggests the framework of recognition that is required for the *polis* to exist. For Aristotle, *nomos*, commonly translated as "law," "custom," or "convention," is not a given, unlike *phusis*, or "nature." The former requires an acceptance or subscription among citizens. This subscription to the common good or law is fundamental to Aristotle's first definition of the *polis* as a partnership or *koinōnia*. The word *koinōnia* is in fact connected to the idea of sharing or holding something in common. Indeed, Aristotle sees the *polis* as a shared enterprise in which citizens or participants pool their resources and efforts toward a common goal, the good life.

Aristotle shows how the city comes into being by means of the formation of various partnerships. He begins with the partnership between male and female, for the sake of reproduction. The other partnership, between master and slave, is for preservation. For Aristotle, the master and slave both benefit from this relationship. Relationships of reproduction and preservation come together to form a household that meets the daily needs of life. As families expand, they come into contact and form villages; as villages expand, they form cities. It is not the size of the villages that makes a city but their self-sufficiency. Resources are pooled to pursue shared virtue and happiness and in this way the fulfillment of an individual's *telos*.

Thus, Aristotle introduces the nature of the city as one that is based on partnership; it is a space of coexistence. He states that the city is clearly a unity, a unity that must derive from a multitude. Human beings are inherently different, and it is from this difference that partnerships are formed. This requires the city to allow for specialization and greater self-sufficiency. Cities for Aristotle are sustained not by complete unity and similarity but by "reciprocal equality." Here, I draw on Aristotle's identification of the importance of coexistence, the common good, and the conflicts that accompany his conception of the *polis*. The citizens of Aristotle's *polis* constitute a relatively homogeneous *demos* compared to most of today's cities, but it is precisely because cities today are heterogeneous and pluralistic that this definition of the city as a partnership, a space of coexistence, becomes more urgent.

Aldo Rossi, in *L'architettura della città* (1966), claims that any Western city has its origins in Greece; Rome may supply the general principles of urbanism, but the constitution of the city and its urban beauty lie in Greece. Rossi distinguishes between the Greek *polis* and the cities of the Orient: the Greek *polis* had no city wall, at least in the beginning, and was characterized by a citizenry scattered over a reasonably large region. He intuits that the city is formed by choice above all else, by something prior to and independent of the physical structure of the city wall:

> The Greek city was characterized by a development from the interior toward the exterior; its constituting elements were its temples and its housing. Only after the archaic period, for purely defensive reasons, were the Greek cities encircled by walls, and in no case were these the original elements of the polis. In contrast, the cities of the

---

10 This view is related to Aristotle's belief that every human being has a *telos*. The concept that links his *Ethics* with his *Politics* is that everything has a purpose, goal, or final end. For instance, an oak tree produces an acorn; the acorn has a natural tendency to grow into a tree. However, not all acorns will grow into trees. It must first encounter the right conditions. Thus, the *telos* for the acorn is to become a tree, and to fully understand what an acorn is we must see this goal or end. Aristotle believed that human beings too have a *telos*, and that human beings are meant to be happy. To be happy, a person has to lead a virtuous life, which requires the fullest use of his or her capacities; the most important capacity is *logos*, which means reason and speech. An individual can only fulfill his or her *telos* and live a full and happy life within a well-constructed political community, or *polis*.

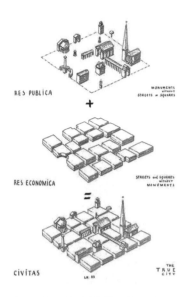

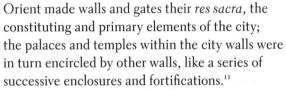

Fig. 9   Athens, Greece, 2008.

Fig. 10   Leon Krier, *The True City*, 1983.

Orient made walls and gates their *res sacra*, the constituting and primary elements of the city; the palaces and temples within the city walls were in turn encircled by other walls, like a series of successive enclosures and fortifications.[11]

Rossi thus highlights the double meaning of the *polis* as Aristotle did: the conception of the city-state. The city refers more to the Acropolis—primitive site of refuge, worship, and governance—and the state refers rather to the extended territory where the citizens lived (fig. 9). Originally, *polis* meant the Acropolis, and *astu* meant the inhabited area. Thus, what linked Athenians to the city was essentially political, not residential. As Roland Martin pointed out, the ties to the abstract idea of the city were more significant for Athenians than the ties to a physical space; they were interested in the form of the city as the political organization most favorable to the moral development of the citizens.[12] From this, Rossi speculates:

> In this ancient organization it seems that the physical aspect of the city was secondary, almost as if the city were a purely mental place. Perhaps the architecture of Greek cities owes its extraordinary beauty to this intellectual character.[13]

The dialectics of abstract and concrete, the domestic space of the family and the political space of free and equal men, housing and monument, center and extended territory, can summarize the way in which the historic European city can be read (fig. 10). The typical European city is composed of an architecture of rule and exception. Housing, the architecture that allows the management of private and family life, is the rule, often bearing the same deep structure that creates entire housing districts—the terrace house, the courtyard block, and so on. The exceptions to this rule are the monuments of the city—churches, town halls, libraries, buildings for the administration of public life. These monuments are built as an expression of the collective will, as something permanent, as singularities in the vast uniformity that surrounds them, as punctuators and concentrations of artistic achievement and capital expenditure. The deep structures of housing and monument differ significantly. The structure that governs the organization of a church into aisles, nave, altar, and transept bears no relation to the arrangement of a house into bedrooms and living rooms. The city as the reification of the idea of what is held in common, as a space of coexistence and therefore a space of plurality, rests on the dialectics of form that Aristotle has bequeathed Western civilization. The city is conceived through its architecture as a common artifact.

3

If the root of the European city is coexistence from free will, the root of the Chinese city can be seen as a code of conduct for coexistence. The formation and preservation

11   Aldo Rossi, *The Architecture of the City*, trans. Diane Ghirardo and Joan Ockman, rev. Aldo Rossi and Peter Eisenman (Cambridge, MA: MIT Press, 1982), 137.

12   Roland Martin, *L'urbanisme dans la Grèce antique* (Paris: E. de Boccard, 1951).

13   Rossi, *Architecture of the City*, 137.

of a harmonious collective culture has been a constant feature of Chinese civilization. Three principal cultural/philosophical concepts were brought to bear: Confucianism, Daoism, and yin and yang (阴阳). These concepts pervade every aspect of life, from statecraft, personal relationships, morals, and ethics to aesthetic production. The conception of the Chinese city is inseparable from the Chinese imperial city from the period of the Zhou dynasty (c. 1046–256 BC) onward. The period of the Zhou dynasty saw the transition of Chinese civilization from a prefeudal to a feudal society. Another factor that sets the Chinese imperial city apart from imperial cities of other cultures is that it is conceived as a whole; its limits are predetermined conceptually and demarcated physically by city walls. Therefore, in China the act of planning is inseparable from the very first act of city making, and both are explicitly guided by written documents. The decision to found a city was decreed by the emperor, exemplifying the expectation that the state would take moral leadership in all aspects of life on earth. It is my argument that to accommodate in advance the multiplicities of life, the city must be conceived as a pliable, adaptive, and aggregative structure. This is the city conceived and reified as a common framework.

The closest Chinese counterpart to Aristotle, Xunzi (荀子; Hsün Tzu, ca. 312–230 BC), accounts for the origins of society and the state:

> If men are to live, they cannot get along without a social organization. If they form a social organization, but have no social distinction, they will quarrel; if they quarrel, there will be disorder; if there is disorder, they will disintegrate; disintegrating, they will become weak; and being weak, they will be unable to dominate other creatures. Hence they will no longer have palaces and homes for habitation. All of which means that people cannot abandon the rules of proper conduct (li 礼) or standards of justice (yi 义)…there is no way of human living which does not have its distinction (bian 辨); no distinctions are greater than those of social distinctions (fen 分); no social distinctions are greater than the rules of proper conduct (li 礼); there are no rules of proper conduct greater than the Sage kings.[14]

In this account of the coexistence of humankind, Xunzi (荀子) adopts a utilitarian approach to stress the importance of hierarchy and conduct (li 礼). A disciple of

Confucius (551–479 BC),[15] Xunzi (荀子) was a realist philosopher who revived and applied Confucian teachings to the critique of state institutions. The most important concept borrowed from Confucius was li (礼). The meaning of li (礼) in ancient China was very wide, signifying present-day "politeness" and "courtesy" as well as "proper conduct," "good manners," and "customs" to be followed by individuals, institutions, and the state. The teaching of Confucius stresses uprightness through the practice of li (礼) as the basis for a harmonious society. It flourished after a period of social disorder and political mismanagement because it advocated the law, ethics, and morality that were sorely needed, from the period of the Zhou dynasty, the Warring States Period (c. 475–221 BC), to the Qin dynasty (221–206 BC).[16] Unsurprisingly, the teaching urges loyalty to a central authority—the emperor—to avoid civil war. It advocates that the state should be guided by compassion and benevolence and should set an example of virtue, as a father does for his family. Confucius believed that moral standards should not be imposed through force but imitated out of respect and admiration. Therefore, the practice of li (礼) for every individual—in his or her relation to others, within the family, community, and state—is imperative for the formation of a harmonious society. A philosophy that urges self-commitment to the community, Confucianism is also a system of secular humanism and ethics that promotes social cohesion and harmony through social responsibility, not religious beliefs.

In Confucianism, the family unit is inherently harmonious, since it is the natural training ground for morality, and it serves as the bridge between individuals and their society; the family is therefore the model for the state. This differs significantly from the viewpoint of Aristotle, who made a clear distinction between the space and interests of the household and those of the polis. The former is bound by blood relations; the latter by the common good that must be derived through politics.

Besides Confucianism, the architecture of the Chinese city is greatly influenced by Daoism and its core concept of yin and yang (阴阳). Like Confucianism, Daoism arose in response to the collapse of prefeudal society during the Eastern Zhou Period (770–475 BC), an era characterized by moral decay and political and economic chaos. Unlike Confucianism, Daoism is a philosophy of non-interference (wu wei 无为). It was promulgated by Laozi (老子), a librarian of the Zhou dynasty imperial court, and emphasizes the acquisition of

14   Xunzi (荀子) in 32 Chapters, c. 298–c. 238 BC; see H. H. Dubs, trans., chapter 5 in The Works of Hsün Tzu (London: Probsthain, 1928); see also Fung Yu-lan, A History of Chinese Philosophy, vol. 1, The Period of the Philosophers (from the Beginnings to Circa 100 BC), trans. Derk Bodde (Princeton, NJ: Princeton University Press, 1952), 279–97.

15   Confucius is the Latinized name of Kung-fu-zu, or Master Kung, who is credited as the founder of Confucianism. A scholar, teacher, and official, he served as an adviser to Duke Ding of the small state of Lu (in present-day Shandong Province).

16   Heerlee Glessner Creel, Confucius: The Man and the Myth (Westport, CT: Greenworld Press, 1972), 13–21.

Fig. 11 Sebastiano Serlio, *Noble Scene*, 1611.

Fig. 12 Sebastiano Serlio, *Comic Scene*, 1611.

Fig. 13 Sebastiano Serlio, *Satiric Scene*, 1611.

knowledge via reasoning, sequential thought, and logic. Its core concepts, yin and yang (阴阳) and *qi* (气), relate to cosmic harmony. The preservation of harmony—maintaining an equilibrium between binary opposites in all aspects and categories of environmental, social, governmental, and aesthetic production—is fundamental. The duality of yin and yang (阴阳) translates to female-male, cold-hot, mountain-water, and so on, and finds its harmonious relations in the conduct that shapes and binds society to all forms of artistic production.

Both Confucianism and Daoism draw heavily from the ancient Chinese understanding of the environment. The term "natural environment" (环境) is associated with morality, human behavior, and ethics. Ancient Chinese artistic production attests to the enhancement of the natural and cosmic environment. Traditional Chinese society views humans and nature within a single system; their survival is mutually dependent. The society and behaviors of humankind suit the natural environment, seeking

equilibrium. Therefore, in the imperial Chinese city, the presence of the natural environment is paramount, exemplified always by the placement of the city between mountains to the north and water bodies to the south. This differs significantly from Western models, which suggest detachment from the immediate natural environment as the source of survival. As pointed out by François Jullien, Greek philosophy treated binary poles as formal, exclusive, and confrontational categories.[17] Aristotle exalts the *polis* as a finite space for association, education, and contemplation, one that is separate from the expanded territory made up of agricultural land and wilderness. Sebastiano Serlio, in his *Five Books of Architecture* (c. 1537 and later), depicted the city in three scenes: noble, comic, and satiric.[18] The first is an orderly composition of the monuments of Rome, the second is a chaotic amalgamation of shops in the market, and the third is a foreboding scene of a village on the verge of being engulfed by nature (figs. 11–13). In the Enlightenment,

17   François Jullien, *A Treatise on Efficacy: Between Western and Chinese Thinking* (Honolulu: University of Hawaii Press, 1996).

18   Sebastiano Serlio, *The Five Books of Architecture: An Unabridged Reprint of the English Edition of 1611* (London: Dover Publications, 1982).

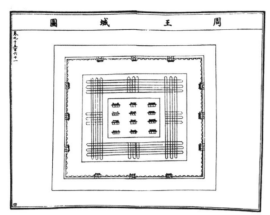

Fig. 14   Wangcheng, *Henan zhi* as preserved in *Yongle dadian* (永乐大典), *juan* 9,561.

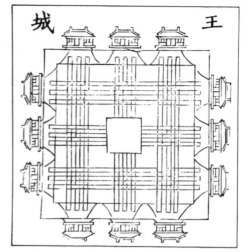

Fig. 15   Wangcheng, Nalan, *Sanli tu*, pt. 1, *juan* 4/2b.

with the rise of Newtonian science, nature was something to be understood, harnessed, and thus subjugated. For the Chinese, the maintenance of equilibrium between opposites—perpetual alternation rather than confrontation or displacement—is the feature that binds the teachings of Confucianism and Daoism. Both influenced architecture and city planning and used the concept of yin and yang (阴阳). Confucius promoted formality, symmetry, and human dominance over the physical environment (yang 阳). Laozi (老子) favored informality and the irregularity of the natural terrain (yin 阴). In the end, architecture followed the way of Confucianism, gardens Daoism.[19]

The ideal Chinese imperial city was first set out in the Kaogong ji (考工记; Record of Trades), a section in Zhou li (周礼; Rituals of Zhou), during the Zhou dynasty, in the late second millennium BC. The text described the plotting of King Cheng's city of Luoyi (雒邑) under the supervision of the duke of Zhou:

> The *jiang ren* (匠人) builds the state capitals, leveling the ground with the water by using a plumb-line (to ensure the posts' verticality), and using their shadows as the determinators of a mid-point. He examines the shadows of the rising and setting sun and makes a circle which includes the mid-points of the two shadows.

> The *jiang ren* (匠人) constructs the state capitals. He makes a square nine *li* on each side; each side has three gates. Within the capital are nine north-south and nine east-west streets. The north-south streets are nine carriage tracks in width. On the left (as one faces south, or, to the east) is the Ancestral Temple, and to the right (west) are the Altars of Soil and Grain. In the front is the Hall of Audience and behind, the markets.

This short passage clearly stipulates the principles and components of the ideal Chinese city. It describes the consideration of the natural forces involved in the preparation of the site, which adheres to the practice of feng shui (风水; the Chinese art of site selection and adaptation). The text also reveals the importance of a geometrically planned city that uses the midpoint as the generator and explains that the ruler's city is constructed from scratch, conceived as a whole, and defined from the outset with clear boundaries. Edged by four walls, the city should be square, although in reality it is often rectangular. The three gates on each wall lead to major routes. The excerpt also pinpoints the locations for the imperial palace, ancestral palace, altars of soil and grain, hall of audience, and markets.[20] When this description was reproduced in later works, it was accompanied by a diagram of the ideal city; the two best-known versions are

19   Gideon Golany, *Urban Design Ethics in Ancient China* (Lampeter, Wales: Edwin Mellen Press, 2001), 66–67.

20   Nancy Shatzman Steinhardt, *Chinese Imperial City Planning* (Honolulu: University of Hawaii Press, 1990), 29–36.

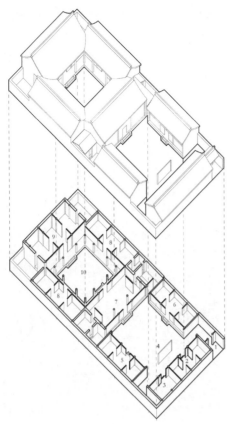

Fig. 16 Quadrangle courtyard house, Beijing.

Fig. 17 Courtyard houses forming a *hu tong* (胡同), Beijing, 2010.

from the early 15th-century encyclopedia *Yongle dadian* (永乐大典; fig. 14) and *Sanli tu* (三礼图; fig. 15). Both encapsulate the principles from the original text, but with one important addition: the imposition of the imperial palace in the middle. All imperial cities in China, over a thousand years, adhered to these propositions.

The city conceived through these ideas evidences the ethics and culture of Chinese civilization. The genesis of the city manifests the ruler's authority to lead in all spheres of human existence. Although it requires the labor and expertise of its citizens, the imperial city is not possible without the tacit involvement of the emperor. The city is thus the construction of the complete reified universe: all under heaven. Clear parallels remain between the ethics and culture through which the city is urbanized today and those of imperial cities: the impetus for construction is state driven. The difference today is the degree of control over the architecture of the city that can be imposed by the state (central and local government). Planning has been largely confined to resource allocation, and the form and building types of the city are driven not

by the ethics of the city but by the logic of the market. The urbanization of the city has become a tool for real estate speculation.

Every imperial city, without exception, is bounded by four walls to form rectangles; additional walls within enclosed the imperial palace complex. As an artifact, the city contains 11 features: four-sided enclosure, gates, defensive projections, clearly articulated and directed space, orientation and alignment, the ward system, accessibility to water, vast size, huge population, siting, and building order.[21]

In contrast to the architecture of the historic European city, with a deep structure that can be understood as the dialectics of rule and exception, the Chinese city is constructed from one dominant type, the courtyard house, and its corresponding deep structure, the courtyard wall. The Chinese courtyard house should not be confused with other courtyard configurations. Here, the courtyard void is not carved out but actually built up by the construction of one- or two-story pavilions (fig. 16). The courtyard houses themselves aggregate to form entire neighborhoods (*hu tong* 胡同, as they are called in Beijing) with very narrow lanes (fig. 17). The Chinese courtyard house does not have an articulated front facade, for it is not intended to be viewed from a distance. It is experienced instead in sequence, as a visitor moves from wall to

21 Steinhardt, *Chinese Imperial City Planning*, 12.

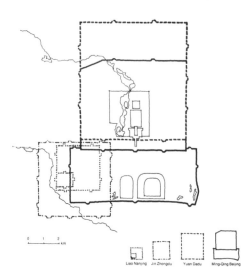

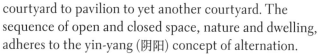

Fig. 18 Historic extension of Beijing through 1948.

Fig. 19 Forbidden City, Beijing.

courtyard to pavilion to yet another courtyard. The sequence of open and closed space, nature and dwelling, adheres to the yin-yang (阴阳) concept of alternation.

This singular deep structure defines the entire city at various scales. For instance, the city of Beijing (from the Qin dynasty onward) has been defined by city walls. The outermost wall delineates the extreme border of the original city while another, on the south, outlines the extension of the city (fig. 18). At ever smaller scales, walls surround the imperial compound, then neighborhoods, and finally the courtyard house. All share the deep structure of walls enclosing an agglomeration of pavilions. It is worthwhile to note that the deep structure of the city is independent of program. That is to say, the same courtyard forms served as family dwelling, administrative office, school, clinic, clan association, and so on. An enlarged courtyard form serves as the Forbidden City (fig. 19).

In the house, the organization reflected family hierarchy—quarters for the elders had high roofs, while those for children and servants were lower. In the Forbidden City, the tallest buildings, with wide spacing and big

pavilions, reflected the emperor as the father of the country. Yet the organization is the same. The city thus physically represents the ethics of Confucianism and the importance of unity, community, harmony, and balance. The ideal society is one that has strong moral values based on the family; individuals are conscious of their ethical responsibilities. Unlike a traditional European city, which has centers of concentration and is marked by an architecture of exception, monuments set apart from housing, the Chinese city can be viewed as a monument in its entirety. Its singular deep structure acts as a self-similar, fractal organizing structure, a neutral form that defines and accommodates all the plurality of city life: a common framework (fig. 20).

4

The recourse to the origin and history of the city to uncover its very essence is not anachronistic. The city, by definition, is a space of plurality, and the multiplicities

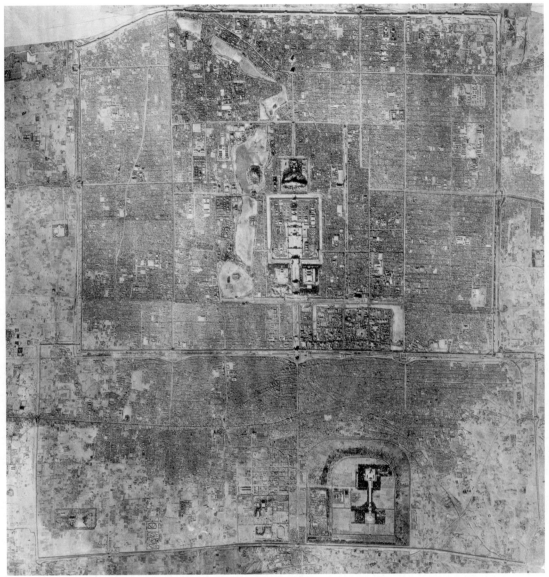

Fig. 20   Aerial view of Beijing, 1943.

Fig. 21 Palazzo della Ragione, Padua, Italy.

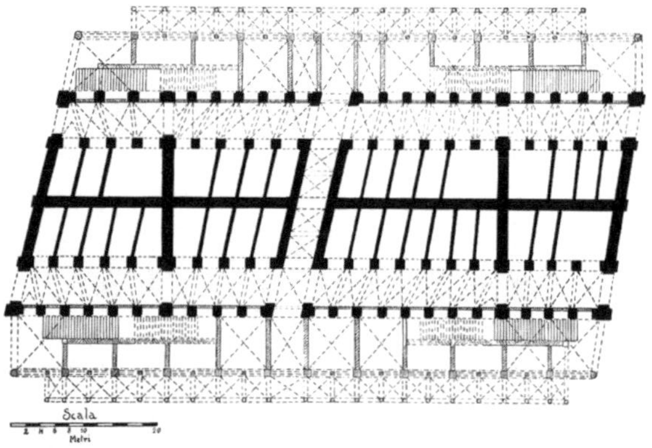

Fig. 22 Palazzo della Ragione, Padua, Italy, ground-floor plan from 1425 to present, according to reconstruction by A. Moschetti; 13th-century walls are in black.

that define the life of the city have architectural and spatial counterparts. The globalization of the contemporary city has cast it even more acutely as a space contested by conflicting demands—a pluralistic space par excellence. To think about the ways in which architecture can respond to the task of defining what is common, through idea and deep structure, is in itself an attempt to create the city as a project. This attempt recognizes that the task for architecture is not to articulate multiplicity through accentuating differences, through an architecture of novelty, but to focus on common ideas and structures.

Despite the epistemological and metaphysical differences that separate European and Chinese conceptions, the city remains a manifestation of the idea of coexistence, a common artifact or framework. An alternative interpretation of Aldo Rossi's early architectural projects offers a way to locate the ideas that are common to the city; then the corresponding deep structure advances an architecture of the city.

The most important concepts put forth by Rossi in his *L'architettura della città* are "urban artifacts" and "collective memory." The book was written in part as a critique of modernism's naive functionalism, in which he claims that the utilitarian and unitary master plan of the modernist city has lost its validity in the face of the realities of urban life.[22] Rossi returned to the historic European city as a site for architectural rejuvenation. The city, through

its architecture, is an artifact of civilization. It is the sum of the culture, politics, and history of its citizens. However, the traditional European city, composed as it is of contrasting architecture, of the rule and the exception, cannot be read as a whole. To resolve this, Rossi proposed the term "urban artifact" to refer to the architecture of the city that is both permanent and propelling. In other words, the urban artifact must both persist over time and participate in the continuous transformation of the city. Through its constancy the artifact becomes a structure that accretes the memory of the city. The urban artifact for Rossi is both the housing and the monuments of the city. The former contains the memory of everyday life; and the latter, its unique characteristics, events, and collective will. The urban artifact, sanctioned by use and acceptance over time, is thus the repository of collective memory.

Rossi cites the Palazzo della Ragione in Padua (fig. 21) as an example of an urban artifact: over time, it has contained a multiplicity of functions that are entirely independent of its form.[23] The building has the character of permanence as well as of force. In other words, the palazzo is an urban artifact because it is transparent in terms of function and independent of any programmatic failure; it is a permanent element because its physical presence remains even as its function changes; it is propelling because it continues to evolve and contribute to

22 Pier Vittorio Aureli, "The Difficult Whole," *LOG* 9 (Winter/Spring 2007): 39–61.

23 Rossi, *Architecture of the City*, 29–61.

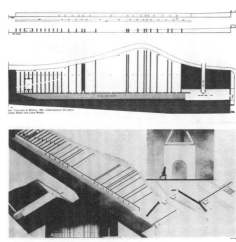

Fig. 23   Aldo Rossi (in collaboration with Luca Meda), pavilion for the 13th Milan Triennial, 1964.

Fig. 24   Aldo Rossi, Gallaratese Housing, Milan, 1969–1973.

the growth of the city despite its permanence. Although *L'architettura della città* did not contain any architectural proposals by Rossi, the concept of the urban artifact would influence his seminal Gallaratese Housing project in Milan (1969–1973).

Conventionally, Rossi's projects are read as monuments, representing a collective memory that is difficult to verify.[24] This reading owes to the Palazzo della Ragione, the example he cited as the urban artifact. However, what is often missed in critiques on Rossi's works is the plan of the palazzo, which is reproduced next to the photograph of the building (fig. 22). This plan represents the deep structure that was crucial to two of Rossi's early projects, a pavilion for the 13th Milan Triennial (in collaboration with Luca Meda) in 1964 (fig. 23) and the Gallaratese (fig. 24). The walls of the palazzo display the same organizational structure as those of the pavilion and the housing project. This was made partially evident in a set of typological diagrams (*schemi tipologici*) published in the article "Due progetti" in the Italian journal *Lotus International* in 1970 (fig. 25).[25] It shows three projects reduced to their most distributive descriptions—the irreducible structures that denote a specific organization of the gallery and the courtyard. Included are the pavilion for the triennial, the upper and ground floors of Gallaratese, and San Rocco, a competition submission for a housing project in Monza (1966).

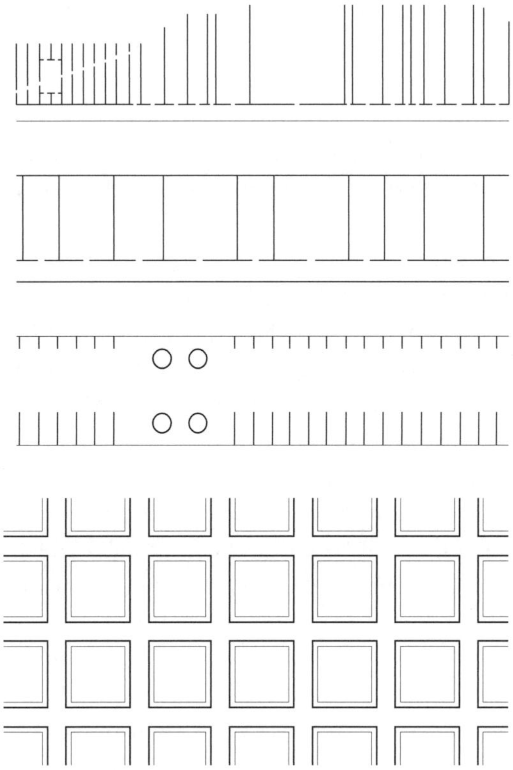

Fig. 25   Aldo Rossi, typological diagrams: pavilion for the 13th Milan Triennial (top); Gallaratese Housing, Milan, upper and ground floors (center); San Rocco, Monza, Italy (bottom).

24   Rafael Moneo, "Aldo Rossi: The Idea of Architecture and the Modena Cemetery," trans. Angela Giral, *Oppositions* 5 (1976): 105–34.

25   Aldo Rossi, "Due progetti," *Lotus International* 7 (1970), 62–85.

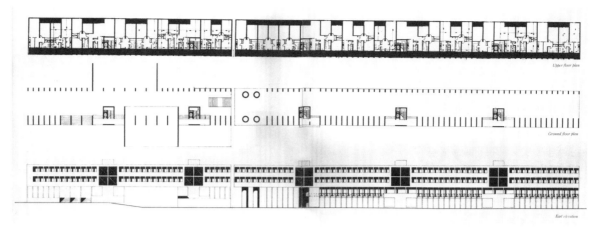

Fig. 26 Aldo Rossi, Gallaratese Housing, Milan: upper-level plan (top), ground plan (center), elevations (bottom), 1973.

This transposition was both possible and necessary for Rossi. It was possible because, for him, the urban artifact is transparent to function—its deep structure is organizationally precise but programmatically indeterminate, that is, typologically specific. Hence the same deep structure can be used for divergent functions. And it was necessary because Rossi wanted to forge a connection, through his concept of collective memory, between architecture and the city. Transposing the deep structure of the palazzo would create that continuity between the past and the present, between the city and the singular architecture project.

Crucially, it is not the *image* of history that is re-created here, that is, a wholesale replica of the palazzo, but an architecture that is *analogous* to the elements of the city: the gallery/street coupling for the triennial pavilion and Gallaratese and the grid/courtyard for San Rocco. All three projects encapsulate in one deep structure a primary element from the city and a building type. Gallaratese is a "slab house" or housing slab block that is also a street (fig. 26). The same is true of the pavilion: it consists of rooms of varying sizes fronting a street, or a pavilion in the form of a gallery/street. The defining element in the deep structure of the gallery/street is a series of parallel walls. These are varied in their distance from one another and also in their length, creating differential depths as well as two rows of piloti-walls. The pliability of the deep structure demonstrates a potential for different degrees of containment, from full enclosures to partial and implied enclosures. The Gallaratese, 182 meters long and 12 meters deep, has a portico on the ground floor at two heights. Connected to an upper gallery by a staircase, the portico is made of walls 3 meters deep and pillars 1 meter deep; both are 0.2 meters thick. Four 1.8-meter-diameter columns mark the entrance, and the entire slab is structured on a bay of 3.5 meters. The rationality that governs this disposition is inherited from the modernists but driven by an analogical, not a techno-scientific, determinism. It is no longer tied to the idea of mass production of a "standard product" or "object type." Rather, repetitive elements form a regulative framework, as common elements for the domestic spaces and for the civic space for meetings and encounters in the giant portico (fig. 27). Although Rossi recognizes the plurality of dwelling requirements,[26] he makes a deliberate distinction between distributive indifference and typological precision and fixity. That is to say, the private and domestic space of the dwelling must fit within an overall common framework, as do the civic spaces. It is precisely in the constant tension of this spatial arrangement—rule and exception, housing and monument, dwelling and street, private and civic—that it is possible to see Rossi's projects as a common framework and not merely as individual monuments.

5

Any attempt to recuperate the idea of the historic Chinese city with the goal of rethinking the developmental city can be informed by Rossi. To define what is common in the city through dominant type touches upon

26 Rossi, *Architecture of the City*, 70.

the very reason why the question of type is raised in architectural theory and history. Type as a heuristic device uncovers architecture's connection to society through a discursive understanding of what is common at every juncture in history when the universal principles of architecture and its accepted conventions have lost their validity. The notion of what is common cannot be reduced solely to a formal or tectonic similitude, like a prevailing style of architecture, nor can it mean just public property or space (as opposed to private).

The dominant type is both the element that constitutes an idea of the city and a reification of the idea of what is common. For this dominant type to be common, it must persist over time and take part in the continuous transformation of the city. Through this capacity to remain permanent it becomes a collective artifact or framework, for it is sanctioned by its acceptance. The capacity for permanence mirrors Aldo Rossi's conception of the urban artifact. While Rossi argues the permanence of urban artifacts through the notion of the collective memory, and uses the historic European city as the site for the identification of the urban artifact, the dominant type is found rather in the context of a globalized production of architecture and is focused on the organizational potential of the deep structure. To draw a connection between type and city is to establish a link between works of architecture and the wider milieu in which the work is produced. It also validates the relevance of the works of architecture outside their own discipline.

Not all dominant types are common frameworks, but they have the potential to be. The first task in attempting to create a common framework is to identify the dominant type and its deep structure. The deep structure can be defined as the irreducible structure that is weathered by use, by time; it bears the traces of daily life or exceptional events. More important, it holds the potential to organize new functions while maintaining a precise spatial arrangement. For instance, the walled courtyard of Beijing can be used as a family dwelling, a temple, or an imperial residence. What it lacks in programmatic specificity it compensates for in organizational precision: the walled courtyard maintains an alternating sequence of covered space and open area, with a gradation of privacy along its circulatory path; domestic, religious, and administrative activities unfold in the same organizational configuration. The deep structure thus acts as a common framework, not only as an administrative tool for the

Fig. 27 Aldo Rossi, Gallaratese Housing, Milan.

formation and management of the imperial city (which emphasizes central control and authority) but also, crucially, as an embodiment of the collective culture that underlies Chinese ethics, culture, and artistic production.

Because deep structure is transparent to function, it is inherently a projective element. That is to say, the same deep structure can accommodate new uses and thus may be transformed in terms of program without any change to its configuration. Using the deep structure of the dominant type offers the opportunity to discover what is common without resorting to the re-creation of an image of the past, a tendency all too often—and wrongly—associated with a typological approach.

So what does a common framework look like for the contemporary Chinese city? It is not what it looks like that is important, precisely because a common framework is an architecture that acts as a background. It is a framework that accommodates the plurality of city life and is in constant alternation with its natural environment. It must maintain a certain formal and organizational coherence, and it must be repetitive and scalable to be recognizable. The common framework is conceived as a singular discursive idea but realized through addition and accumulation. It is most identifiable when it is shared, lived, experienced, and viewed as a whole, as a city—as a collective work of art.

Ten Thousand Things

Notes on a Construct of Largeness, Multiplicity, and Moral Statehood

Jianfei Zhu

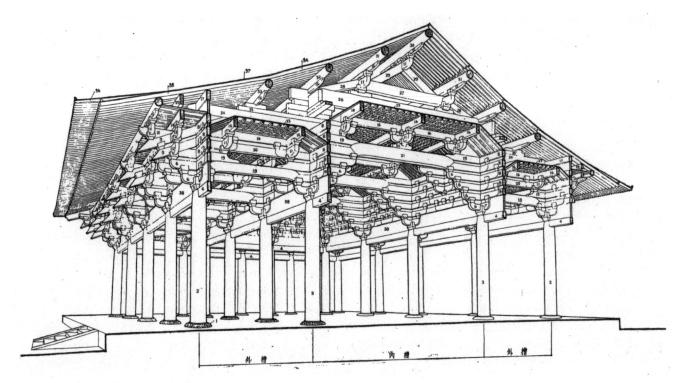

Fig. 1 Sectional perspective of a Chinese timber structure.

We are living in a world of speed, magnitude, and multiplicity. In a new round of "time-space compression," with developments such as digital networking, ideological liberalization, and the urbanization of populous nations such as China, India, and other developing countries (together constituting some 70 percent of the global population), the newly emerged landscape of modernity is unprecedented: it is much larger in terms of size of market and production force, more heterogeneous in terms of a coexistence of cultures, and far more dynamic due to instant transmission of ideas, images, capital, services, and products. These circumstances have fostered a critical interest in magnitude and multiplicity in various academic circles. Rem Koolhaas has written on aspects of the landscape of global modernization in which scale and magnitude recur as an issue, as in "Bigness, or the Problem of Large" in his book *S,M,L,XL*.[1] Michael Hardt and Antonio Negri, in their book *Empire*, have used the concept of "the multitude" to describe a new labor force that is global and mobile in a Marxist diagnosis of the contemporary world.[2]

The work *A Thousand Plateaus*, by Gilles Deleuze and Félix Guattari, which provides a new framework to comprehend nature and society by means of life forces, has been heavily studied in the past two decades by theorists in several fields for an understanding of the emerging condition with its vitalities in a picture that is broader than those framed by categories of ideology and semiotics.[3] These studies are crucial in developing new concepts to comprehend the new condition. However, they are polemical in that they are constructed ideas, with oppositional agendas, developed in a nexus of European-American intellectual currents. As far as critical ideas are concerned, there is little employment of embedded traditions, let alone traditional ideas or categories from China, Asia, or non-Western cultures.[4] This Western/academic field of reference may limit the capacity of these constructs, important though they are, to explain and engage the new global condition.

On another front, since the 1970s and 1980s there has been discussion of an East Asian model of development, a

1   Rem Koolhaas, *S,M,L,XL: Small, Medium, Large, Extra-Large* (New York: Monacelli Press, 1995), 494–516.

2   Michael Hardt and Antonio Negri, *Empire* (Cambridge, MA: Harvard University Press, 2000), 393–413.

3   Gilles Deleuze and Félix Guattari, *A Thousand Plateaus: Capitalism and Schizophrenia*, trans. Brian Massumi (London: Athlone, 1987), 3–25.

4   Deleuze and Guattari refer to many historic cases, yet their theory is a constructed polemic. It aims to move beyond the Western tradition of transcendence to a theory of immanence, yet without a corresponding

tradition. The Chinese tradition is arguably that of immanence; it is evident that Deleuze and Guattari were aware of that but were unable to employ ideas from the Chinese tradition effectively. As such, their work remains an artificial system for a polemic, and they cannot handle contradictions between centering and decentering, oneness and multiplicity, "tree" and "rhizome."

model in which state government, authoritarian and paternalistic, is considered to be efficient in delivering modernization and social improvement, as in Japan and the "mini-dragons" of Singapore, Taiwan, and South Korea. One position in this debate argues that the model is based on the Confucian tradition found in these societies, which in turn is rooted in the Confucianism developed in ancient China. Tu Weiming, editor of *Confucian Traditions in East Asian Modernity*, is one of the key theorists developing this position.[5] Suggesting that Confucian ethics (self-discipline, social harmony, and respect for authority) promoted industrial and capitalist modernization, his thesis amounts to a refutation but also an affirmation of Max Weber's *Protestant Ethic and the Spirit of Capitalism*—it refuted the idea that Confucianism was incompatible with industrial capitalism but also affirmed the importance of ethics for modernization. In any case, Tu's work was about the "Asian miracles" of the 1970s and 1980s. In the 2000s and early 2010s, the rapid development of China seems to repeat these miracles at a larger scale, and with an impact that may be broader and deeper in the context of world history. How might Tu's thesis be reassessed in contemporary times? How might the Confucian tradition of a moral and comprehensive statehood be understood? And what might be the political and cultural implication of Confucianism given China's increasing influence?

Further questions arise when confronting the new global condition with its scale, magnitude, and complex multiplicity, as well as the issue of a rising Chinese or Confucian impact. At what point does the physical condition of largeness begin to acquire critical, qualitative, and cultural information? Can a new framework be developed to address the problem of largeness and multiplicity, one that is not polemic but rather is embedded in a long tradition, so that it is practical, constructive, and ethically balanced? Is there a construct of largeness and multiplicity in the Chinese tradition, and if so, how is it constructed and what is its political, ethical, and epistemological message? What does this message say about the current global condition? This essay presents a Chinese construct of largeness and multiplicity, with a focus on Confucian political ethics and a discussion of concrete practices including systems of signs and the arts of the state.

TWO WAYS OF THINKING

A list of key political thinkers in China might include Confucius, Mencius, Dong Zhongshu, and Zhu Xi; in Europe, Aristotle, Machiavelli, Thomas Hobbes, John Locke, and Baron de Montesquieu. A metaphysical theory invariably serves as a basis for political thought—ideas flow from general philosophy to political ethics. In the case of China, Daoism (Laozi) and yin-yang philosophy are intimately related to Confucian political ethics; in ancient Greece, Aristotle's *Metaphysics* is closely connected to his *Politics* and also to the subsequent political thinking found in works such as Locke's *Two Treatises of Government*. Notable differences exist between the Chinese and Greek/European paths of thinking in the flow from general metaphysics to political ethics.

According to ancient Chinese philosophy, the universe is generated by itself, from within; the universe is immanent; all is here, included and internalized; no outside is possible (all outside relates back to this universe). This metaphysics leads to a moral and familial (or bioethical) political construct, with an emphasis on oneness, from the person to the family, the state, and the universe, as one moral order. For Europeans in classical antiquity, however, the universe is generated by something else, from outside, by something transcendent, ultimately by an external agent, an unmoved mover, the First Cause (God), outside the universe; with this externality, all things can be externalized and opposed to each other, and the world can be abstracted into a pure scheme of absolute opposites, a position that leads to a legal and contractual political construct with individuals and social entities conceived as autonomous and opposed in an open outside.

A CHINESE APPROACH: IMMANENCE, INNER GOOD, AND ONENESS

This Chinese logic of thinking, which leads to Confucian political ethics, has three important ideas: that the world is a "within," and so humans are all inside as well; that there is an inner good in humans, but it is not always manifested, and state leadership is needed to assure this manifestation; and that all entities, from humans to the universe, are related in one moral order. While these three ideas are logically related, they contrast with

5 Tu Weiming, ed., *Confucian Traditions in East Asian Modernity: Moral Education and Economic Culture in Japan and the Four Mini-Dragons* (Cambridge, MA: Harvard University Press, 1996), 1–10, 343–49.

Greek/European thought. In terms of the first idea, that the world is a within, Chinese philosophy conceives of nature as self-generated from within (*zi ran*) through a rational dynamics (*dao* or *tao*) of constant interactions between yin and yang forces, which generates a multitude of "ten thousand things" (*wan wu*).[6] When the universe is self-generated and all are within, humans are also included and embedded, and are related as yin-yang relations, which are not equal and autonomous but bioethically folded or connected—relations between husband and wife, father and son, senior and junior, officials and the emperor, and so on.[7] In his *Metaphysics*, however, Aristotle wrote that the world is generated by an agent from outside, the unmoved mover, the First Cause; with such a conviction, the universe can be conceived as a system of autonomous opposites in an open outside.[8] In *Politics*, Aristotle posited social beings as "citizens" in the forum of city-states;[9] in Locke's *Two Treatises of Government*, individuals are thought of as autonomous and external to each other, poised to compete for resources in a "natural state," as a logical starting point in his theory of government.[10]

For the second idea, Chinese Confucian thinkers have postulated a sequence of ideas on the inner good and the reason for state government. According to these philosophers, there is an inner good in all humans, yet this inner good is potential, not always evidenced; to make it manifest, an emperor with a state government must lead and cultivate humans through moral teaching and exemplification (*li wang yi shan zhi*).[11] In such a conception, state government is conceived first and foremost as a moral agent. There was also a legalist school in China that argued for control and power; yet after synthesis, the Confucian idea remained dominant in the Chinese theory of state authority as moral, familial, and paternal. In European antiquity, by contrast, Aristotle's *Politics* put forward humans as social beings in the city-states as "political animals" in an urban outside, pursuing their own agendas.[12] Centuries later, at the dawn of modern Europe, in the 1690s, Locke's *Two Treatises of Government* offered a conception of humans as

necessarily competing, as in wilderness, in a "natural state"; state government is considered to be a "contract" with the people that protects this right to compete. In addition, this state government must be limited, with a separation of powers to prevent it from corruption.[13]

In the context of the third idea, that of an all-relatedness in a comprehensive moral sequence from the individual to the universe, Confucian thinkers in antiquity proposed that to materialize human kindness and to follow the emperor to manifest one's inner good were merely to follow nature and the ways of heaven. The ideas are expressed in a few well-known passages. One says that it is heaven's intention to establish the emperor with a government to manifest humans' inner good (*li wang yi shan zhi, ci tianyi ye*).[14] Another claims that one is with ten thousand things when one materializes one's inner good (*wan wu jie bei yu wo*).[15] One of the most popular expressions is "the family, the state, and the universe are one" (*jia guo tianxia*).[16] This phrase is associated with a more elaborate expression, a maxim in Confucianism, namely that there is a connectedness of moral functioning from the intention to the mind, the body, the family, the state, and "all under heaven"; for any one of these to work requires all of the previous, in order, to fulfill their disciplined goodness.[17] It also suggests that any one of them is embedded in the overall holistic totality, that is, "nature," "heaven," or "ten thousand things," with a "way" (*dao*) of yin-yang interactions.[18] It is a bioethical and familial oneness, from nature to society and from society to statehood, that is embedded back into nature as a self-justified whole. The key points are inclusiveness and the impossibility of separation and opposition. This inclusiveness differs from the European tradition, which is analytical and oppositional, with a dualistic split and an externalization as a basic conceptual approach. This position is manifested in the constructed opposition, so widely used, between culture and nature, self and other, state and society, state and market, civil liberty and authoritarian regime, individuals and institutions, and the various political parties.

6   *Laozi* (*Lao Tze*) (Hohhot: Yuanfang Chubanshe, 2006), 44 (ch. 25), 74–75 (ch. 42).

7   *Meng Zi* (*Mencius*) (Hohhot: Yuanfang Chubanshe, 2006), 72 (bk. 3, pt. 1, ch. 4); see also Kong Zi, *Lun yu* (*Analects*) (Hohhot: Yuanfang Chubanshe, 2006), 33 (ch. 4), 116, 120, and 124 (ch. 12).

8   Aristotle, Books Alpha, Alpha the Lesser, Lambda, in *The Metaphysics*, trans. Hugh Lawson-Tancred (London: Penguin Books, 1998), 3–39, 43–48, 355–88; see also François Jullien, *The Propensity of Things: Toward a History of Efficacy in China*, trans. Janet Lloyd (New York: Zone Books, 1995), 246–53, and Bertrand Russell, *A History of Western Philosophy* (London: Unwin, 1984), 173–84.

9   Aristotle, *The Politics*, trans. T. A. Sinclair (London: Penguin Books, 1962, 1981), 167–72 (1274b–1276a6); see also Russell, *History of Western Philosophy*, 196–203.

10   Russell, *History of Western Philosophy*, 596–616.

11   *Meng Zi*, 51 (bk. 2, pt. 1, ch. 6); see also Dong Zhongshu's *Chunqiu fanlu* [Luxuriant dew of the spring and autumn annals], quoted in Feng Youlan, *Zhongguo zhexue jianshi* [A brief history of Chinese philosophy] (Beijing: Beijing Daxue Chubanshe, 1985), 231.

12   Aristotle, *Politics*, 59–61 (1253a1–a29); see also Russell, *History of Western Philosophy*, 196–203.

13   Russell, *History of Western Philosophy*, 601–10.

14   Dong, *Chunqiu fanlu*, quoted in Feng, *Zhongguo zhexue jianshi*, 231.

15   *Meng Zi*, 165 (bk. 7, pt. 1, ch. 4).

16   *Meng Zi*, 98 (bk. 4, pt. 1, ch. 5).

17   It is a well-known sentence from *Da xue* [Great learning]. See Zeng Shen and Zi Si, *Da xue, zhong yong* [Great learning and doctrine of the mean] (Hohhot: Yuanfang Chubanshe, 2006), 20–21 (ch. 1).

18   Zeng and Zi, *Da xue*, 20–21; *Laozi*, 44 (ch. 25), 74–75 (ch. 42).

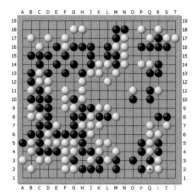

Fig. 2   Weiqi (Go): possible distribution of pieces during a game.

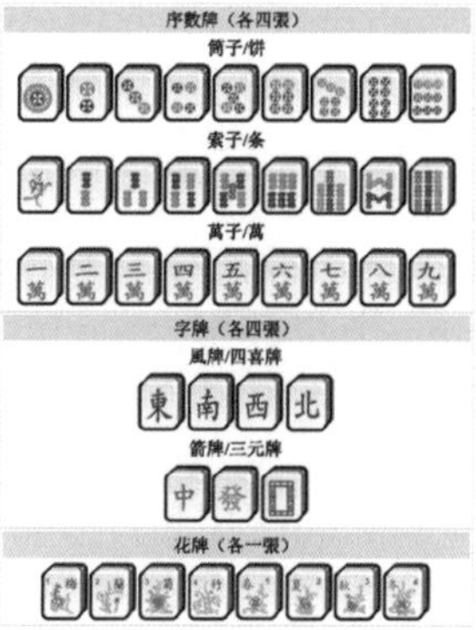

Fig. 3   Mahjong: distribution of the suits; the first five suits have four sets, and the last suit has one set.

INCLUSIVENESS, LARGENESS WITH MULTIPLICITY, AND MORAL STATEHOOD

The core ideas of Chinese Confucian thinking in antiquity have contributed to the formation of a rich and long-standing tradition in the past two millenniums, a tradition that displays three characteristics: inclusiveness, a large oneness with multiplicities included, and moral statehood. First, in Chinese culture and tradition, the universe is conceived as internal and all-inclusive. Second, this culture promotes a conception of oneness that includes a multiplicity of ten thousand things—a large and total oneness with an internal profusion of ten thousand multiplicities, largeness and multiplicity being two sides of the same reality.[19] This conception gives rise to a construct of largeness and multiplicity—COLM—that offers a way to comprehend the world and to build a culture or symbolic system to cope with and to represent this world. Third, in this cultural tradition, state government is considered as morally justified and is within a social and natural oneness that advances from the person and the family all the way to a large social world and natural universe.

These three characteristics contribute to the emergence of a powerful state, with moral and comprehensive leadership, in a state-society hybrid with no "outside," where society, market, religion, culture, and academy are absorbed into the hybrid oneness. A mechanism to achieve this was a nationwide civil examination system established as early as AD 600, a system that was open to all and would select the best students to become government officials based on examinations on Confucian classics. This examination system absorbed the social elite and knowledge production into the state. The state, much expanded, is a COLM, a construct of large oneness with a profusion of multiplicities. The construct itself, generic and not political, is manifested in concrete practices. These practices may be divided into two: the COLM as a way of seeing and knowing the world in the systems of signs and the COLM as a way of governing the world in the arts of the state.

SYSTEMS OF SIGNS

Let us observe the board game of Weiqi (Go), the tiles of mahjong, and Chinese written script, three symbolic systems by which the Chinese see and comprehend the world; their Western counterparts offer useful comparisons. There are many significant differences between chess and Weiqi (fig. 2), for instance.[20] The chess board consists of an 8-by-8 grid with 64 squares. Each side has 16 pieces; in the midst of a game, a player must consider moving 1 piece into 1 square, or position, against a maximum of 64 positions, and against or in relation to some

---

19   By "multiplicity" I mean both numerousness and a coexistence of different kinds of things. Christopher Lee has provided critical observations on the use of this key word.

20   Deleuze and Guattari have compared chess and Weiqi in relation to issues of flow and fluidity; *Thousand Plateaus*, 352–53. My comparison here is instead focused on scale, multiplicity, the range of shifting views, and group phenomena such as a flock of birds.

20 to 30 pieces on the board. In Weiqi, the grid comprises 19 lines in each direction; together these form 361 intersections. One player has 180 pieces, the other 181. In the middle of a game of Weiqi, a player must place one piece on one point or intersection, against a maximum of 361 possible intersections, and against or in relation to some 100 to 200 pieces on the board. In the middle of a game, it is impossible for a player of Weiqi to be as precise as a player of chess, for there are far more positions and far more pieces to scrutinize. The observation has to be large, strategic, and intuitive, as if it were of clouds or flocks of birds flying across the sky. Yet a player still has to look closely when zooming into a specific region; when considering where to place a new piece, the study of existing pieces must be made across several possible areas. In other words, there is a wide range of scales and of locations of areas to review, from global to local, and at a local level, from "here" to "there." So in comparison to chess, Weiqi is large in quantity (pieces and positions), scale (scope of spaces and pieces), and range of changing views (global/local, here/there). The internal profusion of multiplicity occurs in number and in spatial distribution, with minimum content (all pieces are black or white). It is a COLM with purity, a rather abstract construct of ten thousand things.

The tiles in mahjong present instead a system of largeness and multiplicity with semantic messiness or heterogeneity (fig. 3). While a deck of playing cards has 4 suits of 13 cards each, plus 2 jokers, for a total of 54 cards, the pieces in mahjong are far more numerous and semantically complex or "messy." A set of 144 mahjong tiles consists of 4 sets of 3 suits ("pancakes," "strings," and "ten thousands"), each with 9 pieces; 4 sets of 2 suits, 1 with 4 pieces (4 orientations) and 1 with 3 pieces (2 with Chinese characters and 1 with an image of a blank board); and 1 set of 8 pieces (4 flowers and 4 seasons). A pack of mahjong tiles is great in sheer number, in semantic irregularity, and in the range of situations it can generate. So mahjong is large in quantity, semantic openness, and the scope of probability generated. It is also multiple in number and in semantic heterogeneity. If Weiqi is a construct of ten thousand things, mahjong is a construct of ten thousand *different* things. It is inclusive and tolerant of difference; it is a hybrid or a complex totality; it is halfway between system and chaos, a chaotic system that is rational despite its irrationality.

Fig. 4   Yongle dadian, 1408: first page of 2,535th volume.

In the Chinese writing system (fig. 4), there are at least 50,000 square words, or characters. Every character is made up of a few compounds in a square, and there are a few hundred compounds. The compounds are not an alphabet—there is neither a precise number of compounds nor a set of generative rules for assembling the compounds into individual characters. Although there are some consistencies in the use of compounds, they are not rules and do not reliably predict the meaning, pronunciation, or form of a character. Every character has to be learned anew, as an arbitrary given. It is the character, rather than the compounds or strokes, that is the smallest unit of any certainty. Thus, the whole of the written language is composed of tens of thousands of singular characters, each as a basic atom, that is, a beginning or a center for seeing the world or expressing an idea about the world. Further, each character is an abstract figure: it is both abstract and figurative, a visual sign about the world whose visual image (rather than sound) constitutes its primary identity. The Chinese writing system imposes a strong discipline as well as an openness or humbleness in the learning of every new word, and in the process of a student mastering the language (that is, every child in this cultural sphere). It is a construct of both largeness and multiplicity—large in accommodating tens of thousands of

Fig. 5 Wang Ximeng, A *Thousand* Li *of Rivers and Mountains* (section), 1113, color on silk, horizontal scroll, 51.5 × 1,191.5 cm.

singularities and multiple in a radical plurality and openness to these thousands of signs, each of which is a central view to the world. While each character stands between abstraction and mimesis, the whole construct stands between system and chaos. As a primary COLM through which to see and comprehend the world in Chinese culture, the writing system reveals, arguably, how the Chinese think—it is intuitive and abstract, regulated yet specific and open for each case (that is, regulated with no absolute rules), with a mindset that accommodates ten thousand different things.

THE ARTS OF THE STATE

COLMs are manifested not only in systems of signs but in the political system of the state. Comprehensive leadership of society by the state government takes place in many spheres, including moral teaching, academic pursuit, knowledge development, and art practice, as well as religion, economy, and urban construction. The arts of the state—knowledge production, art practice, building construction, and planning of capital cities—are all COLMs that are at once political and something else (epistemological, formal, technological, urban). The Chinese state has always acted as the leader of knowledge production in various disciplines. This practice is most clearly manifested in the writing of historiography and the

assembly of libraries and encyclopedias. The largest books of historiography were made at the imperial court by appointed scholars; the primary case is Sima Qian's *Shiji* (*Records of the Grand Historian*, in the Han dynasty, 91 BC), which covers a history of 3,000 years in 130 volumes with 526,500 printed words.[21] Another well-known example is Sima Guang's *Zizhi tongjian* (*Comprehensive Mirror to Aid in Government*, in the Song dynasty, AD 1084), which covers a history of 1,500 years in 294 volumes with 3 million printed words.[22]

The imperial court is also active in compiling collections of books or encyclopedias of knowledge, especially since 900 (the early Song dynasty). The largest single-edition compilation of books is *Siku quanshu* (*All Books in Four Collections*, in the Qing dynasty, 1782), with 800 million printed words.[23] And the largest encyclopedia as a printed physical book in human history remains the *Yongle dadian* or the *Yongle Encyclopedia* (see fig. 4). Compiled in five years by 2,000 scholars and completed in the Yongle reign of the Ming dynasty, in 1408, it consists of 11,095 volumes with 370 million printed words.[24] The *Encyclopédie,* completed in France in 1780 with 20 million printed words in 35 volumes, may be the closest historical comparison.[25] With these books, the Chinese state was and is acting as a leader in knowledge production and accumulation. The largeness of the collections reflects the power of the centralized and comprehensive state. In these projects, an "empire of signs"—an empire of

21 *Zhongguo da baike quanshu: Zhongguo lishi* [Encyclopedia of China: history of China] vol. 2, (Beijing: Zhongguo Da Baike Quanshu Chubanshe, 1992), 936–37.

22 *Zhongguo da baike quanshu*, vol. 3, 1,618–19; see also

"Zizhi Tongjian," accessed February 17, 2013, http://en.wikipedia.org/wiki/Zizhi_Tongjian.

23 *Zhongguo da baike quanshu*, vol. 2, 966; see also "四库全书," accessed January 25, 2012, http://zh.wikipedia.org/wiki/四库全书.

24 *Zhongguo da baike quanshu*, vol. 3, 1,412–13; see also "Wikipedia: Size Comparisons," accessed August 3, 2012, http://en.wikipedia.org/wiki/Wikipedia:Size_comparisons.

25 "Encyclopédie," accessed August 8, 2013, http://en.wikipedia.org/wiki/Encyclopédie.

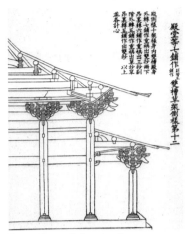

Fig. 6   Yingzao fashi, 1103, volume 31, illustration 4.

printed words—is the sign of an empire; the two COLMs, one political and one epistemological, are one.

The imperial court is also a strong patron of art, including landscape painting. The Academy of Painting was established in the imperial court in the 10th century; it flourished in the Song dynasty (960–1279) and later. The Northern Song dynasty, especially the reign of Emperor Huizong (1082–1135), saw a confluence of the court's interest in fine art and the maturing of the genre of the landscape scroll. At the apex of this confluence is Wang Ximeng and his masterpiece *A Thousand Li of Rivers and Mountains* (fig. 5), which was completed under the influence of Emperor Huizong.[26] Wang served at the inner court and was taught by the emperor, who was himself an accomplished painter and calligrapher. The artist submitted this work, since regarded as one of the greatest landscape paintings in Chinese history, in 1113. Like many landscape scrolls of the time, it is 51.5 centimeters high and 1,191.5 centimeters long. The work is rarely viewed at once; rather it is appreciated bit by bit, viewed slowly across space and over time, as it unrolls in a horizontal direction. The painting depicts a rolling landscape with rivers and mountains at various distances across a wide horizon. Hundreds of details, such as humans, birds, trees, villages, bridges, jetties, ferries, and fishing boats, are scattered on the landscape between the rivers and the

vast sky above. While the scroll reflected an appreciation of the landscape of northern and southern China, it also expressed a political perspective on the land of the state, with its majestic grandeur and richness, since the work was a product of the emperor's court. Such a landscape scroll is also a COLM. It is large and multiple, in the quantity of motifs (hundreds of details), spatial stretch (12 meters), broad range of shifting views (between global and local, here and there), and the ten thousand different things depicted as a great profusion of signs and vanishing points. This COLM is both political and artistic, representing a mixed perspective on the terrain as territory and as landscape, and involving a concern for the state, a supervision of art, and a pure appreciation of form. The empire of signs—here details, views, and centers—again becomes the sign of an empire.

Building construction is another art of the state in the Chinese imperial court. It is an established tradition in China for the imperial government to supervise the building of important structures by publishing books on building methods and standards. The earliest surviving treatise is *Yingzao fashi (Building Method and Standard)* of 1103 (fig. 6), written by Li Jie (1065–1110), a court official in charge of construction in the Northern Song dynasty (960–1126).[27] Other than the *Ten Books* of Vitruvius (from around 33–14 BC), this is the oldest architectural treatise

26   For the emperor-artist relationship in connection with the production of work, see Cai Han, "Beisong Hanlin Tuhuayuan Ruogan Wenti Kaoshu" [Exposition of a few issues concerning the imperial academy of painting and calligraphy in the Northern Song dynasty], *Zhejiang daxue xuebao (Renwen shehui kexue ban)* 36, no. 5 (Scpt. 2006): 176–80; Jiang Xue, "Beisong shuhuajia shengzu nian xiaokao" [Preliminary inquiry into the years of birth and death of artists and calligraphers of the Northern Song dynasty], *Jilin yishu xueyuan xuebao* 94, no. 1 (2010):

26–28; Gu Ping and Yang Yong, "Liangsong huayuan jiaoyu chutan" [Preliminary inquiry into the education system of the imperial academy of fine art in the Northern and Southern Song dynasty], *Nanjing yishu xueyuan xuebao* 6 (2010): 17–25.

27   For *Yingzao fashi,* see *Liang Sicheng quanji* [Complete works of Liang Sicheng] (Beijing: Zhongguo Jianzhu Gongye Chubanshe, 2001), 7:5–27; Pan Guxi and He Jianzhong, *Yingzao fashi jiedu* [Reading and explain-

ing the *Yingzao fashi*] (Nanjing: Dongnan Daxue Chubanshe, 2005); Qinghua Guo, "Yingzao Fashi: Twelfth-Century Chinese Building Manual," *Architectural History* 41 (1999): 1–13; and Joseph Needham, *Physics and Physical Technology, Part 3: Civil Engineering and Nautics,* vol. 4 of *Science and Civilization in China* (Cambridge, UK: Cambridge University Press, 1971), 80–89.

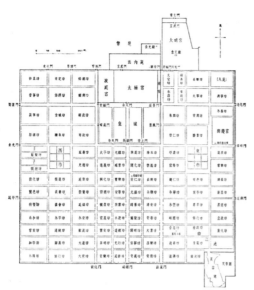

Fig. 7 Chang'an, 583–907.

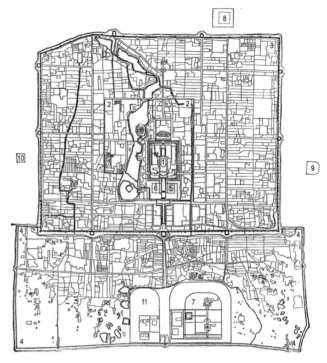

Fig. 8 Beijing, 1420, 1553–1911.

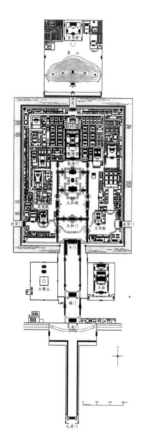

Fig. 9 Palace City of Beijing, central axis, 1420–1911.

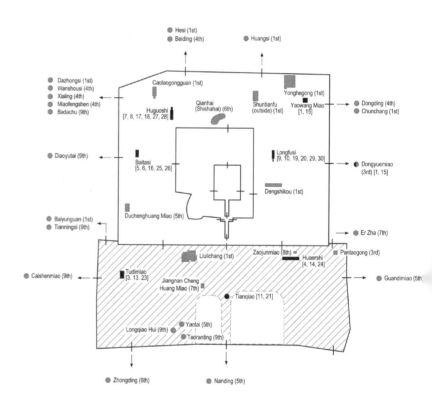

Fig. 10 Distribution of temples in Beijing, 1644–1911.

in the world, published three centuries earlier than Alberti's *Ten Books of Architecture* (1452).[28] The content and the setting of *Yingzao fashi* are different from those of the architectural treatises of Alberti and others. The European authors were humanists, not representatives of the church or state, whereas Li Jie and other Chinese authors were well-educated court officials who wrote the treatises as official guides to practice. While Alberti's *Ten Books* includes significant passages on *venustas* (beauty), addressing proportion and symmetry, and outlines broad expectations for "the architect" and "architecture," *Yingzao fashi* is primarily on technical building methods and the measuring of the use of resources (material and labor).

It is important to single out a few essential aspects of the Chinese text. *Yingzao fashi* was a government project for controlling revenue in capital works (against rising corruption in a prosperous time) and for standardizing the construction of major projects across the nation. The book contained a precise method for specifying resources such as materials and labor but also a standardized procedure for planning and constructing a building and its associated structures. It described how a building was assembled, using precut timber structural members, in an overall modular system. The system allowed reductions and expansions at eight levels or scales, to correspond with the social hierarchy of the functions accommodated. On average, a major hall in a sizable compound would involve a thousand structural members; a larger one or a pagoda, several thousand. A building can be put together in a matter of weeks or months, with a tight collaboration between carpenter-builders, and with structural members known and prepared before assembling. Such a building, in all aspects but especially in the complex timber roof structure, is a micro-universe, a micro-construct of largeness and multiplicity—large in the disciplined coordination of so many small parts and multiple in both the profusion and the variety of materials and parts to be assembled (fig. 1). The key point, however, is the leadership of the state. This state governance of "architecture" in China reflects the comprehensiveness of such leadership over many fields of social life as well as the power of a state capable of delivering this overall leadership. So the case of building again witnesses several constructs of ten thousand things—those of the state, of technology, of art, and of economy of building. If the thousands of timber pieces neatly put together in a Chinese temple or palace

can be likened to an empire of signs, they are also the sign of an empire.

Capital cities are important because they represent, in a condensed manner, the state's administration of the entire country, the functioning of the capital itself, and, indirectly, that of country-wide lower-level administrative centers as well. The largest capital cities in premodern China are Chang'an, of the Sui and Tang dynasties (583–907), and Beijing, of the Ming and Qing dynasties (1420–1911). They were among the most strictly planned, formal, and symmetrical cities in human history (figs. 7–9). Both were roughly square in shape, and both had a long axis of 7 to 8 kilometers. The area of Chang'an was 84 square kilometers, Beijing 60 square kilometers.[29]

A comparison of the Beijing of 1553 and the Rome of 1700—eras when each city had reached its final form but was not yet subject to modern transformation—is instructive.[30] Rome was 13 square kilometers in relation to Beijing's 60. Beijing was about 10 meters in height on average for most of the buildings, with a few high points of 30 to 45 meters. Rome was about 30 to 40 meters on average, with many buildings at 45 meters and the tallest, St. Peter's, at 138 meters. Beijing was vast but low-rise with a sea of courtyards; Rome was small and tall with massive stone buildings. The first was a *field* of mutually internalized spaces; the second was an *object*, or set of objects, standing tall and exposed, especially to the squares and along the city's avenues, which had a visual axis of 1 to 1.5 kilometers to guide visitors toward the monument at the end of the vista. Rome is relatively easy for a visitor to identify and understand in its overall form, whereas Beijing is deep and remote; a visitor staying in one area around a temple may not realize that there are more and more temples behind and farther away (figs. 10, 11), not to mention the palaces and imperial altars hidden from view inside layers of walls. It is in this sense that we may claim that Rome is a city and Beijing is a collection of cities, or a city of cities.

Politics also offers a worthwhile contrast. Rome remains a city-state, a civic and religious realm of a smaller scale, while Beijing is a state-city, a city acting as the seat of government of an empire. Rome evolved locally, from the ground up; Beijing was planned at once and implemented in a top-down process directed by a centralized state. Beijing of 1420 was built in a matter of two to three years (for the palaces, offices, altars, city walls, and city gates) as part of a larger project of

28   Hanno-Walter Kruft, *A History of Architectural Theory: From Vitruvius to the Present* (London: Zwemmer, 1994), 21–29, 41–50.

29   *Zhongguo jianzhu shi* [A history of Chinese architecture] (Beijing: Zhongguo Jianzhu Gongye Chubanshe, 1982), 36.

30   The basic history and general dimensions of the cities of Beijing and Rome are described in many

academic books on architecture; for example *Zhongguo jianzhu shi*, 36 (for international comparison) and 48–52 (for Beijing); and Spiro Kostof, *A History of Architecture* (Oxford: Oxford University Press, 1995), 485–509 (for Rome).

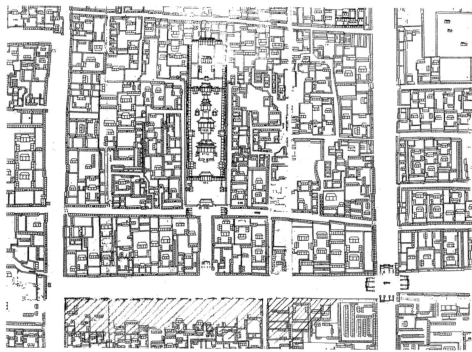

Fig. 11 Beijing around Longfusi temple, 1750.

relocating the capital from Nanjing. It was Emperor Yongle (r. 1403–1424) who moved the capital. His other ambitious projects included the reopening of the Grand Canal; northern expeditions beyond Beijing to resist nomadic forces (leading to later extensions of the Great Wall); various missions to neighboring countries; and the well-known seven maritime expeditions, through Malacca, to western India and eastern Africa, each time for two years with 300 ships and 27,000 people, in 1405–1433 (a few decades ahead of European voyages of discovery).[31] Complementing his geopolitical efforts were his cultural ventures. To sustain an image of the emperor as a leader in learning and moral cultivation, Emperor Yongle wrote in 1409 "Shengxue xinfa" ("The Way of the Sage"), an essay on disciplined cultivation for himself, his officials, and everyone in the empire; and he supervised large compilations of Confucian classics, completed in 1415, as well as the copious *Yongle dadian*.

It is in this context that Beijing was built—the scale and vision of the city were related to the emperor's other projects. Beijing as a city of cities, built around 1420 and expanded in 1553, can be understood as a city of largeness and multiplicity—large in the vast singularity of its formal layout with a central palace and a long axis, and multiple in its profusion of local centers (chiefly temples) and residential communities with religious and commercial life-worlds in the many micro-"cities" distributed over an extended field. The formal duality of a centralized largeness with a dispersed multiplicity of micro-worlds corresponds exactly to a two-level political structure of empire and local society (figs. 9–11). In abstract terms, Beijing can be likened to a scroll painting, a mahjong set, or the game of Weiqi: there is a largeness and an internal profusion, in quantity, scale, and range of views (signs, centers, localities) from global to local and between here and there.

The built environment incorporates several interrelated COLMs: in a single building, in a complex courtyard, in a rich urban area with temples and houses, and in the whole of the capital city. The nesting of a smaller system

31 Jianfei Zhu, *Chinese Spatial Strategies: Imperial Beijing 1420–1911* (London: RoutledgeCurzon, 2004), 17–27; Hok-lam Chan, "The Yong-le Reign," in *The Ming Dynasty, 1368–1644, Part 1*, vol. 7 of *The Cambridge History of China* (Cambridge, UK: Cambridge University Press, 1988), 205–75; and Mao Peiqi, "Chengzu wen huangdi Zhu Di" [The emperor Zhu Di], in *Mingchao shiliu di* [The sixteen emperors of the Ming dynasty], ed. Xu Daling and Wang Tianyou (Beijing: Zijincheng Chubanshe, 1991), 55–89.

within a larger one is perhaps not unusual; what is important is the disciplined inclusion of the multiple in relation to the state, the corresponding profusion of ten thousand things in every system, and the continuation of these several ten thousand things, or multiplicities, in a larger and layered inclusive folding, as if no outside and no autonomous object were possible.[32] In fact, from buildings to urban form, one of the key characteristics of the Chinese tradition is this field of relations and internalizations against the logic of the object and the universal outside.

A NEW MODERNITY

Developed from general metaphysics to specific political ethics, Chinese Confucian thinking has contributed to the formation of a cultural tradition with three key characteristics. First, an emphasis on inclusiveness or internalization indicates that all is related and embedded, with no outside and no split, no dualism or opposition possible. Second, a COLM is established in various aspects of this tradition, from the systems of signs to the arts of the state, from the ways of seeing and knowing to the arts of leading and governing. Finally, a moral and comprehensive statehood, with an all-inclusive approach, assumes a pervasive leadership, absorbing outside and opposition, in a hybrid oneness with society or social lifeworlds. This cultural tradition, as a construct on its own, is not specifically political—it is multifaceted; it is political but also ethical, epistemological, formal, and cultural-symbolic, with a range of manifestations in various spheres including the arts and technologies of the everyday.

The framework outlined above is beyond the issue of ethics and the question of whether Confucian ethics is constructive or not for capitalist modernization, which is Tu Weiming's area of concern, in relation to Max Weber's thesis on ethics. This framework concerns political ethics, but also a broad spectrum of issues concerning metaphysics, epistemology, systems of signs, and various practices and technologies. As such, the ideas are embedded in a rich tradition with many facets. The framework provides an alternative to the polemical theories on magnitude and multiplicity in the work of Koolhaas, Hardt, Negri, and Deleuze and Guattari; the framework is based on long and practiced tradition, with a consequence that it is not necessarily more articulate or polemical but may

be more effective and transformative, with a different concept of logic, ethics, and aesthetics developed over millenniums. It may point to nothing less than a different form of modernity.

At the core of this framework is the idea of a construct of largeness and multiplicity. The COLM argues for inclusiveness, internalization, connectedness, and tolerance of difference and hybridity, for a universe of ten thousand things. It can be employed to forge a new modernity that is critical of the existing model developed from the European tradition; this model is one of externalization and the contract, which emphasizes autonomy, dualist split, antagonism, opposition, and a logic of the object, as discerned in Aristotle and Locke and in the architectural treatises of Alberti and other humanists. The Chinese approach, along with globalization and digital networking, may lead instead to a modernity of internalization, relatedness, and hybridity. For the idea of criticality, for instance, it may refashion the practice to be relational and socially constructive. For the division between state and society, it might suggest a connected approach assuming a hybrid. For the role of the state itself, it could offer a moral and comprehensive leadership beyond a contractual or functionalist approach. For international relations, it might argue for tolerance and understanding of diverse cultures and worldviews, and a broader participation with more nations involved. And for the design of human habitat, it may conceptualize an ecological oneness, or the whole environment as an endless inside, with cities and nature intertwined as a sea of courtyards and gardens, with ten thousand centers and viewpoints across the landscape.

---

32   Readers may benefit from Lothar Ledderose, *Ten Thousand Things: Module and Mass Production in Chinese Art* (Princeton, NJ: Princeton University Press, 2000). While Ledderose has addressed the issue of production with a basic unit, I have focused on a way of seeing and thinking with a construct of largeness and multiplicity, that is, with "ten thousand things." Based on my research, the key issue is not production, let alone production of a unit; instead, the key issue is an epistemological framework.

Spatialization of the Collective

Logic and Dialectics of Urban Forms
in the Chinese City of the 1950s

Ling Fan

Fig. 1   Urban structure of contemporary Beijing.

Contemporary urban development in China has always been characterized and distinguished by its large size. One of the main causes is the state's continual attempt to spatialize the idea of the collective. The state's active involvement in this endeavor can be traced back to the 1950s. The spatialization of the collective is manifested in the coexistence of the collective form and the individual form. By the collective form I mean the speculative developments orchestrated by real estate developers who wish to maximize the land value and challenge the limits of urban managerial criteria. These developments normally consist of generic and repetitive buildings with in-between spaces carefully articulated to meet regulations regarding sunlight, setbacks, and green coverage. The individual form, by contrast, is a singular building that is monolithic, figural, and has clear limits (fig. 1).

Both the collective form and the individual form originated in the 1950s. A comparison of their historical roots reveals not only the spatial differences between them but also, in the relationship between the urban forms and the city, the structural logic of Chinese urban space. The

relationship between urban form and the city is both economic, evidenced since the early 1980s by a series of market and neoliberalist transformations, and political, defined by the nature of the regime initiated when the People's Republic of China was established in 1949. This continuity distinguishes the contemporary Chinese city from European Socialist cities; the latter share the political origin of the former but are undergoing transformation to a post-Socialist condition.

As Fulong Wu has argued, the role of the state did not diminish as China adopted market reforms. Instead, the state redefined its function according to the development of the market.[1] Urban space, the spatialization of the collective, is consistent in its logic, even though the means of production have changed dramatically, from Socialist material production to neoliberal immaterial production. A history of the inception of the collective form and the individual form offers a critical look at the logic behind the contemporary Chinese urban condition and the fundamental question "what is Chinese urban space?"

1   Fulong Wu, Jiang Xu, and Anthony Gar-On Yeh, *Urban Development in Post-Reform China: State, Market, and Space* (London: Routledge, 2007), 309.

Fig. 2 *People's Daily*, 1949: from the city of consumption to the city of production.

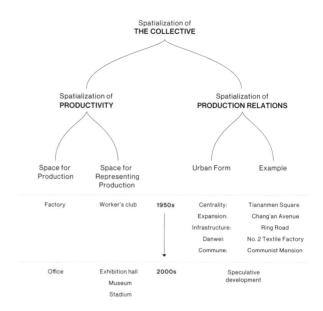

Fig. 3 Spatialization of the collective.

TWO TRANSFORMATIONS: THE DIALECTICS OF THE COLLECTIVE FORM AND THE INDIVIDUAL FORM

Two urban transformations dating from 1949–1950 provide useful context for an analysis of collective form and individual form: the change from consumption to production; and from idea to reality. These two transformations conditioned the emergence of both urban forms and their dialectical relationships.

The history of urban governance by the Chinese Communist Party did not start until 1949. Mao Zedong's "countryside surrounding the city" strategy during the Sino-Japanese War successfully "develop[ed] revolutionary power" in the countryside, where "anti-revolutionary force was relatively weak."[2] Mao's political tactics during the war abandoned the city to the nationalists and to major confrontations with the Japanese. It was only after their victory in the Chinese Civil War that the Communists announced their return to the city in the Second Plenary Session of the Seventh Central

Committee in March 1949. Communists considered the city, both physically and conceptually, to be bourgeois and parasitic. It was condemned as "only consuming, not producing material goods." In his report to the conference, Mao Zedong declared that "the city of consumption" would be transformed into "the city of production": "Only by restoring and developing production in the city and by transforming the city of consumption to the city of production can people's power be consolidated" (fig. 2).[3]

What does it mean to transform the city of consumption to the city of production? What constitutes a productive Socialist urban space? First, the city should be a space for Socialist production; second, the space being productive generates the idea of the (Socialist) city. In other words, the city of production is a spatialization of productivity in both the space for production (such as the factory) and the space for representing productivity (the workers' club, the exposition hall). But the city of production is also the spatialization of production relations—that is, the spatialization of collectivization. The Soviet influence is clear in both types of spatialization, especially the

2   See Mao Zedong, *Why Is It That Red Political Power Can Exist in China?* (中国的红色政权为什么能贵存在), Oct. 5, 1928; *The Struggle in the Chingkang Mountains* (井冈山的斗争), Nov. 25, 1928; *A Single Spark Can Start a Prairie Fire* (星星之火可以燎原), Jan. 5, 1930, "Works of Mao Zedong by Date," Marxists Internet Archive, http://www.marxists.org/reference/archive/mao /selected-works/date-index.htm.

3   Jun Wang, *Beijing Record: A Physical and Political History of Planning Modern Beijing* (Singapore: World Scientific, 2011), 84.

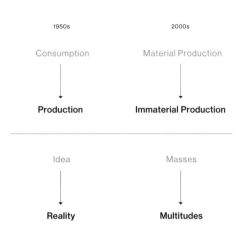

北京市分区计划及现状略图

北京市都市计划要图

Fig. 5 Soviet Advisor Plan for administrative capital of China, 1949 (top); Zhu-Zhao Plan, 1949 (bottom).

1950s   2000s

Consumption   Material Production

↓   ↓

Production   **Immaterial Production**

Idea   Masses

↓   ↓

Reality   **Multitudes**

Fig. 4 Historic and contemporary transformations.

first type. Most of the major industrialization projects of this era were supported financially and technologically by the Soviets. The design of the form was also either directed by Soviet advisers or followed Soviet specifications (fig. 3).

For Mao, it was production relations, more than productivity, that was important. Mao was critical of many aspects of Soviet policy but not of the general project to transform production and collectivization. On the contrary, he thought the Soviets did not go far enough. Mao had two primary objections to the Soviet process. First, he believed the Soviets overemphasized the importance of machinery and technology as the condition for collectivization: tractors before cooperatives. Mao instead emphasized the transformation of the relations of production: "First the production relations have to be changed, then and only then the productive forces can be broadly developed."[4] Second, Mao did not consider the Soviet transformation of ownership radical enough. The collective or communal ownership that the Soviets developed was, for him, only the first step in a process that must

arrive finally at public ownership of both land and means of production (fig. 4).

The second transformation, that from idea to reality, was occasioned by the establishment of a Socialist administrative capital. The vision plan for the seat of government initiated a debate on the question of the Chinese Socialist city and, further, on spatializing a new form of production relations.[5] Two opposite directions were conceived in 1949. Soviet advisers proposed a one-center approach. Taking Moscow as the precedent Socialist city, this scheme located the new administrative programs inside the historic city center and new zones for industrial development, education, and housing around the old city. The one-center system was supported by Chinese architects and planners such as Zhu Zhaoxue, Zhao Dongri, and Xia Nangui (fig. 5).

The second direction was proposed by Chinese architect Liang Sicheng and urban planner Chen Zhanxiang. The Liang-Chen Plan, as it was known, put forward the construction of a new administrative city to the west of the historic city. The north-south axis of the new district

4   Mao Zedong, *A Critique of Soviet Economics* (New York: Monthly Review Press, 1977), 93.

5   Guangqi Dong, 董光器, *Gu du Beijing wu shi nian yan bian lu* (古都北京五十年演变录) (Nanjing: Dong nan da xue chu ban she, 2006), 4.

各基本工作区及住宅与旧城之关系

行政中心与旧城之关系

Fig. 6　Liang-Chen Plan for new Beijing, 1949.

would parallel that of the old city, and the concentric structure of the old city would become polycentric around old and new. This course took into account the land use and the population density (21,400 people per square kilometer) of the old city. Building the new administrative center in the old city could require demolition of about 130,000 houses and relocation of about 182,000 people. Liang concluded that building in the old city "not only increases investment and deteriorates the environment, but also adds traffic complexity since staff have to live outside of the city and commute to work" (fig. 6).[6]

The advantage of the Liang-Chen Plan was that the historic city could be preserved as an artifact while the new town could be developed without the constraints of the old. The new city would represent the new regime, while the old city would offer museums, a memory area, park, event center, commercial district, financial district, school, and cultural facilities. Between the two would be a green belt. An east-west thoroughfare would connect historic city and administrative center.[7] Both Liang and Chen were trained in Western architecture and planning.

Liang earned his degree from the Beaux-Arts-oriented University of Pennsylvania, and Chen was a disciple of British planner Patrick Abercrombie. The architect and planner witnessed the emergence of Western city planning ideas and were informed about the social and physical consequences of urban renewal in Europe and the United States.

While the Liang-Chen Plan was recognized for its preservation of the historic city, it was criticized as utopian and impractical. Because of its clear limit and structure, the historic city can be read as a single gigantic form. Shuishan Yu asserted that the new administrative city emulated the spatial structure of the imperial palace.[8] By duplicating the city center, Liang and Chen attempted to create two legible individual forms, one from the past and one for the future.

In the end, it was the concentric approach that was chosen. Transforming Tiananmen Square turned the Forbidden City into an open form, emphasizing the center. The city wall was replaced by a ring road, altering the historic city boundaries. A major east-west thoroughfare

6   Dong, *Gu du Beijing wu shi nian yan bian lu*, 5.

7   Ruizhi Wang, 王瑞智, and Sicheng Liang, *Liang chen fang an yu Beijing* (梁陈方案与北京) (Shenyang Shi: Liaoning jiao yu chu ban she, 2005), 58.

8   Shuishan Yu, "Redefining the Axis of Beijing: Revolution and Nostalgia in the Planning of the PRC Capital," *Journal of Urban History* 34, no. 4 (May 2008): 571–608.

(Chang'an Avenue) was constructed to allow urbanization to proceed in the outer precincts of the city.

Although the individual form as proposed by the Liang-Chen Plan did not succeed at the scale of a city, at the scale of the superblock it continually manifests the idea of the city. As David Bray argues, "The decision to utilize and modify the old city to the needs of the new regime was not, therefore, simply the result of a reassertion of CCP power at the behest of Mao, nor was it the triumph of Socialist modernization over bourgeois classicism. Rather it was a victory of pragmatism over utopian architectural purism. This decision was crucial because it implied that the new regime would be constructed on the bones of the old."[9] With the physical characteristics of the city largely set, individual forms were positioned in the most appropriate spots in the city in order to change the sense of the city to Socialism. Here, to be appropriate was not to be contextual; rather, it was to contrast and confront, to intervene in the existing city to change the city. Individual form is proactive, not representational. Individual form came into being when the idea of the city transcended the reality of the city.

COLLECTIVE FORM

The development of collective form in the 1950s went through different phases: the neighborhood unit solved problems of population and infrastructure; the perimeter block embedded a strong Soviet influence and political ideology; the parallel block evidenced a tension between political ideology and needs; ultimately the *danwei*, the unification of life and production space, brought together the collective form and the collective institution.

China's urban population rose quickly after the institution of urban production policy in 1949. This increase intensified the urban housing problem, which, after the civil war, was already severe. In a 1947 *Construction Review* article, American-trained architect Dingzeng Wang proposed that housing scarcity in postwar Shanghai could be eased by superblock redevelopment projects and introduced the "neighborhood unit" to improve housing conditions and the welfare of urban residents.[10] First theorized by the American social reformer Clarence Perry in the 1920s, the neighborhood unit delineates the organization of living, transportation, landscape, and services within a housing district.[11]

The neighborhood unit combined a range of early 20th-century visions of collective living into a series of tangible design principles. Clear district boundaries control traffic flow past the neighborhood. School, childcare, and other public facilities are located within walking distance from housing. Grouped local stores are situated at the periphery of the neighborhood. Parks, green space, and playgrounds compose about 10 percent of the district. The neighborhood unit is a design solution that brings together urban functions and social interactions.[12]

Wang's neighborhood unit proposal remained on paper in the republican era. However, Socialist collective living, as well as distribution of material, financial, and human resources, provided an optimum environment for the realization of his ideas. In 1951, Wang realized Caoyang New Village, a 94.63-hectare neighborhood unit development for workers in Shanghai.[13] While Caoyang accommodated a larger population than a neighborhood unit normally would allow, the urban design, with some minor adjustments, followed the basic principles of the neighborhood unit. The plan was divided into three hierarchical levels: neighborhood, cluster, and village. Each cluster had its own childcare, kindergartens, and primary schools, which were located within walking distance (less than 10 minutes) from each other. Community facilities— co-op shops, post offices, cinemas, and cultural clubs— were situated at the center; commercial establishments at the periphery. The street system, bounded by city thoroughfares, was laid out in a flexible pattern to accommodate the unevenness of the site. Shortly after the completion of Caoyang, four Hudong villages based on similar principles were constructed.[14] Together they provided housing for 20,000 residents. At this point, the neighborhood unit idea was also adopted in Beijing, and several residential districts were built.

But the success of the neighborhood unit was provisional. Once the Soviet "Big Brother" movement started in 1952, Soviet influence began to permeate every aspect of Chinese development. The central government conducted a series of measures to learn from the Soviet Union, adapting Soviet technologies, developmental models, and mentality. In the 1950s, more than 10,000 Russian advisers assisted various modernization programs in China, and their opinions often outweighed local attitudes. The neighborhood unit typology was criticized as a remnant of capitalism and fell into disrepute. Soviet advisers promoted instead the perimeter block. An urban

---

9 David Bray, *Social Space and Governance in Urban China: The Danwei System from Origins to Reform* (Stanford, CA: Stanford University Press, 2005), 128.

10 Dingzeng Wang, "Shiqu congjian yu jiejue fang-huang" [Urban redevelopment and housing scarcity], *Jianshe pinglun* [Construction review] 1, no. 2 (1947): 5–6.

11 Duanfang Lu, *Remaking Chinese Urban Form: Modernity, Scarcity and Space, 1949–2005* (London: Routledge, 2006), 19–20.

12 Lu, *Remaking Chinese Urban Form*, 22.

13 Dingzeng Wang, "Shanghai caoyang xincun zhu-zhaiqu de guihua sheji" [The planning of Shanghai Caoyang new village residential district], *Jianzhu xuebao* [Architectural journal], Feb. 1956, 1–15.

14 Lu, *Remaking Chinese Urban Form*, 29–32.

superblock, the perimeter block consisted of four- to six-story apartment buildings on all sides of a semipublic quadrangle with public facilities in the center. The scheme, more directly influenced by a Beaux-Arts concern for formal grandeur than by Marxist theory, stressed symmetrical axes and aesthetically coordinated street facades. During the Stalin era, Soviet planners set their perimeter block against its Western counterpart—the neighborhood unit—claiming that the perimeter block, unlike the neighborhood unit isolated in a suburb, provided "the organic component" of the city and was a more economical approach to urban construction.[15]

The adoption of the perimeter block was concurrent with the key industrial projects, also sustained by Soviet models and technologies, at the beginning of the first Five Year Plan (1953–1957). However, Chinese architects and planners soon found that this typology was problematic in several aspects: the perimeter layout produced a large number of west-facing windows (in China, south-facing residences are preferred; west-facing units are avoided), street-facing units suffered from noise and pollution, and the building orientation and long corridors made cross-ventilation difficult.[16] In a 1956 article on residential planning, architect Ye Wang argued that it was unfair to make people live in west-facing dwellings for no reason other than formalism.[17] In later projects, the perimeter block was less strictly implemented. Parallel slab buildings facing south or southeast gradually replaced the residential buildings in perimeter blocks.

After Stalin's death in 1953, Khrushchev delivered the notorious secret speech in which he negated almost every aspect of Stalinism. The relationship between China and Russia deteriorated. The Soviet ideological impact on architectural form was also deliberately rejected. Starting in 1955, the CCP increasingly emphasized industrial development. Scarcity, economy, and utility, rather than ideological manifestation, became new priorities in housing. The break with the Soviet Union gave rise to a strong sense of scarcity. The "anti-waste" movement received new impetus. The national austerity policy was reinforced: industrialization took priority over all, including quality of life. The perimeter block layout was abandoned in favor of east-west (north- and south-facing) generic slab buildings. This austere architectural figure maximized performance and minimized expenses.[18]

The microdistrict (*mikrorayon*) was another planning principle imported from the Soviet Union. It was defined as a self-contained residential form with an area of 75 to 125 acres and a population of 5,000 to 15,000. During the Stalin era, the microdistrict took the form of the perimeter block. After Stalin's death, the microdistrict idea reemerged and was widely accepted.

The microdistrict concept was introduced to China in 1956 and became the basic unit for residential planning for Beijing. The buildings of a microdistrict were mostly generic and standardized, while the in-between space was much more articulated. The generic building blocks were replaced at various times by different floor plans that spatialized the change of lifestyle. The transposition of architectural and urban debate to the microdistrict was largely a strategic maneuver to revive the neighborhood unit under a new and politically correct name. Dingzeng Wang, originator of the neighborhood unit, was an advocate of the microdistrict. He formulated the principles for microdistrict planning in China: integrating housing and service facilities; discouraging through traffic; grouping housing according to the "service radius," or optimum distance between housing and services; basing the hierarchy and optimum number of community facilities on the number of residents served.[19]

According to Wang's definition, the microdistrict recuperated several ideas from the neighborhood unit. The concept of the microdistrict is inclusive, dissolving the political tension between perimeter block and the neighborhood unit. The microdistrict was implemented in a flexible manner. A project in Beijing might be significantly different from one in the south of China. The spatial organization of the microdistrict was influenced more by immediate local context than by any overarching formal principle. The microdistrict was easily adaptable to and negotiated between political ideologies. In fact, both the idea and the space of the microdistrict carry weight in contemporary Chinese cities.

A final collective form of this period was the *danwei*. A project-based development model had come to be the main mode of urban land development. These projects, including factories and institutions, advanced as work units, or *danwei*.[20] It would not be an exaggeration to contend that it is the foundation of urban China. The *danwei* "is the source of employment and material

15   Lu, *Remaking Chinese Urban Form*, 31.

16   Junhua Lü, Peter G. Rowe, and Jie Zhang, eds., *Modern Urban Housing in China, 1840–2000* (New York: Prestel, 2001), 128–30.

17   Ye Wang, "Guanyu juzhuqu guihua sheji xingshi de taolun" [Discussion on the planning of the form of the residential district], *Jianzhu xuebao* [Architectural journal], May 1956, 51–57.

18   Lü, Rowe, and Zhang, *Modern Urban Housing*, 128–30.

19   Dingzeng Wang and C. Xu, "Juzhu jianzhu guihua sheji zhong jige wenti de tantao" [On several issues in residential planning], *Jianzhu xuebao* [Architectural journal], Feb. 1962, 6–13.

20   Anthony Gar-On Yeh and Fulong Wu, "The New Land Development Process and Urban Development in Chinese Cities," *International Journal of Urban and Regional Research* 20, no. 2 (1996): 330–53.

Fig. 7 Individual and collective forms in Beijing, 1950s.

Fig. 8 Collective form in Beijing, 1950s.

support for the majority of urban residents; it organizes, regulates, polices, trains, educates, and protects them; it provides them with identity and face; and, within distinct spatial units, it forms integrated communities through which urban residents derive their sense of place and social belonging. The importance of the *danwei* is further highlighted by the fact that any person who does not have a *danwei* is considered to be 'suspicious' or even 'dangerous.'"[21]

The physical form of the *danwei* might consist of a superblock or multiple superblocks. The neighborhood unit, perimeter block, parallel block, and microdistrict can all be found in the *danwei*. Some of the *danwei* were funded directly by the ministries and departments of the central government. Those *danwei* formed virtual "factory towns" inside municipal territories, though they were more powerful than the municipal government. The *danwei* is a specific yet generic Socialist institution that integrates ideology, governance, space, and individual identity (fig. 7).

Collective form was intended to integrate production and living to increase efficiency and convenience for management. The wall and the enclosed form have been put forth by scholars as the prototypical spatial characteristics of the *danwei*. However, it appears from urban panoramas and other documentation from the 1950s that the wall was not prevalent. In fact, due to the campaigns of the Great Leap Forward and the People's Commune, walls were even demolished to support communitarian exchange and

sharing. The wall may have become prevalent as a consequence of the problem of scarcity at the end of the 1950s. In the Socialist system, the *danwei* was both the producer and the consumer of material. In fact, the abolishment of the pure consumption class did not reconcile the social conflict that was formerly caused by class contradiction. The social conflict still existed between the *danwei* and the city. The reason can be traced back to the beginning of this system: the *danwei* were built without consideration of each other or of services. And the lack of coordination emerged as a focus of concern. In 1953, the central government in its report to the central CCP stated, "Factories are constructed according to our plans, but cities are not; factories are managed well but cities are not."[22] The next year, it was decided that comprehensive urban planning should be enacted, in particular to support national industrial construction. In the first Five Year Plan, the primary task for urban planning was to further 156 key industrial projects, many of which were sponsored by the Soviet Union.[23] However, that planning effort was already obsolete. The conflicts between the *danwei* and the city mounted during the Great Famine and the three years of economic readjustment between 1959 and 1961. Scarcity detached the *danwei* from the city. *Danwei* were responsible for individual living needs and built a large number of residential structures without permits. (*Danwei* cheated by reporting small, redeveloped, and temporary construction projects but instead building large, new, and permanent structures.[24]) Thus, the *danwei* as a collective

21 Bray, *Social Space*, 5; also see Xiaobo Lü and Elizabeth J. Perry, eds., *Danwei: The Changing Chinese Workplace in Historical and Comparative Perspective* (Armonk, NY: M. E. Sharpe, 1997).

22 Cao Hongtao and Zhu Chuanheng, eds., *Dangdai zhongguo de chengshi jianshe* [Urban construction in contemporary China] (Beijing: China Social Science Press, 1990), 40.

23 Yeh and Wu, "New Land Development," 177.

24 Lu, *Remaking Chinese Urban Form*, 86.

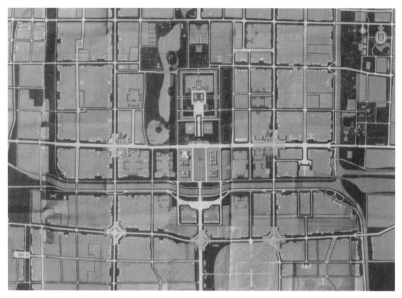

Fig. 9 Master plan proposal, city and individual forms, 1950s.

form supported individuation within. It is because of this tolerance that Mao did not regard the *danwei* as complete collectivization (fig. 8).

INDIVIDUAL FORM

Although the overall transformation to collectivization achieved significant improvement in productivity during the first Five Year Plan, Mao launched the much more radical Great Leap Forward at the beginning of the second Five Year Plan. The Great Leap Forward was an economic and social campaign; as reflected in planning decisions from 1958 to 1961, it aimed to use China's vast population to rapidly transform the country, via industrialization and collectivization, from an agrarian economy into a modern Communist society. Development of China's agricultural and industrial sectors would occur in parallel to eliminate the chasm between urban and rural. The government sought to take advantage of the available supply of cheap labor, avoiding the import of heavy machinery, and to avoid both the social stratification and technical bottlenecks involved in the Soviet model of development. Its solutions were political (production relations) rather than technical (productivity). Distrusting technical experts, Mao and the party sought to replicate the strategies used in the 1930s after the Long March:

"mass mobilization, social leveling, attacks on bureaucratism, disdain for material obstacles."[25] Mao also advocated a further round of collectivization modeled on the Soviet Third Period for the countryside, where existing collectives would be merged into People's Communes. At the end of the 1950s, more than 90 percent of farmers belonged to communes.[26] The People's Commune movement was also quickly introduced to the city and coexisted with work units (fig. 9).

The urban form most suitable to accommodate the People's Commune was open to question. The Communist Mansion in Beijing was one of the most extreme cases. Different from the *danwei*, the Communist Mansion was an individual form, a social condenser almost in the manner of Soviet Constructivism. The Communist Mansion sheltered hybrid programs in a single structure: two-bedroom apartments, bachelor dormitory, kindergarten, hostel, canteen, club, communal kitchen, and store. Nine stories high, the building was equipped with the first residential elevator system in China. There were chandeliers on every stair landing. The individual form envisioned a new way of living. There were no private kitchens or living rooms; meals were served in the communal dining hall, and spacious public areas were available in the building. Children would live with their parents when young and then move to dormitories (figs. 10, 11).[27]

25   Kenneth Lieberthal, "The Great Leap Forward and the Split in the Yenan Leadership," in *The People's Republic, Part 1: The Emergence of Revolutionary China, 1949–1965*, vol. 14 of *The Cambridge History of China* (Cambridge, UK: Cambridge University Press, 1987), 304.

26   Wen-shun Chi, "The Ideological Source of the People's Communes in Communist China," *Pacific Coast Philology* 2 (April 1967): 62–78.

27   Ling Fan, "Revisiting a Built Communism," *Monu: Magazine on Urbanism* no. 18 (April 2013).

Fig. 10   Communist Mansion, Beijing, 1959.

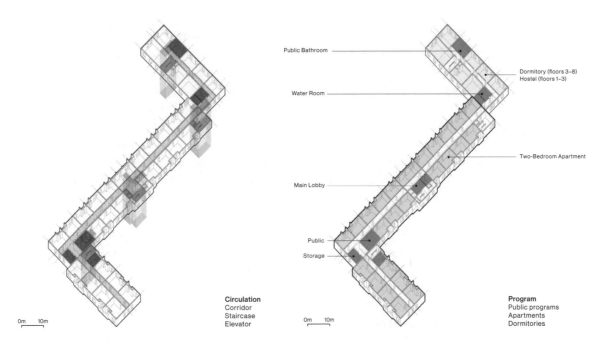

Public Bathroom

Water Room

Main Lobby

Public

Storage

Dormitory (floors 3–8)
Hostel (floors 1–3)

Two-Bedroom Apartment

Circulation
Corridor
Staircase
Elevator

0m   10m

Program
Public programs
Apartments
Dormitories

0m   10m

Fig. 11   Communist Mansion, Beijing: typical floor.

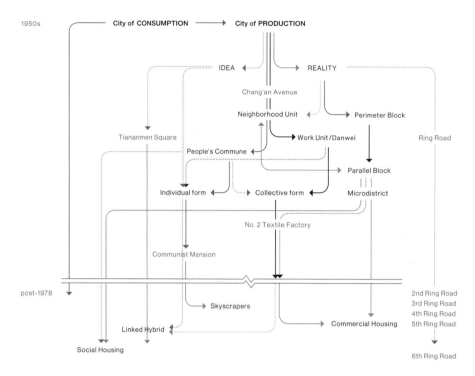

Fig. 12   Logic and dialectics of urban form.

Individual form was not invented by the Communist Mansion but emerged shortly after 1949. Architectural intervention was the most effective way to quickly and economically change the sense of the city from an imperial one to a Socialist one. Compared with collective form, which coordinated production and consumption, individual form projected the new idea of the city in its accommodation of new Socialist programs. Generally large in size, individual forms represented a contrast to the immediate urban context. Construction of individual forms reached its apex at the end of 1950s, as the country was approaching its 10-year anniversary. The most famous individual forms were the Ten Great Projects, public buildings erected in Beijing in 1959. These structures were part of the architectural and urban initiative that accompanied the Great Leap Forward and were completed in 10 months. Also undertaken at this time were an expansion of Tiananmen Square and a program of art commissions for the Ten Great Projects. (Two subsequent art campaigns for these buildings were conducted, in 1961 and in 1964–1965.) The architecture of the buildings

was a mixture of three main tendencies: International Style modernism, Stalinist Socialist realism, and a historicism based on traditional Chinese architecture.[28] The buildings were designed by the Beijing Institute of Architectural Design working with the Beijing Planning Bureau and the Ministry of Construction. The Ten Great Buildings transformed Beijing with monumental architecture typical of such national capitals as Washington, DC, Paris, and Moscow.

Located next to major roads or public spaces, individual forms connect with the city directly and strategically. The individual form was strongly influenced by Stalinist precedents, as well as by the iconic buildings of the École des Beaux-Arts and the mixed-use architecture of Constructivism and the modernist metropolis. Unlike collective forms, every individual form has its own story and identity. The Ten Great Projects are concentrated on both sides of Chang'an Avenue, while the Communist Mansions rise abruptly from the urban fabric in strong contrast to both courtyard and neighborhood units. They are landmarks, even monuments. Situated at critical

28   Peter G. Rowe and Kuan Seng, *Architectural Encounters with Essence and Form in Modern China* (Cambridge, MA: MIT Press, 2002), 107–37.

points, these buildings function like Chinese acupuncture: they confront the city to project the idea of the city.

THE LEGACIES OF INDIVIDUAL AND COLLECTIVE FORM

Collective form and individual form act in different ways. The former reconstructs urban territory by disconnecting from the city, while the latter encounters the city by connecting with it. Collective form, composed of generic buildings with an articulation of the space in between, is rarely credited to an architect; most such buildings were constructed according to a standard drawing set. Inside the generic buildings, and inside the in-between space, a certain degree of individuation was allowed. Individual form, by contrast, was always designed collectively by architects and decided collectively by party leaders and respected professional experts. Both the Great Hall of the People and the Museum of Revolution and History on Tiananmen Square were designed through a series of collective design processes. However, individual forms differed from each other. Individual form needs to project, through unique articulation, a precise idea. Though comparable in their massing, the Great Hall is almost three times larger than the museum. Spatial strategies are distinct: the Great Hall is almost a solid mass, while the museum is more porous and richly layered. The relatively similar facades hide the palatial, closed courtyard form of the Great Hall and the open courtyard form of the Museum of Revolution and History. Yung-Ho Chang has argued that the unlike spatial structures and like facades of these two buildings anticipated a split in architectural practice in contemporary China.[29] The palatial type has led to grand governmental aesthetics; the courtyard form to a more subtle, intellectual approach (fig. 12).

Collective form persists in China today. The vocabulary of city development aligns with the characteristics of collective form, which is reflected in its nomenclature: from a Socialist managerial theory (Big Yard) to a reformist notion of marketized area (Small District) and then to a concept to reconnect with the city and urbanity (Megaplot). All were similar in size and formation, whether "big," "small," or "mega": collective form is adaptive. Its resilience rests in its ability to allow individuation. In the Socialist market economy, the greatest assets of most of the *danwei* were the land they occupied, not their

products or productivity. A large number of *danwei* were privatized; these new entities then became developers. One example is the Beijing Paper Mill Factory. Once privatized, the factory became the developer for Steven Holl's Linked Hybrid project.[30] Individuation in collective form has progressed from space and spatialization to system and social structure.

Individual form, on the other hand, gradually lost its validity after the failure of the Great Leap Forward and the People's Commune. But starting in the 1980s, some individual forms have come back to the urban scene as the spatialization of the Socialist market economy. These post-reform individual forms are not proactive but representational. Individual forms in the 1950s were fragmented and premature attempts to realize the idea of the city. It is because of the close connectivity between the idea of the city and the individual form that the individual form has been reactivated in the context of marketized collective forms—speculative housing and office development. In these cases an individual form can sharpen the vitality of the city—not through a combination or a hybrid but through the encounter between collective decisions and individual actions.

Although marketization and neoliberal policy have advanced unprecedented development, an updated form of state control still endures. The idea of the collective has changed and adapted to a different sociopolitical context. Yet in comparison to the instability of the spatialization of the collective, the relation between the city and collective form or individual form is stable. In the Socialist market economy, the collective form individualizes the collective (spatial enclosure and managerial regulation segregate the space in the plot from the city, creating an antagonism between the city and collective form), while the individual form collectivizes the individual (the contrast to the city in scale, figure, and visual presentation projects the idea of the collective not as a reality but as an exemplar).

29 Yung-Ho Chang, "Zhang vs. Zhang: Symmetry and Split: The Development of Chinese Architecture in the 1950s and 1960s," in *Chinese Architecture and the Beaux-Arts*, ed. Jeffrey W. Cody, Nancy Shatzman Steinhardt, and Tony Atkin (Honolulu: University of Hawaii Press, 2011), 301–14.

30 Cressica Brazier, Ling Fan, and Tat Lam, "Cong xiao qu dao da yuan dao chao ji jie qu" [From big to small to mega-zone: reading large-scale development of Chinese cities through social and spatial structures], *Shi Dai Jian Zhu: Time and Architecture* 3 (2009): 28–37.

Analysis: Xiamen

A City of Three Types

Yuan Zhan, Roy Yu-Ta Lin, Dingliang Yang

Fig. 1   Boardwalk along Lujiang Road.

Xiamen is a city of 3.5 million people in southeastern China. Located on the Taiwan Strait in Fujian Province, it consists of a large island, Xiamen Island; the small Gulangyu Island; and the surrounding mainland. It was originally a small military outpost, became a burgeoning port during colonial times, and has grown into a modern and rapidly urbanizing city. Xiamen is acutely affected by its geopolitics. Island geography, proximity to Taiwan, and situation on the periphery of China's mainland have thrown into sharp relief the political and economic pressures that have shaped China's cities, providing fascinating insight into the nature of Chinese urbanization and the Chinese city today (figs. 1–3).

The urban condition of Xiamen may be understood through urban history and built forms as well as through data and maps. The city has, over time, developed specific architectural paradigms. These paradigms are not necessarily visual or functional; they may also be organizational. Political, social, and cultural forces, along with the history of the city, have shaped the primary architectural types; an analysis of these types, in turn, provides insight into the forces prevailing at the time of their production.

Three phases in the growth of Xiamen—as a city of defense, as a city of commerce, and as a city of development—have distinct correlating types. For the city of defense, it is the quadrangle courtyard house. Found throughout China, this category of residence embeds the inner hierarchies and cultural notions of the world, clan, and family. The city of commerce is characterized by the *qilou*, or shop-house. The *qilou* was advanced as Chinese overseas investment aiming for commercial profit and active street space brought foreign urban planning methods to Xiamen. The city of development brought forth the megaplot. A large parcel of land for high-rise construction, the megaplot promotes economic growth and rapid urbanization. It is used more as an instrument of financial speculation than as a means to provide places for living.

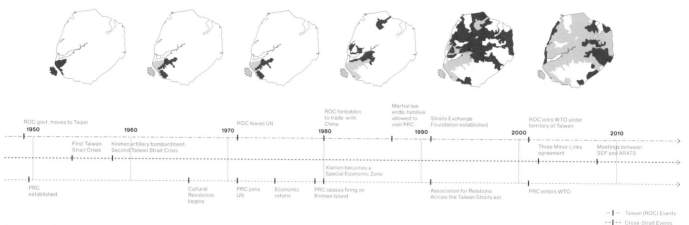

Fig. 2   Development of Xiamen.

COURTYARD HOUSE

Xiamen's position on the periphery of mainland China has given rise to two often contradictory functions for the city: military/defense and commerce/trade. The port, nearness to foreign lands, and the island topography support both naval and trading purposes. Which role prevailed was often decided by centralized powers.

The defensive nature of the city was embodied in the edict that created its first urban element: the wall. Zhou Dexing, governor of Fujian Province, reported in 1387: "Building a 425-zhang (1,417 m) wall with the height of 3-zhang (approximately 10 m) in Xiamen."[1] The building of the wall marked the official establishment of the city. Its location, on the western tip of the island, was selected for military considerations. Mountains on the east offered protection; the harbor was ideal for a naval base; and proximity to the mainland meant easy supply routes to the rest of Fujian Province.[2]

Xiamen was originally planned according to the precepts of traditional Chinese cities set out in the Kaogong ji (考工记; Record of Trades), part of Zhou li (周礼; Rituals of Zhou), a description of all manners of procedures and customs. Once the city was enclosed by a wall, the territory was divided into a matrix of grids. The palace and administrative agencies were located in the middle; quadrangle houses filled the surrounding area (see page 26, fig. 15).[3] The rationale behind this configuration can be traced to two cultural concepts. The first is "tianyuan di fang" (round heaven and square earth), which stipulates that land be divided into grids to contain urban activities.[4] The second is the cultural significance of the center. Governing power must reside in this most important area. Confucian ideas were also influential within the society, politics, and culture of ancient China; one key conviction is that the family is the basic social unit of the city, and that the dwelling for the family, the quadrangle house, should express this unit in built form (figs. 4, 5).

The quadrangle house, the first dominant type in Xiamen, shares the three key qualities of cities in ancient China: self-similarity, spatial hierarchy, and repetition of elements at various scales. These characteristics manifest in built form the classical Chinese idea "all under heaven," the idea that there is no outside or other and that there is a political order across China by which all conflicts are resolved within the system. In this way, the development of early Xiamen is linked to fundamental ideas of Chinese culture and identity,[5] and the idea that the city and its dominant type each express the other is reinforced.

Self-similarity and homogeneity of elements are evidenced in the plan of the courtyard house. The house was not a continuous volume with a courtyard puncturing the middle; instead, small rectangular buildings, each the same size and containing three rooms, were arranged to form the courtyard. Seven of these small buildings were

1   Kai Zhou, *Xiamen zhi* (1839; Daibei: Daiwan yin hang, 1961), 35.

2   Zifeng Zhou, *Jin dai Xiamen cheng shi fa zhan shi yan jiu, 1900–1937* [A study of the urban history of Xiamen, 1900–1937] (Xiamen: Xiamen University Press, 2005), 17.

3   Nancy Shatzman Steinhardt, *Chinese Imperial City Planning* (Honolulu: University of Hawaii Press, 1990), 29–36.

4   Steinhardt, *Chinese Imperial City Planning*.

5   Steinhardt, *Chinese Imperial City Planning*.

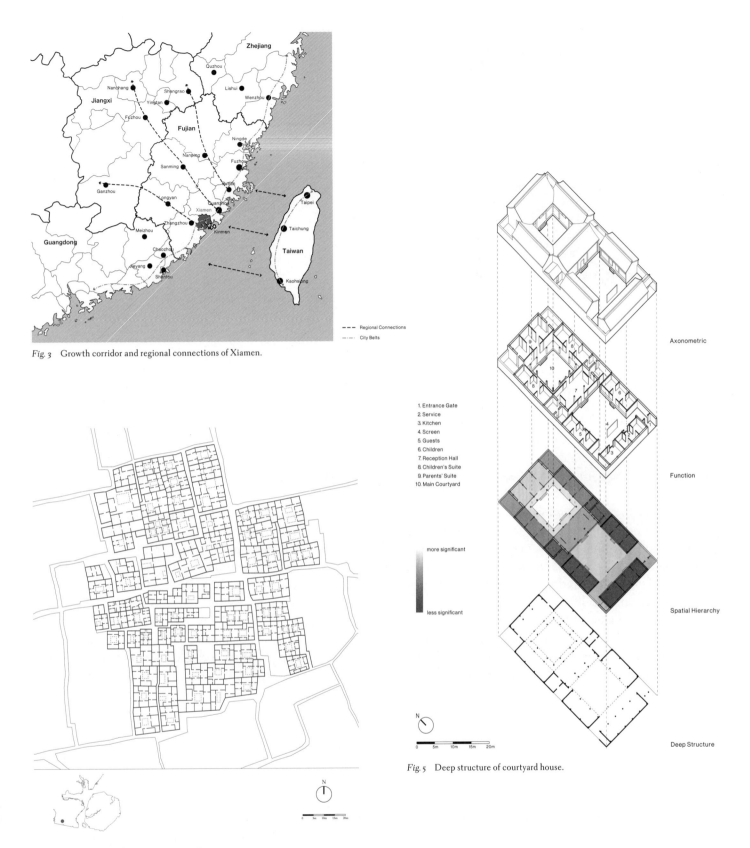

Fig. 3 Growth corridor and regional connections of Xiamen.

Fig. 4 Plan, courtyard houses in Xiangan, Xiamen.

1. Entrance Gate
2. Service
3. Kitchen
4. Screen
5. Guests
6. Children
7. Reception Hall
8. Children's Suite
9. Parents' Suite
10. Main Courtyard

Axonometric

more significant

less significant

Function

Spatial Hierarchy

Deep Structure

Fig. 5 Deep structure of courtyard house.

Fig. 6 Early courtyard houses with distinct
Minnan gables in central Xiamen.

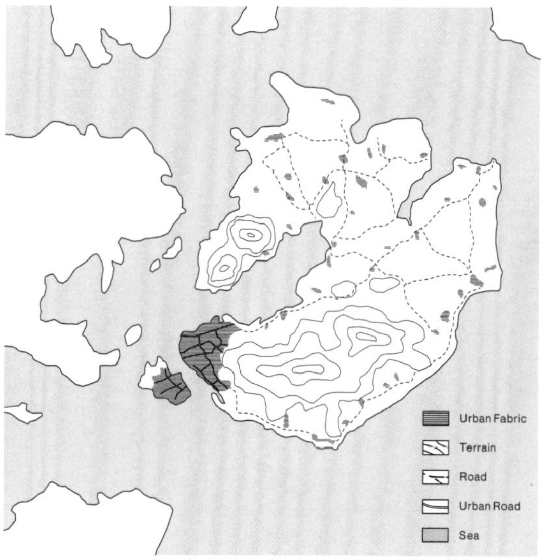

Fig. 7 Urban roads in Xiamen, 1920s.

Urban Fabric
Terrain
Road
Urban Road
Sea

assembled to produce a house with two courtyards. The
exact dimensions of a quadrangle courtyard house were
not fixed, but the proportions of the rooms and spaces
were similar from one to another. The edge of the house
was defined not by the buildings themselves but by a wall
that ran around the perimeter of the site.

The importance of a room was indicated by its placement in the plan. Primary and secondary spaces denoted
the family hierarchy. In the typical layout, the courtyard
was a centralized common space that accommodated the
family's daily activities. Rooms at the north, facing south,
were more dignified, sheltering the ancestor shrine, parents' bedroom, and the living room that received guests.
Rooms in the east and west wings were for the children.
Front rooms, the least desirable, housed the servants and
also contained the storeroom and kitchen. The position of
rooms in relation to the sequence through the dwelling
also demonstrated status. The central route, and thus the
central spaces, was the most dignified; privacy increased
toward the back of the house.

The quadrangle house manifests an idea that was
repeated at different scales in ancient Chinese cities. The
central palace at the heart of the city was in essence a
large quadrangle house that hosted many more family
members and officials. Even the city itself shared the same
structure: a collection of individual buildings surrounded
by a wall. Within the individual courtyard house, the

scalability of elements is apparent in the plan. The
arrangement of the three rooms in the individual buildings—two peripheral rooms with a common central
room—corresponds to the relationship between four
peripheral buildings and a common courtyard.

Perhaps unsurprisingly for a city devoted to defense,
the courtyard spaces of individual dwellings provide much
of Xiamen's open space; there was no large open public
area. Streets were not planned but were formed by the
aggregation of many dwellings (fig. 6).

As families became smaller and lost their importance
as a political unit within Chinese society, the quadrangle
house lost its unique and dominant place within the
urban context. Contact with the outside world was more
frequent; trade and commerce were transformed into
important aspects of life, bringing different influences to
the city. The dominant architecture of Xiamen became
less aligned with traditional Chinese culture and more
receptive to Western models.

QILOU

The *qilou* (or shop-house; the literal translation is "riding-
horse building" because it projects into the street like the
forequarters of a horse) was the dominant type in Xiamen
from the 1920s to the 1960s. After the political instability

around the turn of the century subsided and more trading links were established, an increasing number of returning Chinese émigrés brought Western architectural and urban models into an increasingly active commercial and trading city.

In 1628, Emperor Chongzhen issued an edict that Xiamen was to be restricted to military use. All commercial activity was ordered to be halted. Emperor Kangxi of the Qing dynasty (1644–1911) continued this policy, consolidating the city's position as a key component in the defense of China's eastern coast.[6] Xiamen also became an administrative and political center for the region.

Despite Emperor Chongzhen's edict, in the later years of Emperor Kangxi's reign (c. 1662–1722), increasing population pressures and the proximity to Taiwan and other developing Southeast Asian countries gave rise to business activities.[7] A century later, Emperor Jiaqing issued orders making Xiamen the "commercial gateway" to Fujian Province. The transition from military port to commercial city was greatly accelerated by the Opium Wars in the 19th century. The Treaty of Nanjing signed by the Chinese and British governments in 1842 named Xiamen and four other cities treaty ports, opening them to foreign trade. The treaty marked the transformation of Xiamen into a commercial and trading hub with strong ties to the rest of the world.

Gulangyu, the smaller of Xiamen's islands, was occupied by the British, furthering the transfer of Western practices into the old city: modern urban infrastructure, commercial environments, Western living conditions, and many outside investors. To capitalize on the circumstances of Gulangyu, and also to attract outside investment, the Xiamen city council instigated urban planning policy to reform and modernize the city. These efforts included demolishing the old city wall, improving infrastructure, and creating commercial streets (fig. 7). Approximately 60 to 70 percent of the 13.3-million-yuan cost was financed by the overseas Chinese community, and between 1920 and 1927, Xiamen was slowly transformed into a "modern city."

This period saw the first roads built to foreign standards, such as Zhongshan Road and South Simin Road.[8] Shops for high-end goods, large company offices, and department stores moved onto the newly built roads. The formation of this new commercial district was accompanied by open public space (fig. 8) and its architectural

Fig. 8 Mahjong players in Bailuzhou Park: much of the life of Xiamen is outdoors.

Fig. 9 Qilou along Zhongshan Road.

corollary, the *qilou*, which supports commercial activity within the space of the street (fig. 9).

Until the 1920s the *qilou* was common in Southeast Asian colonial cities such as Singapore but not yet in mainland China. Several factors had a role in its introduction to and subsequent dominance in Xiamen. Among the returning Chinese foreign nationals were scholars and urban planners who were trained in Western schools. Lin Guogeng (1886–1943), from Fujian Minhou, who became head of the Municipal Engineering Bureau, studied in Britain and considered transportation planning and construction to be the basis of urban reform.[9] Other emigrants returned from Japan, Taiwan, and Southeast Asia, where the *qilou* was already common. Bringing investment and knowledge they opened businesses and shops in newly built *qilou*. Between 1927 and 1931, 26 large real estate companies with an investment

6   Jinming Li, "Sixteenth-Century Chinese Overseas Trade Development and the Rise of the Moon Port," *Journal of Southeast Asian Affairs* 18, no. 4 (1999).

7   Ng Chin-Keong, *Trade and Society: The Amoy Network on the China Coast 1683-1735* (Singapore:

Singapore University Press, National University of Singapore, 1983).

8   Zhou, *Jin dai Xiamen*, 166.

9   Zhou, *Jin dai Xiamen*, 130.

Fig. 10 Plan, *qilou* along Zhongshan Road.

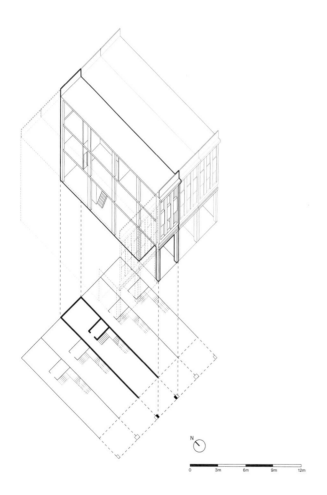

Fig. 11 Deep structure of *qilou*.

of over 30 million yuan were established by returning Chinese emigrants.[10]

The *qilou* could not have become prevalent without the new roads. Zhongshan Road, one of the most successful new commercial streets, was half a kilometer long with a 15-meter vehicular roadbed and a 3-meter pedestrian walkway (fig. 10). Columns along the edge of the walkway created an arcade, and forming the inner facade of the arcade were the *qilou*. The quadrangle courtyard house remained at the rear and center of the blocks.

Unlike the disposition of *qilou* in Singapore or Malaysia, in Xiamen there is no clear block grid. Instead, the city's *qilou* were built at a time when the planning principles associated with colonization were beginning to affect the traditional Chinese urban fabric. Linear groups of courtyard houses were demolished to clear the way for the new shopping streets; little attempt was made to integrate the streets and their buildings into the existing fabric. The dictates of commerce imposed a logic on the city, creating a new spatial hierarchy and form of public space.

One *qilou* is 4 to 5 meters wide and 20 to 30 meters deep. A cover extends from the front of the *qilou* 2 to 3 meters over the arcade. The long, thin figure allowed many storefronts to be accommodated along a relatively short street. Most *qilou* are three stories; the shop is about 4.5 meters high, and the second-floor storage and third-floor living and sleeping areas are about 3 meters high (fig. 11).

Qilou owners displayed goods in the front shop windows, which were sheltered by the arcade. The facades of

10   Jinzhi Lin, *Introduction to Overseas Chinese Investment in Domestic Enterprises in Modern Times* (Xiamen: Xiamen University Press, 1988), 80.

Fig. 12 "One Country, Two Systems" sign on Xiamen Island at closest point to Taiwan's Kinmen Islands.

the upper floors were used for advertisements; small openings admit sunlight and natural ventilation. Few *qilou* have inner courtyards, since the courtyard decreases the area for the store. The spatial hierarchy is linear, with the shop of primary importance. The disposition and function of rooms is driven not by the family unit but by commercial requirements.

The covered arcade mediates between the private space of the shop and dwelling and the public space of the street. Unlike the courtyard house, which internalizes common space within the unit, the *qilou* externalizes common space at the building and in the street. Private space is pushed inside and upward.

By forming the very structure of the street, the *qilou* is not only a tool for commercial activity; it is synonymous with the idea of the city of Xiamen as a place of commerce and trade. This conception was a radical break from the former city, which was based on traditional Chinese principles. The new public space within Xiamen allowed members of the public to imprint their own identity and also introduced the idea of the market into the urban realm.

MEGAPLOT

The megaplot, or large building site, allows the state to urbanize rapidly and efficiently by shifting to developers the investment required to install infrastructure; its architecture has been the dominant type in Xiamen since the 1980s. Xiamen's military past did not entirely recede until the early 2000s with the signing of new trade agreements between China and Taiwan; before that the threat of military conflict with Taiwan hindered its growth for much of the 20th century. Following the most active period of the Chinese Civil War, engagement shifted to the islands of Xiamen and Kinmen, and Xiamen's growth was restricted to the west side of the island. The military confrontation lasted until 1979, when the People's Republic established diplomatic relations with the United States and the conflict was transformed into a war of propaganda (fig. 12). It was only with the calming of rhetoric and hostilities between the two countries that the eastern part of the island began to develop.

Deng Xiaoping championed rapid growth at the Second National Conference on Science and Technology

Fig. 13 Central Xiamen: the growth of the city creates a uniform sea of urbanization that
isolates and defines islands of nature (hills and lakes).

in 1978, the year he began serving as China's "paramount leader": "Where conditions permit, some areas may develop faster than others; those that develop faster can help promote the progress of those that lag behind, until all become prosperous." This speech led to the program "Reform and Opening Up," or "Socialism with Chinese Characteristics," adopted by the People's Republic. On August 26, 1980, the Standing Committee of the Fifth National People's Congress approved the implementation of Special Economic Zones in Guangdong Province; in 1980, Xiamen was nominated as an SEZ and was officially defined as a "developmental city."

The SEZ brought competition, free trade, regulatory freedom, and direct foreign investment to Xiamen. The city itself became a tool for economic growth; its prosperity legitimized the government's policies. After 15 years of high-speed development, Xiamen was a new metropolis of modern high-rises (fig. 13). In 1992, Deng Xiaoping visited Xiamen and guaranteed the city 20 more years of growth and development.

Xiamen's designation as an SEZ coincided with the improvement in Cross-Strait relations, and this state of affairs played a significant role in Xiamen's urban development. Major new infrastructure projects included Xiangan Tunnel, built to connect to a newly developed peripheral district in the northeast, and the Xiamen International Conference and Exhibition Center, erected on the east side of the island as an anchor for international events (figs. 14, 15). Certain developments were started based on the anticipation of a peaceful reunification. Wu Yuan Wan, a large mixed-use project at the northeast of Xiamen Island, was named the "five fates." The label implied a close relationship with Taiwan and aimed to encourage former mainland Chinese to return.

The architecture of the megaplot is the most typical building type of the SEZ period of Xiamen, and of urbanization throughout China. Large parcels of land are transferred, by way of state support, to private developers, who take on the burden of creating infrastructure. The majority of megaplots are populated by residential towers

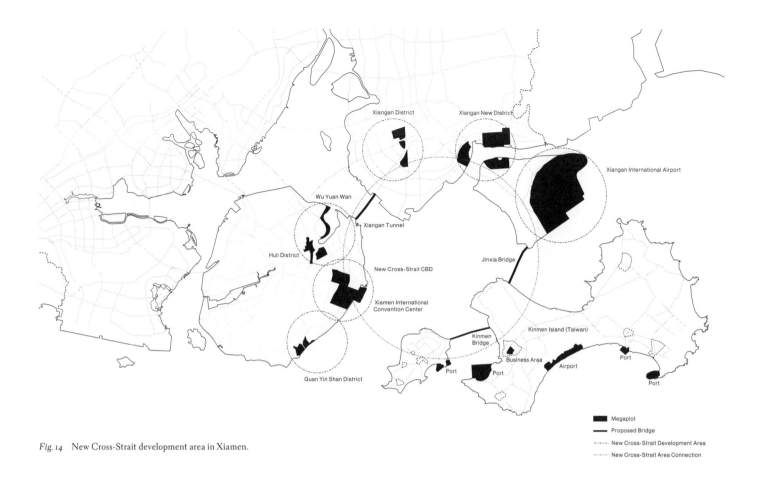

Fig. 14 New Cross-Strait development area in Xiamen.

Megaplot
Proposed Bridge
New Cross-Strait Development Area
New Cross-Strait Area Connection

Xiangan District
Xiangan New District
Xiangan International Airport
Wu Yuan Wan
Xiangan Tunnel
Huli District
Jinxia Bridge
New Cross-Strait CBD
Xiamen International Convention Center
Kinmen Island (Taiwan)
Kinmen Bridge
Business Area
Port
Airport
Port
Port
Port
Guan Yin Shan District

Fig. 15 Model for the Xiamen master plan for 2020 at the Xiamen Planning Exhibition Hall.

Fig. 17 Future Coast, a gated community on a megaplot in Jingkou, a mainland suburb of Xiamen.

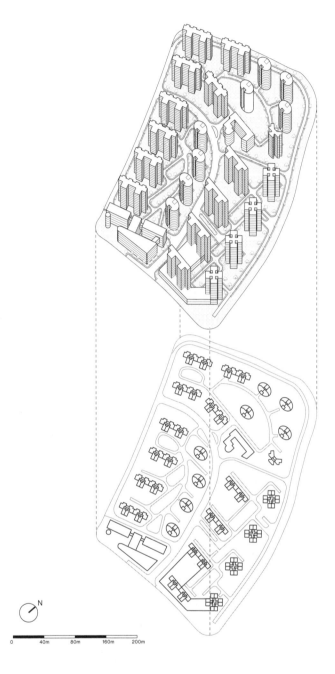

Fig. 16 Deep structure of megaplot.

or blocks, with a small amount of retail; however, in some megaplots commercial and retail are the dominant uses. East Haicang New District, a new area in Xiamen, illustrates that the form of the megaplot is a direct product of certain regulatory conditions. The massing is determined by planning regulations set by the central government, such as setbacks from main roads, distances between towers, and density and ground coverage. Because the goal is to maximize development capacity and thus profit, density is always increased to the most that is allowable, resulting in homogeneous fields of towers. The generic nature of the megaplot makes land transactions and planning easy and fast. Redundant infrastructure fractures the space of the city since all megaplots require a periphery road around the site that duplicates the road provided by the city (fig. 16). Generally isolated and islandlike, they lend themselves to gated communities or luxury enclaves, an antithesis of the public space of the street (fig. 17).

The floor plans of the high-rise towers that compose the megaplot achieve a remarkable yet unsurprising degree of homogeneity (fig. 18). The residential towers accommodate four units per floor; a compact circulation core aids in achieving maximum efficiency of space. Ventilation requirements for the kitchens and bathrooms create gaps between apartments in what is termed the "butterfly" plan. Once the most efficient floor plan has been formulated, it becomes the template for every building on the megaplot (fig. 19). Recent development of megaplots, while following the same planning principles,

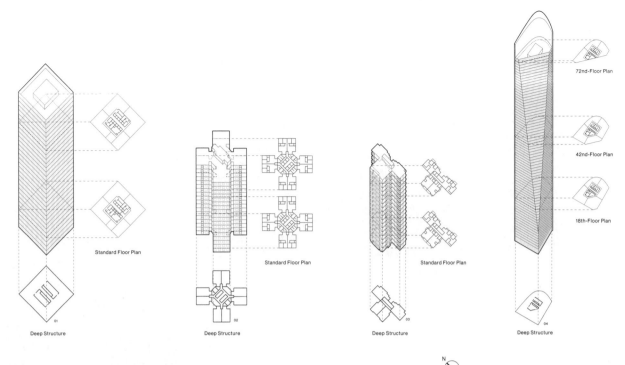

Standard Floor Plan

Standard Floor Plan

Standard Floor Plan

72nd-Floor Plan

42nd-Floor Plan

18th-Floor Plan

Deep Structure

Deep Structure

Deep Structure

Deep Structure

Fig. 18   Deep structure of high-rise as rule and exception.

Fig. 19   Royal Garden, a development on a megaplot.

Fig. 20   Center of Xiamen with three dominant types: courtyard house, *qilou*, high-rise.

Fig. 21   Main street of Dongzhai Village with construction of Morning Light over the Sea, a megaplot development, in the background.

Fig. 22   Liang Ann Financial District.

has turned to more exotic forms to keep attracting investment. The Liang Ann Financial District in east Xiamen uses the super-high-rise as a symbol of technological capital to attract both funding from the central government and foreign investment, especially from Taiwan (fig. 22).

PAST, PRESENT, FUTURE

The development of these three dominant types in Xiamen demonstrates a clear tendency: what started as a common space forged by family relations within the courtyard house has been exposed and fragmented as the city has modernized and expanded (fig. 20). If the courtyard house created a common space for a family unit, and the *qilou* a more dispersed common space in the street, the megaplot is a collection of discrete private areas with a few common spaces. It fosters a complete atomization of the social space of the city. While the economic and political forces that underlie this drastic change are not unique to Xiamen or indeed to China, certain factors make their impact particularly dramatic here. The use of the megaplot as a financial instrument for economic development, where homes are built more for speculative purposes than for housing people, has not only increased the pace of urbanization but has shifted consideration away from the civic dimension of the city (fig. 21).

Another trait exclusive to Xiamen that has had a major impact on the city's development is its geopolitical situation, namely its proximity to Taiwan. Projects proposed by the city government take advantage of the improving relations between China and Taiwan. The central government in particular regards the city as an instrument to achieve political and economic ends. A new airport in the eastern periphery of the city is expected to be a joint venture with the Kinmen government; the Jingxia Bridge will furnish a direct link between Dadeng Island, on the outskirts of Xiamen, and Kinmen Island, easing the crossing from China to Taiwan. According to Li Peng, deputy director of the Taiwan Research Institute at Xiamen University, these schemes used the claim of improved relations with Taiwan as a means to attract funding and support from the central government.[11] Such political machinations serve only to further accelerate the detrimental qualities of urbanization, treating development as a display of political intention rather than as a response to the city's needs.

An examination of Xiamen's two historic dominant types as well as the one of today suggests that there are alternatives that relate to the history of Xiamen. Returning these ideas to the city might generate new typologies and city spaces, at once offering respite from the spatial poverty of the megaplot and embodying the idea of the city.

11 Li Peng, interview with the authors, February 28, 2013.

The Xiamen Studio:
An Introduction

These studio projects are based on a typological approach to the problem of the city. An investigation into and redefinition of the city reveals its persistent architectures, or dominant types. Any attempt to define type is an attempt to define what is typical; what is most typical is common to all. Thus, type is an effective heuristic device through which to locate commonalities. The goal of a search for what is common in architecture is not formal or tectonic similitude but a commonly held idea that invests architecture with a social and political role.

THE MEGAPLOT AND THE DEVELOPMENTAL CITY

Varying from 4 hectares in urban areas to 40 hectares in city peripheries, the megaplot is a systematic and streamlined planning apparatus that allows for swift urbanization. The state requires developers to supply the investment for infrastructure, taking on the responsibility only for widely spaced infrastructure such as perimeter roads.

Megaplots are represented in city planning documents by land-use color patches. With neither architectural nor spatial attributes, the megaplot offers to development a tabula rasa. Planning parameters typically produce freestanding towers in large, unconsolidated open spaces or colossal superblocks; the luxury housing development is an enclosed gated community while the cheaper housing tract consists of monotonous rubber-stamped blocks. The idea of the city as a common space is lost.

The developmental city, or the city conceived and constructed through megaplots and used primarily as a developmental tool, has been instigated mainly by speculative capital. The urbanization of the megaplots results in the dissolution of the city as a legible artifact: it is bereft of civic dimension or public sphere. The ensuing sea of enclave urbanism does not constitute the idea of the city, either in the European tradition, as a space of partnership or coexistence, or in the Chinese tradition, as a framework with a clear and legible deep structure that regulates spaces and social relations. In response, the studio conceived and designed a common framework for the city, accommodating housing, work space, outdoor space, and related civic function or functions.

XIAMEN

Four distinct ideas of the city arose from the studio's investigation into the city of Xiamen: the city as an archipelago, the city of juxtaposed dominant types, the city of geopolitical assertion, and the city of the megaplot. The city as an archipelago exists on two scales. At the overall scale of geography, the city is defined as an island through its separation and limits to its physical development. At the scale of the city, growth has created a uniform sea of urbanization that isolates and defines islands of nature: the hills in Xiamen. The city of juxtaposed dominant types establishes the physical structure of Xiamen. The courtyard house, the *qilou*, and the megaplot mark not only particular moments of urbanization but also bear specific social, cultural, and political organizational characteristics.

The city of geopolitical assertion manifests the activities of local and national governments in the physical development of the city. Growth in specific areas is deliberately stunted or accelerated according to political expediency, resulting in uneven spatial development. In this manner, the city indexes power relations peerlessly. The city of the megaplot—an expanse of generic high-rise tower blocks—is the most ubiquitous.

The two sites for the studio projects illustrate the developmental strategy adopted by Xiamen: creating a ring of centers that connects the city to its hinterland. Yuandong Lake, adjacent to the old center of Xiamen at the southwest of the island, is the city's administrative, commercial, and cultural heart. According to the latest master plan for the city, it will be one of two central areas on the main island and thus is the site for much current redevelopment. Within Yuandong Lake is an island that represents the condition of Xiamen in miniature. It is situated in the center of a vast and sprawling hinterland yet has firm boundaries set by the lake. It is connected to the mainland yet unmoored in the city, set apart, a island within an island.

Liang Ann Financial District is situated on the northeast tip of the island and forms part of what is considered the new center to the east. This area of Xiamen is being developed as the typical developmental city in China is, with large megaplots parceled out from random districts. The site, the Lakeside Business Center, a new central business district for Xiamen, is part of the Lakeside Reservoir District. If Yuandong Lake can be defined by its geographical and contextual specificity, Liang Ann Financial District can be defined by its very genericness. It is a rectangular plot bounded on all sides by roads and setbacks. Adjacent plots will not relate to this site; this site will not relate to them. The image of the city is a fiction intended to build political support and encourage developer involvement.

COMMON FRAMEWORKS FOR XIAMEN

Each studio project proposes a common framework for the city of Xiamen. A common framework is the deep structure of the city, the structure that embodies the space of coexistence. Such an accommodative framework promotes inclusivity through exacerbating difference. Suggesting a common framework insists that a certain degree of control, through architecture, is necessary in order to cultivate meaningful difference; it insists that the city is first and foremost a space of plurality. The common frameworks proposed by the studio achieve control through an ability to frame, absorb, sequence, mark, enclose, layer, limit, separate, compress, and imprint.

Much contemporary development considers landscape to be opposed to the city; nature is to be subjugated to urbanism. The studio projects instead put forth an idea of landscape that highlights its organizational potential as a structuring element for the city. This understanding supports a conception of landscape and architecture in which the two are mutually involved. Binary opposites that are constantly in alternation, architecture and landscape generate an equilibrium of opposing forces.

Christopher C. M. Lee

Xiamen as Green Archipelago

Sonja Cheng, Waqas Jawaid

The collision of nature and city is a defining feature in the urban planning of Xiamen; each is intensified in contrast to the other. A "city created within a garden," Xiamen is a kind of urban archipelago: islands of dense development are nestled in a sea of green. However, Xiamen is quickly losing this quality as tower after tower is built by private developers.

Unlike Beijing, where the quadrangle house is the dominant type, Xiamen has resisted a singular characteristic structure in favor of three. The first is the quadrangle house. These informal constructions are ad hoc and additive; there is no standard grid. Houses are built next to and on top of one another; leftover space becomes circulation and common outdoor areas. The building type grows through incremental additions to form a villagelike construction. The common space in this assemblage is not superfluous; it is formally defined and densely programmed.

The second type is the *qilou*, or shop-house, which makes up most of the old city center. Shop-houses form an arcaded street on the ground level and contain housing above. The third building type is the megaplot with tower. In 1980, Xiamen was made a Special Economic Zone in order to attract foreign investment. Neither the quadrangle house nor the shop-house could meet the needs of the city as it grew. The tower—dense, efficient, and quick to construct—took over as the dominant type.

Our project attempts to combine qualities from all three types: the common spaces of a collection, or village, of courtyard houses; the vibrant street life of the *qilou*; and the efficiency of the tower. The site, at the southwest corner of Yuandong Lake, is a microcosm of Xiamen in its juxtaposition of architecture and landscape. The proposal will infuse the developmental framework of Xiamen to allow for heterogeneity and a regeneration of city life. A notable component of the project is common space. Common space, as distinguished from public space (open, undefined, and unprogrammed), is formally defined and programmatically specific. Common space enables individuals to come together and form an identifiable community.

A grid of civic program—library, school, fitness center, restaurant, entertainment venue, and so on—is organized in linear strips. Each civic component is paired with a landscape condition; for instance, the peach tree (*Prunus persica*) is assigned to the school strip because the peach symbolizes the rewards of patience and hard work. In the legendary orchard of Chinese goddess Xi Wangmu, peach trees flowered only after 3,000 years and their fruit made the eater immortal.

The grid, a continuation of the existing city grid, rotates and shifts in scale to accommodate the three dominant types. As large objects, the building typologies define common space within the megaplot in the same way that the dominant types have determined smaller areas of common space. Spaces for living, working, and commerce are urban islands, each a moment of "exacerbated difference" providing an area that inspires varying degrees of collaboration.

The grid defined by civic components brings together courtyard house, shop-house, and tower yet also acts as a separate entity; it proposes a framework that permits possibility, expansion, and flexibility. Spacing within the grid is varied to support a dense development of common spaces; recombining the spaces in the deep structures of buildings in Xiamen makes these areas available.

The ideal Xiamen, represented by this project in microcosm, reimagines how people live and work by bringing the heterogeneous vitality of the city within walking distance of residential areas. It is an idea and a model for future development in Xiamen that preserves and amplifies the essence of the place: a city created within a garden.

Site plan. The project preserves and amplifies the essence of Xiamen: a city created within a garden.

An island within the larger sea of urban fabric, the project proposes a framework that permits possibility, expansion, and flexibility.

The Collective Perimeter

Aanya Chugh, Lik Hang Gu

In many urbanizing regions throughout Asia, the central business district acts as the de facto city center. Characterized by an accumulation of towers in a dense center, the CBD affects an image of the city that reflects on the ability of the developer to accumulate capital and bear the cost of advanced building technology. The city as a collective space formulated for the common good—the Aristotelian definition of the city—is irrelevant, if not wholly absent. Nor does the CBD bear any semblance to traditional Chinese collective space.

One conception of collective space in China is offered by the courtyard house, where small rectangular buildings share inwardly oriented common areas. The most privileged spaces are typically those that are the most concealed from the exterior and the farthest from the entrance. This introverted notion of collective space manifests itself at the scale of the city and at the scale of the building. According to architectural theorist and historian Jianfei Zhu, this collectivity expresses the relational nature of Confucianism and Daoism, which is based on maintaining opposites in equilibrium. In the Fujian *tulou* (circular courtyard house), for instance, an introverted nature and central-facing disposition suggest common ownership of the center. Although this type is oriented defensively inward, it is nevertheless highly collective.

Xiamen's current urban development is characterized by top-down master planning, a byproduct of China's market Socialism. Paradoxically open-ended, planning policies do not limit future growth, suggesting that urbanization must result in endless expansion. This project negates these received assumptions by redeploying the circular logic of the Fujian *tulou* at an urban scale. Instead of a dense, vertical center, low-rise housing and commercial spaces are arrayed to frame a vast expanse of open space.

The outside landscape, designed to draw people in, slopes gently downward. At the center, this relationship is inverted: the landscape builds up for privacy and for the central open space. This inner void is reserved as a retreat, where meandering pathways offer respite from the metropolis.

The building enclosing the park twists, or migrates, to accommodate commercial space and housing in a pliable, continuous framework. The bearing of the structure changes dramatically at the thresholds between functions, operating defensively for housing and in a more porous manner for office and commercial space. Through the constant inversion of convexity and concavity, the overall form entertains various perceptions of individual and collective space. Within the folds of the building are pockets of public space that vary in scale and program, from small parks to large public areas. These external spaces convey a sense of privacy even though they are directly connected to the more public commercial space.

The malleable nature of the structure accommodates both housing and commercial space. Variation lies in the elevation. Housing units of different sizes are positioned within a fixed perimeter. Leftover spaces in the plan translate to open spaces in section. These areas are connected by stairs to produce common spaces within the facade. The collective spaces therefore exist at the urban scale, within collections of units, and as balconies, within the units themselves.

The project offers an alternative to the typically gridded megaplot parcel. Density occurs at the perimeter of the plot in close proximity to the twisting, crenulated building. Density generated in this way may take on a diversity of forms. Here, it is informed by the context of Xiamen and other Chinese precedents. Unlike most CBDs, which impart an image of economic progress through iconic high-rise clusters, the project puts forward a strategy by which the city center may be made more dense without compromising an experience of collectivity.

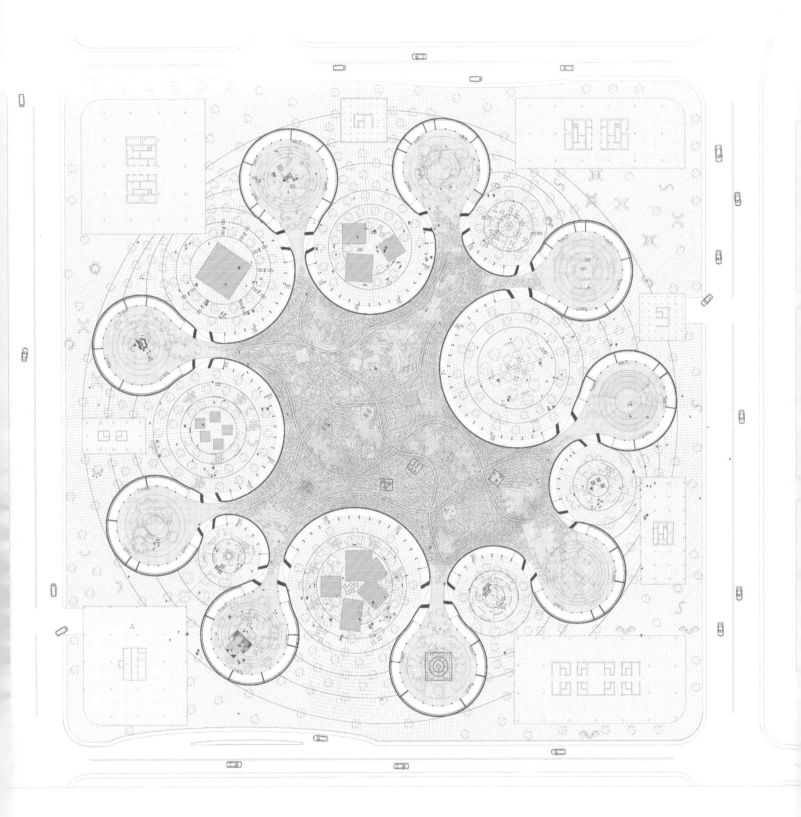

Site plan. The project offers an alternative to the typically gridded megaplot parcel. Density occurs at the perimeter of the plot in close proximity to the twisting, crenulated building.

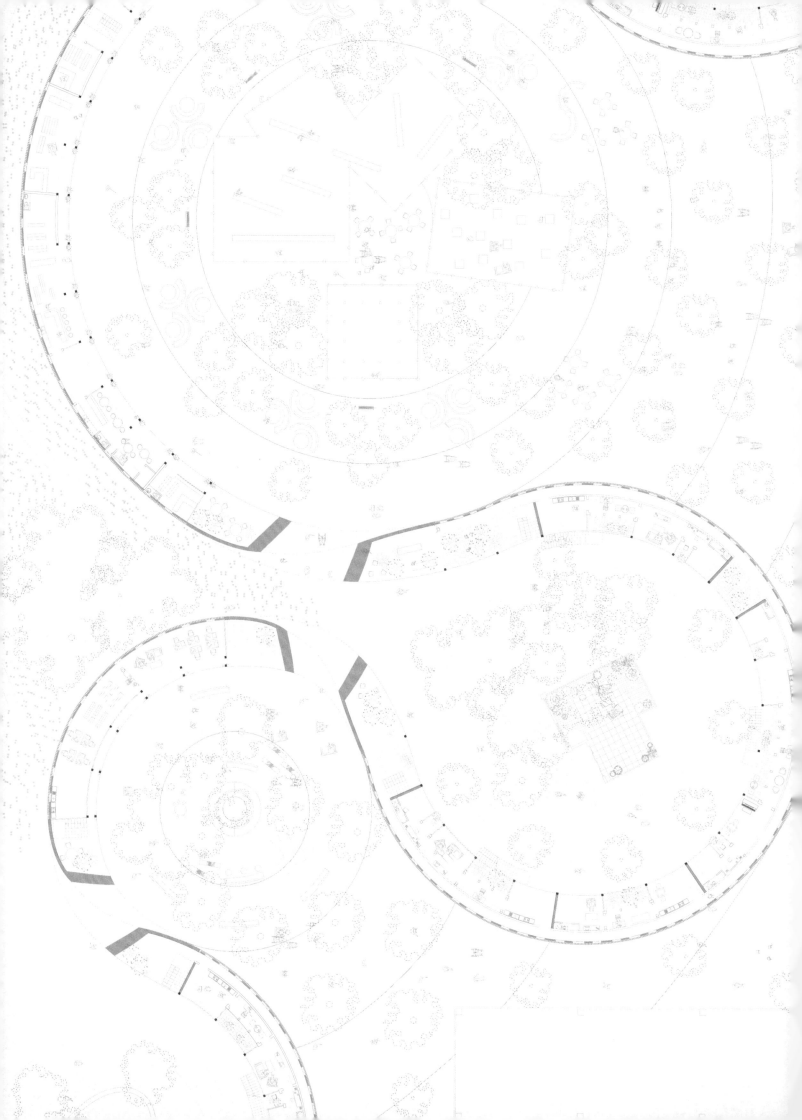

Fragment model. The project puts forward a strategy by which the city center may be made more dense without compromising an experience of collectivity.

Fragment plan. Within the folds of the building are pockets of public space that vary in scale and program, from small parks to large public areas.

The Two Sides

Roy Yu-Ta Lin

The relationship between mainland China and Taiwan has been a matter of contention since 1949. While the political situation remains unsettled, financial and economic cooperation has served to create closer ties. In the region of the Taiwan Strait, economic ties were evidenced by the 2001 Three Minor Links agreement between Xiamen Island, Kinmen Island, and Taiwan Island. By transforming Xiamen and Kinmen into interrelated economic entities, the agreement changed the eastern part of Xiamen Island from a military no-man's-land to an area ripe for development.

As part of the Xiamen master plan for 2020, a central business district is proposed as an economic hub for this newly connected region. In general, a CBD is a symbol of capital accumulation, an image of confidence to attract investors. It does not respond well to a granular urban fabric; it is indifferent, homogeneous, and inevitably not of a human scale. In other words, the CBD is the megaplot par excellence. This proposal, instead of taking the idea of the CBD for granted, uses the *qilou*, Xiamen's shop-house, as an urban framework for reconceptualized accommodation for contemporary living and working.

The *qilou*, an Asian version of a European arcade, is common throughout Xiamen. It reflects the local climate, alludes to colonial intervention, and incorporates a programmatic mix that is typical of the region. As a dominant type, the shop-house embodies a common memory. A linear garden, which draws on the deep structure of the *qilou*, represents a street running east-west between two rows of shop-houses. The party walls of the shop-houses, which run north-south, organize live-work units of varying sizes. Some of these walls extend to enclose a series of urban "pockets" that house different programs.

As in the *qilou*, each office unit has a sequence of exterior space, transitional corridor space, interior space, and in some cases, back alley. Shared courtyards are formed between every two clusters. Degrees of access and privacy are established by the treatment of landscape.

Inscribed over the site and encompassing the living units is a perfect circle. The contrast of fine grain and geometric circle gives the project a strong identity within the city. Like the corridor of the *qilou*, the circular space is transitional, a locus for interaction and collaboration.

A sinuous park stretches from one edge of the circle to the other, separating the project into two sides and providing an area for several civic programs. The most significant of these is a library for the history and culture of China and Taiwan. The facade is blank and the structure is narrow, reflecting an unsettled political state and a limited historic period.

While the architecture of the CBD creates an absolute and common framework for the site that works at various scales, the landscape identifies and creates difference between the two sides. It is composed of productive plant species from both Xiamen and Taiwan: fruit trees, vegetables. The region where pathways from opposite directions overlap is planted with rice, a crop prevalent in Xiamen and Taiwan alike. The rice paddies are shared and cultivated by both sides.

The reinterpretation of the *qilou* reimagines the space for working, living, and cooperation. It manifests the political circumstances of the region as it rejects the use of a generic CBD to represent a unification glossed over by economic convenience. By transforming the dominant type into a common framework, the project captures an idea of the city based on political, cultural, and social realities. This common framework, both as architecture and landscape, forms a rich ground where the two sides can interact, cooperate, benefit without compromising.

Site plan. The contrast of fine grain and geometric circle gives the project a strong identity within the city.

Fragment model. The party walls of the shop-houses organize live-work units of varying sizes.

Ground-floor fragment plan. While the architecture creates an absolute and common framework, the landscape identifies and creates difference between the two sides.

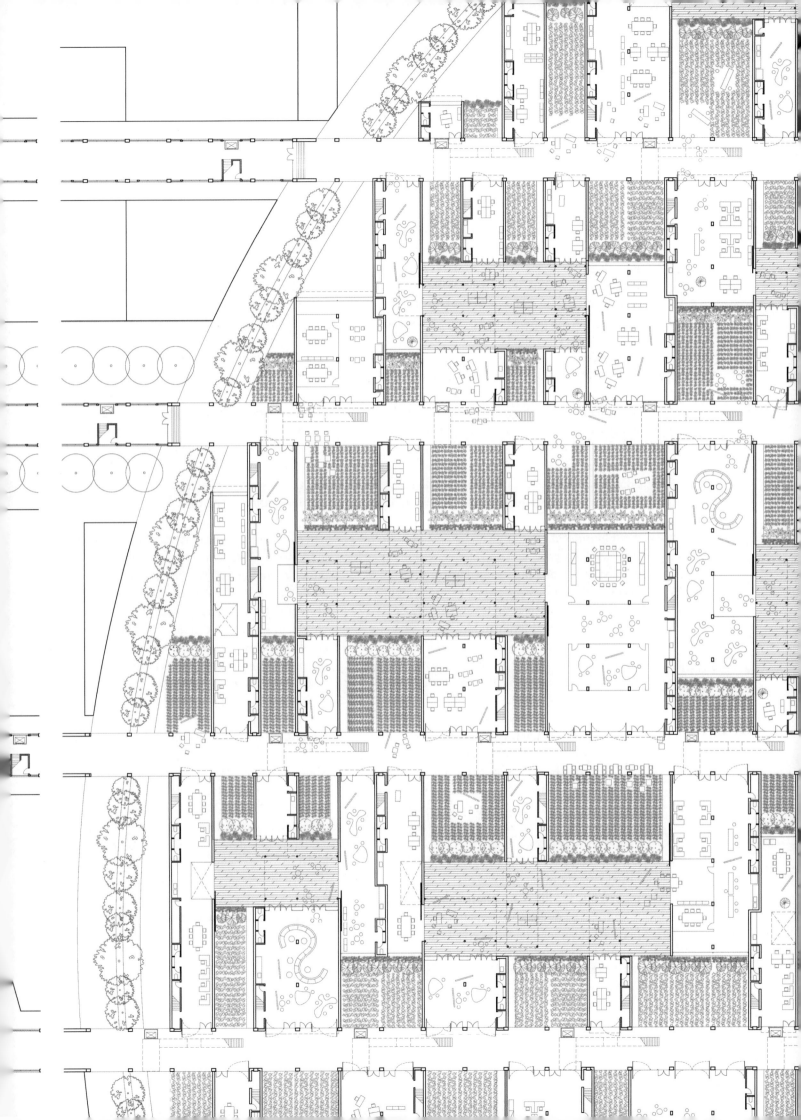

The City Room: Captures of Xiamen

Ryan Otterson, Michael Leef

In Xiamen, the space of urbanization is separate from the space of the city. The unbounded space of urbanization promotes continuous economic growth. The megaplot is the primary mechanism for this urbanization. The space of the city, by contrast, is a negotiation between areas of housing and the public realm. Cities are spaces of voluntary gathering, of commonality and difference.

Public spaces within urbanized Xiamen are too big and impersonal, and there are too few of them outside the historic center. They fail to capture the interaction, pluralism, and community that define civic life. An exception is Xiamen's central park, where the spaces are appropriated and reappropriated in rich and diverse ways. The outdoor space of the park takes on the life of the city.

This project proposes a revised relationship between landscape and architecture within the context of Xiamen and its rapid urbanization. A new mechanism of space making resists the dissolution of city space in urbanizing areas. Japanese architect Fumihiko Maki's concept of a city room, a momentary capture of the continuous flow of the city, proposes a means by which the traditional central business district, a tract of dispersed towers, may be counteracted.

Informing the idea for the city room in Xiamen is the common space shaped and defined by two exemplary projects. The Neue Nationalgalerie in Berlin by Mies van der Rohe and Duisburg Nord by Latz + Partner supply, in their deep structure, both typological precedents and a clear idea of the city room in terms of architecture and landscape.

The Neue Nationalgalerie offers a city room raised by a plinth and defined by a floating steel roof. While the interior room is a place apart from the city, its glass walls open the view and play on the interaction between city and city room. Duisburg Nord arranges an isotropic grid of trees on an abandoned industrial site. The even grid fills the voids between industrial artifacts, measuring a series of rooms that unifies the disparate structures. The industrial artifacts serve as meaningful exceptions in the park landscape.

The site in Xiamen is a future CBD—not a city, but a space of urbanization. City life is likely to disappear from this megaplot development, as it has in existing ones. The city room is inserted into the center of the planned CBD, an intervention that provides a contrast to the surrounding high-rises. In accordance with Maki's conception of the city room, the CBD and the landscape must be structured to capture the continuous flows of the city. The utilization of a ubiquitous, seemingly endless landscape, which gives definition to an otherwise generic field, questions the spaces of urbanization in the CBD.

This field of landscape is a multilayered system of offset isotropic grids in which a porous umbrella of living quarters above defines the various city rooms. The even field of landscape is given meaning only where it overlaps with the umbrella above. Vertical circulation cores and entrances—points of contact with the ground—are shared between the housing units above and the programmatic components below; the field of landscape becomes a negotiated plane where lawn is either playground, schoolyard, meeting room, or park.

Our project also contributes to the series of dominant types—courtyard house, *qilou* (shop-house), megaplot—that has been identified in Xiamen. A new dominant type might manifest a redefined idea of the city in Xiamen, whether it punctuates the fabric of megaplots (unlike contemporary developments) or takes on new forms of higher density, new programs, and new types of urban fabric. This dominant type would be characterized by a ground plane of "captures" rather than one of uninterrupted or undefined fields.

Axonometric. The project proposes a revised relationship between landscape and architecture within the context of Xiamen and its rapid urbanization.

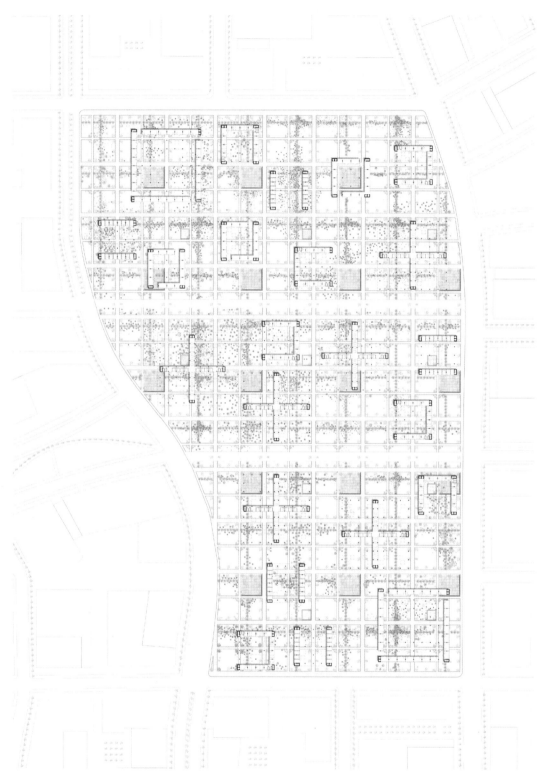

Site plan. The utilization of a ubiquitous, seemingly endless landscape, which gives definition to an otherwise generic field, questions the spaces of urbanization in the CBD.

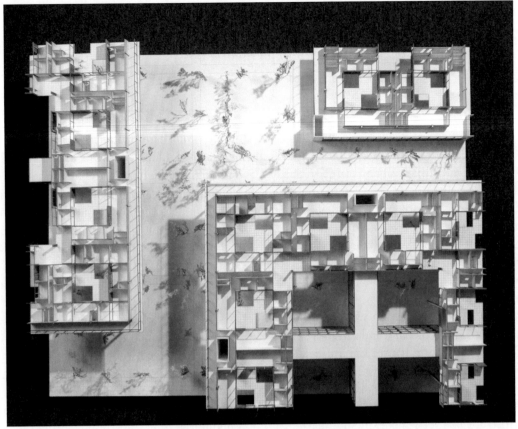

Fragment model. Residential units occupy the umbrella canopies.

The even field of landscape is given meaning only where it overlaps with the umbrella above.

Sequential Urbanism

Ryley Poblete

Since the 1960s, a shift in the interpretation of the public realm in China has been paired with a devolution of the relationship between the public and private realms. The urban condition of Xiamen is the result of four distinct phases of development. Each of these phases may be defined by a specific urban measure that attempted to mediate between the public and private space of the block. The historic precedent for development—the first phase—was premised around the concept of the lane and the alley, defined by the *qilou* (shop-house) and the *cuo* (courtyard complex), respectively.

In the next stage of development, the *qilou* was introduced in Xiamen by returning émigrés from British colonial settlements in Southeast Asia. With the insertion of the *qilou* into the urban framework came the fortification of the street front and the insulation of neighborhood communal space. As local populations increased, more public space was consumed, eventually eliminating the alley.

The third phase, the city of micro-regions, saw megablocks used to create self-sustaining communal and industrial areas. The mediated space defined by the *qilou* was contracted; the bar building with its increased setbacks was ushered in. Infrastructure took over as the definitive planning element, creating vast chasms in the urban fabric as semipublic mediated space was obliterated.

The most recent phase of development accelerates the process of insulation. Megaplots, often subdivided by function, are populated by homogeneous fields of towers. These constellations of islands are divided by infrastructure and parceled for financial viability.

This project seeks to replicate the public and semiprivate communal space lost over the various phases of development in Xiamen by using the megaplot to mediate between disparate elements of the urban grid. The ordering of urban space into a sequence of realms—whether housing and housing, housing and office, office and landscape, or housing and landscape—is defined by the bidirectional party wall, the fundamental element of the *qilou*. The party walls generate a new type of bar building, and when these bars are placed on the site they create framed space that is transformed into the public realm. The bars themselves are subdivided into communal space and residential units. The aggregations of units are thus defined by the multiplicity of units, sponsoring variation at the level of the unit, the housing block, and the site plan.

The terrain between the bar buildings is defined as a space of topographical, hydrological, botanical, and programmatic diversity. It is not a transitory field of superficial landscaping; nor is it a podium. Rather the ground densifies in certain areas to increase space for specific functions. The system is organized around the concept of the *lang* (a corridor-room that unifies the rooms in a Chinese courtyard house). The multiplication of the *lang* creates a series of framed spaces that together foster difference.

The arrangement becomes a network for circulation and also accommodates programs for the city. The programming of the landscape itself constructs a layering of difference. Disparate topographical and hydrological conditions augment the programmatic elements. Their implementation within the structure of the *lang* opens the public spaces to the city and the inhabitants.

The project takes the mediating quality of the semipublic layer of the city to the scale of the megaplot. The public space at the scale of the framed landscape, the communal space at the scale of the neighborhood bar, the programmatically active ground: these afford a field of rooms for the city. Ultimately the project recuperates a semblance of the lost order of spaces. A fabric of new construction that seeks to stitch together distinct elements of the city relieves the monotony of the island urbanism plaguing the Chinese city today.

Axonometric. Urban space is ordered into a sequence of realms by the bidirectional party wall.

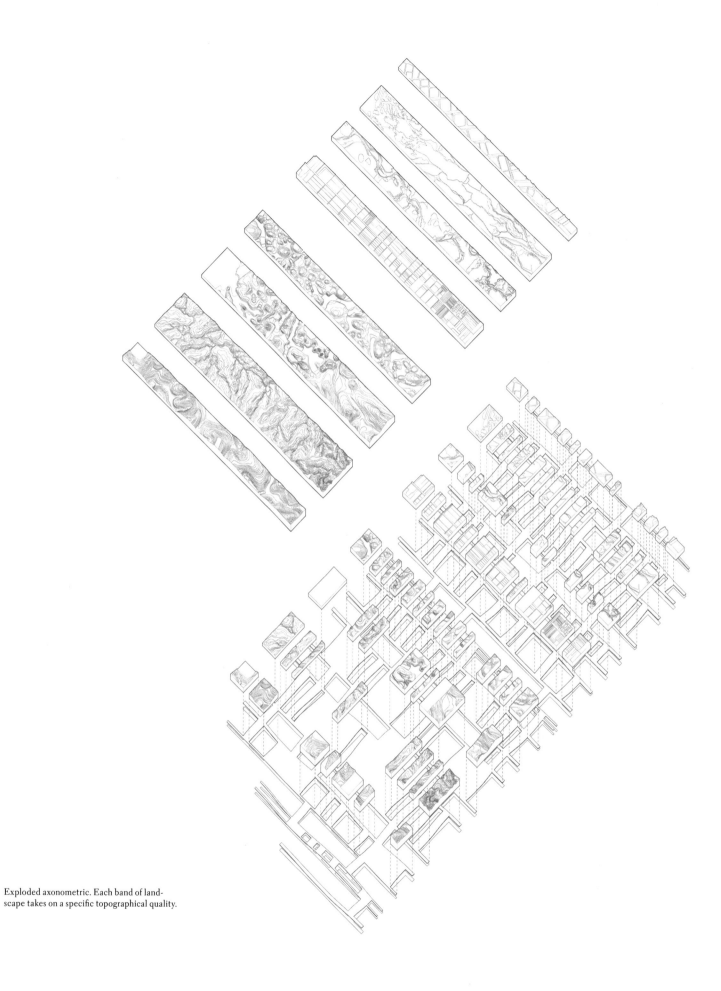

Exploded axonometric. Each band of landscape takes on a specific topographical quality.

Site plan. The landscape is framed at different scales, from the scale of the city to the scale of the dwelling.

Production of Nature: Reframing Xiamen

Matthew Scarlett, Jisoo Yang

Xiamen is unique among China's developing frontier cities, in large part due to a commitment by the city planning department to preserve and expand green space. Nevertheless, the existing paradigm of development relies heavily on the megaplot and the narrow logic of real estate speculation. Landscape elements are typically restricted to interstitial spaces between buildings. This reinforces a perception of Xiamen as a "city in a park," where landscape, considered to be a continuous, endlessly proliferating field condition, is utilized primarily as a tool to soften rapid urbanization.

In considering the modern city, Henri Lefebvre noted in *The Production of Space* that one of the illusions that defines the predominant conception of space is "the realistic illusion," or "the illusion of natural simplicity." The HOK master plan for the new Liang Ann Financial District, envisioned by the government and its investors as a step in the economic collaboration with Taiwan, suffers from this problematic conceptualization. HOK uses green space as it is used elsewhere in Xiamen, to fill borders and setbacks, attempting to "naturalize" the overall image of the city. In short, it exemplifies Lefebvre's palliative component: green space surrounds individualistic and often ludicrous architectural objects in a manner that will most likely result in a completely fractured urban experience.

This project, which occupies the same territory, runs counter to predominant notions of capitalist development in China, endeavoring to reorient landscape in the district toward the experience of the event. Through a framework of limits and juxtaposition, it develops a "park in a city." Established building types in China, including the courtyard house, the lane house, and the *qilou* (shop-house), provided useful sources for the project.

The quadrilateral courtyard house, an assembly of pavilions, creates an interior landscape that serves as the focal point of the architecture. Lane housing, most commonly found in Shanghai, likewise presents an architectural typology that folds exterior and interior space into an interrelated entity. The famous *qilou* of Xiamen feature a continuous exterior arcade. The hard boundaries between outside and inside, public and private, are reduced at ground level, and the captured space along the facade is permeable and inclusive.

In our project, architecture fades into the background and frames three landscape types with different scales and orientations: the garden courtyard, the productive lane, and the utopian escape. The formal qualities of the garden courtyard are derived primarily from the courtyard house. The essence of the landscape originates from an intimacy of scale and a relationship with the indoors. The lane garden, a strip of open space delimited on both sides by buildings, suggests a reinterpretation of the productive landscape. Adjacency between architecture and landscape expands the notion of useful green space beyond the solely agricultural. Finally, the central open space, a romantic vision of nature as an escape, dramatizes the pastoral, which to most people in Xiamen characterizes the identity of the city. As landscape is brought to the fore and the city recedes, the cultural significance of nature is replenished.

While it is an established custom in Xiamen to enjoy open-air social events, both the demands of the knowledge economy and the presence of mobile technology increasingly allow work to occur in unlikely spaces. The proposal offers a less structured and potentially more collaborative work environment that extends beyond the boundaries of an individual office building or apartment tower. Most important, by proposing a framework for the city that stems from architectural specificity, richness of landscape, and spectrum of urban activities, the project puts forward the possibility of intensifying a sense of collective memory and shared experience.

Site plan. As landscape is brought to the fore and the city recedes, the cultural significance of nature is replenished.

Site model. The central pastoral landscape is framed by thin, linear housing blocks.

Site model. Counter to predominant notions of capitalist development in China, the project positions landscape as an integral part of the city.

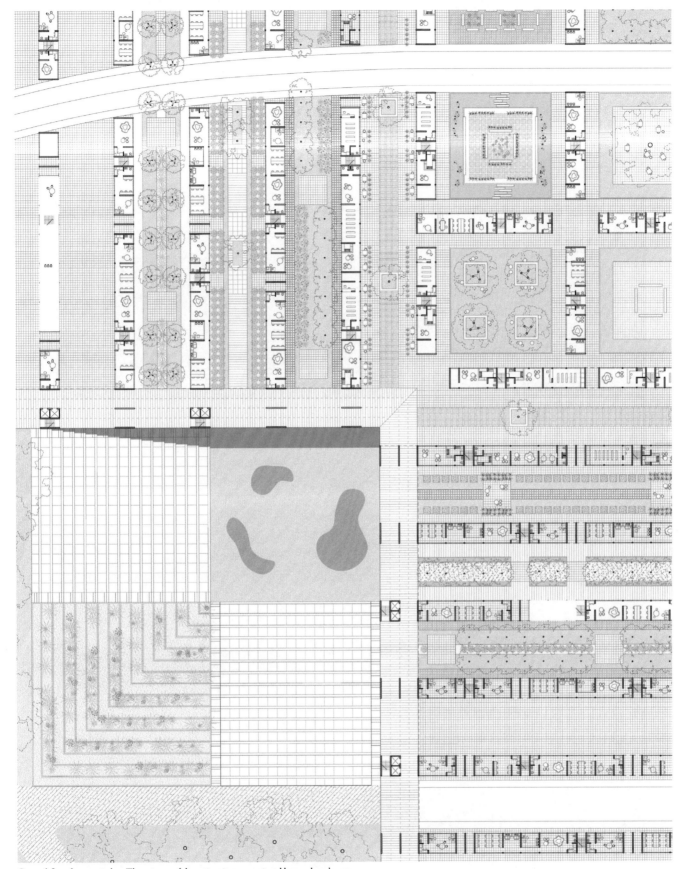

Ground-floor fragment plan. Three types of deep structure—courtyard house, lane house, and *qilou*—form the project.

The landscape of the utopian escape dramatizes the pastoral.

The landscape of the productive lane suggests a reinterpretation of the productive landscape.

The landscape of the garden courtyard is derived primarily from the courtyard house.

Architecture fades into the background and frames three landscape types with different scales and orientations.

The Urban Sift: Exacerbated Proximities

John Martin Tubles, Jonghyun Yi

In China, the megaplot is a fast and effective tool used by the government, through developers, to urbanize rapidly. The ground condition produced in association with the megaplot is fragmented and antagonistic to any kind of common space. The pervasive use of the extruded tower block changes the scale and overall skyline of the city, and it transforms the spatial character of the district into one with little relation to its recent past.

The figure-ground plan created by the megaplot in Xiamen illustrates the city's attitude toward the appropriation of public space, along with the dilemma of the freestanding building in the modern city. The buildings, or figures, are unmoored objects in an expanse of ground, a striking contrast to the rich urban fabric of traditional European cities. The buildings of a megaplot are disconnected from adjacent areas, and the residual open spaces are turned into bleak parks.

This project critiques the megaplot's anonymous relationship with the city by means of an architecture defined by intimacy, thinness, and specificity. A series of medium-rise wall-blocks creates an egalitarian mat condition, a porous space on the ground and a vital screen on the vertical plane. Situated in the center of the Liang Ann Financial District, adjacent to an array of generic tower blocks, the project traverses a proposed green corridor. The mat intervention softens the divide between the high-rises and the park, favoring a serendipitous stroll of meanders and discoveries.

Key to our proposal is a sense of compression that creates an intense proximity between two thin wall-blocks. The architecture of thinness and fineness impresses on the private and common realms closeness, friction, and compactness, qualities not found in the megaplot. The relationship of figure to ground, however, does not re-create the traditional city fabric of Xiamen. Instead, an open ground plane makes use of thin walls, piloti, and landscape elements to frame space. Degrees of porosity, as opposed to hard barriers, are arrayed to form areas of extreme, streetlike compression or open, plazalike expansion. The porosity repositions the connection between residential district and landscape to one of proximity, interaction, and integration.

The underlying structure of the architecture, thin parallel walls, distinguishes the disposition of figure and ground. The correspondence between the two is not neutral; the allocation of figure and ground generates hierarchies, programmatic zones, and circulation routes and sets larger, more anonymous park areas apart from smaller communal gardens. The landscape reflects the principles of the architecture at a larger scale. The open spaces engage and transgress the boundaries of the site, melding the plot with the surrounding area. The elements of the landscape are themselves architectural and act as an urban sift—a fine urban grain that allows pedestrians to traverse the open spaces via multiple routes.

The logic of the site plan extends to the design of architectural details. Residents store their belongings within translucent walls composed of shelves and thin screens, producing unique and ever-changing shadows that will animate the facade. Urban life is characterized by an awareness of others, which fosters a sense of commonality. The architecture presents these traces of everyday living in an effort to move away from the isolation often typical of the megaplot and the high-rise.

The figure-ground correlation put forward by this project mitigates the segregation of the lone tower yet does not resort to the image of the traditional European city. It is an attempt to reinterpret the common spaces of Xiamen through its dominant type, favoring neither object nor fabric, architecture nor landscape. The landscape and architecture act in unison and in alternation to reify the idea of the city as a common framework.

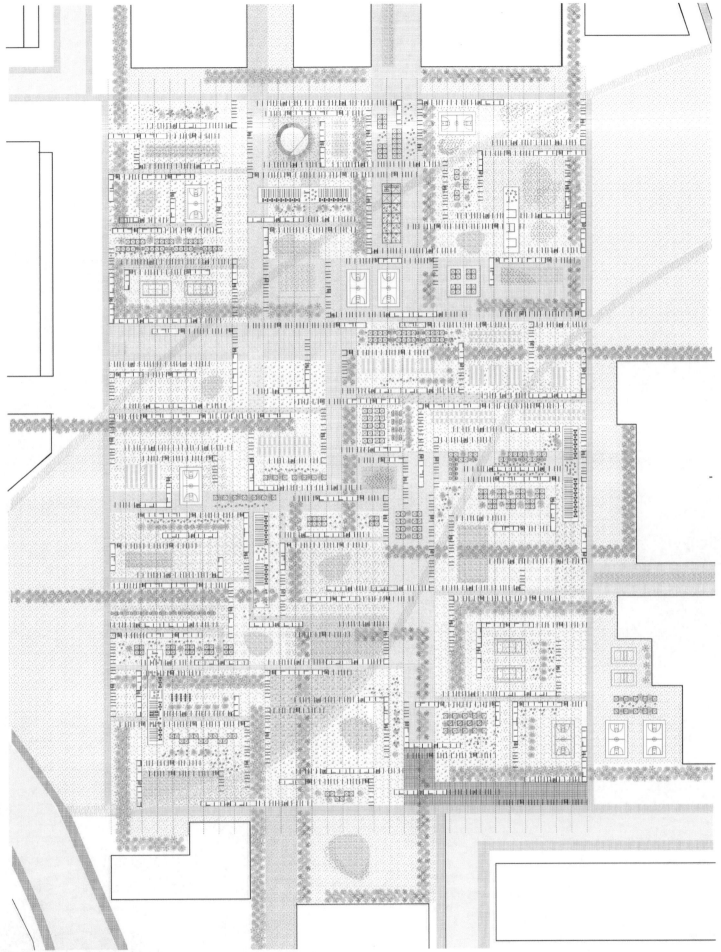

Site plan. Degrees of porosity are arrayed to form areas of streetlike compression or plazalike expansion.

Cross-Border City

The Border as a City

Christopher C. M. Lee

Fig. 1   Macau's Hengqin (left) and Cotai (right), 2012.

Borders are not commonly associated with a city's density, richness, and concentration of economic, cultural, and political life. They serve, rather, to separate nations and to host immigration checkpoints and infrastructural crossings; these are degraded spaces to pass through quickly, not worthy destinations. However, many rapidly urbanizing areas today are situated at borders that separate two spaces with fundamentally different socioeconomic and political statuses, be they nation-states or cities. These developing borderlands include the urbanized area along the US-Mexico border (El Paso/Juarez, San Diego/ Tijuana); Johor Bahru and Iskandar at the border between Singapore and Malaysia; and Shenzhen/Hong Kong and Macau/Zhuhai between mainland China and its special administrative regions. The recent and rapid urbanization at these locations is affected by the flow of global capital, which locates the points of greatest polarity for the extraction of profit: cheap and abundant labor in Mexico and Shenzhen, expansive land for development in Johor, and legal gambling in Macau, at the doorstep of mainland China. As many border scholars have argued, the

urbanized borderlands are spaces of exploitation and exclusion, with acute economic and social inequality and political disenfranchisement.[1] However, they possess many of the same characteristics as cities: they are dense, economically vibrant, and most important, spaces where strangers meet, spaces of coexistence.

My aim here is to understand, and attempt to conceptualize, the space of the border as a city or, more precisely, as a cross-border city. Macau is a paradigmatic example of a cross-border city (fig. 1). Although it is indeed unique, a former Portuguese colonial city in the southern tip of China, it shares characteristics of cross-border cities elsewhere. The cross-border city is an example of architecture as a common framework for the city, precisely because the border is not merely something that separates but also something that accommodates: these borders absorb, thicken, feather, and broaden in different parts of the city. And at points they become a specific architecture, an architecture of the city. The term "cross-border" suggests an exportation from one zone to another as well as an incursion, sometimes violating or

1   Henk van Houtum and Ton van Naerssen, "Bordering, Ordering and Othering," *Tijdschrift voor Economische en Sociale Geografie* 93 (2002): 125–36; Henk van Houtum, Olivier Kramsch, and Wolfgang Zierhofer, *B/ordering Space, Border Regions Series* (Burlington, VT: Ashgate, 2005).

suspending a sovereign boundary. Instead of assuming a belief in the determinism and absolute authority of so-called scientific planning and economic development or a pessimism adopted by many a disinterested architect or urbanist, who accepts everything and offers nothing, I attempt here to conceive of a project for the city through an understanding of the city itself, its perceived shortcomings and strengths, and always through its architecture. It is when architecture can offer an alternative model, without being completely subservient to the status quo, that it revalidates its cultural, political, and social relevance in its wider milieu.

CITIES AND BORDERS

The city is often discussed as a clearly delimited space, a defined center. The border, conversely, is presented as a line that separates, a frontier often far from areas of concentrated inhabitation. Clearly, the tropes used to describe and understand the city fall short when the subject is the outcome and process of urbanization in the borderlands. Saskia Sassen's observations in "When the Center No Longer Holds: Cities as Frontier Zones" and Richard Sennett's elucidation of the difference between boundaries and borders illuminate the interdependency between the idea of the city and the idea of the border.

According to Sassen, the more complex and global a city is today, the more it behaves as a frontier. These global cities, with their transversal borders, are in fact more impenetrable than conventional transnational borders:

> The large complex city, especially if global, is a new frontier zone. Actors from different worlds meet there, but there are no clear rules of engagement. Where the historic frontier, as seen from imperial centers, was in the far stretches of the "colonies," today it is deep inside those imperial centers.[2]

This statement is an expansion of her *Global City* thesis of 2001,[3] in which she observed that the processes that drive the formation of the global city find their expression in the clustering of multinational corporations in central business districts in different cities around the world. Such clusters have two defining characteristics: the homogenization of spaces where the corporations are located (the CBD in London's Canary Wharf, for instance,

is almost indistinguishable from certain districts of Manhattan) and the extreme disjunction between these spaces and their contexts in terms of both built form and social and cultural content. Her later essay argues that global cities are more tightly bordered today due to increased global flows of capital, information, and population groups; gated communities are one example of this bordering. Far from making a borderless world, and contrary to popular belief, these spaces are impenetrable. Goods may travel through customs checkpoints, and capital through binary codes supplied by international banks, but immigrants and tourists require documentation for movement and access. There are two distinct sets of travelers: those who have unimpeded access to multinational corporations—professionals involved in the global economy—and those who do not. Trade agreements enacted by the World Trade Organization and others allow professionals to circulate across borders and move freely within the networks that connect more than 75 global cities—such networks are essentially transversal borders that cut through conventional state borders. The professionals who move through these spaces are separated radically from the working-class and poor migrants—no skilled smuggler or amount of luck or courage can get the latter groups across these borders. The transversal borders make the city ever more polarized and politicized, fostering a common cause that can unite citizens of the city and not the nation. The free movement of capital but not labor has concentrated economy and society in zones where two financial and political frameworks meet, in other words, at the periphery, the borderlands. The city has arrived at the border at the same time that the center is ever more bordered and impenetrable.

If the border and the city are mutually involved in the contested space of urbanization today, then Richard Sennett's call to shift attention away from the center, and toward the border, offers a reminder of the importance of modulation and time in the design of urban spaces. Sennett uses analogies from the natural world to define the difference between boundaries and borders. Borders are zones in a habitat where organisms, due to the meeting of disparate species or physical conditions, become more interactive. Like a membrane, borders contain nourishment but also permeate selectively. Boundaries are rather limits, territories marked by scent and sound beyond which a particular species does not stray. This distinction informs Sennett's ambitions for an open city,

2   Saskia Sassen, "When the Center No Longer Holds: Cities as Frontier Zones," *Cities* 34 (October 2013).

3   Saskia Sassen, *The Global City: New York, London, Tokyo* (Princeton, NJ: Princeton University Press, 2001).

in both process and built form, and especially in borders between communities.[4] As a demonstration, he cites his work—which he considers "a failure"—on a regeneration project in New York's Spanish Harlem. The border between Spanish Harlem, one of the poorest communities in the city, and the neighboring district, one of the richest areas in the world, is 96th Street. Sennett's team placed a new market not on this border but at the heart of the community, 20 blocks away. He opined, however, "By privileging the center, community-based planning can...weaken the complex interactions necessary to join up the different human groups the city contains."[5] He concludes that they should have placed the market right at the border.

It is important to note that both Sassen's conceptualization of transversal borders in cities and Sennett's plea for reexamination of city borders are driven by an implicit desire to strive for the city as an ideal—a city that is more open, equitable, modulated, and diverse. This ideal is true if we are to understand the city, through Aristotle and Hannah Arendt, as a space of both coexistence and plurality, where the accommodation of difference is settled discursively among equals.[6] And for Sennett, the value of difference afforded by the city lies in the opportunity for regular encounters with people of unlike social, economic, and political backgrounds, as opposed to the routine daily meetings that do not make an impression on the consciousness, as Arendt once observed.

In this way, the border or, more precisely, the latent potential of the architecture of borders in a city thus acts like a membrane. Its modulation and flexibility can bring together diverse social, cultural, and economic functions. The border offers a density of urban life necessary for the anonymity and difference that create friction and exchange—in other words, the most fundamental purpose and characteristic of the city as a common framework.

CITIES IN CITY-REGIONS

A cross-border city owes its existence and identity to its other across the border. Increasingly border cities are nested in an intricate web of interconnected cities within a wider city-region that straddles nation-states. One of the defining qualities of a city within a city-region is the

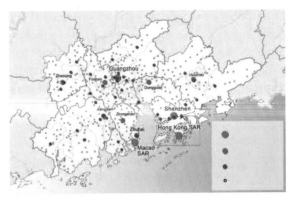

Fig. 2 Pearl River Delta, 2009.

way in which it defines its identity and competitiveness by exacerbating its difference in relation to other cities. In many respects, the effort to define itself has been the persistent feature in the development of Macau ever since the Portuguese arrived in the 1550s to trade with China. Macau is defined by its relation to and comparative difference from mainland China—it offered access to goods and services that were unavailable and often prohibited on the mainland.[7] The tendency to capitalize on comparative difference is more pronounced when neighboring cities are at dissimilar states of development and administered under varying political systems. Macau became a special administrative region of China at the time of the 1999 handover; while sovereignty lies with China, Macau remains largely autonomous. In this arrangement, Macau is bound to its other, Zhuhai, and is one component in a larger network of cities that forms a city-region—the Pearl River Delta, the most economically efficient city-region in the world today (fig. 2).

City-regions function as essential spatial nodes in the global economy and as distinctive political entities on the world stage. They are central to the economic, cultural, and political life of contemporary urbanized and globalized societies. City-regions support the entire spectrum of economic activity, from manufacturing to services, from low-tech to high-tech. Today, there are more than 20 city-regions with populations in excess of 15 million and a further 300 city-regions with populations in excess of 1 million.[8]

4   Sennett has discussed this idea for an open city in various articles and lectures, including the 1998 Raoul Wallenberg Lecture "The Spaces of Democracy" at the University of Michigan; the 2013 lecture "The Open City" at the Harvard Graduate School of Design; and the essay "The Public Realm," accessed May 23, 2014, http://www.richardsennett.com/site/SENN/Templates / General2.aspx?pageid=16.

5   Sennett, "Public Realm."

6   See Aristotle, *Politics*, trans. Ernest Barker (Oxford: Oxford University Press, 1995), 7–37; and Hannah Arendt, *The Human Condition* (Chicago: University of Chicago Press, 1958), 28–67.

7   I use the terms "comparative difference" and "comparative advantage," instead of the more common "difference" and "competitive advantage," because the difference that defines border cities arises out of a direct comparison between them. That is to say, "comparative

difference" refers to a difference of opposites rather than to a difference of variety.

8   Allen J. Scott, John Agnew, Edward W. Soja, and Michael Storper, "Global City-Regions" in *Global City-Regions: Trends, Theory, Policy*, ed. Allen J. Scott (Oxford: Oxford University Press, 2001), 11.

The rise of global city-regions is triggered by the nature of global economic activity, which currently transpires in extensive cross-national networks in which the flow of labor, investments, goods, products, ideas, technology, and services is unimpeded by national sovereignty or jurisdiction. The simultaneous proliferation of multi-nation blocs—EU, NAFTA, ASEAN, APEC, and so on—has intensified the formation of this agglomerative transborder urbanization, leading to the gradual depletion of the sovereign political autonomy of individual states along with a reduction in the effectiveness of borders to contain and shape urbanization.

In Asia, these emerging global city-regions include the Beijing-Tianjin Economic Area, Delhi Mumbai Industrial Corridor, Pearl River Delta, and ASEAN. The regions are moving beyond their initial function—low-cost factory to the world—to become integrated territorial platforms with a high concentration of productive networks, allowing competition in the global market. For example, as the most developed economic center in China, the Pearl River Delta accounts for more than 13.38 percent of China's economic output; it occupies only 0.45 percent of the country's land area.[9]

The process of urbanization within emerging city-regions is no longer confined by or directed within national boundaries; the criteria for creating successful urban plans requires understanding and accommodating demands and pressures from multiple and often conflicting origins. Furthermore, the center-periphery model of urbanization is no longer adequate in view of the fact that the spatial structure of global city-regions tends toward an archipelago (polynodal framework) of concentration: the centers of different, mutually dependent economies within a city-region often appear far from established urban cores or even on the borders. Cities in global city-regions attract low-wage service workers as well as high-value knowledge workers and creative professionals. This heterogeneous population is crucial for the vitality and competitiveness of the city but also gives rise to the problems of uneven development, income disparity, and social inequality. These tendencies are played out in the urbanization of the borderlands.

THE CHARACTERISTICS OF CROSS-BORDER CITIES

Due to its physical location, landform, history, and political status with China, Macau can be described and conceptualized as a cross-border city through four distinct and interrelated characteristics. The first is the tendency toward the exacerbation of difference, which has led to single-program urban developments and the creation of a city constituted of distinct parts, with each part indexing episodic political and economic convulsions. Macau's monoprogrammatic urban developments are synonymous with the gambling industry; it has secured its place as China's capital of gambling and is, in fact, the only city in China to permit gambling. The territory is the world's fourth-richest per person, with a per capita GDP in 1986 of $90,000, higher than that of Switzerland, the United States, or the United Kingdom.[10] The GDP in 2013 was more than $50 billion, owed largely to the gambling industry; in 2012, gambling was responsible for a disproportionately high 45.9 percent of GDP. Paradoxically, Macau has experienced its most significant and rapid economic growth since its December 20, 1999, reunification with China. The adoption of Deng Xiaoping's "One Country, Two Systems" ensured success for Macau, strengthening its physical and comparative advantage. In less than a decade, it was transformed from the "seedy sideshow of nearby Hong Kong"[11] to the largest gambling hub in the world and, in terms of per capita GDP, the richest place in Asia. The transformation was further accelerated in 2002, when Macau's chief executive, Edmund Ho Hau Wah, outlined a long-term economic strategy based on the gambling-led tourism and service industry. In the same year, he ended Stanley Ho's 40-year monopoly over gambling, awarding gaming concessions to Wynn Resorts, Las Vegas Sands, and MGM Mirage (all based in Las Vegas) and Galaxy and Melco Crown (both based in Hong Kong, the latter controlled by Stanley Ho's son Lawrence). Stanley Ho's Sociedade de Jogos de Macau retains its license.[12] Macau has surpassed Las Vegas to become the world's biggest gaming market. The gaming industry was worth $6.85 billion in 2006 and $45.32 billion in 2013; 70 percent of the city's tax revenue comes from gambling.[13] Supplemented by visitors to Macau's historic center, which was awarded UNESCO World Heritage status in 2005, gaming has

9   Construction Department, Guangdong Province; Development Bureau, Hong Kong SAR; and Secretariat for Transport and Public Works, Macau SAR, "Building Coordinated and Sustainable World-Class City-Region, Public Digest," 2009, 31.

10   Angela Monaghan, "China's Gambling Capital Macau Is World's Fourth-Richest Territory," accessed August 12, 2014, http://www.theguardian.com/world/2014/jul/02/macau-china-gambling-capital-fourth-richest-in-world-per-capita.

11   Craig Duncan, "City Profile: Macau," Cities 3, no. 1 (February 1986).

12   Stanley Ho's daughter, Pansy Ho, together with MGM Mirage Las Vegas, now owns the MGM Mirage Macau.

13   Statistics and Census Service, Macau SAR, "Macau in Figures," 2013.

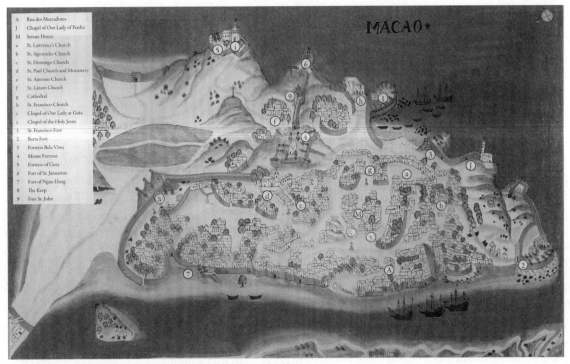

Fig. 3   Macau with the Portuguese settlement sandwiched between the Chinese villages of Barra (south) and Mong Há (north), late 17th century.

Fig. 4   Macau, 1590s.

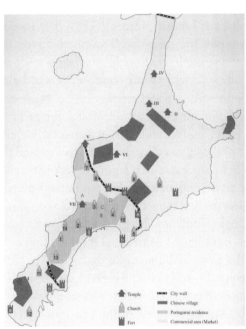

Fig. 5   Macau, 1634.

boosted tourism to ever higher numbers: 22 million travelers in 2008 and 29.3 million in 2013, higher than tourism in Hong Kong, which has a bigger land area.

But the seed for the city of parts and the tendency for the exacerbation of difference were planted as early as 1557, when the Portuguese obtained the leasehold to the small peninsula. The landscape then was mountainous; flat areas in the south and north accommodated eight Chinese villages in two areas, Barra and Mong Há (fig. 3). The Portuguese settled along Bahia Praia Grande and immediately erected churches, with plazas in front, on top of hills. Naturally, the churches and forts overlooked the urban and coastal areas (fig. 4), elevating the prominence of religious buildings and securing the best defensive position for the forts. One-story residential buildings grew incrementally around the hills, adapting to the terrain and producing winding streets and the "organic" fabric of settlement still evident today. This importation of a medieval Iberian city to south China represents the incursion of a city model from one tradition into the territory of another. The tripartite structure of 16th-century medieval Portuguese Christian society—feudal militarized aristocracy, religious order, common people—is manifested in Macau's forts, churches and convents, and housing, respectively. A defensive wall surrounds the ensemble. The city that grew out of this incursive settlement made no attempt to be contextual or to integrate with its surroundings. It is by being absolute that the city as a settlement exerted its presence, identity, and autonomy in an unwelcoming foreign land (fig. 5).

The limited land area—9.3 square kilometers—and the use of the city as developmental tool caused the city to grow in sudden spurts, contributing to and entrenching the city's tendency to behave as distinct parts. The population swelled from 500 (1561) to 40,000 (1640) to 461,100 (2007); population density as of 2009 was 49,580 inhabitants per square kilometer, eight times that of Singapore or Hong Kong and nine times that of Tokyo.[14] Macau's urban growth, from 1577 to the present, can be seen in numerous phases of land reclamation and extensive territorial expansion. Among the most distinct parts of the city are the old Portuguese center (now a UNESCO heritage site), the former Chinese villages of Barra and Mong Há, the casino areas of ZAPE (Zona de Aterros do Porto Exterior), the high-rise courtyard blocks of NAPE (Novos Aterros do Porto Exterior), the high-rise "butterfly" towers of Taipa, and the Las Vegas casinos of Cotai. This city of parts

transpired between 1557 and 1794 (old center; Chinese villages), 1912 and 1957 (ZAPE), 1957 and 2005 (NAPE; Taipa), and 2005 and the present (Cotai).

Centered at the Largo do Senado, the historic center of Macau was initially acquired by the Portuguese for trading. Adjacent to the former port of Praia Grande, it stretches from the Church of St. Augustine southwest to Avenida de Almeida Ribeiro, the Church of St. Dominic, and the ruins of St. Paul and Monte Forte hill. The narrow, winding cobbled streets, squares, and urban form reflect the medieval city of Lisbon. After settlement, the Chinese villages were absorbed slowly by the Portuguese, and today the medieval fabric of the historic center is juxtaposed to the tenement housing and warehouses along the Inner Harbor of the Macau Peninsula. At the time of the ZAPE expansion, roads began to radiate outward from the churches and squares of the historic area, resulting in unusually thin triangular blocks. The fragment between the center and ZAPE is composed predominantly of three- to five-story blocks, with services and amenities on the ground floor and housing above. This dominant type is an adaptation of the Portuguese peristyle courtyard, but on tighter building plots with narrower frontages.

Two abrupt shifts along two parallel roads, Avenida do Dr. Rodrigo Rodrigues and Avenida da Amizade, mark ZAPE and NAPE. The former is dominated by high-rise towers, the latter by high-rise courtyard blocks. The ZAPE expansion is punctuated conspicuously by the Casino Lisboa of 1970. The casino, now synonymous with the city's image of gaming tourism, extended Macau's business district from Largo do Senado along Avenida de Almeida Ribeiro toward the southeast corner of the peninsula. The master plan for NAPE, designed by Álvaro Siza, incorporates courtyard blocks on a northeast-southwest grid. The courtyards, demarcated by U-shaped perimeter blocks, admit light and open space, unlike the congestion and perceived unhygienic conditions typical of buildings in the old city. The courtyard type represents the introduction of modern urban planning practices to Macau, which addressed not only physical organization but industrial, social, and welfare services; open hills for recreation; and reservoirs. To the north, near the Gongbei border crossing, are low-income housing and slums.

The adjacent islands of Taipa and Coloane were also subject to land reclamation. Taipa's original landscape included two hills with a lake in between. The island began to lose its rural character in 1974 when Governador

14   U. W. Tang and N. Sheng, "City Profile: Macao," *Cities* 26, no. 4 (August 2009).

Fig. 6   The Venetian Macao and the Cotai Strip, 2013.

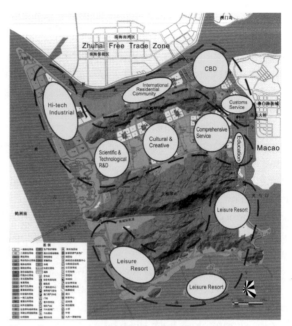

Fig. 7   Strategic master plan of Hengqin New Area, 2012.

Fig. 8   Gongbei border crossing from Zhuhai, 2013.

Nobre de Carvalho Bridge, linking the island to the peninsula, was built.[15] Following on the bridge construction were an airport, hotels, casinos, and housing; the housing is dominated by high-rise towers, generally about 30 stories, of a type imported from Hong Kong. Highly inflected facades, which allow maximum ventilation for all habitable rooms as well as service spaces for the individual apartment units, produce plans that resemble the outline of a butterfly. Each unit protrudes individually from a central core (see page 162, fig. 23). The butterfly type stands in notable contrast to the housing blocks on the peninsula.

Undoubtedly the most audacious and conspicuous addition to the city, yet another of its distinct parts, is Cotai. This reclaimed land of 5.2 square kilometers was planned in 1992 to provide housing for 150,000 residents, easing the housing crisis on the peninsula. But when the gaming monopoly ended in 2002, and the need arose for a piece of land to host megacasinos and their accompanying conventions and entertainments, the stipulated land use for this area was overturned. And so arose a wholesale re-creation of the Las Vegas Strip (fig. 6). The Sands Venetian Macao registered the name Cotai Strip in 2007; it is now synonymous with the whole casino area. The most significant shift in this part of the city is the size of the developmental plots, which measure an average of 257,250 square meters, approximately 50 times larger than the average building plots on the peninsula. Following on the Venetian, the biggest casino in the world, were the Four Seasons (2008), City of Dreams (2009), and Galaxy Macau (2011). All share a similar design, and all are self-enclosed developments devoted to keeping an audience within an environment of gaming and leisure. They are truly enclaves unto themselves, isolated from their immediate competitors and the city outside.

The growth spurts of the city, as exemplified in its stages of development, demonstrate the city's tendency to become denser, coarser, and more impenetrable; to rise higher; to occupy larger footprints; and to isolate its constituents (see "Macau: Land Reclamation," pages 164–73). In this sense, Macau is no longer a city of parts but a city of enclaves. Land reclamation, offering as it does a tabula rasa condition, is an attractive way to meet the challenges of growth. The promise of a new beginning for the perpetual exacerbation of difference finds its logical outcome—parts of the city so unlike that they completely alienate the city itself.

15 Two more link bridges were subsequently built, the Friendship Bridge in 1994 and the Sai Van Bridge in 2004.

Closely related to exacerbation of difference is separated integration, an oxymoron of sorts, and the second characteristic of Macau as a cross-border city. Urban developments that display a tendency for separated integration are positioned in close proximity and well integrated, yet maintain a separation that serves individual identity, resulting in uneven development. The borders of Macau are themselves a mechanism that generates separated integration, crucial in establishing its cultural, political, and economic identity. Developments on either side of the Macau border are intended to promote specific economic strategies, urbanizing via a staging of comparative difference. For instance, Hengqin New Area, a reclaimed district straddling the islands of Da Hengqin and Xiao Hengqin (Big Hengqin and Small Hengqin) adjacent to Cotai, is to advance a knowledge-based economy (fig. 7). It capitalizes on the hotel, conference, and leisure facilities of Cotai and at the same time offers vast tracts of land for campus- and science-park-based developments, a model that Macau cannot support. Such initiatives entrench the mono-economic nature of the city. Between 2001 and 2011, employment in Macau's gambling and tourism industries increased from 45.3 percent, already exceptionally high, to 60.3 percent; in the same period, manufacturing decreased from 19.8 percent to 3.4 percent. Such concentration ultimately has an adverse effect on the local population. The economy does not provide diverse opportunities for employment, especially to residents who aspire to futures other than those offered by the gaming industry. In time, this overspecialization will empty Macau of its citizens.

While the border plays a role as a line that separates, it also has the opposite effect: it creates intense points of integration at strategic locations along its length, the third characteristic of cross-border cities. As neighboring cities develop different yet complementary programs at their borders, people (and goods) surge across administrative boundaries—for work, education, and leisure—at these border crossings. With the establishment of Zhuhai as a Special Economic Zone in the 1980s and the handover of Macau in 1999, cross-border integration and flows have increased even further. Unsurprisingly, this situation has led to the creation of numerous border crossing facilities at various points along the Macau/Zhuhai and Macau/Hengqin borders. The largest and busiest is the Gongbei border crossing (fig. 8), which handled, in 2013, more than 200,000 people in a day and 100 million in a year. Two

Fig. 9   Novos Aterros do Porto Exterior (NAPE; new Outer Harbor reclamation area).

Fig. 10   Model, Cotai City master plan, 1999.

Fig. 11   Zoned map, Cotai City master plan, 1999.

large immigration halls on either side of the border interlaced with transport networks add up to a degraded urban space—behemoth buildings stranded on a sea of tarmac, dislocated from the immediate city due to sheer scale and impenetrability, and despite the very large number of footsteps hosted, remaining a conduit for passing through rather than dwelling in.

The fourth characteristic of the cross-border city is that it is a contested territory. This condition poses a fundamental challenge to the question of citizenship and identity. Fifteen years after the handover of Macau to China, the Macanese still perceive themselves as a group separate and unique from mainland Chinese. The border crossings stand as a physical and symbolic structure that holds inward migration and the dilution of identity at bay. Local residents see "the border as a symbol of Macau's autonomy, which needs to be preserved: because of differences in identity and culture, because of the better political system or because of economic advantages."[16]

Apart from contestation from across the border, the alienation of citizens from their own city also occurs within the border, affected again by the need for the exacerbation of difference to gain a comparative advantage. This contestation and alienation are often played out on reclaimed land. In the three major districts of reclamation—ZAPE, NAPE, and Cotai—what was originally intended for housing to ease the severe congestion on the peninsula quickly gave way to casinos and their associated leisure facilities. In ZAPE, first the Lisboa and then the Grand Lisboa casinos forestalled the opportunity to produce a mixed-use business and housing district; in fact, the facilities have turned large parts of the district into pawn shops, jewelry shops, and massage parlors that cater to the casino tourist. Likewise, the NAPE expansion was meant to be a district of mid-rise courtyard housing designed by Siza, but the blocks were densified and scaled up to such a degree that the architect chose to relinquish his authorship of the project (fig. 9). The urban uniformity afforded by the grid and the courtyard blocks was violated when the plots adjacent to Nam Van Lake were amalgamated to produce the mammoth swaths of land required for the gambling floors of the MGM Macau and Wynn Macau. Inserting the casinos not only disrupted the continuous urban grain of NAPE but terminated the finer northeast-to-southwest routes to the waterfront. Where ZAPE and NAPE lost their most prime locations to casino developments, Cotai lost its entire territory. Instead of Cotai City, a new housing district

16   Werner Breitung, "Macau in the Eyes of a Border Scholar" in *IIAS Newsletter* 64 (Summer 2013): 25.

for Macau (figs. 10, 11), a magnified replica of the Las Vegas Strip has risen.

Contestation over territory takes place not only at and within the border, but across the border, on land leased for development through the reconfiguration of the border. The recent relocation of the University of Macau to Hengqin is the result of the propensity of cities to compete and cooperate in equal measure (fig. 12). This recently completed cross-border development, 20 times the size of the former Taipa campus, will remain under the administration of Macau for 50 years through a land-lease arrangement. Here, Macau overcame its land shortage by relocating an immense programmatic element. Hengqin, on the other hand, will capitalize on Macau's drive to diversify its economy. The relocation of the university amounts to the incursion of a fragment from one city into another territory; large infrastructural links—the new Lotus Bridge—act as an umbilical cord. The increased cross-border flow of tourists, workers, and now students and likewise the insertion of the university campus into mainland China contribute to a questioning of the stability of the Macanese identity and sense of autonomy that have persisted for hundreds of years.

ARCHITECTURE FOR CROSS-BORDER CITIES

Although it is a place of difference, of separation, of dispute, the cross-border city boasts many qualities that bolster the idea of the city as a space of plurality. These qualities are reified in an architecture that is legible and common to all even as it is expressed in disparate dominant types in particular cities. In the imperial cities of China—with a structure that persisted until 1948—the dominant type is the quadrangle house. Walls generate an irreducible and singular structure that defines the organization of the city, from the single-family quadrangle to the walls that demarcate the sequential spaces of the Forbidden City to the very city walls that limit and define the city as a mandate of the emperor. Conversely, in Greek cities, the birthplace of the *polis*, the space of economics (household management) and the space of politics (the public realm) are separated. This detachment finds its manifestation in the articulation of the acropolis as an archipelago surrounded by a sea of housing. As for the cross-border city, the encapsulation of the idea of the city lies in the way the border can be conceived and articulated. This expression may occur at several scales at different locations: the borders between two states or administrative regions; the liminal space that separates the city; and the articulation of this liminal space itself.

In response to the shortcomings of the cross-border city, future urban developments in Macau should seek to rebalance the tendency toward exacerbation, albeit without eliminating the value of comparative difference between cities and parts within the city. After all, this counterposition is never a static one: it is in constant alternation between polarities, and consideration should be given to the needs and demands of the marginalized—disposed migrant workers and alienated citizens alike. The strategies I propose are restricted to those that are able to directly shape the physical structure and space of the city, and that can be enacted through architecture and urban design. For instance, I exclude the ideas of resource allocation on the regional scale and of administrative cooperation between different provincial governments.

The first strategy must involve the introduction of industry-specific urban developments, which will contribute to the diversification of Macau's economy. In particular, a knowledge-based economy may be cultivated in key locations in the city. The relocated University of Macau, intended to support development of the Hengqin New Area, is one example, but the typological outcome of the campus falls short of the promise and potential offered by such a model.[17] The second strategy involves the reconfiguration of the borderlands and borders themselves. These spaces can be intensified to support competition and cooperation. Integrating parallel functions on both sides of the border will support the further densification of these points, for they are already served by rich infrastructural networks and animated by transient populations. The effort should extend from the creation of space to pass through to the creation of space to dwell in. A third strategy involves transferring specific developments and growth pressures to the other side of the border. The criteria for dispersing and decanting should not be based on size alone (as it was with the relocation of the University of Macau). Instead, a specific program or a dominant type, as part of a complete development, must provide the key economic driver. This way, the decanted piece of city is not a severed limb but a functioning organ in a host city. All these strategies should strive toward the creation of a more equitable city.

17   As it stands today, the University of Macau remains an isolated campus, bounded by a moat and fences that cut it off from any involvement with its surroundings. Modeled after Ivy League campuses, the university demonstrates little understanding of Macau's urban history, the way spaces are used in its subtropical climate, or the programmatic elements that typify a thriving space for learning.

Fig. 12   University of Macau, Hengqin, 2013.

Beyond furnishing open spaces for recreation and cultural amenities—the primary goal of urban regeneration projects today—the key to a fairer city is the provision of an affordable and dignified home for every citizen. Easing housing congestion on the peninsula is an urgent task considering population density and escalating housing prices; given Macau's GDP, it should not be an insurmountable one. Imposing trade-offs and other conditions on new developments, especially those led by casinos, will not hinder the attractiveness of these ventures as business investments.

These strategies will support a cross-border architecture that is, in essence, an idea and model of the city that can be transplanted to another territory. Through juxtaposition, the city becomes crystallized and its uniqueness exacerbated. Macau's current incarnation as a city of parts, with each part an almost direct importation of a model from elsewhere—Lisbon in the peninsula, Hong Kong in Taipa, and more recently, Las Vegas in Cotai—demonstrates this conception. The crystallization of the idea of the city of Macau can offer an alternative strategy to sustain Macau's unique heritage beyond the present tropes of preservation and cultural tourism. When this model is propagated elsewhere—from one part of the city to another or across the border entirely—the heritage of the territory will be involved in the growth of the larger city-region and in the collective imagination of its citizens.

Developing such a crystallization relies on Sennett's distinction between the boundary and the border and involves the reconceptualization of the border crossings of Macau as an architecture that reifies the cross-border city. At points of entry, the border and its supporting facilities may be reimagined as a frame or a wall containing housing, work spaces, public amenities, spaces for learning, and immigration checkpoints. The frame/wall defines and delineates fragmented or residual spaces in the borderlands, bringing an absolute clarity to the organization of the degraded urban space, and in turn makes the city a visible and legible whole. The surfaces of the frame and the wall are inflected and feathered, admitting movement, air, and view—in other words, the frame and the wall behave also as porous space.

In fall 2013, my studio at the Harvard Graduate School of Design developed this idea in a series of design projects. Yun Fu and Chen Hao Lin's "Collective Border: The Latent Project of Gongbei" (pages 176–81) utilizes a frame of housing for students, researchers, and cross-border knowledge workers. The scheme encapsulates the degraded and superfluous tarmac of the Gongbei checkpoint and transforms it into a park for the city. The existing immigration checkpoint buildings on both sides of the border will be transformed, in stages, into cultural and educational buildings and facilities. Border checkpoints are then dispersed around the perimeter of the frame, allowing multiple entry points into the city. In 2049, when the administrative border of the SAR disappears, the remaining architecture will stand as an artifact that not only contains the memory of the border but reinforces the idea of Macau as a cross-border city integrated with the mainland but retaining a sense of cultural and social autonomy.

Navajeet KC and Josh Schecter's "Marked Difference: Inscribing the City of Parts" (pages 192–97) envisions two sinuous walls that trace the border between Macau and Zhuhai and converge to form the border crossings. This proposal recasts the symbolic "city gate" as a permeable wall of housing and work space passed through by the tourist and resided in by the cross-border worker. Utilizing a similar strategy in "A Few Sharp Lines" (pages 186–91), Ashley Takacs and Gabriel Tomasulo offer two walls that act as an elongated immigration checkpoint. Entry and exit points are located at strategic positions along the axis between Gongbei and Ilha Verde. The double wall captures and heightens the qualities of the sites it traverses along its length, framing these locales as public spaces with specific programs and amenities.

Fabiana Alvear, Hao Chen, and Jing Guo's "Spaces of Exception: Housing as a Common Framework for Cotai" (pages 198–203) attempts to return Cotai to its intended purpose—affordable housing for the city. It does so by treating the border as a series of horizontal layers: the enormous gaming floors of the casinos are hidden at basement level, freeing the ground plane for housing. Casino amenities are shared with the city, and programs associated with the gaming industry—pawn shops, jewelry shops, and so on—are clearly separated and constrained. Thus, the casinos become spaces of exception, tolerated because they enable the provision of housing for the city. Expansion of the casinos is regulated by a series of alternating bands of housing and landscape. These bands may be seen as Sennett's permeable border: they define and demarcate, absorb and allow permeation. More important, they regulate and administer an urban plan that allows the close coexistence of housing and casinos.

Reconceptualizing the inherent architecture and spatiality of the cross-border city gives rise to alternative models for urbanization. The developmental brief that drives these architectural and urban propositions is not dictated solely by the market but instead is informed by the need to manifest the idea of the city as a plural and equitable space for coexistence.

The concept of the city as a border and vice versa is not confined to urban development in the borderlands. The contemporary global city is structured with transversal borders that are often more impenetrable than the conventional borders between nation-states. The more global the city, the more intense the conflict between what is generic and specific, global and local, privileged and dispossessed. The more cities are connected through trade, communications technology, and cheap transportation, the more they will behave as cross-border cities. The conflicts and challenges that these cities pose as a contested space should not obscure the potential that they offer in their diversity and promise of equitability. No longer bound by citizenship through nationality, or through any single social or cultural identity, these cities are shaped by difference and multiplicity. For distinction to exist legibly and coexist meaningfully in these circumstances, the city can exist as a city of parts that, despite its clear definition, allows the permeation of one part to another at its borders. The permeable border is structured by the architecture of the city in parts, acting as both a limiting and a permitting framework, a framework for the accommodation of difference, a common framework; in other words, the border as a city.

Borderlands as Urban Space

Contexts for 21st-Century Chinese Cities

Piper Gaubatz

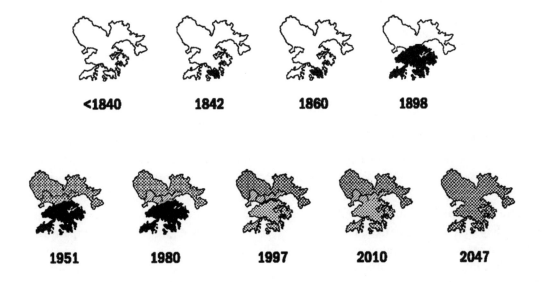

Fig. 1   Dissolution of borders in the Pearl River Delta, 1840–2047.

At the 1893 World's Columbian Exposition in Chicago, a young historian, Frederick Jackson Turner, mounted the podium and addressed the American Historical Association. His words, spoken in a hall in what was to become the Art Institute of Chicago, began an academic and popular conversation that continues to this day about the role of frontiers and borderlands in shaping history and national identities, cultures, and institutions. He began by quoting from the census superintendent's report on the 1890 survey: "Up to and including 1880 the country had a frontier of settlement, but at present the unsettled area has been so broken into by isolated bodies of settlement that there can hardly be said to be a frontier line." The remainder of the talk presented his theory: that the experience of the frontier had shaped American identity. He concluded: "Now…the frontier has gone, and with its going has closed the first period of American history."[1] The "isolated bodies of settlement" referenced in the census report were cities. As Turner observed, "These trading posts, situated so as to command the water systems of the country, have grown into such cities as

Albany, Pittsburgh, Detroit, Chicago, St. Louis, Council Bluffs, and Kansas City."[2] The development of cities marked the end of the frontier; cities, by definition, had no place in a frontier region.

Among the many subsequent critics of Turner's agrarian frontier hypothesis was Richard Clement Wade, who brought frontier cities into the discussion of both frontier history and urban studies.[3] Nonetheless, it was only in the late 20th century, as borders and border cities became increasingly central players in the rapidly shifting global economy, that they have come to the forefront of urban studies, and that concepts of frontiers and borders have been applied to the analysis of cities and urban life more generally. As Saskia Sassen contends, "Cities are one of the key sites where new norms and new identities are *made*" and thus constitute a new frontier zone.[4]

The century-spanning conversation about frontiers, borderlands, and the role of cities within them provides a context for Sassen and others to consider borderlands as urban space and cities as frontier zones. While "frontier cities" were once considered peripheral, "border cities"

1   Frederick Jackson Turner, *The Frontier in American History* (New York: H. Holt, 1920).

2   Turner, *Frontier in American History*.

3   Richard Clement Wade, *The Urban Frontier: The Rise of Western Cities, 1790–1830* (Cambridge, MA: Harvard University Press, 1959).

4   Saskia Sassen, "When the Center No Longer Holds: Cities as Frontier Zones," *Cities* 34 (October 2013): 68; italics original.

play an increasingly central role in the globalizing world, with the Chinese developmental cities at the core of contemporary globalization. The changing nature of borderlands and the conditions of borderland space have a strong impact on the development of cities on the Chinese frontiers and the possibilities for developmental border cities in contemporary China.

BORDERLANDS

The concept of "frontier" evokes ungoverned or less-governed territories of interaction between large political, cultural, or economic regimes. The Roman *limes*, for example, were more conceptual and transient outer zones of the empire than they were specific or fixed territorial limits.[5] Although frontiers were a key unit of analysis during much of the 20th century, the end of the century saw a discursive shift from frontiers to borders as scholars turned toward the increasingly fluid configurations of formal border regions and the processes of "bordering," "debordering," and "rebordering" (fig. 1).[6]

Whereas frontiers were often characterized as lawless, creative, and ambiguous, the concept of "border" evokes bounded spaces generated through legal, political, and economic designation of the limits of territorial authority. They might be regulated, legislated, managed, controlled, defined, defended, and precisely demarcated by structures such as fences or walls. Frontiers, borders, and borderlands are simultaneously distinctive geographical spaces and conceptual zones of ambiguity and/or transition.

In the context of geography, the term "frontier" has been used most often to connote a region of intersection between the peripheries of two or more regions; "border" suggests a specific delineation and demarcation of territory; and "city" refers to a defined space of concentrated settlement. The cartographic representation of these elements highlights their difference: frontiers are areas; borders are lines; cities are points. But this simplifies the fact that the "lines" formed by borders may well anchor functional zones that span both sides of the border. Hence the term "borderlands" is growing in use to describe a space bisected by a border.

The spaces of frontiers, borderlands, and border cities are often analyzed in the context of spatial scale. These spaces can be perceived as a continuum of nested territorial scales, each of which can be considered in terms of its border functions, from the sometimes vast reaches of the frontiers to the more defined areas of borderlands and border cities. This hierarchical spatial framework has been produced in the context of political, economic, and social change. One of the great global geopolitical projects of the industrial era, beginning with the European age of exploration and colonization, has been to find increasingly precise ways of demarcating and negotiating borders. As precision map-making technology has progressed from sextants to satellites, and territorial boundaries have been defined, contested, and redefined, borders have both increased in their precision and blurred in their functions. Moreover, institutions that rely on carefully delineated borders and the spatially differentiated policy regimes that accompany them have proliferated, from modern states to multinational corporations (which, despite their border-crossing reach, take advantage of differential policies in areas such as labor, taxation, and environmental protection).

This institutionalization of the definition and demarcation of borders at multiple scales has generated increased interest among urban scholars in the phenomenon of "border cities." Border cities are more than just cities situated in close proximity to a border. Jan Buursink, for example, suggests that a better definition may be cities that depend for their existence, in one way or another, on a border.[7] They may have existed before the border, but the border function is now paramount to their political, economic, cultural, or social raison d'être. In this understanding of border cities, contemporary border regions are increasingly perceived as fluid and transient realms where multiple scales of authority and shifting configurations of power and resources generate complex and malleable landscapes despite the seemingly fixed nature of the border itself: border cities concentrate these interactions.

Frontier and borderland concepts have also entered discussions of the intra-urban scale as scholars use them to analyze the relationships between neighborhoods and other territories within cities. Such discussions follow from Kevin Lynch's identification of boundaries and edges in *The Image of the City*.[8] Werner Breitung argues, for example, that the differential and overlapping scales of authority in Chinese cities generate political, physical, sociospatial, psychological, and functional border dynamics within cities; Thomas Wilson observes that frontiers

5   Friedrich Kratochwil, "Of Systems, Boundaries, and Territories: An Inquiry into the Formation of the State System," *World Politics* 39, no. 1 (1986): 27–52.

6   Xiangming Chen, *As Borders Bend: Transnational Spaces on the Pacific Rim* (Lanham, MD: Rowman &

Littlefield, 2005), 265; Gabriel Popescu, *Bordering and Ordering the Twenty-First Century: Understanding Borders* (Lanham, MD: Rowman & Littlefield, 2012), 15.

7   Jan Buursink, "The Binational Reality of Border-Crossing Cities," *GeoJournal* 54 (2001): 7–19.

8   Kevin Lynch, *The Image of the City* (Cambridge, MA: MIT Press, 1960).

within cities are seen as zones of varying width and definition where cultures interact and intersect in dynamic and significant ways.[9]

Analysis of frontiers, borderlands, and frontier cities as artifacts of multiple, nested scales of territoriality provides a linkage between the physical conceptualization of these places as areas or regions and the abstract conceptualization of "frontier" and "border" as functional concepts or processes. Sassen's "cities as the new frontiers," for example, are spaces of concentrated interaction between cultures, classes, and corporations; they may be far removed from politically designated borders. In the complex contemporary world of geopolitics, globalization, mobility, and hybridity, borders can be theorized in terms of politics, power relationships, economics, cultures, and societies; they can be described through their functions, their political delineation, or their landscapes; they can be simultaneously ambiguous and clear.[10] Canadian political theorist Emmanuel Brunet-Jailly has argued for a theory of borders based on four different analytical lenses: market and trade flows, multiscale policies given multiple governments/jurisdictions, distinct political power held by borderland communities, and distinct borderland cultures.[11] Functional definitions seem particularly common for contemporary borderlands, so much so that "border," "deborder," and "reborder" have been introduced as verbs to describe the processes of establishing, weakening, and strengthening border functions.

Moreover, as political geographer John Agnew observes, different conceptualizations of borders and borderlands, which once clearly identified them as distinctive places, may even challenge their very existence. In the discussions of borders in the contexts of spaces of flows (economic, political, social, and cultural), global economic and political regimes, and citizenship and identity, as identity retreats from the state to other affinities, such as ethnicity or religion, the significance of borders may be substantially diminished.[12] Nonetheless, borders and borderlands continue to have an intensely territorial aspect. As Wilson explains,

> Territory and territoriality still matter to social scientists who are interested in borders, boundaries and frontiers. When approaching the issues of place, space and identity, territory remains the principal ingredient in territoriality. Territory is an inescapable agent of social and political differentiation and integration. But territory has also become one of the many concepts that have been recently asserted to be in decline as a basis to social life, in what is seen to be a globalized world that has shed its former national and normative constraints.[13]

Cities play a pivotal role in the mobile, fluid borderlands of the 21st century; they serve as focal points and places of intense interaction within the borderlands.[14] They are "lived spaces challenged and inspired by international boundaries."[15] They are the destinations of migrants, the hosts to trade ranging from black-market street vendors to multinational corporations, and the spaces and landscapes where identity is produced and reproduced through both the daily lives of the local citizenry and state policy and practice.

FIVE CONDITIONS OF BORDERLAND SPACE

"I Know Who I Am"

My father was a Portuguese mountaineer
My mother a Taoist of Chinese descendent
And I, well, I am an Eurasian
One hundred percent Macanese!
. . .
My heart is Luso-Chinese
My mind is Sino-Portuguese
And in spite of all my pride
I know how to be casual about it.
I've got a little bit of Camoens
And Lusitanian faults
And on some occasions
Confucian thoughts
. . .
I can say the Ave Maria
as well as the *o mi to fo*.[16]

—Li Anle (also known as Lee Lok,
or Leonel Alves 李安樂), 2010

9   Werner Breitung, "Borders and the City: Intra-Urban Boundaries in Guangzhou (China)," *Quaestiones Geographicae* 30, no. 4 (2011): 55–61; Thomas M. Wilson, "Territoriality Matters in the Anthropology of Borders, Cities and Regions," *Revista Cadernos do Ceom* 25, no. 37 (2013): 199–216.

10   John Agnew, "Borders on the Mind: Re-Framing Border Thinking," *Ethics and Global Politics* 1, no. 4 (2008): 175–91.

11   Emmanuel Brunet-Jailly, "Theorizing Borders: An Interdisciplinary Perspective," *Geopolitics* 10 (2005): 633–49.

12   Agnew, "Borders on the Mind."

13   Wilson, "Territoriality Matters."

14   Sassen, "When the Center"; Mark B. Salter, "To Make Move and Let Stop: Mobility and the Assemblage of Circulation," *Mobilities* 8, vol. 1 (2013): 7–19.

15   Willem Van Schendel and Erik de Maaker, "Asian Borderlands: Introducing Their Permeability, Strategic Uses and Meanings," *Journal of Borderlands Studies* 29, no. 1 (2014).

16   This poem, written in Portuguese, was quoted in Cosima Bruno, "Contemporary Poetry from Macau," *Interventions* (2013): 1–20. It was originally published in

Although identity is complex as it is constituted in every contemporary city, it is particularly complex in border cities. The economic, social, political, and cultural dynamics and interconnections of border regions generate specific, overlapping conditions for shaping urban space. These conditions, or characteristics, can be loosely classified as liminality, hybridity, mobility, security, and mediation. The five conditions signify the fundamental functions and processes that produce and reproduce the distinctive elements of these cities through the interplay between urban identity expressed through elements of permanence[17] as these five fluid characteristics adapt to changing border regimes.

Liminality

We may see Macao as a dialectical image, the liminal moment where dream and waking meet.[18] Liminal spaces are transitional spaces, where one thing becomes another in the context of fluid power and mobility. Originally identified with transitional identity during cultural rites of passage, and later with a relatively unstructured, transitional state within communities,[19] liminality implies that the spaces between well-defined types may be in a constant state of transition as cross-border influences generate a range of conflicting and contradictory processes. As Deljana Iossifova observes, cities in urban borderlands might be "spaces of exclusion, or the bounded milieu of marginalized groups," or "spaces of contestations, of genesis and change."[20] Liminality influences the landscapes of border cities as changing power relationships, economies, and populations repurpose urban space as transitions take place that disrupt the futures projected by the built environment. Liminal areas "can be understood as containing conditions that allow for new forms of organisation to occur, as emergent circumstances that embody genotypes or conditions not found in the quotidian or conventional."[21] Liminality and its concomitant ambiguities of identity, landscape, and type are the norm in borderland cities.[22]

Hybridity

The new government has cultivated a hybrid identity [in Macau], including local, national and international identities, believing that these can advance not only nation building but also the economic goals beneficial to governance. Contrary to common wisdom, the process of identity making is not a clear process of differentiating "the other" from "the self" and repressing "the other" but is instead a process of incorporating the identities of "the other."[23]

Border cities are often characterized by hybridity—whether in language and culture, landscapes, or architecture. As different peoples and structures meet, new forms emerge that are distinct from those in the core areas. While it is perhaps easy to argue that many, if not most, large contemporary cities are characterized by various forms of hybridity as distinct migrant cultures have intersected, border and borderland cities may demonstrate several forms of hybridity. Those border city regions that are bisected by an international boundary are subject to intense disruption in the urban fabric since each side of the border is governed by different spatial planning and management policies, yet in the case of a relatively porous border, hybrid forms may develop through the direct apposition of the differing spatial systems.

Mobility

Mr. A lives in Macao, but crosses the border 1–2 times per day. He is one of those with a dual car licence, which allows him to drive on both sides. He had a factory in Zhuhai before and still does business in the mainland...

Mrs. B is a mainland resident. She has lived in Zhuhai since 1989, where she met a man from Macao. They married and she gave birth to a child in Macao in 1998. Since then [as of 2004] she has lived in Macao on two-year visas.[24]

Christopher Kelen and Lili Han, eds., *Poetas Portugueses de Macau (Portuguese Poets of Macau)* (Macau: ASM, 2010).

17   Christopher C. M. Lee and Sam Jacoby, "Typological Urbanism and the Idea of the City," *Architectural Design* 81, no. 1 (2011): 14–23.

18   Tim Simpson, "Macao, Capital of the 21st Century?" *Environment and Planning D: Society and Space* 26, no. 6 (2008): 1,053–79.

19   Victor Turner, *The Ritual Process: Structure and Anti-Structure* (New York: Aldine, 1969); Arnold van Gennep, *Les Rites de Passage: Étude Systématique des Rites* (Paris: Picard, 1909).

20   Deljana Iossifova, "Searching for Common Ground: Urban Borderlands in a World of Borders and Boundaries," *Cities* 34 (2013): 1–5.

21   Joshua Bolchover and Peter Hasdell, "Opening the Frontier Closed Area: A Mutual Benefit Zone" (paper presented at the Fourth Conference of the International Forum on Urbanism, Amsterdam, Nov. 26–28, 2009),

http://newurbanquestion.ifou.org/proceedings/5%20 The%20Transformation%20of%20Urban%20Form/ full%20papers/D64-2_Bolchover_Joshua_Opening%20 the%20Frontier%20Closed%20Area_Reviewed.pdf.

22   Wilson, "Territoriality Matters."

23   Wai Man Lam, "Promoting Hybridity: The Politics of the New Macau Identity," *China Quarterly* 203 (2010): 656–74.

24   Werner Breitung, "Living with Borders—Overcoming Borders," *Revista de Cultura* 9 (2004): 18–29.

Border regions have become intensifiers for a wide range of mobilities, from the movement of people to the movement of capital. Cities play an integral part in these mobilities. As Neil Brenner explains, recent state policies to focus transnational capital and urbanization, while sometimes directed toward traditional metropolitan cores, increasingly "are also articulating vast grids of accumulation and spatial regulation that cascade along intercontinental transportation corridors; large-scale infrastructural, telecommunications, and energy networks; free-trade zones; transnational growth triangles; and international border regions."[25] Border regions and their cities have become increasingly central as conduits of transnational capital flows, and in numerous instances have eclipsed the prosperity of core metropolitan regions.[26]

Different types of urban mobilities either enable or confine. According to Saskia Sassen, two distinct bordered spaces "cut across traditional borders"—the cross-border space of corporations and capital, which enhances protection and opportunity, and the cross-border space of migrants, which can vary from opportunity to capture and detention. She observes that "the city can become a refuge, and even more important, a space where powerlessness becomes complex and in so doing enables the powerless to make a history and to make the political."[27] The most common mobilities in contemporary border cities are those of migrants and day workers, capital, and trade.

Security

Daily security patrols from the Macau and Zhuhai police forces and perimeter surveillance will be enough to deter illegal immigrants from trying to enter the territory via the University of Macau's (UM) Hengqin campus, Macau Customs told Business Daily.

On August 21, mainland police officers arrested four people for allegedly attempting to climb over the fence surrounding the Hengqin campus . . .

"At the fence surrounding the campus, there is [sic] also surveillance cameras that should act as an effective tool against any illegal entry attempt," the spokesperson added.

Official news agency Xinhua reported that the mainland authorities stopped 117 illegal immigration attempts during the three-year campus construction.[28]

The apparatus of security is a necessary condition in cities located on borders. It must always intercede in the ordering of the landscape, but the extent to which it defines the urban landscape varies with the relationship between the territories on either side of the border. At one extreme, the cities of Baarle-Nassau, Netherlands, and Baarle-Hertog, Belgium, have a relatively secure relationship combined with a complex and interleaved international border that runs through houses and shops, down sidewalks, and between structures. The border is delineated by brass plaques and studs in the pavement (fig. 2).[29] At the opposite end of the spectrum, the border defenses surrounding the contested Spanish cities of Ceuta and Melilla, which are located on the Mediterranean shore of Morocco, include double or triple metal fences, thermal and infrared cameras, pepper spray, and razor and barbed wire, all of which attempt to stem the tide of potential migrants across the only land borders between Africa and Europe (fig. 3).[30] While the border at Baarle-Nassau/Baarle-Hertog, although a genuine international border, appears as little more than a visual curiosity in the urban landscape, the borders at Ceuta and Melilla/Morocco fundamentally define the cities, their landscapes, and their identities. The extent to which the border itself becomes a defining physical feature of a border city depends on the particular political moment. As the relationships between the countries on either side of the border change, so too must the level of security infrastructure that defines the border as an element of urban infrastructure.

Mediation

Macau is a cluster of islands mediating the terra of China to the South China Sea estuary . . . "Dreaming of islands," writes Deleuze (2004), "is dreaming of pulling away, of being already separate."[31]

25 Neil Brenner, "Theses on Urbanization," *Public Culture* 25, no. 1 (2013): 85–113.

26 Joachim Blatter, "From 'Spaces of Place' to 'Spaces of Flows'? Territorial and Functional Governance in Cross-Border Regions in Europe and North America," *International Journal of Urban and Regional Research* 28, no. 3 (2004): 530–48.

27 Sassen, "When the Center," 68.

28 Stephanie Lai, "No Fears over Hengqin Illegal Entry: Police," *Macau Business Daily*, September 12, 2013, www.macaubusinessdaily.com/Society/No-fears-over-Hengqin-illegal-entry-police.

29 Alon Gelbman and Dallen J. Timothy, "Border Complexity, Tourism and International Exclaves: A Case Study," *Annals of Tourism Research* 38, no. 1 (2011): 110–31.

30 Xavier Ferrer-Gallardo, "The Spanish-Moroccan Border Complex: Processes of Geopolitical, Functional, and Symbolic Rebordering," *Political Geography* 27 (2008): 301–21.

31 Tim Simpson, "Tourist Utopias: Las Vegas, Dubai, Macau," Asia Research Institute Working Paper Series No. 177 (Singapore: National University of Singapore Asia Research Institute, 2012), https://ari.nus.edu.sg/Assets/Uploads/docs/wps/wps12_177.pdf.

Fig. 2 Café in Baarle-Nassau, Netherlands, on the border with Belgium; the border is marked on the ground.

Fig. 3 Border fences between Spanish Ceuta and Morocco.

According to Gabriel Popescu, "an essential aspect of state borders is their double meaning as lines of separation and contact in space. Whenever a line is drawn between two groups of people, that line acquires two meanings simultaneously. On the one hand it separates the two groups, while on the other it brings them into mutual contact."[32] Border cities mediate different regimes and scales of production, capital accumulation, culture, and society; they mediate the economic, social, political, and cultural relationships between countries and/or spatial territories; and they articulate the material aspects of power relationships between the two sides. As Xiangming Chen explains, "The relationship between the global and the local is strongly mediated by the in-between status and role of transborder subregions."[33]

CHINESE FRONTIERS, BORDERS, AND CITIES

Chinese empires waxed and waned over the vast expanses of the Asian continent from ancient times to the present. For the Chinese, the far-ranging frontiers defined the extent of the civilized world; maintaining the frontiers was a project synonymous with maintaining the integrity of the empire. The Great Wall, built and rebuilt in varying configurations over a span of centuries beginning in the third century BC, symbolizes the Chinese conceptions of inner and outer space, core and periphery, homeland and frontier. The Chinese imperial project was anchored to the landscape through systems of frontier and border outposts that extended political, military, economic, and social control to far-flung regions, shaping the movement of people and goods across vast territories. These outposts were established at regular intervals to protect and resupply trade, military, and communications routes. In many cases they developed into small cities or towns. The Chinese establishment of cities within non-Chinese areas joined indigenous and Chinese urban traditions to produce a distinctive style of frontier urbanism.[34]

Historically, China's western continental frontiers and eastern maritime frontiers were quite different, though cities in each frontier region fulfilled the five conditions of borderland cities. The contrast between western and eastern frontiers can be seen in the development of Hohhot, now the capital of the Inner Mongolian Autonomous Region on the frontier with Mongolia, and Guangzhou, now the capital of Guangdong Province adjacent to Hong Kong and Macau.

32 Popescu, *Bordering and Ordering*, 26.

33 Chen, *As Borders Bend*, 39.

34 Piper Gaubatz, *Beyond the Great Wall: Urban Form and Transformation on the Chinese Frontiers* (Stanford, CA: Stanford University Press, 1996), 3.

Fig. 4 Hohhot, 1909.

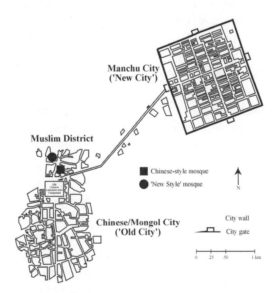

Manchu City
('New City')

Muslim District

Chinese/Mongol City
('Old City')

Chinese-style mosque

'New Style' mosque

N

City wall

City gate

0   .25   .50   1 km

Fig. 5 Hohhot, early 20th century.

The western, interior frontiers of China were the zones where Chinese homelands, over the course of history, intersected with a wide range of "other" homelands—such as those of the Mongols, Tibetans, or the Turkic peoples of China's northwestern frontiers. Thus, the history of the interior frontiers was written through the intersections of territories and punctuated by trade and military cities that concentrated the interactions between these different peoples. This western frontier zone expanded and contracted over the course of China's history as subsequent empires gained and lost territory. The greatest expansions of the western frontier came with the two distinct periods of the Silk Road—one spanning the years from about 115 BC to the third century AD, and the second from the 7th century to the 14th century. During these periods, overland trade required securing the frontier zone from the Chinese heartland west into central Asia.

The cities of China's western frontier zone developed an interesting, if contradictory, urban form that was at once *more* and *less* true to Chinese urban ideals. The military commanders who established the cities often built square, walled core areas as direct replications of ancient Chinese ideal cities, without the adjustments and nuances imposed by geomancers and other experts in the establishment of eastern Chinese cities. These square or rectangular walled areas became the official "shapes" of the cities as represented on maps, with characteristic street grids, orientation to the cardinal directions, and symmetry. Outside the central walled areas, however, hybrid settlements of traders and non-Chinese migrants developed. These were often walled either with an attached outer wall or in a physically separate "twin city." Thus, the frontier cities maintained the ideal in their core areas while executing irregularly shaped and noncompliant urbanism in their peripheries. The cities were frequently rebuilt or expanded in response to the changing power dynamics along the frontier. In this manner, the form of the cities supported, mediated, and secured the liminal, hybrid multiplicities and mobilities of frontier politics, economies, cultures, and identities. For example, the city of Hohhot began its history as a Mongolian monastic center and trading center during the mid-16th century when the Mongol leader Altan Khan sought trade with the Chinese empire across the Great Wall. Although historic depictions of the city (fig. 4) portray a symmetrical, idealized twin-city form with only two settlements of

apparently equal size—the "Chinese" city on the west, the "Manchu" city on the east—the western city was actually an irregularly shaped hybrid of square, walled Chinese administrative complex, Mongol temple town, and Muslim quarter. The walled Chinese complex, which is all that would have been depicted in the historical record, was actually much smaller than the formal, walled military and administrative Manchu city to the east (fig. 5).

Thus, over the course of its history, the Mongol settlement grew into a complex multinational hybrid of settlements including the Chinese administrative center, the Manchu military complex, the Muslim quarter, and the Mongol town, which itself incorporated a number of large walled monasteries and temples.[35] In this manner, the physicality of multifaceted sociospatial structure was complemented in the inland frontier cities by their multiple functional roles, which mediated the political, economic, military, and cultural interactions between empires and anchored the vast trade and military routes that secured the Chinese empire's hold on interior Asia. Hohhot, for example, served as a major center for administering trade and managing security in the borderlands between China proper and Mongolia. By the mid-18th century, the city was dominated by four distinctive institutional forces that facilitated these functions: the military command for the northwestern region of the Chinese empire; the civilian administration, which extended the reach of Chinese imperial power toward the grasslands and deserts; a set of banking/trading organizations, headquartered in Hohhot, that managed the massive trade of livestock between Mongolia and China; and the regional Mongolian monastic hierarchy, which was also centered in Hohhot. Each of these institutions contributed to the management of border functions throughout the region and generated appropriate urban space to accommodate their functions and employees.

In contrast to the western frontiers, the eastern maritime frontier was sustained through centuries of coastal trade. With few exceptions, there was no territory-to-territory interaction. Rather, the borderland cities became hybrid spaces as traders, missionaries, and adventurers from far-flung ports chose to sojourn for periods of time on Chinese shores. The Muslim communities of eastern China, for example, had for 500 years maintained contact with the Arab world through sea trade.[36] Chinese seaports were home to traders who brought not only trade but culture to contribute to the development of unique and

35   Gaubatz, *Beyond the Great Wall.*

36   Piper Gaubatz, "Looking West Toward Mecca: Muslim Enclaves in Chinese Cities," *Built Environment* 28, no. 3 (2002): 231–48.

Fig. 6 Treaty port of Shanghai, 1930.

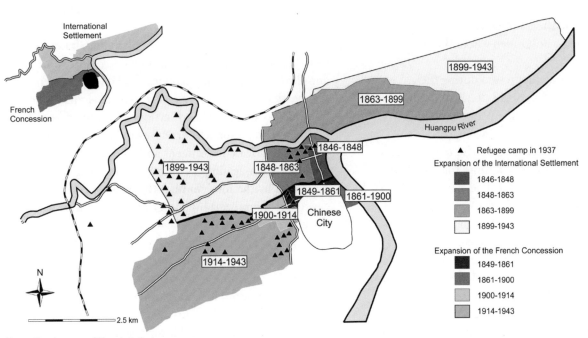

Fig. 7 Development of Shanghai, 1846–1943.

cosmopolitan centers. Chinese historians tell of mosques and other structures built in "foreign styles" in the coastal cities from the 10th century onward.[37] But until the arrival of large numbers of Europeans to the post–Opium War coastal cities of the mid-19th century, the border functions of Chinese seaports were moderated by the small numbers of foreign traders to set foot in China. Nonetheless, those who arrived and settled for periods of time—largely from the Indian subcontinent or the Arabian Peninsula—had a marked impact.[38] Archaeologists have discovered numerous relics of Hindu temples and Islamic mosques in the cities of the eastern seaboard.

The city of Guangzhou, for example, began as a Chinese walled fort, known as Panyucheng, when the Qin army established a base there in 214 BC. Located along the Pearl River not far from what was to become Hong Kong, the fort was expanded multiple times as it grew into a trade center. Unlike the practice of inland cities, where trade was often confined to markets within the walled center where it could be controlled and taxed, Guangzhou carried out its trade at the port, outside its walls. By the sixth century BC a small settlement had developed for foreign traders across the river from the city. As one Chinese annalist wrote in about 750 BC, "On the river (of Guangzhou) there were merchantmen belonging to the Po-lo-men (Indians), the Po-sseu (Persians), the K'ouen-louen (Malays), and others besides of which it is difficult to determine the number… There were also three monasteries of the Po-lo-men where Brahmans were residing."[39]

Most of this trade was suppressed during the extended periods of the Ming (1368–1644) and Qing dynasties (1644–1911) as the Chinese empire turned inward. A succession of edicts banning coastal trade began in the 14th century, which gave rise to an increase in piracy along Chinese coasts.[40] During the mid-17th century, there was even an order, called the "frontier shift," for coastal communities to relocate inward about 10 miles to preserve the security of the coastline.[41] At that time, the Chinese emperor envisioned a China surrounded by protective frontier zones on all sides— continental frontiers on the north, west, and south, and the maritime frontier on the east. Guangzhou was able to maintain some foreign trade, but in 1720, the empire imposed limits; subsequently, foreign trade was confined to 13 Chinese-operated trading companies that operated in what had been the foreign settlement area across the

river from the city. In response to the closure of China to foreign trade, both Macau and Hong Kong grew as bases for European missionaries and traders who sought entry into China.

The city of Guangzhou (then known to foreigners as Canton) exemplifies both the development of these coastal cities and the contrasts between the coastal cities and the inland frontier cities. Eventually, the closed nature of the Chinese empire led to war when the British challenged China for the right to trade. In 1842, the British victory over the Chinese in the first Opium War, which had begun in Guangzhou, led to the establishment of "treaty ports" along the coast—extraterritorial border cities where a broad mix of foreign corporations established manufacturing and trade concerns that came to dominate many aspects of the Chinese economy (fig. 6).

Guangzhou, the other mainland treaty ports, Hong Kong, and Macau exemplify a new type of border city that developed in China following the Opium Wars. These cities all had both the maritime border characteristics typical of most port cities and an inland border between the extraterritorial/colonial settlements and China—a distinctive form of borderland/border city on the eastern Chinese frontiers. The spatial configuration of these settlements was highly regulated, with a clear distinction between what was "foreign" and what was "Chinese." Territory demarcated by walls, open spaces, or guard posts was complemented by disjunct logics of urban space. The foreign concessions in Shanghai, for example, were legible through their monumental architecture and through density and land use. While the French Concession included large residential villas surrounded by gardens, the oval walled settlement that had been the Chinese town before the arrival of the Europeans was dense and crowded. Refugees and labor migrants gathered in the concessions in informal camps (fig. 7).

Thus, by the 19th century, the frontier cities of the east coast shared certain border characteristics with the cities of the interior: they were the liminal focal point of the transition from tradition to modernity; the hybrid landscapes of multinational settlement; the primary mechanism of Chinese efforts to secure the frontier; the primary spaces for movement of people and goods; and the spaces of mediation between the Chinese empire and the overseas empires that sought entry into China.

In Guangzhou, a treaty port was opened on an island between the former foreign settlement area and the city

37   Gaubatz, "Looking West."

38   John Chaffee, "Diasporic Identities in the Historical Development of the Maritime Muslim Communities of Song-Yuan China," *Journal of the Economic and Social History of the Orient* 49, no. 4 (2006): 395–420.

39   Kanshin quoted in John Guy, "Tamil Merchant Guilds and the Quanzhou Trade," in *The Emporium of the World: Maritime Quanzhou, 1000–1400*, ed. Angela Schottenhammer (Leiden: Brill, 2001), 283–308.

40   Tonio Andrade, "The Company's Chinese Pirates: How the Dutch East India Company Tried to Lead a Coalition of Pirates to War against China, 1621–1662," *Journal of World History* 15, no. 4 (2004): 415–44.

41   Chin-Keong Ng, *Trade and Society: The Amoy Network on the China Coast 1683–1735* (Singapore: Singapore University Press, 1983), 51.

Fig. 8   Canton Fair, 1958.

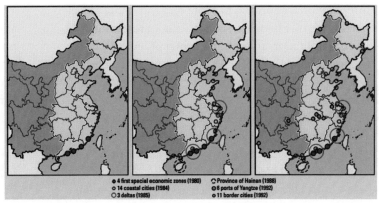

● 4 first special economic zones (1980)   ◔ Province of Hainan (1988)
○ 14 coastal cities (1984)   ◑ 6 ports of Yangtze (1992)
◯ 3 deltas (1985)   ◉ 11 border cities (1992)

Fig. 9   Special Economic Zones in China.

itself, which was divided between the French and the British.[42] Unlike the situation in Hohhot, in Guangzhou the institutions shaping the border functions included not only the Chinese military and civil administration and Chinese trading firms but also two different extraterritorial foreign authorities and foreign trading concerns. Religious institutions were present but not as a dominant force. This multiplicity of Chinese and foreign institutions was characteristic of most of the eastern border cities from the mid-19th century through the mid-20th century. The authority of the domestic and foreign powers was clearly differentiated and generated sharp contrasts in the way urban space was shaped and administered in different parts of the city.

Immediately after the establishment of the People's Republic of China in 1949, however, the foreign corporations and residents of the treaty port cities left or were deported, the eastern border was all but closed, and most of these cities lost their bordering functions. But more recently, during the post-1979 reform era, border cities have played a pivotal role in the transition from the inward-looking China to the new emphasis on global engagement that has characterized China and its cities

since the inception of the reform era, Deng Xiaoping's 1992 southern tour, and the increasing globalization of 21st-century China. This is particularly true of the cities of the Pearl River Delta—Hong Kong, Shenzhen, Guangzhou, and Macau—whose landscapes and livelihoods have been tied to the quest for new forms of economic development within the context of global geopolitics.

From 1957 to the early 1980s, the Canton Fair—an annual trade fair in Guangzhou that permitted foreign corporate representatives usually denied access to China a chance to enter a heavily managed environment to conduct trade with state-run industries—was one of the few means of entry to China for foreign nationals (fig. 8). The border control point for travel to the fair from Hong Kong was located at Shenzhen, a small village. Pre-reform fairgoers, shepherded directly to Guangzhou, had little developmental impact on Shenzhen. But after China's economic reforms were announced at the end of 1978, the Pearl River Delta, with its proximity to the European territories of Hong Kong and Macau, became one of the first regions to experience new urban development driven by China's outward reorientation of its economy.

42   Piper Gaubatz, "Understanding Chinese Urban Form: Contexts for Interpreting Continuity and Change," *Built Environment* 24, no. 4 (1998): 251–70.

In 1980, China designated its first four Special Economic Zones—free-trade zones modeled on Shannon, Ireland's 1960s free-trade zone—to launch this economic transition. The SEZs created international "border" spaces within or adjacent to other cities as they fostered controlled trade with multinational firms. Two of these SEZs were located in the Pearl River Delta: Shenzhen, adjacent to Hong Kong, and Zhuhai, adjacent to Macau. Designation of the SEZs here (and eventually in many more cities) fostered an entrepreneurial approach to economic and spatial development (fig. 9). Shenzhen, in particular, grew from a low-rise, utilitarian agricultural center of fewer than 200,000 inhabitants at the end of the 1970s to a gleaming high-rise metropolis of more than 7 million by the early 21st century.[43]

More recently, a new scale has been added to the urban system in China as the state has enabled the formation of large city-regions designed to coordinate development and environmental planning. Many of these—especially the Beijing-Tianjin-Tangshan region, the Changjiang River Delta, and the Pearl River Delta—include in their structures border functions and one or more border cities. Similarly, China has established 17 "border economic cooperation zones" since 1992, and has recently begun to experiment with free-trade zones (the first is in Shanghai; 12 more have been authorized), in a clear effort to make use of the economic advantages of border cities and regions. These state-led initiatives channel development funding into these cities and regions, which will culminate in increased urban development along international borders.

Today, Chinese cities are home to about 10 percent of the world's population. China's GDP is second only to that of the United States. A vast proportion of that economy is produced, managed, and traded in and through the eastern cities. In this sense, the developmental border cities are core players in the world economy. As they have grown at a staggeringly fast pace, and in all dimensions, from economy to built-up area, they have become destinations for labor migrants and hosts to creativity and innovation. They are home to rising wealthy and middle classes but also are centers of poverty and rising inequality; are proving grounds for some of the world's most innovative experiments in green urbanism but also are plagued by some of the world's worst urban pollution.

Macao people are border people. They live close to a political border, and this border has a very significant impact on their lives. Their identities, their thinking and their everyday choices are influenced by this spatial setting—as much as they are influenced for example by living in a Chinese, post-colonial or urban environment.[44]

When Frederick Jackson Turner rose to speak at the World's Columbian Exposition, he envisioned the development of the frontier as a linear process with defined starting and ending points. The work of the frontier was accomplished: it had shaped the American character through agrarian challenge. With the maturation of cities in the American West, the time of the frontier was past. What Turner failed to envision was the role of perpetual, though constantly shifting, frontiers and borders in shaping space and identity. As Xiangming Chen explains, "As borders get pushed and pulled by both domestic and global forces, border regions develop their own distinctive transborder (sub)regional character and structure that in turn reorganize broader national and local political and economic spaces into a new transnational space."[45] Turner was right to identify the creative force of frontier and border dynamics. But he failed to recognize the figurative role of cities in this process and could not imagine a world in which the cities located in the borderlands would play a central role.

Today's borderlands are defined by their cities; and borderland conditions define the spaces of those cities. These conditions are liminal: border conditions are in a constant state of change, and they are characterized by hybridity as landscapes and identities are negotiated, produced, and reproduced through the border's mediating functions. While the apparatus of security is a condition of borders, mobility is also key, thus establishing a shifting dynamic between fluid flows of people, capital, goods, and ideas and control of those flows.

In China, the central role of present-day border cities is manifest in the cities of the eastern border region. The contemporary configurations of the five border conditions are strongly differentiated between China's maritime and interior frontiers. In the interior, on the north, west, and south, some borderland cities are experiencing a renaissance as they benefit from the reestablished trade between China and its bordering

43 Weiping Wu and Piper Gaubatz, *The Chinese City* (New York: Routledge, 2013).

44 Breitung, "Living with Borders."

45 Chen, *As Borders Bend*, 4.

countries. For example, along the northern and western borders, the newly independent countries of central Asia seek primary resources such as oil, coal, timber, and meat and dairy products. While Hohhot is once again a headquarters for firms trading in meat and dairy products produced in the Mongolian grasslands, cities in central Asian China, such as Urumqi, are growing with both foreign and domestic demand for oil. These cities are centers for transitional economies and societies and continue to host hybrid, mobile societies where the homelands of China's different peoples meet and migrants and traders come and go. They accommodate a substantial military presence as China secures its borders and serve as the locus for the mediation of economies and cultures across the borders.

Yet mobility, mediation, and hybridity are much less intense in the interior cities than they are in the eastern border cities. The interior cities continue to lag behind the eastern coastal cities, which have become the center of the new economy, in development and foreign investment. Mobility is one of the key characteristics of these cities, primarily in the sense that rural-to-urban labor migration has become a defining aspect of their economies, growth, and development. This in turn generates new hybridities, not only between peoples of different origins but between peoples of different economic classes as well. The mediating function of the eastern border cities, with their role as new focal points in the relationship between the global economy and interior China, has intensified as well. Guangzhou, for example, has become an important node in a network of Pearl River Delta cities, including Hong Kong and Macau, which produces about 40 percent of China's total exports. The major conurbations of the eastern border—especially the Pearl River Delta and the Shanghai region (Changjiang River Delta)—have intensified both their border functions and their economic centrality in China's newly configured and constantly changing relationship with the global economy.

Macau and Its Borders

Peter G. Rowe,
Har Ye Kan

Fig. 1 Defense map of Macau, 1679–1682.

In today's world of alleged globalization, two impetuses often compete. One works toward leveling differences among places by lowering the transaction costs of moving around and being comfortably both here and there. The other works in an opposite direction, actively seeking to maintain and even celebrate differences among places and their spaces of local and unique experience. The Pearl River Delta is currently involved in this struggle as China, through both overarching development plans and regional interests, seeks to increase urbanization, improve access, and generally unify the delta region into a more potent ensemble where boundaries and borders are either erased or significantly weakened. Consequently, distinct places of the past, with particular histories, sovereignties, and manners of occupation—Guangzhou, Hong Kong, and Macau, for instance—let alone relative newcomers in this regard—Shenzhen, Dongguan, Zhongshan, and Zhuhai—are being reordered if not harmonized into some semblance of a coherent whole in which each has a largely predetermined role to play. In this interplay, the former Portuguese territory and now Chinese special administrative region of Macau seems most likely to be simply annexed as a site subject to the subsequent ebb and flow of activity due to its almost insignificantly small size and loss of borders. It is, after all, only 29.2 square kilometers in size and a little over half a million in population.

It is important to recognize that borders and boundaries, both literal and figurative, are necessary to contemporary life. They help bring order and understanding to environments, especially during times of dramatic change and spatial transformation. In fact, it is precisely via coming and going in space and time that it is possible to achieve both the exhilaration of being somewhere else and the peace of being home. Put another way, familiarity and comfort within urban environments require borders within borders in order to render feelings of a sense of place, thresholds, portals to more private realms, and margins for framing life's encounters and experiences. Without borders, there can really be no "there" there. Moreover, when connected to less individual and more collective experiences, "good" and "appropriate" borders make for meaningful and lasting territorial and temporal definitions that benefit all. At the same time, these definitions also raise questions about what constitutes "good" and "appropriate" borders in any specific instance.

THE SHIFTING BORDERS OF MACAU AND THE AOMEN

Since the early 16th century, a significant feature of Aomen, or the gateway to the Chinese mainland formed by the islands of Hengqin, Taipa, and Coloane, adjacent to the peninsula on which sits the Ma Kok Temple, has been the numerous realignments of borders. With regard to the Portuguese settlement of Macau—derived from the Fujianese Ma Kok—these shifts have come by way of occupation, seizure, land reclamation, exercise of sovereignty, exceptionalism in use, district designation, defense, modernization, and integration with neighboring areas and sea links, along with cultural attitudes of mind, language, and customs and ebbs and flows in balances of power. Throughout much of the history of the region, the process by which borders are shifted has had at least two distinguishing traits. The first is the sheer multiplicity of movements, generally in an expansive direction. The second, which differs from what has occurred in neighboring Hong Kong and elsewhere, is the evasion of strict or statutory border delimitations. For the most part, shifts in borders have been accomplished by physical means, although they have also occasioned changes in both local and external perceptions of Macau as a place.

In addition to its physical borders, Macau possesses broad temporal borders that coincide with three periods of occupation and orientation. The first, beginning more or less in the 1550s, comprised "shared sovereignty" with China and then with the dual monarchy of Spain and Portugal; part of this era is what is sometimes referred to as the "golden age" of Macau. The second, commencing in 1849 with the assassination of Macau's governor João Maria Ferreira do Amaral and ensuing reprisals by the Portuguese, was characterized by the "colonial governorate." The third, beginning in the 1970s with the dissolution of the Salazar dictatorship in Portugal, continued through the agreement to return Macau to China in December 1999 and until the present. With few exceptions, these temporal demarcations also shifted gradually or unsteadily.[1]

BEGINNINGS

The Portuguese first came to Macau in 1513, when Jorge Álvarez arrived to begin moving into Chinese waters from Portuguese holdings in Malacca and Goa. These trade explorations were rebuffed by China—in 1530, Guangzhou was reopened to foreign, but not Portuguese, trade. After Jesuit missionary Francis Xavier went to Macau in 1552, Portuguese traders began settling there in 1553 and resumed trade with Guangzhou in 1554. In 1557, Portugal obtained the leasehold of Macau by agreeing to pay an annual fee and formally founded the settlement under the name of "City of the Name of God, Macau." By 1564, the population of the new settlement was estimated to be around 900, with a large number of Jesuits. In 1568, the Portuguese successfully defended the seas around Macau and the Pearl River Delta against attacks by pirates preying on the incipient coastal trade. This engagement involved some 100 vessels, 1,500 guns, and 3,000 to 4,000 men on the pirates' side; the Portuguese numbered far fewer. Such battles set a pattern for the years to come: stout defense on the part of those in Macau against potentially overwhelming odds earned good will from the Chinese along with permission to build fortresses on the peninsula.[2] By 1573, the Portuguese began to pay ground rent as a part of their leasehold on Macau, and the Chinese constructed a barrier gate—the Portas do Cerco—at the narrow isthmus between Macau and the mainland. This first border crossing was essentially aimed at preventing Chinese from crossing into Macau in much the same manner as was to occur elsewhere in China (fig. 1).

In 1580, back on the Iberian Peninsula in Europe, the dual monarchy united the Spanish and Portuguese crowns in a manner strongly favoring Spain. Macau entered into a 60-year era of substantial trading and international prominence—the golden era. Macau was strengthened considerably at this time. In 1582, China affirmed the land-lease arrangement, essentially conveying Macau to the Portuguese for 500 *taels* of silver, annually assigned to adjacent Zhongshan County. The Senado da Câmara, or municipal senate, was established in 1583 as the administrative body for the settlement; by 1586, Portuguese authorities accorded Macau the status of a self-governing city. Additional institutions, such as a university, were formed by 1597 as the Portuguese presence became more

1 Historical accounts of Macau include Charles R. Boxer, *Macau Three Hundred Years Ago* (Lisbon: Fundação Oriente, 1993); R. D. Cremer, ed., *Macau: City of Commerce and Culture, Continuity and Change* (Hong Kong: API Press, 1991); Geoffrey C. Gunn, *Encountering Macau: A Portuguese City-State on the Periphery of China,* 1557-1999 (Boulder, CO: Westview, 1996); Zhidong Hao, *Macau: History and Society* (Hong Kong: Hong Kong University Press, 2011); Steve Shipp, *Macau, China: A Political History of the Portuguese Colony's Transition to Chinese Rule* (Jefferson, NC: McFarland, 1997).

2 Shipp, *Macau, China,* 24–31.

permanently established.[3] During this time, one of the keys to economic success was active trade with Japan; direct trade with the nation was banned in China, and the Portuguese played the role of go-between.[4] Macau also became part of Portuguese trading conduits back to Malacca and through the Indian Ocean to Goa and then to Lisbon, as well as from Guangzhou to Nagasaki and, via Manila, to Mexico, largely in Spanish hands at the time. From a European perspective, the Portuguese, through Macau, virtually monopolized trade with China.

COMPETITION FROM OUTSIDE

Dutch ships first appeared in the Pearl River Delta in 1601, partway through this era, and subsequently sought to trade with China and break Portugal's trading hegemony. This confrontation resulted in attacks on Macau by the Dutch in 1602 and 1603 and invasion attempts in 1604, 1607, 1622, and 1627. During the 1622 attack, an 800-strong Dutch force was repelled by 150 Portuguese defenders under Captain-Major Lopo Sarmento de Carvalho. Jesuit priest Jeronimo Rho fired cannon from the vicinity of the Fortaleza de São Paulo do Monte, sited on a hill overlooking the battlefield, and blew up much of the Dutch gunpowder. According to a map of the time, the Dutch, their fleet anchored off the coast of the Bahia de Caclihas, landed near today's Islamic mosque and cemetery and made their way inland before returning across Guia Hill. Some 200 to 300 Dutch invaders were killed, but only two combatants on the Portuguese side.[5] By the time of the final invasion, contemporary depictions show that the Portuguese settlement was substantially enclosed by an east-west defensive wall and nine cannon emplacements, which split the peninsula more or less in two; another wall crossed the peninsula adjacent to Barra Hill.[6] The area outside of the wall to the north was occupied by six Chinese villages and substantial areas of agriculture; commercial activity occupied the zone immediately beside the Portas do Cerco. Several Chinese villages also occupied the area in the south both inside and outside of the wall near Barra Hill (fig. 2).

One factor that seemed to encourage the Dutch maritime forces, at least initially, was that the Portuguese deployed large ships, or *carracks*, displacing up to 12,000 tons. Smaller boats made the passage between ship and dock. The *carracks* were slow and vulnerable to attack,

especially in comparison to faster and more compact Dutch vessels, and soon the Portuguese developed much smaller and speedier ships—the so-called *galiotas*, which had up to 400 tons in carrying capacity.[7] Portugal's relatively uncontested, or well-defended, maritime border around and within China's seas altered significantly in 1631 when the Dutch seized Malacca, severing the trade route between Macau and Goa and severely hampering Portuguese trade. In 1639, the lucrative trade with Japan ended; in 1640, the dual monarchy itself. By 1685, the Portuguese monopoly on trade with China ended, largely at China's behest.[8]

The British had attempted to enter the China trade as early as 1637, setting up an office of the East India Company in Macau in 1715 and routinely making port there while conducting business upriver in Guangzhou. In 1802, a British invasion attempt was thwarted by the Chinese. Meanwhile, in 1808, the Portuguese once again endeared themselves to the Chinese by subduing a much larger pirate fleet of *Wakō* from Japan: 730 men and 118 guns subdued some 3,000 junks, 20,000 men, and 1,500 guns.[9] The British later increased pressure on China: in 1833, Lord Napier came to Macau and attempted to bypass the exclusive *cohong* arrangement for trade in Guangzhou, eventually leading to British occupation of what became Hong Kong.[10] In 1837, Chinese opposition to the opium trade led to war, which was decided in favor of the British in 1842. The Treaty of Nanjing opened treaty ports and foreign trading facilities in Guangzhou, Amoy, Fuzhou, Ningbo, and Shanghai. Shortly thereafter, in 1845, the Portuguese crown declared Macau a free port. Governor João Maria Ferreira do Amaral immediately began to pursue expansionist policies, tax local Chinese residents, and expand Macau's territory beyond its generally recognized borders, devastating Chinese property and even demolishing the local Chinese customs house. This exercise of power ushered in the absolute rule of Portugal rather than the prior shared sovereignty between Portugal and China. It also resulted in Amaral's assassination in 1849 at the hands of mainland China; in response, the Portuguese seized Taipa, the island to the south of the Macau Peninsula.[11]

3   Shipp, *Macau, China*, 195–96.

4   Shipp, *Macau, China*, 39–40.

5   Shipp, *Macau, China*, 43–47.

6   Fengxuan Xue, *Aomen wubainian: Yige teshu Zhongguo chengshi de xingqi yu fazhan* [Macau through 500 years: Emergence and development of an atypical Chinese city] (Hong Kong: Sanlian Bookstore, 2012), 23.

7   Shipp, *Macau, China*, 39.

8   Shipp, *Macau, China*, 197.

9   Shipp, *Macau, China*, 64.

10   Hao, *Macau: History and Society*, 21–24.

11   Shipp, *Macau, China*, 198.

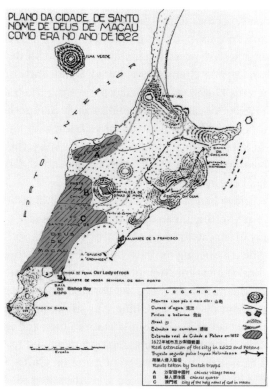

Fig. 2 Macau, 1622.

Fig. 3 Macau, 1889.

During the second half of the 19th century, the Portuguese colonial presence dominated Macau. Throughout the dual jurisdiction of China and Portugal, which had weathered political and other ups and downs in the 16th, 17th, and 18th centuries, neither side had been quite able to obtain complete control.[12] Between 1862 and 1887, for instance, Portugal and China conferred over the matter of Macau as a Portuguese colony. The Treaty of Friendship and Trade of 1887 confirmed perpetual occupation of Macau by Portugal—but evaded the question of border delimitations. This position was restated during another round of talks in 1909. Meanwhile, Ilha Verde, or Green Island, to the northwest of the peninsula and close to the isthmus with the mainland, was integrated into Macau in 1890, probably for its defensive advantages—hilly terrain and a prospect over the Porto Interior, or Inner Harbor, area. In this period, the Portas do Cerco and the border with the Chinese mainland received renewed attention,

alongside substantial public works improvements to Macau and immaterial though important institutional arrangements like the 1867 subordination of the legal system to the Portuguese Civil Code.[13]

Toward the end of the 19th century, if not earlier, the broad territory of populated Macau remained within the original peninsula (fig. 3). It was essentially comprised of two cities, one covering most of the eastern and southeastern side, which was occupied primarily by the Portuguese, and the other on the western side, adjacent to the extensive Inner Harbor, which was occupied primarily by the Chinese. At the north was some agricultural land. Hilly terrain and ridge lines provided something of a border or boundary between these precincts; the Portuguese generally adhered to the higher terrain. A rough line of demarcation ran from the Jardin e Gruta of the wealthy Portuguese merchant Manuel Pereira (built in 1770 and later rented to the English East India Company) past the site of the old defensive wall (built around 1579 to the west of São Paulo and the Jesuit redoubt of Fortaleza do Monte) and then to the west of

12 Philippe Forêt, "Globalizing Macau: The Emotional Costs of Modernity," in *Globalization and the Chinese City*, ed. Fulong Wu (London: Routledge, 2006), 108–23.

13 Shipp, *Macau, China*, 75.

the thicket of government buildings in the area of Largo do Senado and the Leal Senado building and finally south to Barra Hill at the tip of the peninsula.[14] Today, 25 or so locations on the Portuguese side of this line constitute a UNESCO World Heritage site, which was designated in 2005. Prominent Portuguese defensive features included the region of Guia Hill and the Fortaleza da Guia, built between 1622 and 1638 against attacks from the sea on the east near the mouth of the Pearl River Delta; the Fortaleza de Mong Há, to the north facing the narrow isthmus to the Chinese mainland where the first inhabitants of the peninsula settled; and the Barra Hill fortifications in the south.[15]

Perhaps the most notable feature of Macau's landscape was the Bahia Praia Grande and its esplanade, which inscribe a crescent across the southwest portion of the peninsula, from Barra Hill northeast toward Guia Hill. This area became a celebrated summer promenade. Banyan trees planted close to the beach lined the approximately one-kilometer path, which was protected by a granite wall. Along the parallel Rua da Praia Grande were Government House; other official buildings, consulates, and residences; and at the southern end, the Hotel Boa Vista, resplendent in pastels. Macau's sea breezes and more benign climate drew many of Hong Kong's wealthy residents there in summer months.

The geographical and ethnic boundaries that separated the littoral, or waterfront, area from the downtown sector, and Portuguese institutions from Chinese stores, including shop-houses, are relatively easy to locate in Macau's urban fabric.[16] Residents formed several communities, each with its own subculture, that met although seldom merged: Cantonese immigrants, Portuguese bureaucrats and merchants, the Catholic Macanese group (Portuguese-speaking, Chinese-looking, often with both Portuguese and Chinese heritage), and international travelers and merchants.[17] Marriages between Portuguese men and Chinese women were not formalized for the first centuries of Portuguese rule, perhaps not until the end of the 19th century.[18] Religion also differentiated Macau's population. In one instance, the bishop of Macau rejected the consolidation of Chinese trade in Macau for fear of "contamination" from Protestant foreigners.[19] Even today, Macau's politics are largely about associations: close-knit communities have developed, socially and historically, based on kinship, clanship, profession, or industry. The

overall population of Macau stood at 12,000 inhabitants in 1830, with 26 percent European, primarily Portuguese, roughly doubling from the 17th century. With Macau's participation in the infamous "coolie trade" in 1851, alongside the British, the population surged to nearly 30,000 inhabitants, mostly Chinese.[20]

PRESSURES OF MODERNIZATION

In 1910, Portugal became a republic following a revolution that deposed the monarchy and brought a largely progressive regime to power. The most immediate impact on Macau was replacement of the prevailing picturesque and nostalgic colonial image and identity with a drive toward modernization. Historically, Macau had been important for speculative rather than commercial activity; at the beginning of the 20th century, the economy was dominated by rice import, fish export, fireworks manufacture, and gambling, first permitted around 1851 in the form of *fantan* salons. "Political isolation, economic irrelevance, and the sedimentation of its port had combined to keep Macau somnolent and picturesque," human geographer Philippe Forêt has written.[21]

In keeping with its earlier history, this modernizing impulse brought accommodation of modern ocean-going shipping. Industry was nurtured to replace, at least in part, the dependence on trade. Although new port proposals had been made since the 1880s, serious preparations for land reclamation and port development began with the creation of the Outer Harbor Commission in 1919. By 1924, the construction of Patane Port was completed near Ilha Verde, which had been linked to the western side of the peninsula in 1912. Reclaimed land was set aside for brick factories, cement plants, timber yards, and dry docks. Work on the Porto Exterior, or Outer Harbor, began in 1923 and was completed in 1927 (fig. 4). A trade fair inaugurated Zona de Aterros do Porto Exterior (Outer Harbor land reclamation), or ZAPE, in 1928.[22] Land reclamation on the eastern side of the isthmus provided a site for a horse track; further land was set aside for industry; and a diked area in between formed a reservoir. The efforts to convert Macau into an industrial city with direct access to maritime trade met with modest success. The Macau Chinese Chamber of Commerce was created, and in 1928, the treaty between

14   Xue, *Aomen wubainian*, 67.

15   Steven Bailey and Jill C. Witt, *Strolling in Macau: A Visitor's Guide to Macau, Taipa and Coloane* (San Francisco: ThingsAsian Press), 50–85.

16   Forêt, "Globalizing Macau," 109.

17   Forêt, "Globalizing Macau," 110.

18   J. A. Berlie, "Society and Economy," in *Macau 2000*, ed. J. A. Berlie (Oxford: Oxford University Press, 1999), 23; personal observation, September 2013.

19   Hao, *Macau: History and Society*, 35.

20   Berlie, "Society and Economy," 25–26.

21   Forêt, "Globalizing Macau," 119.

22   Forêt, "Globalizing Macau," 119–22.

Portugal and China was renewed—avoiding still the issue of Macau's border delimitations. Back in Portugal, amid rampant corruption and state bankruptcy, a dictatorship was installed under António de Oliveira Salazar, ushering in, in 1933, the so-called Estado Novo along with a period of state corporatism and pro-fascism.

Further underlining Macau's determination to modernize was the landfill created in Bahia Praia Grande between 1931 and 1939, which cut the Rua da Praia Grande between São Francisco Garden on the east and the government offices toward the west off from the sea. But with a nod to the old cultivation of tourism, Macau granted monopoly rights to casino gambling to the Tai Xing Company syndicate, which opened its first casino in the Central Hotel near the Leal Senado. When Japan invaded China in 1937, Portugal's neutral status meant refugees fleeing mainland China flooded Macau. The city's population, which had expanded to about 160,800 inhabitants by 1928, stood close to 300,000 during World War II.[23]

After the war, many of the Chinese refugees returned to China, and Macau renewed its ties with places like Hong Kong. The territory became a Portuguese province in 1951, shortly after the outbreak of the Korean War, and joined the United Nations embargo against China. Not surprisingly, the relationship between China and Macau deteriorated, resulting in the 1952 Barrier Gate Incident and subsequent Chinese restriction on food imports to the city. After the war, Portugal made Macau an "overseas province" in 1955; defined exports from Macau to other Portuguese territories as duty-free in 1957; and declared Macau a tourist center, with full authority to establish gambling, in 1961. As a result of this last move, all casino rights in Macau were transferred from Tai Xing Company syndicate to Stanley Ho's Sociedade de Turismo e Diversões de Macau, or STDM, and later subsidiary Sociedade de Jogos de Macau, or SJM. Casinos soon lined the swath of reclaimed land under ZAPE more or less adjacent to the Avenida da Amizade.[24] During the mid- to late 1960s, the Cultural Revolution in the People's Republic of China disrupted daily life in Macau. Conflict between Macau police and local leftists resulted in violent demonstrations in 1966. But modernization and commercialization continued apace (fig. 5). In 1964, Taipa and its coastal boundaries were remade, and in 1969, the 2.2-kilometer causeway and bridge linking the Macau Peninsula to Taipa was completed along with Estrada do

Isthmus, still farther to the south, linking Taipa with Coloane. The 8.7-square-kilometer Coloane Island grew notably in population with the causeway link, although it still remained primarily a natural preserve with the picturesque Coloane Village on its southern coast. Portugal had occupied Taipa and parts of Coloane since about 1864, although the territory was often disputed until pirates were more or less eradicated in 1910.[25]

MODERN MASTER PLANS

About 1974, radical change came to Macau, including the question of who was to control the land and its borders. Portugal's bloodless, left-wing military coup, or Carnation Revolution, ushered in the Third Republic and rid the country and its colonies of the dictatorship of Salazar and his successor, Marcelo Caetano. Devolution of colonial power was slower in Macau than in other Portuguese colonies: administrative change was not seen until the Sino-Portuguese Joint Declaration on Macau in 1987 and formation of the Basic Law Drafting Committee, charged with preparing a constitution-like document for Macau for the period between its transfer to China in 1999 and its becoming part of China in 2049. Meanwhile in 1979, a secret agreement between the Portuguese and the Chinese affirmed Macau as a Chinese territory under Portuguese administration and extended Stanley Ho's casino monopoly until 2001. As part of the handback to China, Portugal extended citizenship to Macanese residents. The Basic Law was adopted by the Chinese in 1993. In 1979, the planning firm of John Prescott and Palmer and Turner prepared master plans for the extension of reclaimed lands and for the city. Portuguese architect Álvaro Siza became involved in planning the Novos Aterros do Porto Exterior (new Outer Harbor reclamation area), or NAPE, between 1982 and 1988, subdividing this area into a relatively fine grid of blocks with a height restriction of 22 meters, later increased to 80 meters.[26] Development at this time favored tourism and gambling, rather than commerce. Also included in Macau's land area by 1990 were reclamations on the northeastern edge of the peninsula and around the Ilha Verde expansion. Additional segments of Bahia Praia Grande were also filled in, including the essential occlusion, between 1995 and 2000, of the earlier bayfront from the sea by the Aterro da Praia Grande. Further extensions

23   Forêt, "Globalizing Macau," 111–12; Berlie, "Society and Economy," 25–26.

24   Shipp, *Macau, China*, 199; Thomas Daniell (presentation, University of St. Joseph, Macau, September 20, 2013); Gaming Inspector and Coordination Bureau, Macau SAR, *Location Map*, February 16, 2014.

25   Bailey and Witt, *Strolling in Macau*, 116–39.

26   Daniell, presentation.

of Taipa and Coloane, including the seaward development of Macau International Airport in 1995, were made at this time, and two new sea links to the peninsula south of Taipa were constructed, including the Ponte da Amizade, or Friendship Bridge.

The advent of the Cotai Strip in about 2004, occasioned largely by the liberalization of gambling and the opening of competition beyond STDM, brought more changes to Macau. The Cotai Strip consists of reclaimed land that effectively unites the islands of Taipa and Coloane, in the south, into a single land mass. Building on properties in this new land area were the recipients of newly granted gaming concessions: Galaxy and Melco Crown from Hong Kong and Wynn Resorts, Las Vegas Sands, and MGM Mirage from Las Vegas.[27] The number of "keys," roughly equivalent to rooms or suites, is expected to continue to grow, from the current level of 26,000 to 60,000.[28] Regulation encouraged by the Chinese has placed something of a cap on casino operations in Macau. Nevertheless, the combined operations of 34 casinos, including both Stanley Ho's and the new arrivals, employ 21 percent of Macau's workforce of 323,000; the gaming industry has proven more attractive to employees than smaller businesses, to the detriment of the latter. Even more striking, the concentration of casinos has been estimated to be six times more than anywhere else in the world, including Las Vegas.[29] Between 2008 and 2012, gambling revenues grew an average of 29 percent annually.[30] In December 1999, Macau was transferred back to China. It is now a special administrative region of the People's Republic of China; in 2049, the Basic Law will terminate and Macau will be fully integrated into China.

PRESENT JURISDICTIONS AND FUTURE PLANS

The area of the Macau Special Administrative Region is currently 29.2 square kilometers. It comprises the Macau Peninsula, at 9.3 square kilometers; Taipa and Coloane, at 6.7 and 7.6 square kilometers respectively; and the Cotai Strip, at 5.6 square kilometers. The region has more than doubled in area since 1912, when the land area was 11.6 square kilometers (fig. 6). This expansion is quite remarkable, even in the fluid realms of East and Southeast Asian city-states.[31] Population distribution is very uneven,

however, with almost 85 percent of the approximately 600,000 inhabitants on the peninsula, 14 percent on Taipa, and less than 1 percent on Coloane. Population growth in Macau has remained relatively stable since 2006 and earlier; 95 percent of residents are of Chinese descent, and 5 percent of Portuguese or other descent. This preponderance of Chinese has been a conspicuous aspect of Macau since as early as the mid-19th century. In addition, about 100 million visitors arrive in Macau each year, including cross-border workers, tourists, and some travelers who stay for extended periods.[32] On average, the daily population flow of workers represents about 10 to 15 percent of the total population and is driven, in part, by the fact that jobs, particularly in the gambling and related service industries, are available on the peninsula, and the cost of housing is higher in Macau than in neighboring Zhuhai. With a per capita GDP of about $35,000 to $40,000, Macau's inhabitants are wealthier than their near Chinese neighbors but not as rich as, for instance, residents of Hong Kong. Income disparity is also high in Macau, skewed in favor of a relative few involved in gambling and affiliated enterprises. In fact, gambling contributes 45 percent of the annual GDP, with finance and real estate contributing about 18 percent and wholesaling and retailing about 12 percent.[33] The majority of Macau's exports—67 percent—go to Hong Kong and mainland China; exports to the United States and Europe amount to a combined 10 percent. Both in visitors and exports, Macau is largely a regional and local phenomenon, although with relatively significant flows in both cases.[34]

Income disparity is one of the main issues confronting Macau. It is due, in part at least, to the significantly higher incomes to be made within the gambling and associated industries and to the continuing marginalization of non-gambling enterprises. Fully 99 percent of all businesses in Macau have less than 100 employees; 92 percent have less than 10.[35] There exists a clear need to diversify the economy or, rather, to strengthen sectors that compete with the gambling industry for employees.

Population density on the Macau Peninsula is about 50,000 inhabitants per square kilometer, quite high even for East and Southeast Asia. China, for instance, has generally targeted average urban densities of about 10,000 people per square kilometer. Overcrowding, along with

27 "New Macau Casinos Have Luck of the Draw in Second Expansion Phase," Reuters, March 12, 2014, http://www.reuters.com/article/2014/03/12/us-macau-expansion-idUSBREA2B09D20140312.

28 Lao Long, director of Department of Urban Planning, conversation with authors, September 18, 2013.

29 "The Rise of the Low-Rollers," Economist, September 7, 2013, 63.

30 "Rise of the Low-Rollers," 63; "Macau GDP and Economic Indicators," Economist Intelligence Unit Country Report: Macau, generated June 13, 2013 (London: Economist Intelligence Unit).

31 Long, conversation; Public Works and Transportation Bureau, The Brief of Macau's Urban Planning and Regional Cooperation (Macau: Government of the Macau SAR, 2013), 6.

32 Public Works and Transportation Bureau, Brief, 7.

33 "Macau Economic Indicators," Economist Intelligence Unit Country Report: Macau, generated June 13, 2013.

34 "Basic Data," Economist Intelligence Unit Country Report: Macau, generated June 13, 2013.

35 Hao, Macau: History and Society, 66–67.

Fig. 4   Macau, showing Inner Harbor and Outer Harbor, 1927.

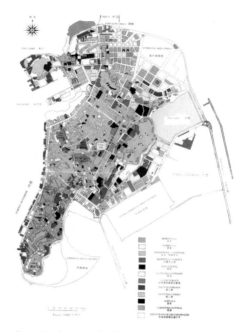

Fig. 5   Land-use map for the Macau Peninsula, 1964.

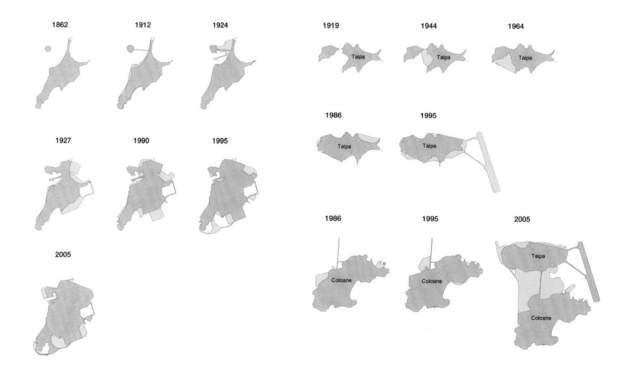

Fig. 6   Changes in Macau's Coastline, 1862–2005.

dilapidated living conditions, is present in many areas of the peninsula. Some shift in the population to other parts of Macau, such as Taipa, would relieve this condition. With high densities and modest road space comes traffic congestion, which is another matter in question in Macau even though more than 30 percent of commuters travel by bus and another 30 percent or more walk. Air pollution, particularly noticeable in denser parts of the city, is a related concern. Overcrowding also leads to a relative scarcity of affordable housing, particularly within attainable rental markets. Short of wholesale removal of residents to areas in Macau south of the peninsula, availability of housing will continue to be limited by a scarcity of developable land, particularly land with reasonable proximity to employment, including the newer casinos. Finally, orderly development in various areas of Macau has been hampered by an absence of both effective plan making and a reliable regulatory framework. This absence was addressed in part starting in 1986 with urban planning guidelines; today the Macau Special Administrative Region is in more robust condition.[36] Nevertheless, more headway needs to be made, especially on such issues as property consolidation. Lack of public open space within or near urban areas is yet another concern for the region.

Macau has made several plans to alleviate these problems (fig. 7). China's central authorities have granted permission to add 3.5 square kilometers of land at several points along the existing coastline.[37] Approval, not necessary for earlier land reclamations, was required because the SAR authority has no water rights. (The prior circumstances are one of the sources of border ambiguity, although it mattered less then than it does today, with China's increasing assertion of jurisdictional hegemony.) Of the new land areas, 53 percent will accrue to the Macau Peninsula, particularly in an island linked to the mainland on the east, between the planned staging and border crossing facilities of the Hong Kong–Macau–Zhuhai sea link, currently under construction; an extension of NAPE; and the full enclosure of the former Bahia Praia Grande. The remaining land reclamation will occur along the northern perimeter of Taipa, associated with the three bridge links between Taipa and the peninsula. An additional link between Taipa in the vicinity of the airport and the new island expansion on the east of Macau has also been proposed. Land use across these expansions is mixed, with significant areas of public open space, particularly where there is access to the coast. In fact, the coastal perimeter of Macau will be increased by 26 kilometers, a rise of about 54 percent, even though the land area will grow by only 12 percent.[38] These land reclamations and extensions will relieve density on the peninsula in a manner that keeps the overall urban footprint of the city both compact and diverse.

The second major aspect of Macau's future plans is the construction of a light rail system. Because of the area's geography, in conjunction with the difficulty of installation in dense urban areas, the system will be located close to or at the edges of the peninsula.[39] This disposition will maximize pedestrian access to the system. The 50 kilometers of track will be constructed in two phases, with extension into Taipa, the Cotai Strip, and on to the airport.

New links to the mainland (and until at least 2049, border crossings) are also included in plans for Macau in addition to the enduring Gongbei border crossing (on the site of Portas do Cerco). New interchanges will be placed at the boundary with Zhuhai on the northwest and with Hengqin Island in the south, across from Cotai. Hengqin Island, currently undeveloped, is planned as something of a free-trade zone, with significant urbanization, including the relocation of the University of Macau in 2009 (fig. 8). Another significant connection is the sea link from Lantau Island in Hong Kong, which crosses about 35 kilometers of the Pearl River Delta estuary to Macau and on to Zhuhai. This construction will form a major connection between the Pearl River's thriving east bank and its developing west bank. The sea link is also a physical manifestation of the regional ambition, at least by those in authority, to tie Guangzhou, Shenzhen, Hong Kong, Macau, Zhuhai, and Zhongshan more closely together. As conceptualized in the Reform Plan for the Pearl River Delta of 2008 to 2020, this consolidation will enhance the competitive advantage and continued economic and urban development of the region. Each center has a role to play, and Macau is designated as a world-class venue for tourism and leisure. This urban integration is being promoted by, among others, the Planning Study on the Co-Ordinated Development of the Greater Pearl River Delta Townships, the Regional Cooperation Plan on a Quality Living Area, and the Study on the Action Plan for the Bay Area of the Pearl River Estuary.[40] This is not unusual within China; similar activities are taking place in prominent coastal zones, like Bohai Bay in the north,

36 Long, conversation.

37 Public Works and Transportation Bureau, *Brief*, 24.

38 Public Works and Transportation Bureau, *Brief*, 19–20.

39 Long, conversation.

40 Public Works and Transportation Bureau, *Brief*, 30.

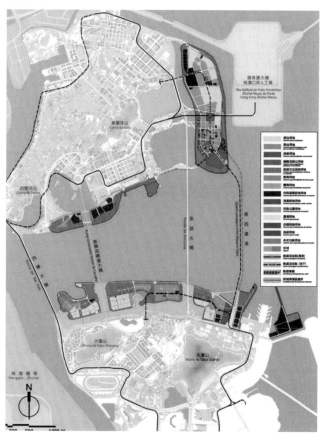

Fig. 7 Land-use map for planned land reclamations, 2011.

Fig. 8 Satellite photograph of Macau and Hengqin, 2010; the star identifies the new location of the University of Macau.

and elsewhere, as in the Changjiang Delta Region in the center.

It is worth noting that improvements in Macau have led to less independence and fewer physical and virtual boundaries. It is almost as if the constant shifting that has occurred in both borders and boundaries of various kinds since the early 16th century is coming to a close with regard not only to actual movement but to real and imaginary boundary divisions. This suspension may have both positive and negative effects on Macau. A leveling of differences in property and other economic values with neighboring areas, for instance, could relieve overcrowding and make available greater lifestyle choice. The social costs associated with daily, weekly, and other cyclical migratory flows may also diminish. Employment opportunities, along with educational and other community service provisions, might be provided more easily off-site in bordering communities. The recent University of Macau expansion on Hengqin Island is a case in point. Access to Macau will be improved simply by virtue of freer flows of movement. On the other hand, it is reasonable to expect that the uniqueness of Macau, and its historically propelled cultural identity, stands to be lost, even though the awareness of such losses has grown more prevalent. One of the main reactions to globalization, after all, has been a stout defense of regional difference, cultural clarity, and localism.

TOWARD GOOD AND APPROPRIATE BORDERS

Given that Macau may become almost borderless in the relatively near future, it is worth considering the borders or boundaries that might remain, at least the physical ones. Three processes are at work in defining these borders. The first is the preservation of Macau's heritage in its UNESCO World Heritage sites. These efforts should extend to adjacent areas to form a fitting context for the sites themselves, though this leads to a host of further deliberations. The second process involves manipulating the current balance of power. Influential actors, like the casinos and other financial and related businesses, may be capable of taking care of themselves, but they require guidance as well as assistance in minimizing negative externalities, like crime and other forms of social disruption. At present, there are two rather distinct zones of gaming and attendant activities, one centered around

Avenida da Amizade on the Macau Peninsula and the other at Cotai. It is worth considering associating these zones with the historic area more closely, given the blurring of margins between an underworld and colonial and other presences in forming Macau's cultural identity. The third process takes into account appropriate space for outdoor recreation and leisure activity. In the context of Macau, these activities could have both urban and wilderness aspects, especially given the relatively deserted and picturesque landscape of Coloane. Although outdoor occupations are not characteristic of Macau's past, except perhaps for erstwhile promenades along Bahia Praia Grande, these activities coincide strongly with Macau's new emphasis on leisure.

The World Heritage district, known as the Historic Center of Macau, covers 25 sites, primarily in a sweep from the A-Ma Temple to the south of the Macau Peninsula to the Casa Garden to the north, as well as the Fortaleza da Guia on Guia Hill to the east (fig. 9). The district incorporates not just the monuments but their immediate vicinities and the routes running between them. In effect, the boundaries of the area may be considered an itinerary for observation and appreciation. A buffer zone outside the district largely conforms to geographical features, like ridge lines and edges, and to entire areas, like Guia Hill. This buffer zone is intended for conservation, regeneration, and street renewal, all in concert and scale with the historic landmarks. The World Heritage District is 0.16 square kilometers, and the buffer zone 1.1 square kilometers, typical for urban heritage sites elsewhere. Appropriate maintenance of this zone will require control over any rebuilding that might take place and government funds for repairs, preservation, and beautification. Ironically, one of the factors that has preserved Macau's historic area is the density of occupation and pattern of small property ownership. Although decreasing population density would improve the quality of life in Macau, any shift to new and improved redevelopment will require relatively strict supervision. In both the historic district and the buffer zone, firm boundaries and monitoring of construction and use will be essential to Macau's future identity. If not, the risk of an overrun and essentially placeless zone will be too high.

Gambling activity has been restricted in Cotai by limiting keys, or access to adjacent hotel and other accommodations. Development in the area and connections to Hengqin will provide relatively convenient

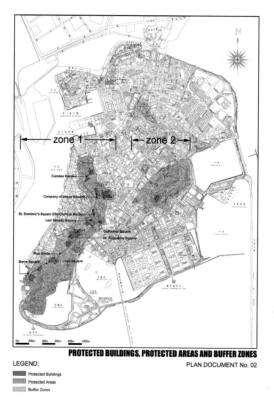

Fig. 9 Historic Center of Macau World Heritage site.

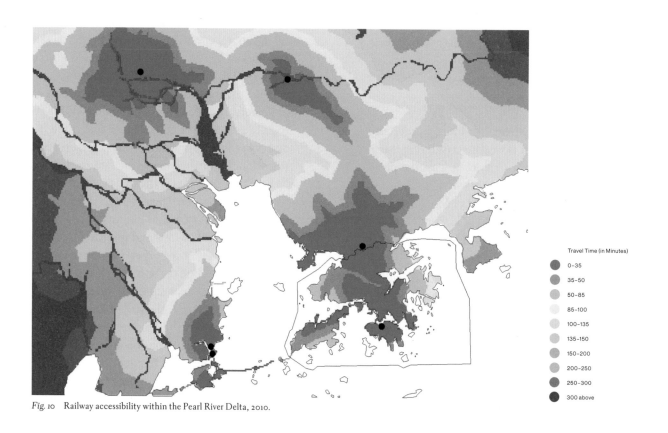

Fig. 10 Railway accessibility within the Pearl River Delta, 2010.

housing for service workers and others. Proximity to the airport and to the new Hong Kong–Macau–Zhuhai sea link will also effectively curb expansion on the Macau Peninsula by providing superior regional accessibility to the Cotai area (fig. 10). Indeed, the combination of local infrastructural incentives and constraints, along with effective limits on building supply, seems likely to guide, cohere, and circumscribe casino and casino-related development in a way that will allow it to thrive but not to take over other areas of Macau. On the peninsula, the Avenida da Amizade strip through the ferry terminal provides similar high-quality access. The planned connections to the new sea link will support these efforts. In short, the opportunities and constraints already in place are likely to support reasonably orderly development of casinos and related activities at and near where they are today and sustain something of the bifold identity of Macau intact.

Protection and maintenance of areas for public open space and recreational activity will surely require both definition of borders and stipulation covering the use of natural boundaries, particularly between sea and land. Topography has consistently played a role in Macau's history, especially with regard to higher ground and defensive positions. The seven or so hills on the peninsula, together with the top of Ilha Verde, should be preserved, along with the peaks of the former Taipa Grande and Taipa Pequena. They have so far resisted development and have been or could be maintained as parkland preserves. To provide diversity in options for recreation, Coloane, particularly south of Estrada do Altimo de Ká-Hó, should be off limits to intensive or non-recreational development, as should be the beaches and fishing villages stretching from Coloane Village in the southwest to the Bahia de Hác Sá to the east. In fact, the entire area could and should be considered an integrated parkland preserve. Village activities would thrive within the relatively protected environment. Another area slated for recreation is the coastal shoreline, particularly the more or less continuous access to the water's edge. The new land additions proposed for Macau appear to anticipate such an eventuality through the provision of strips of green open space. Precedents for public shorelines are ample elsewhere in the world; sharing the shoreline with light rail, if handled well, particularly around station stops and in regard to the transit alignment itself, will help to activate and populate these areas, bringing the city back to the waterfront as in earlier times. Significant portions of the Macau Peninsula are appropriate for this kind of activity, including the proposed new addition to the northern coastline of Taipa.

Running through all three of these processes of border or boundary definition and the separation of particular territories from Macau's broader whole is a relatively consistent connection with the past, as well as a distinct usefulness in the present and future. Each approach preserves and promotes an aspect of Macau that has secured and continues to secure its particular character. Taken together, all three processes have made Macau unique both symbolically and practically. Even if Macau's borders and boundaries have stretched through territorial expansion, they have remained present at least in kind. It is this consistency and long-term continuity, from the 16th all the way to the 20th century, that will continue to help Macau preserve its identity in the world. Aspects of Macau will change and change again, but it is only with these three ways of defining border or boundary conditions that Macau will retain something of its eternal identity.

Analysis: Macau

Structure of the City

Fabiana Alvear, Hao Chen, Yun Fu, Jing Guo,
Navajeet KC, Chen Hao Lin, Josh Schecter,
Ashley Takacs, Gabriel Tomasulo

Fig. 1   Aerial view of the Venetian Macao, Cotai Strip, with Hengqin in the distance.

A former Portuguese colony and a present-day linchpin in China's emerging Pearl River Delta city-region, Macau is defined from within and without as a territory of spatial conflict. Within, Macau has been transformed from a city of parts, with a rich conurbation of historic and modern urban forms, to a city of enclaves, with different parts that exist side by side but never interrelate. Due in part to a century of extensive reclamation of land and liberalization of gambling, Macau has become identified with the rapid development of casinos and of high-rise housing that is segregated from the rest of the city. Undeveloped, vacant, or residual land is a place of tension, negotiating needs for less congested housing, speculative real estate, and casino construction.

Outside the borders of Macau, spatial conflict arises in relation to near neighbors (fig. 1). The city shares physical borders with Zhuhai and with Hengqin Island. While these territories are separate and in some cases contradictory, they are also interdependent. Differences between the areas are exploited as positive and negative attributes alike are exchanged across the borders. In addition,

specific models of development, transposed and transplanted, inflect ongoing cross-border engagement.

The border is malleable, constantly redefined and transformed, in part physically due to the large reclamation projects but also notionally due to Macau's status as a special administrative region (a temporary political entity, in this case set to expire in 2049) and the changing economic and social policies that dictate relations to mainland China. The border constructs, on one side, a fragmented urban scenario (with some areas for local residents and others for temporary occupants); on the other side, the city of enclaves. This model is not a wholesale repudiation of the existing border condition; rather, it suggests that a city can mend itself by exploiting and reshaping its most peripheral element, the border.

ONE COUNTRY, TWO SYSTEMS

The differences between Macau and Zhuhai lie principally in the asymmetric distribution of resources and

Fig. 2 Macau, city of parts: figure-ground.

Gongbei Housing
FAR: 6.97
GFA: 332,657 sq m
Plot Coverage: 49%
Avg. Building Height: 11 stories

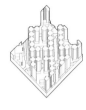

Areia Preta Housing
FAR: 6.01
GFA: 307,255 sq m
Plot Coverage: 38%
Avg. Building Height: 13 stories

Siza Courtyard Housing
FAR: 6.68
GFA: 279,611 sq m
Plot Coverage: 53%
Avg. Building Height: 8 stories

Historic Center
FAR: 3.43
GFA: 175,192 sq m
Plot Coverage: 60%
Avg. Building Height: 5 stories

Peninsula Casino
FAR: 9.84
GFA: 398,043 sq m
Plot Coverage: 46%
Avg. Building Height: 14 stories

Cotai Casino
FAR: 9.50
GFA: 593,847 sq m
Plot Coverage: 83%
Avg. Building Height: 12 stories

Taipa Housing
FAR: 6.12
GFA: 296,793 sq m
Plot Coverage: 39%
Avg. Building Height: 12 stories

Coloane Housing
FAR: 0.66
GFA: 20,252.12 sq m
Plot Coverage: 17.8%
Avg. Building Height: 2 stories

Fig. 3 Parts of Macau.

industries. That is to say, something abundant on one side is often absent on the other. This asymmetry results from at least two characteristics of present-day Macau: its geography and its compliance with China's "One Country, Two Systems" policy, which effects a series of specific social, economic, cultural, and political consequences. This condition invites, almost warrants, exploitation from both sides.

Macau is barely one-fifteenth the size of Zhuhai's metropolitan area. The scarcity of land on the peninsula results in extremely limited space for housing and institutions. The search for and planning of uncongested space have led to multiple forms of land agreements and policy alignments with China. For instance, relocating the University of Macau campus to Hengqin enabled a vast expansion and epitomized a new form of cross-border collaboration.

Macau grew, organically and over centuries, as a city composed of different parts (figs. 2, 3). The parts, differentiated by density and type across the urban landscape, were enriched by a strong sense of identity, historical continuity, and especially by the synergies of their differences. Various areas in Macau demonstrate the range of economic, social, political, and spatial experience in the city and summarize the complex urban landscape of Macau.

The parts may be identified through prevalent, prominent, or significant building types, that is, dominant types. Dominant types in Macau include high-rise, high-density housing (typical of the Zhuhai–Macau Peninsula exchange; figs. 6, 8) and the resort/casino and high-end residential model (characteristic of Cotai and Hengqin Island; fig. 7). The difference between dominant types lies not only in their built form but in their occupants/residents. High-density housing, in both Zhuhai and Macau, is defined by a plinth and towers. While density and aggregation do not necessarily correspond, new developments on both sides of the border display congruencies nevertheless. Resort/casino buildings likewise share similarities across the physical and infrastructural borders of the region. Cotai's casino type, for instance, has been exported (without the gambling component) to Hengqin in the form of leisure/resort developments. These new projects capitalize on their proximity to Macau and on discrepancies in the costs of goods and services in the two different economies.

The expansion, collaboration, and exchange over time between Macau and its neighbors have contributed to a situation in which the lands are defined more by their similarities across borders than by their differences in terms of economy and politics. Cross-border exchanges and forms of development dilute the cultural and spatial identity of Macau's urban landscape and simultaneously reduce the tension and exploitation of differences.

In fact, the exchanges and export of development types have constrained the differences between Macau and Zhuhai to the city of Macau itself. Macau has been transformed into a city of enclaves, clearly evident in Cotai and Hengqin. The available land in these areas is consigned to gambling and leisure pursuits. The projection toward Hengqin could have been an opportunity to diversify the economy of Macau; instead, it supports existing patterns of speculative real estate and fails to improve quality of life for the Macanese. Cotai, the reclaimed land between Taipa and Coloane, was initially planned as a predominantly residential area but was soon transformed into an area of resort urbanism. The revision of the plan for Cotai depicts a trend that dispossesses the city of its citizens as well as of its legibility as a city of parts. While these tendencies may improve the economy of Macau, they result in conflicting urban conditions and untenable housing densities.

Macau's position as an island/peninsula will ensure that its distinctive border condition is maintained. It will remain a key gateway to the Pearl River Delta, and its urban models of resort megablocks will be replicated across Hengqin. The task for future development, then, becomes one of considering the interaction and collaboration between the different parts of the city, connecting the systems of parts into a whole and avoiding support for the fragmentation typical of contemporary forms of development. If development continues on its current tack of "Macanese exclusion," it will end in drawing off the local population and turning Macau into a city of temporary occupants.

Fig. 4   Zhuhai-Hengqin-Macau border zone.

A   Gongbei Border Crossing
Pedestrian/vehicular
Daily Max.: 350,000 (500,000 planned)
Gates: 98 manned, 80 unmanned
Open: 1574, 1870, 2004

B   Guangdong-Macau New Access Project (New North Border Crossing)
Pedestrian
Daily Max.: 200,000
Gates: 40 manned, 30 unmanned
Open: 2014

C   Macau-Zhuhai Cross-Border Industrial Zone
Vehicular
Daily Max.: n/a
Gates: 6
Open: 2004

D   Macau-Zhuhai Ferry
Pedestrian
Annual Max.: 1.4 million
Gates: n/a
Open: n/a

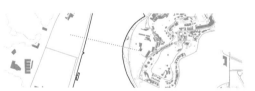

E   Wanzai-Barra Tunnel
Pedestrian
Daily Max.: n/a
Gates: n/a
Open: 2016 (projected)

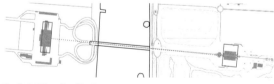

F   Cotai Frontier Post
Pedestrian/vehicular
Daily Max.: 70,000 pedestrians, 10,000 vehicles
Gates: 24 manned, 12 unmanned
Open: 1999

Fig. 5   Border crossings.

Macau's borders are coincident with its coastline. Eight formally distinct zones comprise the Zhuhai-Hengqin-Macau border, each arising from different topographical features and the history of incremental land reclamation throughout the archipelago. Border crossings exist at four points; two more are planned (figs. 4, 5). The vast majority of people cross the border on foot. Despite legislation allowing Macanese-licensed cars to drive in Hengqin, the planned new border crossings will be dedicated solely to pedestrians. Overall, the China side of the border is less concentrated in terms of development, but the densities tend to approach each other near crossings.

Zone One: Gongbei/Canal dos Patos

The border between Macau and Zhuhai is defined by the shallow and marshy Canal dos Patos. The canal meanders northeast from Macau's inner harbor and terminates at the Gongbei isthmus. Two mounds shape the canal's path. The larger of the two, Ilha Verde, a separate island as recently as 1915, is 30 meters high. The second is 7-meter-high Sun Yat-Sen Park, which was reclaimed in the late 1980s. Gongbei border crossing, dating back to 1574 and the original point of crossing between Portuguese Macau and imperial China, occupies this territory. It is still the most used crossing and can accommodate both pedestrians (350,000 per day at peak times) and vehicles. The Guangdong-Macau new north border crossing, which crosses Canal dos Patos, is a planned pedestrian gate 800 meters to the southwest of Gongbei. It is anticipated to process up to 200,000 pedestrians daily.

Zone Two: Inner Harbor

At the west of the peninsula, the Inner Harbor is Macau's historic port. It has taken on a distinctive rectilinear form as a consequence of incremental land reclamations. Abutting the harbor is the Macau-Zhuhai Cross-Border Industrial Zone. The border crossing here consists of six gates dedicated to industrial traffic serving manufacturers on both sides of Canal dos Patos.

Zone Three: Chinatown Piers

This straight portion of coast just south of the Inner Harbor consists of a series of fishing piers numbered 1 to 34. The border is defined by the Wanzaizhen River, consistent in width for much of its length. Macau's Inner Harbor Ferry Terminal, located at Pier 14, processes 1.4 million passengers annually through its border checkpoint. Ferries depart every half hour between 8:15 am and 4:30 pm.

Zone Four: Barra/Sai Van

Known as Barra, "inlet" or "bar," this part of Macau was reclaimed in 1996. The thin strip of land follows a curve that encloses Sai Van Lake. This territory is home to the Macau Tower as well as to a large public plaza. Avenida Panorâmica do Lago Sai Van, a five-lane road that crosses to Taipa by way of Ponte de Sai Van, runs along the waterfront. A planned tunnel originating from the Barra bus terminal, on the Avenida Panorâmica do Lago Sai Van, will allow pedestrians to cross to Wanzai, the area of Zhuhai just north of Hengqin.

Zone Five: The Bridges (Future Cross-Gate City)

Three bridges traverse the 1.7-kilometer channel between the Macau Peninsula and Taipa. This channel was at one time the major corridor between the Inner Harbor and the South China Sea. On the Chinese side of the border, the channel forms the division between Wanzai and Hengqin Island. A high-tech central business district on an island off the northeastern tip of Hengqin is currently planned.

Zone Six: Taipa Island

The borders of Taipa, originally mountainous and jagged, have been smoothed by a series of reclamations and by the construction of a major highway along the west coast. The mountainous interior is further separated from the water by housing towers. A dog track occupies much of the flat land to the south.

Fig. 6 High-density tower housing, north Macau.

Fig. 7 Interior of Wynn Macau.

Fig. 8   High-density housing, north Macau.

Fig. 9   Zhuhai Checkpoint, Gongbei border crossing.

Fig. 10 Regional transportation routes.

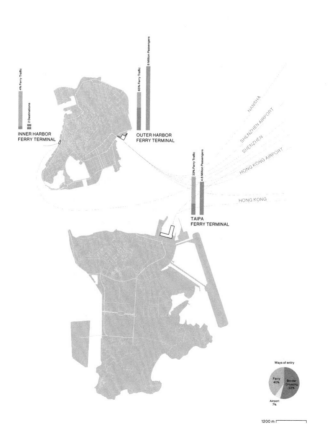

Fig. 11 Ferry connections to Macau.

Zone Seven: Cotai

Reclaimed in the 1990s, this part of Macau is best known for its casinos. The coastline is straight. The northern half of Cotai faces the central part of Hengqin, largely undeveloped, while the southern half faces the new University of Macau campus, which is connected back to the peninsula by a one-kilometer tunnel. This crossing, Cotai Frontier Post, opened in 1999 and is the newest border crossing in Macau. It was designed to handle 70,000 pedestrians and 10,000 vehicles daily, but due to sparse development on both sides of the border, it currently operates at about one-fifth capacity.

Zone Eight: Coloane Island

The most mountainous and sparsely populated part of Macau, Coloane retains much of its natural coastline. Coloane Village is clustered around a shallow bay punctuated by long fishing piers and stilt houses. There are no border crossings between Coloane and mainland China.

INFRASTRUCTURE

Since losing its status as a dominant shipping port in the 19th century, Macau has been a peripheral territory with regard to infrastructure, particularly in comparison to other cities in the region (fig. 10). For example, Hong Kong's airport handles 56 million passengers and 4 million tons of cargo a year, making it one of the busiest airports in the world; in 2012, Macau's airport saw only 6 million passengers and 220,000 tons of cargo.

Other regional transportation infrastructure, such as rail, follows the same pattern. The Zhuhai rail station, newly built, has a capacity of 18 million rides a year; yet intercity rail does not stop, and is not planned to stop, in Macau. The ferry system is well utilized, perhaps because it is one of the only efficient ways to get to Macau, other than walking across the border from Zhuhai or Hengqin. However, the construction of the Hong Kong–Macau–Zhuhai sea link, slated to be completed in 2015, will tie the city directly into the larger Pearl River Delta, completing a loop that circumscribes the growing region. The bridge will shorten the trip between Hong Kong and Macau from 4½ hours to 40 minutes. This is the only major regional connection planned for Macau, aside from current expansions to the ferry terminals, so it will play an important role in connecting the city to the larger economic region.

Far more people enter Macau by land and sea than by air. Macau's two public land border crossings with China account for 54 percent of overall visitor traffic to the city; of these, 92 percent passes through Gongbei (fig. 9). Gongbei is foremost based on historical patterns but also because it is close to the downtown area of Zhuhai. Zhuhai's new rail station, directly adjacent to the site of the new north border crossing, will support this trend, at least until the full development of Hengqin Island, which will increase travel to Cotai.

Forty percent of visitor traffic to Macau passes through the ferry terminals (fig. 11), with the Outer Harbor Ferry Terminal, on the east side of the peninsula across the delta from Hong Kong, handling most passengers. This state of affairs will most likely change when construction is complete on the Taipa Ferry Terminal, to the south. Capable of shuttling 15 million passengers a year, this facility will bypass the peninsula entirely, bringing many visitors straight to the casinos of Cotai. The final 6 percent of visitors to Macau enter through the airport; this traffic will likely remain low.

Getting around the city is very much a work in progress. Macau is heavily congested, especially in the peninsula, due to small streets and extreme density. A public bus system covers most of the peninsula and Cotai with 63 bus lines operated by three different private companies. A secondary bus system exists solely to transport people to the casinos. Every major casino has a fleet of these free buses, which generally skirt the interior of the city, leaving from Gongbei or one of the ferry terminals and depositing visitors directly at the casinos' doorsteps (figs. 12, 13).

The newest and perhaps most consequential development for Macau's infrastructure is a planned light rail system. The first phase, currently under construction, will run from Gongbei to the casino developments in Cotai. When it opens, it will have a capacity of 300,000 rides per day. With the completion of the second phase in 2020, capacity will jump to 532,000. This is roughly comparable to Boston's public transport system, which provides 628,000 rides per day for a population of 636,000. To avoid the challenges of building infrastructure within the city, the rail route is almost entirely on the periphery. In the first phase of development, walking

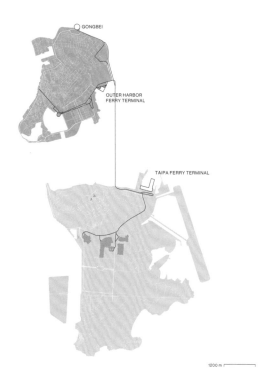

Fig. 12   Casino bus routes.

Fig. 13   Casino bus stop at Gongbei border crossing.

times between the rail system and certain parts of the city will exceed 25 minutes; the second phase, which will create a complete rail loop around the edge of the peninsula, will lower walking times. Like the rail route, all of Macau's major arteries and recent additions skirt the edge of the city. This infrastructure at the periphery carries visitors to the casinos rather than to the city center. It is possible that the center of Macau will move away from its traditional site in the peninsula toward the relentless development of the south.

DOMINANT TYPES

A city is defined as much by its architecture as by its urban form or infrastructure. Understanding a city typologically involves a study of its dominant architecture. Certain types of building may be identified as dominant through repetition; through historic, cultural, or political importance; or through position. Two of the principal dominant types in Macau are the casino, which is not only the primary economic driver of the city but forms the majority of the modern skyline of Macau, and high-rise, high-density housing, which continues to be the main form of housing for the majority of residents in the city.

Casinos

Since the liberalization of gambling, casinos have dominated, literally, conceptually, and politically, the development of the city. Located on reclaimed land, with oversized plots that dwarf the adjacent neighborhoods, the casinos are worlds unto themselves. The evolution of the casino in Macau may be seen in a comparison between the Casino Lisboa, the first casino built to capitalize on legalized gambling, and the Venetian Macao, the largest and most successful of the Cotai casinos.

High-Rise, High-Density Housing

High-rise, high-density housing is concentrated in Gongbei and NAPE. Gongbei predominantly provides public housing for the poor; NAPE supplies market-rate housing for local professionals. High-rise housing is also distributed in Coloane (premium market-rate residential towers as well as public housing) and Hengqin (student

housing for the new university campus). Three categories of high-rise, high-density housing appear in Macau. Before the 1980s, the wall type, the dominant type for public housing, was mostly found in Gongbei. The courtyard type was developed by Álvaro Siza for NAPE; it was intended to have a significantly reduced floor area ratio and a high degree of flexibility in regard to housing and office space. The tower type, imported from Hong Kong, is found all over Macau, with the highest concentration in Gongbei. While the trend in the development of collective housing is for the floor area ratio to increase alongside the area per resident, the pressure of Macau's high population density seems to have reversed this direction.

Casino Lisboa, the first hotel/casino built after the government granted monopoly gambling rights to the Sociedade de Turismo e Diversões de Macau, is one of the most famous hotel/casinos of the city. The original casino and 12-story round hotel tower were built in 1970 by Stanley Ho, Teddy Yip, Yip Hon, and Henry Fok on reclaimed land at the terminus of a primary avenue on the Macau Peninsula. An extension of 270 rooms was added in 1991; the hotel now provides 927 rooms.

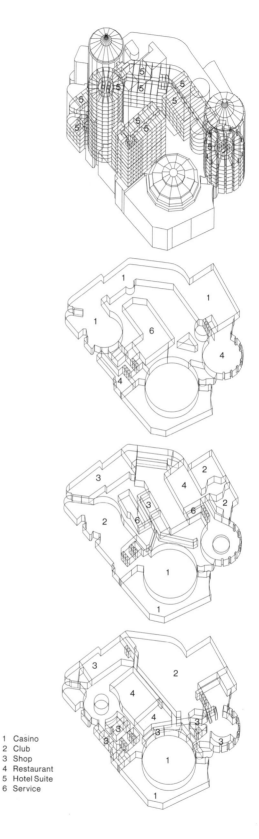

1   Casino
2   Club
3   Shop
4   Restaurant
5   Hotel Suite
6   Service

Fig. 14   Deep structure of Casino Lisboa.

Fig. 15   Programmatic components of Casino Lisboa.

CASINO: VENETIAN MACAO

Completed in 2007, the Venetian Macao is a hotel and casino resort on the Cotai Strip. Owned by Las Vegas Sands, the casino is modeled on the Venetian Las Vegas. Lead architects were Aedas and HKS. The Venetian Macao consists of a 40-story hotel with 3,000 suites (110,000 square meters); a casino with 3,400 slot machines and 800 gambling tables (51,000 square meters); convention space (1.1 million square meters); a 15,000-seat arena; and retail (150,000 square meters). The Venetian Macao is the largest casino in the world and the largest single-structure hotel building in Asia.

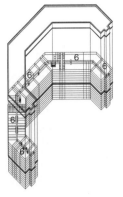

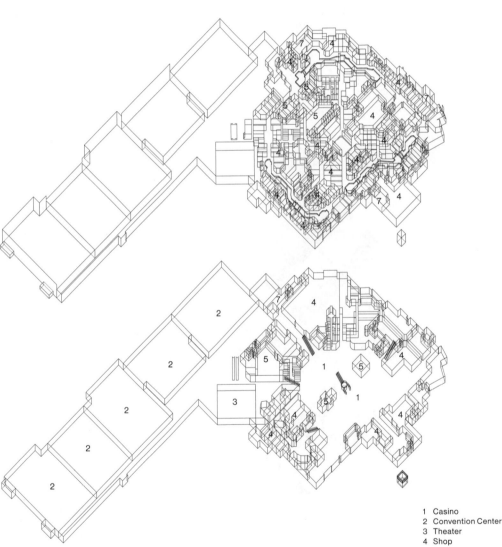

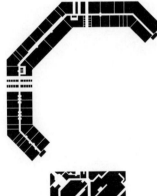

1 Casino
2 Convention Center
3 Theater
4 Shop
5 Restaurant
6 Hotel Suite
7 Service

Fig. 16 Deep structure of Venetian Macao.

Fig. 17 Programmatic components of Venetian Macao.

Housing of the wall type is typically found in Gongbei. Buildings are about 20 stories high. The building footprint occupies the entire site, and the FAR is about 17.5. The typical wall complex houses 2,340 residents; the area per resident is 8.4 square meters. The buildings are composed of identical parts repeated along a linear axis. Towers are generally serviced by elevators and three sets of stairs; there is no circulation between towers. Air wells pierce tower interiors, allowing cross ventilation; common space for the residents is provided on the roof and in throughways at ground level. This public route allows non-residents to penetrate the wall. Apartments are organized along single-loaded corridors that wrap the air wells. Major rooms face the exterior; service rooms look to the interior. Commercial programs occupy the first two levels, with housing above.

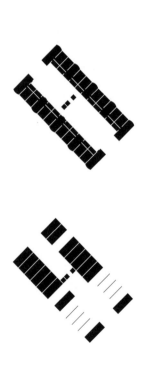

Fig. 18   Deep structure of wall housing.

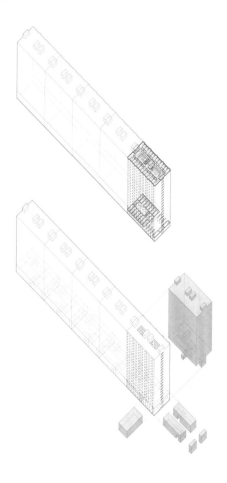

Fig. 19   Circulation and programmatic components of wall housing.

The FAR of Álvaro Siza's courtyard housing is significantly lower than that of the wall type: 6.7, with 1,456 residents per building. Area per resident is more generous: 32.4 square meters. The courtyard type consists of four identical L-shaped parts. Each module is serviced by elevators and two sets of fire stairs; the modules do not share circulation. Apartments are arranged along a single-loaded corridor, with major rooms opening to the outside and service spaces ventilating to the corridors. Various apartment types are provided. The large courtyard delineated by the towers sits on a podium two floors above ground level. Parking and commercial activities occupy the podium; some of the commercial activities, such as kindergartens, cater specifically to residents.

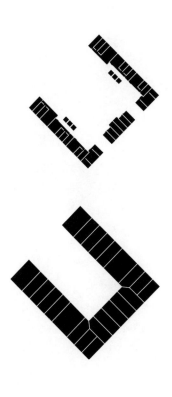

Fig. 20   Deep structure of courtyard housing.

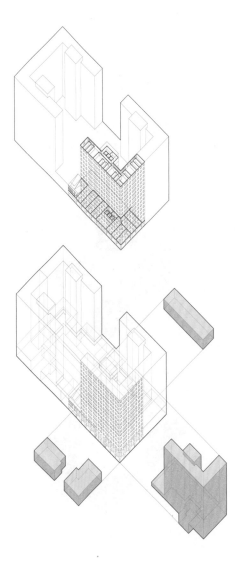

Fig. 21   Circulation and programmatic components of courtyard housing.

The newest type of high-rise, high-density housing in
Macau is the tower type. As manifested in Macau, the
tower is a direct import from Hong Kong. At 14.4, FAR is
higher than that of the courtyard type but lower than that
of the wall type. A tower complex generally houses 2,688
residents; the area per resident is 20.7 square meters.
Tower complexes consist of identical towers sitting on a
podium, which usually defines the perimeter of the development block. Elevators and fire stairs service each tower.
Public space is in the podium; a fire break level at the 13th
floor is sometimes used as common space for residents.
There are typically eight apartments per floor; these radiate out from the core, with all rooms ventilating to the
outside. This disposition produces the highly articulated
facades and deep recesses that have labeled such buildings "butterfly towers." Shops line the street edges of the
podium; parking for residents is provided on the second
and third levels.

Fig. 22 Deep structure of tower housing.

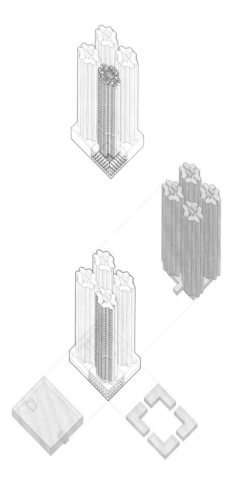

Fig. 23 Circulation and programmatic components of tower housing.

Fig. 24 View from Macau's Inner Harbor toward Wanzai.

Analysis: Macau

Land Reclamation

Fabiana Alvear, Hao Chen, Jing Guo

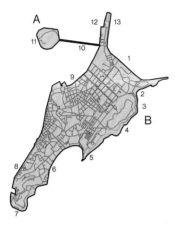

1	Avenida de Venceslau de Morais
2	Ramal dos Mouros/Estrada de D. Maria II
3	Estrada do Reservatorio
4	Avenida do Dr. Rodrigo Rodrigues
5	Avenida de Lisboa
6	Avenida Dr. Stanley Ho
7	Avenida da Republica
8	Rua do Almirante Sergio
9	Avenida Marginal do Lam Mau
10	Avenida do Conselheiro Borja
11	Rua da Ilha Verde
12	Avenida de Artur Tamagnini Barbosa
13	Estrada dos Cavaleiros
14	Avenidas dos Jardins do Oceano
15	Estrada Lou Lim Ieok
16	Avenida Padre Tomas Pereira
17	Avenida Son On
18	Avenida Wai Long
19	Estrada Governador Nobre de Carvalho
20	Rua Correia da Silva
21	Avenida Olimpica
22	Estrada de Seac Pai Van
23	Estrada do Altinho de Ká-Hó
24	Estrada de Nossa Senhora de Ká-Hó
25	Estrada de Hac Sá
26	Rua Tres dos Jardins de Cheoc Van
27	Avenida de Cinco de Outubre

A	Ilha Verde
B	Macau Peninsula
C	Taipa Grande
D	Taipa Pequena
E	Coloane Island

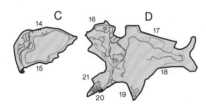

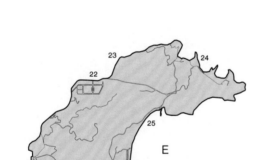

One of Macau's defining characteristics is its ever increasing land area; continual growth in turn generates a constantly redefined coastline. Since the early 20th century, Macau has more than doubled its size by means of land reclamation, and future works will enlarge the city by a further 10 percent. The various areas typically belong to large urban projects, each of which is characterized by a dominant type.

1915–1934

The first major extension of Macau added surface area to Ilha Verde, the Macau Peninsula, Taipa Grande, Taipa Pequena, and Coloane. The dominant types were the patio house (as seen in the Mandarin's House, which dates from the mid-19th century, in the historic center) and the tenement house.

Total Area: 11.6 sq km
Macau Peninsula: 3.4 sq km
Taipa Island: 2.3 sq km
Coloane Island: 5.9 sq km

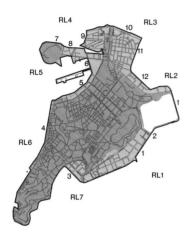

1	Avenida da Amizade
2	Avenida do Dr. Rodrigo Rodrigues
3	Avenida Dr. Mario Soares
4	Rua do Almirante Sergio
5	Rua da Ribeira do Patane
6	Avenida do General Castelo Branco
7	Estrada Nova da Ilha Verde
8	Estrada do Canal dos Patos
9	Avenida do Comendador Ho Yin
10	Avenida Norte do Hipodromo
11	Avenida Leste do Hipodromo
12	Estrada Marginal da Areia Preta
13	Avenida Son On
14	Estrada da Ponta da Cabrita
15	Estrada Governador Nobre de Carvalho
16	Avenida Olimpica
17	Rua de Viseu
18	Avenida dos Jardins do Oceano
19	Estrada de Seac Pai Van
20	Estrada do Altinho de Ká-Hó
21	Estrada de Nossa Senhora de Ká-Hó
22	Estrada de Hac Sá
23	Rua Tres dos Jardins de Cheoc Van
24	Avenida de Cinco de Outubre

RL1	ZAPE (Zona de Aterros do Porto Exterior)
RL2	Areia Preta Reclamation
RL3	Hipodromo Reclamation
RL4	Ilha Verde Reclamation
RL5	Pai Chi Kei Reclamation
RL6	Inner Harbor Reclamation
RL7	Praia Grande Bay Reclamation
RL8	Taipa Grande Reclamation

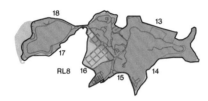

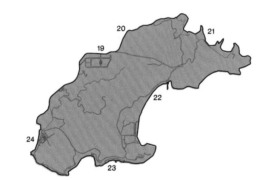

1936–1964

Reclamation projects included the organization of the Porto Interior (Inner Harbor), west of the Macau Peninsula, where the dominant type was the tenement house; the Hipodromo to the east of the connection with the mainland (high-rise tower) and Ilha Verde to the west (high-rise wall); Areia Preta (high-rise tower, tenement house); and ZAPE, or Zona de Aterros do Porto Exterior (Outer Harbor land reclamation; high-rise tower, Casino Lisboa).

Total Area: 13.8 sq km
Macau Peninsula: 5.2 sq km
Taipa Island: 2.6 sq km
Coloane Island: 6.0 sq km

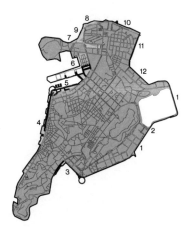

1	Avenida da Amizade
2	Avenida do Dr. Rodrigo Rodrigues
3	Avenida Dr. Mario Soares
4	Rua das Lorchas
5	Avenida Marginal do Lam Mau
6	Rua Norte do Patane
7	Estrada do Canal dos Patos
8	Praca das Portas do Cerco
9	Avenida do Comendador Ho Yin
10	Avenida Norte do Hipodromo
11	Avenida Leste do Hipodromo
12	Estrada Marginal da Areia Preta
13	Estrada de Pac On
14	Avenida Wai Long
15	Estrada Governador Nobre de Carvalho
16	Rua de Coimbra
17	Estrada Governador Albano de Oliveira
18	Avenida dos Jardins do Oceano
19	Estrada de Seac Pai Van
20	Estrada do Altinho de Ká-Hó
21	Estrada de Nossa Senhora de Ká-Hó
22	Estrada de Hac Sá
23	Rua Tres dos Jardins de Cheoc Van
24	Avenida de Cinco de Outubre
RL9	Taipa Reclamation

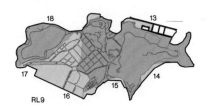

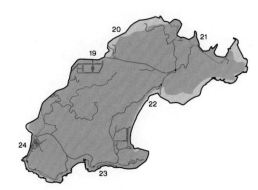

1965–1985

In this period Taipa Grande and Taipa Pequena were joined into a single island.

Total Area: 15.1 sq km
Macau Peninsula: 5.5 sq km
Taipa Island: 3.3 sq km
Coloane Island: 6.3 sq km

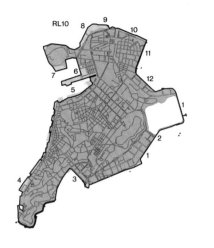

1	Avenida da Amizade
2	Avenida do Dr. Rodrigo Rodrigues
3	Avenida Dr. Mario Soares
4	Rua das Lorchas
5	Avenida Marginal do Lam Mau
6	Rua Norte do Patane
7	Traversa da Ilha Verde
8	Estrada Marginal da Ilha Verde
9	Estrada do Canal dos Patos
10	Avenida Norte do Hipodromo
11	Avenida Leste do Hipodromo
12	Estrada Marginal da Areia Preta
13	Estrada de Pac On
14	Avenida Wai Long
15	Estrada Governador Nobre de Carvalho
16	Rua de Coimbra
17	Estrada Governador Albano de Oliveira
18	Avenida dos Jardins do Oceano
19	Estrada de Seac Pai Van
20	Estrada do Altinho de Ká-Hó
21	Estrada de Nossa Senhora de Ká-Hó
22	Estrada de Hac Sá
23	Rua Tres dos Jardins de Cheoc Van
24	Avenida de Cinco de Outubre

RL10	Ilha Verde Reclamation
RL11	Taipa Industrial Area Reclamation
RL12	Coloane Reclamation

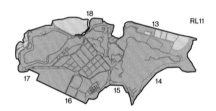

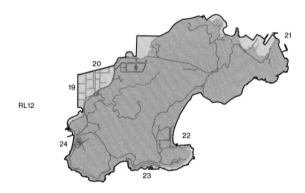

1986–1995

This period saw less than the usual expansion of Macau. Three small reclamation projects added land on the peninsula, Taipa (where the dominant type was the high-rise tower), and Coloane. The reclaimed land at the north of Taipa is used for industrial purposes.

Total Area: 16.6 sq km
Macau Peninsula: 5.8 sq km
Taipa Island: 3.7 sq km
Coloane Island: 7.1 sq km

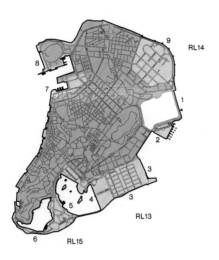

1	Avenida da Amizade
2	Outer Harbor Ferry Terminal
3	Avenida Dr. Sun Yat-Sen
4	Avenida de Sagres
5	Avenida Panorâmica do Lago Nam Van
6	Avenida Panorâmica do Lago Sai Van
7	Avenida Marginal do Lam Mau
8	Avenida do Parque Industrial
9	Avenida do Ponte da Amizade
10	Avenida Nordeste da Taipa
11	Macau International Airport
12	Avenida do Aeroporto
13	Avenida dos Jogos da Asia Oriental
14	Estrada do Istmo
RL13	NAPE (Novos Aterros do Porto Exterior)
RL14	Areia Preta New Reclamation
RL15	PRBPG (Praia Grande Rehabilitation Plan)
RL16	Macau International Airport

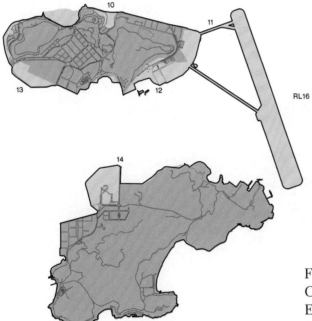

1996–1999

Four large reclamation projects characterize this period. On the peninsula, NAPE, or Novos Aterros do Porto Exterior (new Outer Harbor reclamation area), was initially envisaged as a separate island; due to construction problems, it was appended to the peninsula. NAPE was intended for mixed-use buildings (where the dominant types were the high-rise courtyard type and the new casino/hotel tower type). Land reclamation in Areia Preta extends the land toward the north of the peninsula for residential development. A project in Praia Grande, at the southern tip of the peninsula, was largely dedicated to hotel and tourism development. Finally, Macau International Airport was built with connections to Taipa.

Total Area: 21.3 sq km
Macau Peninsula: 7.7 sq km
Taipa Island: 5.8 sq km
Coloane Island: 7.8 sq km

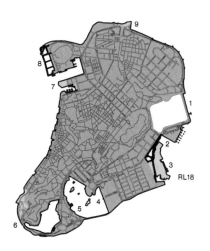

1   Avenida da Amizade
2   Outer Harbor Ferry Terminal
3   Macau Fisherman's Wharf
4   Avenida de Sagres
5   Avenida Panorâmica do Lago Nam Van
6   Avenida Panorâmica do Lago Sai Van
7   Rua do Fai Chi Kei
8   Avenida do Parque Industrial
9   Avenida Norte do Hipodromo/Portas do Cerco
10 Avenida Nordeste da Taipa
11 Macau International Airport
12 Estrada do Istmo/Cotai Strip
13 Avenida Marginal Flor de Lotus
14 Estrada Flor de Lotus (elevated)

RL17   Cotai Reclamation
RL18   Macau Fisherman's Wharf Reclamation

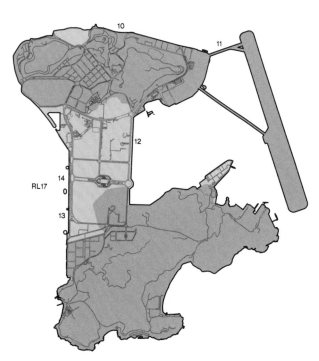

2000–2005

The Cotai reclamation project joined Taipa and Coloane Islands. The 1999 plan for the district envisaged the land for residential and public uses, with only a small area for tourism. The plan was altered in 2002, and Cotai became primarily a district of resorts and casinos (with the resort/casino tower, characterized by plinths of interiorized spaces for shopping and gambling topped by high-rise hotel towers, as the dominant type).

Total Area: 25.4 sq km
Macau Peninsula: 8.5 sq km
Taipa Island: 6.2 sq km
Coloane Island: 7.6 sq km
Cotai: 3.1 sq km

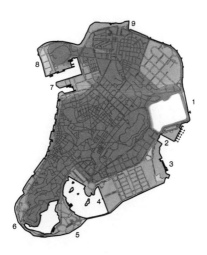

1   Avenida da Amizade
2   Outer Harbor Ferry Terminal
3   Macau Fisherman's Wharf
4   Avenida de Sagres
5   Rua Torre da Macau
6   Avenida Panorâmica do Lago Sai Van
7   Rua do Fai Chi Kei
8   Avenida do Parque Industrial
9   Avenida Norte do Hipodromo/Portas do Cerco
10 Avenida Nordeste da Taipa
11 Macau International Airport
12 Avenida da Nave Desportiva
13 Avenida do Aeroporto
14 Ponte Sai Van

RL19   Cotai Reclamation

2006–2011

This period sees more expansion in Cotai, again assigned to resort/casino development. The Macau Peninsula does not grow during these years.

Total Area: 28.6 sq km
Macau Peninsula: 9.3 sq km
Taipa Island: 6.5 sq km
Coloane Island: 7.6 sq km
Cotai: 5.2 sq km

1 Avenida da Amizade
2 Outer Harbor Ferry Terminal
3 Macau Fisherman's Wharf
4 Macau Science Center
5 Macau Tower
6 Avenida Panorâmica do Lago Sai Van
7 Rua do Fai Chi Kei
8 Avenida do Parque Industrial
9 Avenida Norte do Hipodromo/Portas do Cerco
10 Terminal Maritimo Provisorio da Taipa
11 Macau International Airport
12 Macau International Airport Extension
13 Macau University

RL20 Cotai Reclamation
RL21 Macau International Airport Expansion
RL22 Praia Grande Bay Expansion (Zone B)

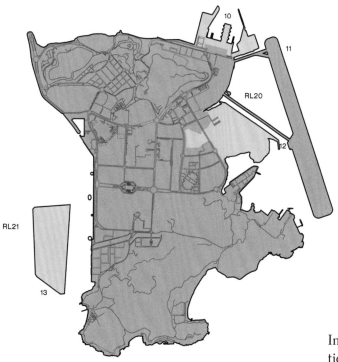

2012–2013

In this period, Macau's territory is expanded via reclamation but also via lease. The University of Macau was relocated to a new campus in Hengqin, 20 times the size of the former institution. The campus itself is the dominant type, and the strategy of leasing on the mainland represents a new method for growth and collaboration between Macau and China. Also at this time, land is reclaimed for future airport development, and work begins on a project at Praia Grande Bay, known as Zone B.

Total Area: 29.9 sq km
Macau Peninsula: 9.3 sq km
Taipa Island: 7.4 sq km
Coloane Island: 7.6 sq km
Cotai: 5.6 sq km

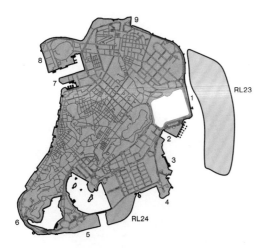

1 Avenida da Amizade
2 Outer Harbor Ferry Terminal
3 Macau Fisherman's Wharf
4 Macau Science Center
5 Macau Tower
6 Avenida Panorâmica do Lago Sai Van
7 Rua do Fai Chi Kei
8 Avenida do Parque Industrial
9 Avenida Norte do Hipodromo/Portas do Cerco
10 Terminal Maritimo Provisorio da Taipa
11 Macau International Airport
12 Macau International Airport Extension
13 University of Macau

RL23 Zone A
RL24 Zone B
RL25 Zone C
RL26 Zone D
RL27 Zone E1
RL28 Zone E2

2014–2040

In the next 20 to 30 years, the expansion of Macau's territory will comprise five large reclamation projects. This series of interventions, which represents the final phase of such land reclamation projects, will increase the surface area by 3.5 square kilometers.

Total Area: 33.4 sq km
Macau Peninsula: 9.3 sq km
Taipa Island: 7.4 sq km
Coloane Island: 7.6 sq km
Cotai: 5.6 sq km
Zone A: 1.38 sq km
Zone B: 0.47 sq km
Zone C: 0.33 sq km
Zone D: 0.59 sq km
Zone E: 0.73 sq km

The Macau Studio: An Introduction

The studio projects that follow are based on a typological approach to the problem of the city. An investigation into and redefinition of the city reveals its persistent architectures, or dominant types. Any attempt to define type is an attempt to define what is typical; what is most typical is common to all. Thus, type is an effective heuristic device through which to locate commonalities. The goal of a search for what is common in architecture is not formal or tectonic similitude but a commonly held idea that invests architecture with a social and political role.

BORDER CITIES, CROSS-BORDER CITIES

The challenges facing the former Portuguese colony of Macau are daunting. Though the gambling industry is responsible for 45 percent of GDP, the casinos offer uneven development. The city must wean itself from an over-dependence on gaming and its associated programs. It is increasingly evident that the future of Macau is tied to its position in the Pearl River Delta, the most populous and economically vibrant city-region in the world. One of the defining characteristics of a city within a city-region is the way in which it defines its identity and competitiveness by exacerbating its difference in relation to other cities. As a border city, and as a special administrative region of China, Macau has continued its largely autonomous focus on developing what is unavailable or forbidden across its borders, specifically its unique cultural heritage and its gambling industry. The tendency for neighboring cities to develop different yet complementary programs at their borders triggers large daily surges of people—for work, education, and leisure—across administrative boundaries.

The recent relocation of the University of Macau to China's Hengqin exemplifies the propensity for cities to compete and cooperate in equal measure and illuminates the ambiguous border condition of Macau. Relocating entire urban quarters or large programmatic elements across its borders, into the expansive mainland, is one way for Macau to overcome its overwhelming land shortage. The relocation and incursion of a fragment of the city into another territory, with a connection via large infrastructural links, transforms the border city into a cross-border city.

This cross-border city is, in essence, an idea and a model of the city that can be transplanted to another territory. When a city is juxtaposed with its other, the identity of each is crystallized, the uniqueness of each exacerbated. It is precisely through its urban history that it can be argued that Macau stands as the paradigmatic cross-border city: it is Lisbon in South China, Hong Kong in Taipa, Las Vegas in Cotai.

The cross-border city offers a strategy, beyond the tropes of preservation and cultural tourism, to sustain Macau's unique heritage. Making manifest the idea of the city of Macau, when it is propagated elsewhere, enmeshes its heritage in the growth of the larger city-region and in the living collective imagination of its citizens.

THE ARCHITECTURE OF BORDERS

The problem of the cross-border city is encapsulated in Macau in one dominant type: the border-crossing checkpoint. The design task for the studio was to conceive a border-crossing facility that acts as a common framework, accommodating housing and work space, plus an additional provision currently lacking in Macau. The projects bring together two ideas: the border city and the cross-border city. In a border city, the act of crossing borders is a daily activity for residents and workers alike. Despite the inconvenience of the border checkpoints, the border demarcates two different administrative regions in China and, in so doing, heightens a sense of political autonomy and cultural identity for the Macanese. As Macau becomes ever more integrated with Zhuhai and Hengqin, the balance between separation and connection, cooperation and competition, uniqueness and commonality requires rethinking. The cross-border city, like the new University of Macau campus, is an idea that offers the opportunity to transport large objects or civic functions across the border, releasing open spaces for the city to breathe.

These ideas of the city and challenges of urbanization correspond to architectural, landscape, and infrastructural responses and problems. The student investigations turned the border from a line into a space, asserting its concreteness through an architecture that reified the border as a cross-border city.

PROJECT SITES

The studio developed six projects for three different sites, each a current or proposed border-crossing facility. These sites represent three different border conditions in Macau: dense hubs, urban hinterlands, and virgin territory. Studio projects are inserted into a congested and chaotic city gateway, a highly contextual if neglected part of the city, and an almost tabula rasa condition respectively.

The first site, Gongbei border crossing, is the principal gateway between Macau and mainland China. It is located on the initial crossing point between Macau and the mainland, the gate into the city, Portas do Cerco, which still stands. Half a million people (almost the total population of the city) can pass through this crossing every day. The border is not a peripheral entity but a fundamental part of the city and a major transport hub. The site for the projects is just south of the border crossing in an area that intermixes public plaza, road infrastructure, sports grounds, government office buildings, and dense residential blocks.

About 800 meters to the west of Gongbei border crossing, in the Ilha Verde district, is the second site, the planned Guangdong-Macau New Access Project (new north border crossing). The facility, open around the clock, will accommodate only pedestrians, up to 200,000 daily. Projects here consider not only the border crossing but nearby sites, as well as the impact on the area as a whole. Ilha Verde, one of the first areas of reclaimed land in Macau, is a hinterland of the island, an enclave of light industry.

The third site, Cotai Frontier Post, links newly reclaimed land in Cotai to newly reclaimed land on Hengqin. True to its name, the checkpoint is located on the frontier of the city's development. Large casinos, resorts, and a golf course are currently under construction on the land adjacent to the border crossing; in Hengqin are planned large resorts and gated communities. The checkpoint can process 70,000 people and 10,000 vehicles per day. The projects for this site, the largest of the three, address both an anti-city yet collective urban condition and a nondescript yet precarious landscape condition.

Christopher C. M. Lee

Collective Border:
The Latent Project of Gongbei

Yun Fu, Chen Hao Lin

Historically, the space of the border is separate from the space of the city. Valued and shunned in equal measure for its proximity to foreign territories, the border is often a place of cultural diversity and economic prosperity, but it is also inherently unsettled and prone to conflicts. The city takes an ambivalent stance toward the border, at once attracted by its flow of people and goods but cautious of its volatility.

Gongbei border crossing, the main point of entry to Macau, sits amid the densest and most closely linked districts of Macau and Zhuhai, yet it is surrounded by a 300-meter empty zone offset from the border. Between the border and the center of Macau is a further buffer area, this one consisting of low-cost, high-density housing. Gongbei can process more than 300,000 people a day, yet the border is strangely absent from the experience of the city. Checkpoints circumvent the city and deliver visitors directly to the casinos.

For a city contemplating both its identity in the contemporary world and its fluctuating sovereignty (in fact, it is set to expire in 2049), the spectacle of the cross-border flow should be celebrated rather than concealed. The space of the border should become a collectively defined civic space, and the city and its identity and cultural heritage should endure in common memory after the border expires. The border is the ideal site to bring investments in facilities for cultural programs into the city. Defined collectively, the border is a latent project that will develop in anticipation of 2049.

Macau is a city of parts, and these parts are becoming increasingly narrow in program. Recent economic development aims to diversify into cultural tourism and creative services. However, due to intense congestion on the peninsula and the dominance of casinos in Cotai, such diversification is proving difficult. This project, with a prospect of 50 years, considers the expiring border at Gongbei as the last piece of open land on the Macau Peninsula and reexamines the relationship between the border and the city.

The project attempts to facilitate the conversion from the space of the border to the civic space of the city as it is transformed into the largest park on the Macau Peninsula.

In the first phase, the space of the border is captured in a rectangular frame of 400 by 500 meters. This abstract figure will consolidate the fragmented components of the border into a clearly defined space. During construction of the frame, Gongbei border crossing will continue to function; at completion, the frame will take over as the border crossing.

The frame is composed of thin six-story residential towers with one apartment per floor. Apartment types accommodate different occupants. Between the buildings are various courtyard spaces. Two-meter gaps between the towers will serve as the new border crossings.

The second phase converts the retired checkpoint buildings into facilities for cultural programs and knowledge production. The Zhuhai checkpoint building, with its centralized organization, becomes a performance center and galleries. The Macau checkpoint building will house in its modular bays a library, laboratories, workshops, and studios. The long building is cut into three parts to allow connection through the site.

Phase three cultivates the landscape of the park. Larger facilities are positioned to take advantage of existing structures and buildings. Basketball courts, tennis courts, amphitheaters, and paved squares reuse the foundations of existing buildings. Jogging paths and landscaped areas sit atop below-grade traffic tunnels, shopping malls, and parking garages.

In 2049, the park will become completely open. Mature and established, it will be protected from speculative development and continue to provide a civic space in the densest part of Macau. The frame and new programs of the border preserve the collective memory, identity, and heritage of the city.

Satellite view. Gongbei border crossing, 2049.

The unsettled space of the border is converted to the civic space of the city.

Site plan. The space of the border is captured in a frame of 400 by 500 meters.

Site model.

Fragment model.

Corner fragment plan. Current border facilities are reimagined as cultural venues.

Urban Respite: Reframing Density

Yatian Li, Mina Nishio

With a high population density and an extreme flow of visitors, Macau may be deemed a cross-border city. Its local and visiting populations are concurrent yet disproportionate. The city's dependence on its gaming and tourism industries has largely shaped its present urban condition and its recent development, or lack thereof. Macau is characterized by continual expansion in tourism and gaming but also by stagnation and neglect in providing for residents and fostering the local context. This conflict is emphasized at the Gongbei border crossing.

The historic center of the Macau Peninsula supports the liveliness and richness of local city life. Yet the area is treated with indifference and severely underserved in urban and public programs and in provisions vital to the local quality of life. With its current extreme density, adding housing only exacerbates the problem; adding cultural facilities and public open space, on the other hand, would contribute to and enrich the local fabric and city life.

If the city is understood as a shared space, with a dominant type and underlying deep structure that are emblematic of an idea of the city and thus common to its inhabitants, the deep structure (and life) of Macau is in its streets. The city, both local and visiting populations, comes together in these active spaces. The streets act as an element that unifies the developed and stagnated sides of Macau. A framework that can organize new programs while still maintaining a precise spatial arrangement, the streets as the deep structure of Macau can be used to mediate between the two aspects of the city.

Situated at the border between Macau and Zhuhai, Gongbei border crossing offers the opportunity to present to visitors a first impression of the city. Yet it fails to do so, acting as a checkpoint and point of immediate dispersal rather than as a threshold or transition. This project both addresses the inadequacy of the current border crossing as a gateway to the city and intervenes in the local neighborhood fabric with relevant and crucially needed cultural programs and public space.

The deep structure of the streets establishes a common framework that extends the urban organization of the adjacent neighborhood onto the site. But the proposal utilizes columns rather than walls (and buildings) to define streets and blocks, allowing for an openness and fluidity of space. The typical relationship between street and block is reversed in response to the need for open space: open spaces are in the blocks, cultural programs are in the streets. Each street is associated with a different program and thereby takes on a distinctive character: east-west streets as "staying" spaces (exhibition gallery, arts and music studios, and so on); north-south streets, lined with small commercial shops, as "passing" spaces. Each block is subdivided into adjacent "rooms" of landscape. The series and gradations of public and outdoor spaces throughout the site are indirectly derived from the internal logic of the urban block. With the urban fabric extended up to the border crossing, visitors arrive directly into the city, into Macau's vibrant street life.

A similar deep structure of streets and rooms is implemented in other locations throughout Macau, serving to highlight moments in the city and also to unify the urban fabric via an identifiable common framework. These urban insertions attempt to instigate change and reactivate the stagnant and untouched core. Not only do they become for visitors points of encounter and recognition within the city, but they provide within the local neighborhoods previously unavailable cultural programs and public spaces. Enriching and reinvigorating the scarce moments of respite in the congestion and density of Macau, the organization of streets and rooms reestablishes the city as a collective space of coexistence.

Satellite view. Macau with urban insertions.

Isometric. The relationship between street and block is inverted.

Site plan. The streets of Macau are extended to the border crossing.

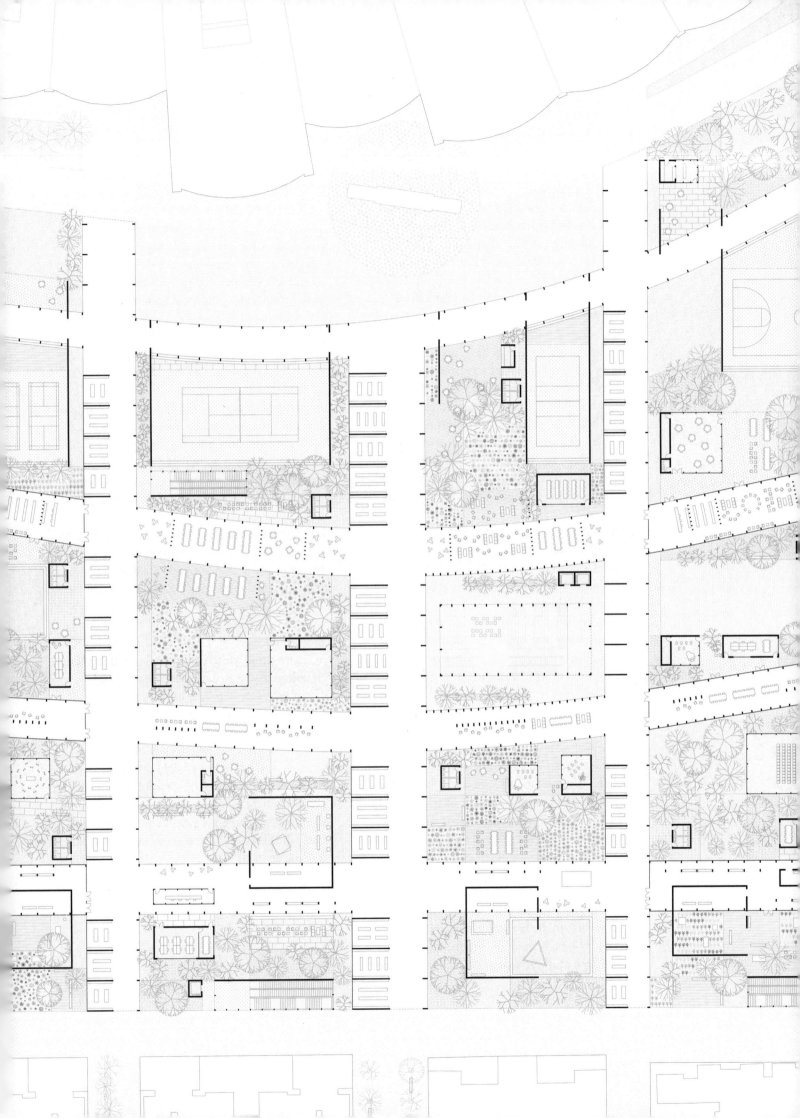

A Few Sharp Lines

Ashley Takacs, Gabriel Tomasulo

Macau has exhausted its ability to reclaim land from the sea, and any remaining open land has been earmarked for casino development. Thus, any further territorial expansion must lie in leasing land from mainland China. The northern border between Macau and Zhuhai is home to densely populated, programmatically and topographically diverse programs and infrastructures. Sun Yat-Sen Park, one of the city's largest green spaces, hugs the southern edge of the border. The park's ability to serve the city is limited, however, severed by a highway from the densest parts of Macau. The border itself is defined by the partially silted-in, polluted, and inaccessible Canal dos Patos. The canal winds through the city, playing a role in the isolation of another of Macau's large green spaces, the hill at Ilha Verde. The southwestern end of the canal cuts through the center of the Macau-Zhuhai Cross-Border Industrial Zone; spanning the canal are one small bridge and a pair of customs facilities. These moments define an axis of relatively isolated islands along a straight line that runs from the southwest to the northeast across Macau and Zhuhai.

Intervening materially in Macau requires both an encompassing urban vision and a localized architectural sensitivity. The axial arrangement of features along the border suggests the layout of a campus. A new university makes a precise incision through the patchwork of northern Macau, unifying disparate zones of program while revealing the richness inherent in their adjacency. A cross-border zone of cooperation, the campus takes the no-man's-land within the border as a productive space of education and cooperation, acts as a new gateway, and defines an urban center at the edge of two cities.

The campus is composed of simple and repeated architectural elements chosen for programmatic flexibility and figural clarity: walls, rooms, and plinths. Two four-story bars—7.5 meters wide, 19 meters apart—run the length of the site. The bars touch the ground lightly, preserving free movement at grade into and through a series of captured public courtyards. Thin structural fins support the bars. The fins are punctured at ground level by a covered pedestrian walkway, creating an enfilade. The fins and floor plates operate as a basic frame, providing incomplete enclosure: the structure will eventually be enclosed by the kind of varied, personalized facade treatment endemic to Macau.

Spanning the bars are programmed roofs that define rooms and plinths that lift off the ground to accommodate topography. The plinths that carry the campus across the water also function as border crossings. The spaces captured between the bars are reprogrammed as a system of interconnected public parks. The rooms created by these roofs, plinths, and parks structure the entire campus as an urban-scale enfilade that distributes public and campus programs across the site: hanger, research/prototyping facility, greenhouses, art museum, theater, and more.

The roof of the bars maintains a position 27 meters above sea level. This consistency gives rise to a constantly changing relationship between building and landscape. These integrate in different ways: the roof of the museum is an occupiable extension of Ilha Verde, and the theater appropriates the slope of the hill as an amphitheater.

This project strives for two seemingly incompatible goals: to structure the city through a common framework and to disappear into the various contexts it passes through. The insistence on the single line allows the inhabitants to experience Macau's interwoven densities, topographies, and histories as a coherent sequence. Serving local and regional ambitions alike, the project generates a new knowledge center at the core of an emerging city-region and germinates desperately needed economic innovation for Macau itself.

Satellite view. A single line cuts across distinct territories.

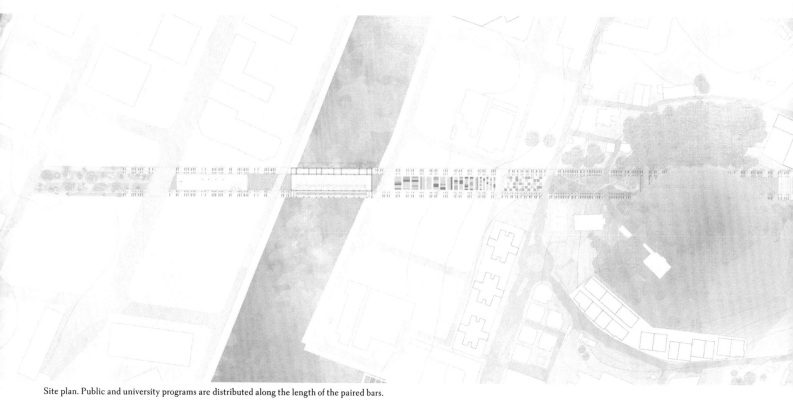

Site plan. Public and university programs are distributed along the length of the paired bars.

Section. The roof of the bars maintains a constant height.

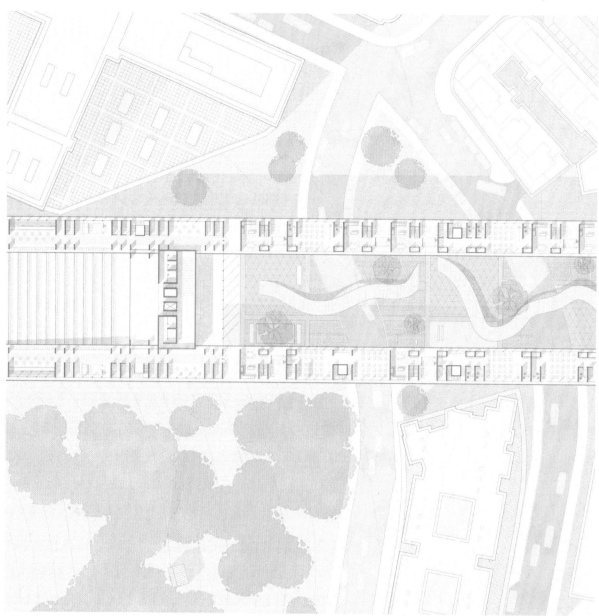

Ground-floor plan detail. The two bars are for classrooms; in between are public services and public parks.

Topography defines use; building and landscape integrate in different ways.

The structure takes on the materiality of its context.

Marked Difference:
Inscribing the City of Parts

Navajeet KC, Josh Schecter

Poised at the intersection of the European city, the Chinese city, and the developmental city, Macau occupies a unique position among the rapidly developing urban centers of the Pearl River Delta. Since its inception, the city has crafted an identity at once independent of and beholden to a set of external ideas. Shifting colonial borders and geographical expansions have resulted in an urban fabric of startling adjacencies. The architectural element of the wall, in various manifestations, has played a fundamental role in maintaining and defining these adjacencies.

Macau now confronts the dissolution of this identity. As the city approaches political integration with China in 2049, it must move beyond a single-industry economy (gaming) or risk being identified solely as a "city of leisure." In this context, the Guangdong-Macau new north border crossing plays a crucial role in defining Macau's future. Drawing inspiration from the history of the wall in Macau, from its ability to create barriers, gates, and rooms, this project strives to become the mechanism that preserves Macau's existence as a city of parts.

In its most basic sense, the wall is a barrier, manifesting the point of encounter between a city and its surroundings. As in many European cities and in Macau itself, walls and other barriers have become inscribed into the fabric of the city, even after the barrier ceases to exist. Following this convention, the project marks the existing limits of Macau, impressing the current border into the fabric of the city, and at the same time originates a new framework for future negotiations with China.

Although a wall affords a city cohesion, it also defines the activity within its limits, generating a "city room." The hills of Macau, originally used as defensive positions at the city's edge, have been encased by centuries of development. Now, however, they provide a respite for the residents. The hills on either side of the new border crossing lack this frame of current development,

providing an opportunity to replicate these vital spaces of the city. The new city rooms will, like the other hills in the city, operate as charged focal points for assembly.

While the border and the city rooms provide an overall form for the wall, individual sections are crafted to respond to their immediate surroundings. Each building is comprised of two bars, one occupied by living and common areas, the other by work space. The L configuration rests on a plinth and frames a central courtyard, a smaller city room nested within the wall.

The ability of a wall to generate development rests on the points of interaction between the two sides. The deep structure allows the buildings to react to their context, accommodating more apartments in some areas (near the parks and the Zhuhai rail station) and more work space in others (at the border crossing). The semi-private city rooms elsewhere in the project are transformed into a series of paths that direct visitors to crossing points. Instead of framing a courtyard, the L "zips" across the border, connecting with its counterpart on the other side, producing a single cross-border complex directly above the existing political boundary.

The project aims to restructure the current and future cross-border condition. Macau is presented with the opportunity to carve out a space of interaction that balances its identity as a city of parts with its role in the Pearl River Delta city-region. By extending this space of interaction into both Zhuhai and Macau, the wall acts as a focal point for development. One day in the future, the wall, engulfed by the fabric of the city and stripped of its role as a border crossing, will remain as an echo of Macau's former identity, another boundary marked and absorbed by the city of parts.

Satellite view. Two walls come together to create the crossing.

Site plan. The wall, a boundary marked and absorbed by the city of parts, echoes Macau's former identity.

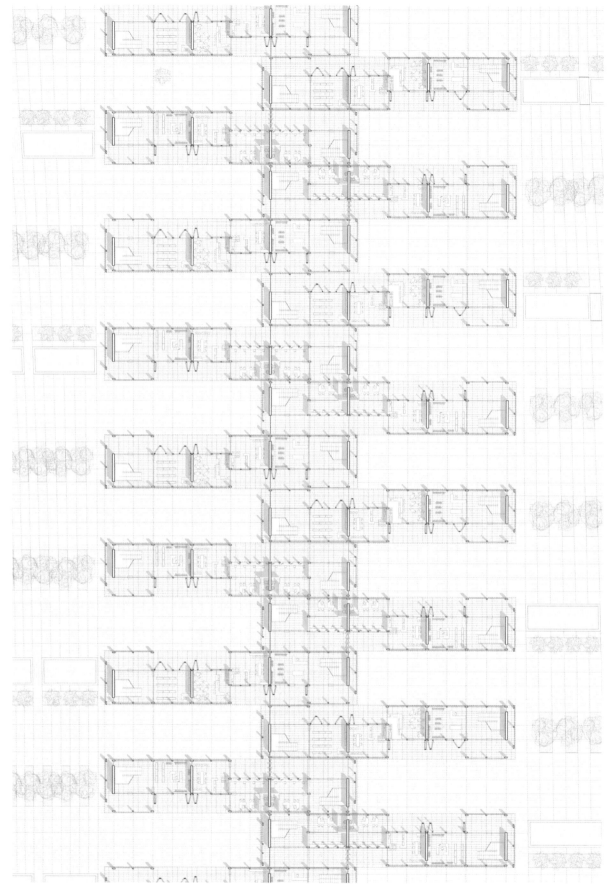

Plan detail at border crossing. The blocks extend across the border, producing a single complex.

The blocks trace the border, creating a center at the former edge.

Spaces of Exception:
Housing as a Common Framework for Cotai

Fabiana Alvear, Hao Chen, Jing Guo

Macau, a territory of spatial urban conflict, has been defined and redefined by layers of landscape and infrastructure. Once a city of parts, with variations in density and type across its urban landscape, Macau is now characterized by a model of development and pattern of occupation, across borders, that have transformed it to a city of enclaves.

Macau belongs to both its permanent residents (more than 500,000) and its temporary occupants (16 million). The population density is exceptionally high; public spaces are confined to a contested landscape. Temporary occupants interact with fragmented, highly capitalized, and interiorized spaces in the city. The conflict between the need to decongest the peninsula and the desire to expand the casinos manifests in vacant land, which becomes a place of tension.

The border and its built manifestation become the space where Macau's populations coexist. While the expansion and collaboration across borders provides a new framework for development and education, any effective development strategy must re-create the city of coexisting parts, disrupting the city of enclaves and providing spaces of exception. This project proposes the Cotai Frontier Post as a catalyst for urban development. A common framework for Cotai—one that shifts the existing border and redefines it as ground—advances a tool to return the island to the city.

The border as a space of coexistence provides grounds for public and private amenities alike. The new infrastructure defines spaces that furnish the freedom casino developers expect for their projects. Spaces of exception are defined by the border and road infrastructure; these infrastructure rings allow the space for coexistence and double as checkpoints that offer entry to Macau and to casino drop-off points. Contrasted with the incoherence in the rings of exception is consistent housing. An organizational logic generated by various dominant types and their corresponding programs dictates the terms of the contrast. By reinterpreting and redefining relationships among dominant types—high-rise, high-density housing and casinos—the proposal returns Cotai to the city of Macau; provides an opportunity for spatial, social, and economic integration; and promotes economic diversification. The deep structure and aggregation model of the housing rely on a differential grid dominated by alternation between solid and void, building and landscape, public and private.

Transferring the border checkpoint to nodes within Cotai requires the public to move through the spaces of exception and encounter the city and its multiple parts in the same space. The space of exception and the undulating structure capture the collective space, define the perimeter of the site, shelter public spaces, and delineate grounds for private and public occupancy. The exceptions exist at multiple layers and multiple scales. The landscape, mediator between housing and gambling, presents exceptions that reverse the void condition of gambling.

The exceptions become cross-border incursions of political and economic implication. These are not artifacts of collective will or large historic monuments; rather, they are agonistic spaces, incompatible with each other but existing as islands of concessions, spaces of negotiated difference. They exacerbate the interiorized condition of casino culture and liberate the ground level for public amenities and green spaces. The strategy reconstructs the notion of Macau as a city of parts, and the spaces of exception provide a framework for collective living by reorganizing the border. This larger framework in turn structures future development in a Macau that sustains a collaboration with its borders and maintains its identity.

Satellite view. New development in Cotai benefits residents, not casinos.

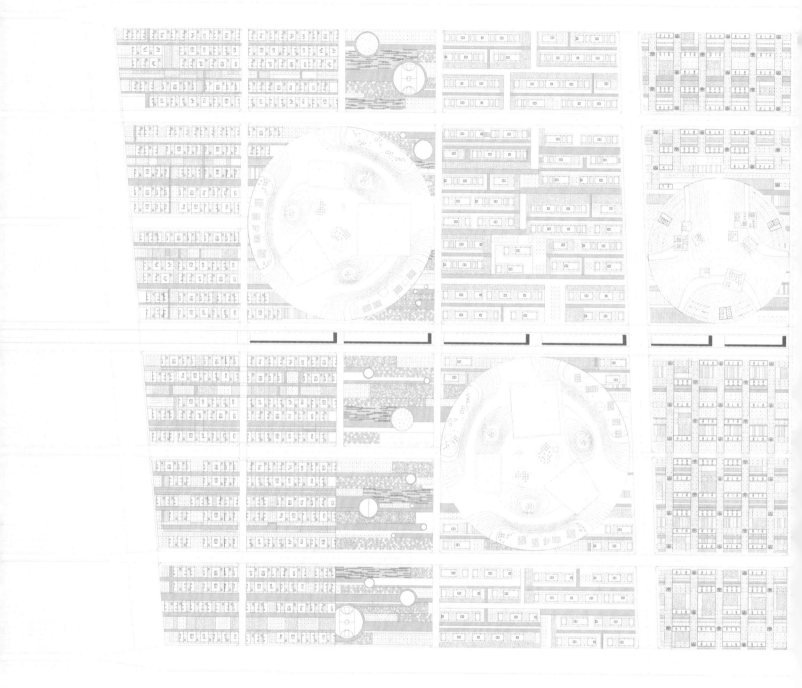

Site plan. Circular spaces of exception are set against residential areas with a finer grain.

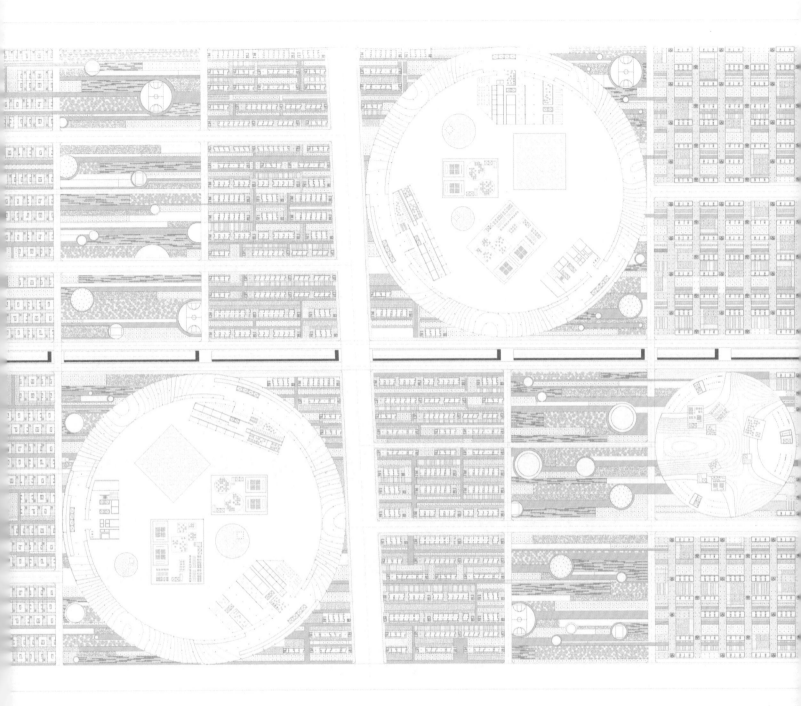

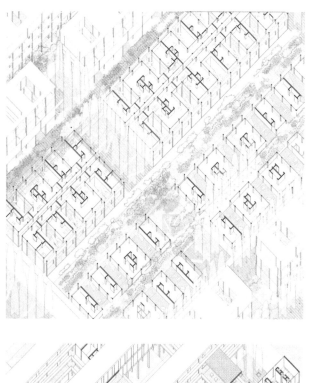

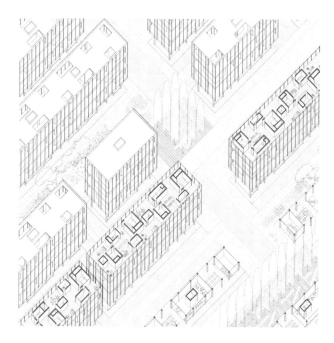

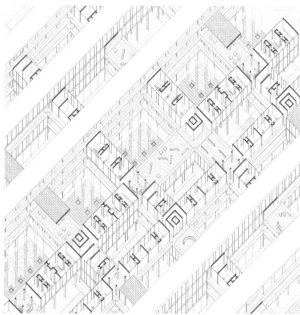

Axonometrics. Courtyard block typology and shop-house typology.

Axonometrics. Tower typology and wall typology.

Site model. Landscape strips give rise to various building types.

The Distributed Border

Rae Pozdro, Sung Joon Chae

Development in Cotai is defined by isolated, dispersed megaplots that lack the cohesion provided by an urban fabric. Cotai's detachment and homogeneity of development create an unsustainable economic and social climate. The location of Cotai Frontier Post, the site for this project, is isolated and lacks diversity, largely because of its position relative to Cotai Strip and the border with Hengqin. In fact, the fractured form of the border facility is partly responsible for the isolation of Cotai. Because entry is allowed at only a single point on the border, traffic is concentrated along the main corridor. Additionally, a lack of small-scale infrastructure discourages any development independent of Cotai's casino industry. As a consequence, the development remains segregated from other urban programs. The overwhelming profitability of and associated public revenue from gambling means that there is little incentive to develop the land for alternative functions.

Cotai Strip also perpetuates the homogeneity of development in this area. Speculative investment has encouraged the government to provide very large plots of land in order to maximize profit. Cotai's low density and wide land tracts reflect this strategy, which leads to monotonous, dehumanizing environments.

In order to liberate itself from the gaming industry's dominance, Cotai needs to be able to access the diverse industries and markets developing across the border in Hengqin. The project facilitates Cotai's economic integration with Hengqin to stimulate non-casino economic growth. Cotai's landscape must be fundamentally restructured to foster alternative modes of building and occupation, promoting growth by bringing more diverse programs to this district.

The landscape is restructured under a framework of strip and wall. Dividing the land into long strips maximizes the surface area shared between different programs, forming a framework that supports great programmatic diversity. At Cotai, long, linear elements constituting the border, which stand apart from their context, would bring about a multitude of different points of interaction.

Six existing roads are extended as bridges from Hengqin to Macau, organizing a set of evenly spaced pedestrian paths across the site. These bridges serve to transport people but also provide institutional space zoned for free trade—an incentive to build in Cotai. The bridges act as walls, breaking up the land underneath into smaller, occupiable lots.

The Cotai Strip is drawn down to the site from its position to the north, continuing the structure of the area. This incursion links the site to its context and also establishes, at the edge of the strips, a boundary for the casinos. The strips themselves are used for housing developments.

New border stations are built where the bridges meet the strips. Distributing the border across the site facilitates crossing at numerous points and encourages spread-out, smaller-scale development. The programs within the strips sustain Macau's existing structure, and the long walls that slide across the strips force different programs to interact. In this way the border extends long fingers into Cotai and Hengqin, thickening into an occupiable zone that is distinct from adjacent frontiers even as it integrates them.

The landscape of Cotai, a set of isolated points that lack any consistent urban fabric, is activated and united by the introduction of an element of difference, the wall. The action of insertion redefines the border crossing between Cotai and Hengqin both by creating free-trade zones of interaction and by helping Cotai achieve greater economic diversity.

Satellite view. Checkpoints in the form of inhabitable bridges are dispersed
along the border to develop a new commercial area in Cotai.

The bridges define smaller-scale plots for development.

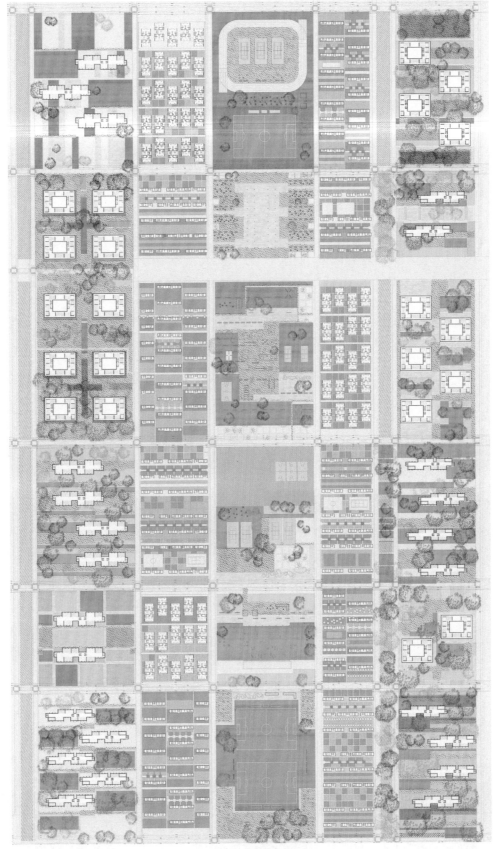

Site plan. Long strips organize a coherent framework of diverse types, generating a new city fabric for Cotai.

The Countryside as a City

The Countryside as a City

Christopher C. M. Lee

Fig. 1 Xiancun, Guangzhou, 2013.

To turn the countryside into a city is an act of foolery, if not outright scandal, especially if the city is one of the dense, overdeveloped, speculated, and polluted coastal cities of China. But I believe the opposite to be true. The city and its qualities of prosperity, civility, and stimulation can be infused with the very essence of the countryside to transform the rural areas of China into unique habitats. In doing so, the entrenched contrast between the countryside and the city—the rural-urban divide, which is responsible for the broadest form of social inequalities in China—can be ameliorated.

Indeed, with the rate of urbanization in China reaching the 51 percent mark in 2011, the next phase of economic and social development will be focused on the urbanization of its rural areas. In 2014, Li Keqiang announced that the state's urbanization target of 70 percent, which will affect 300 million people by 2025, will come not from the expansion of large cities but from the growth of rural towns and small cities.[1] A continuation of the Building a New Socialist Countryside program of 2006, which was developed against a backdrop of rural

unrest and an urgent need to secure food production, this drive toward urbanization attempts to reverse migration from rural areas to the city, uplift living standards in rural areas, and safeguard farmland from further speculative developments. This form of urbanization can currently be divided into three broad categories: the reconstruction into higher-density developments of villages stranded in the city; the demolition of villages to make way for urban developments at the edges of the city; and the wholesale demolition, amalgamation, and rebuilding of villages into new towns (figs. 1–3).

China's rural urbanization should not be mistaken for the suburbanization of the United States or the creation of low-density picturesque garden cities in Britain. Nor is it the transformation of rural areas into dense urbanized cores, a transformation driven primarily by a glut of speculative housing. Beyond upgrading basic infrastructure and sanitation, the challenge in rural urbanization is to imagine a self-sufficient place that can support a dynamic economy, provide cultural and intellectual stimulation, and offer a respite from the inequalities and divisions that

1   "Li Keqiang Urges More Urbanization to Support China's Growth," Bloomberg Business, Nov. 21, 2012, accessed July 23, 2014, http://www.bloomberg.com/news/articles/2012-11-21/li-keqiang-urges-deeper-urbanization-to-support-china-s-growth.

Fig. 2   Zhengzhou Architectural Design Institute, Yang Zhuang New Agricultural Town, Zhongmu County, Henan Province, 2013.

plague the developmental city. In other words, the city in the countryside must be conceived as a space of equal and plural coexistence, one that oscillates between the polarities that have defined the spatial habitation of Chinese civilization: natural and constructed, carefree and restrained, peasant and urban worker, physical and mental. Therefore, the binary between rural and urban cannot be abolished, for they are defined in contraposition to one another.

Often the role of design can seem insignificant in light of the more transformative tool of policy and the more urgent task of basic provision of sanitation, power, and communication. This assessment is especially the case when attempts to redesign rural areas start from the typical impulse to make them more urban. But with less density and infrastructure and a smaller budget, the ensuing design is a knock-down version, a utilitarian affair. In fact, the idea of urbanizing the rural misses the point and is the first mistake of architects and urban designers when they approach this matter. Instead, it is important to eschew the deterministic scientism of urban planning and

design and recognize that the countryside is as much a cultural and political construct as it is a manifestation of policies and autocratic bureaucracy. Doing so conceptualizes an altogether different understanding of a space of coexistence, one that is neither fully urban nor fully rural.

RURAL URBANIZATION AND VILLAGES

Numerous and continual efforts to transform rural China, from 1949 to the present, have revealed the unique social and political landscape of the country. The binary structures of rural and urban have become evident. Also apparent is an emphasis by successive state efforts—with the broadly similar goal of eliminating the big gaps between peasants and urban workers, country and town, manual and mental labor—on coordinating balanced development between the two domains.

The rural-urban divide, generally, is the outcome of an urban-centric, industrialized-economy-geared development model. In China, this type of development began

Fig. 3   City edge, Zhengzhou City, 2014.

with setting up treaty ports in the 19th century. These served to propel coastal cities ahead of rural areas in terms of economics, culture, and politics. Even then, rural residents were moving to the cities to find work and to escape famine and instability; they have faced discrimination ever since. This push and pull has persisted, and by 1983, more than 200 million rural residents had moved to the cities.[2]

To control population movement, especially rural-to-urban migration, the state implemented the household registration, or *hukou*, system, in 1958. It is a two-part "internal passport" for all Chinese nationals determined by place of registration (residence) and type of registration (employment). Employment status is inherited through the mother. Each individual is thus conferred a position in society—a birthright for some, a curse for those born on the wrong side of prosperity. Household registration enacts the binary structure by controlling grain supply, non-staple food and fuel supply, housing, and means of production; access to education, employment, and medical treatment; pension labor protection; military service; and right to marriage and child bearing.[3] In all but the

last, urban residents have the advantage. In sum, migration between rural and urban is controlled not only through the provision of public goods but by the most basic right to exist—a rural resident will not have access to public goods in urban areas and vice versa.[4] Before Deng Xiaoping's market liberalization in the early 1980s, with the exception of forced migration during the Cultural Revolution (1966–1976)—when city residents, especially urban youths, were sent to work in rural areas and frontier regions following Mao's exhortation to learn the true nature of revolutionary society from the peasants, a movement propped up by the slogan "Up to the Mountains and Down to the Villages"—all internal migration in China was highly controlled.

With the *hukou* system exacerbating the divide between the rural and the urban, the physical space of rural areas and villages in China was distinguished, in comparison with its Western counterparts, for instance, by collectivization. After the Communist Revolution of 1949, rural land was owned collectively by peasants and urban land by the state. An aerial survey of the

2   Weiping Wu and Piper Gaubatz, *The Chinese City* (New York: Routledge, 2013), 93.

3   Zhou Daming, "On Rural Urbanization in China," *Chinese Sociology and Anthropology* 28, no. 2 (1995): 10.

4   The registration of a rural resident can be changed only through employment by an urban employer as a skilled rural resident, admission to university, marriage to an urban resident, or when his or her land is acquired for development and subsumed into an urban area.

Fig. 4 Aerial view of agricultural fields and villages, outskirts of Zhengzhou City, 2014.

Fig. 5 Aerial view of agricultural fields, Iowa, United States, 2014.

Fig. 6 Chen Yanning, *Mao Zhuxi Shicha Guangdong Nongcun (Chairman Mao Inspects a Village in Guangdong)* propaganda poster, 1972.

Fig. 7 Dazhai Village, Shanxi Province, 1970.

countryside reveals compact villages, each housing several hundred people and spaced one kilometer or so apart, scattered over agricultural fields (fig. 4). The villages are geometrically regular and, with their axial symmetry and intersecting grids of north-south-oriented paths and roads, echo the spatial structures of Chinese urban places.[5] In the American Midwest, by contrast, solitary farmsteads and clumps of trees, spaced at roughly the same distance, neatly punctuate a gridded expanse of privately owned agricultural land (fig. 5).

During the period between 1945 and 1987, spanning the rule of Mao Zedong and Deng Xiaoping, the countryside underwent tremendous change and upheaval. The era began with a revolutionary zeal for total collectivization, which led to a great famine, and ended with a controlled and limited form of commoditization of farming. As outlined succinctly by Ronald G. Knapp, the countryside experienced five phases of change in these 42 years.[6] The first 10 years, 1939 to 1949, were a recovery from the ravages of the Japanese occupation. The land reform of 1950 introduced categorized classes in rural areas: landlords and rich, middle-income, and poor peasants. Land, housing, and equipment were confiscated from landlords and redistributed to poor peasants. Landlords' surplus houses were converted to public use. The early phase of redistribution, with the elimination of land rents, saw improved rural life for the peasants, who could retain their agricultural output, adding 100–150 kilograms of grain per capita.[7] Construction was limited in this period, with efforts concentrated on upgrading basic infrastructure and dwellings and ensuring a shelter for every villager. The work included the proper maintenance of manure pits, cleaning of polluted ditches and ponds, elimination of pests, improvement of water quality, and construction of public toilets. By 1956, the state declared the movement to upgrade villages a success, although the morphology of rural areas remained largely unchanged.

In February 1958, the National People's Congress announced the Great Leap Forward, marking the beginning of commune building in rural China. The campaign was masterminded by Mao to propel China to an industrialized economy, with the goal of overtaking Britain in steel production within a mere 15 years. By 1961, this grassroots industrialization had brought about "deaths estimated at up to 46 million from coercions, forced labour and, finally, the worst manmade famine ever seen on earth... The plan was that China would 'walk on two legs' with capital-intense heavy industry in the cities and state-run rural communities combining agriculture and small scale industrial production."[8] The Great Leap Forward marked a crucial transformation of the countryside. It led not only to the building of communes but to the collectivization of production and, inadvertently, to the collectivization of consumption and the total abolition of private life (fig. 6).

By the end of 1958, a total of 25,000 communes had been established, each averaging 5,000 households;[9] the corresponding three-tier organization—commune, production brigade, and team—changed the social structure and fabric of the countryside. More than 750,000 backyard furnaces were set up to smelt iron and steel from "pots and pans, bicycles and door knobs, scrap metal, scissors, jewels and children's pendants—the melting down of cooking utensils served the subsidiary purpose of forcing the owners to eat in the commune canteens."[10] One hundred million people labored at furnaces and associated enterprises. The scale of Mao's industrialization moved labor from the fields to industry, decreasing the working hours devoted to agricultural production; coupled with unsuitable methods of farming, this situation led to reduced agricultural outputs and thus the great famine. Moreover, the iron produced was unusable; it was quietly shipped to secret depots.

Certain communes were created by consolidating dispersed hamlets and villages into single sites to increase the efficiency of agricultural production. Communal facilities included mass canteens, small schools, clinics, meeting halls, and recreation grounds. Housing was reduced to dormitories, linear blocks containing dwelling units of two rooms per family; kitchens and toilets were shared. Families were supposed to live in separate quarters, even husbands and wives. Many of the new communal buildings involved alterations to and destruction of "temples, lineage halls, and other structures that expressed aspects of traditional sociocultural reality then in disrepute."[11] Often referred to as the Dazhai model,[12] the communes created from the amalgamation of villages were urban in character, a product of their gridded and compact layout, functional zoning, and use of brick and concrete (fig. 7).

5 Ronald G. Knapp, ed., *Chinese Landscapes: The Village as Place* (Honolulu: University of Hawaii Press, 1992), 48.

6 Knapp, *Chinese Landscapes*, 47–72.

7 Knapp, *Chinese Landscapes*, 48.

8 Jonathan Fenby, *The Penguin History of Modern China: The Fall and Rise of a Great Power, 1850–2009* (London: Penguin Books, 2008), 396.

9 Fenby, *Penguin History of Modern China*, 399.

10 Fenby, *Penguin History of Modern China*, 400.

11 Knapp, *Chinese Landscapes*, 54.

12 Held up by Mao Zedong as the Socialist model for development, Dazhai consists of 82 households farming 80 hectares of rocky and hilly land in the semi-arid area in Taihang Mountains in Shanxi Province. It gained its reputation from the way in which the villagers overcame natural disasters by rebuilding their homes in caves and on carved-out terraces on the hilly site. See Christopher L. Salter, "Dazhai Village, Shanxi: A Model Landscape," in Knapp, *Chinese Landscapes*, 193–210.

After Mao died in 1976, his disastrous economic policies were discontinued. A period of economic reform was ushered in under Deng Xiaoping. The third plenary session of the 11th Central Committee of the CCP in December 1978 was a watershed moment. Policies were enacted to purge leftist elements and correct past mistakes. The main economic set piece was the household responsibility system, a limited and controlled form of commodification of the agriculture economy; it allowed surplus produce to be sold on the open market. The responsibility system diversified the economy and eased the reliance on agriculture. To alleviate rising unemployment in rural areas, development was directed to the cities, creating jobs that triggered a migration from rural to urban. Net income per capita rose quickly, prompting a housing boom. In the countryside, this surge, whether realized in new buildings or extensions, involved nearly one in three households. Although the process of concentrating dispersed hamlets continued—the "learning from Dazhai" model—many rural residents moved to multistory developments or expanded their homes for the next generation. Accompanying the construction of housing in the villages was an increasing commercialization, with the gradual insertion of workshops, small retail shops, and restaurants, as well as the emergence of peddlers, making for weekly mobile markets. By 1983, communes were abolished, transformed into the Township and Village Enterprises.

From 1991 to 2013, with a market economy taking hold, the rapid urbanization of cities further accelerated rural-to-urban migration. From 1979 to 2009, China's urban population grew by 440 million to 622 million; 340 of the 440 million increase can be attributed to migration.[13] This relocation inevitably set off a series of imbalances and inequalities. Migrant workers from rural areas, having no access to public goods in cities due to the *hukou* system, left their children in the villages with their grandparents. Villages began to lag economically. During market reform, income per capita for urban residents was two and a half times higher than that of rural residents;[14] today it is three times higher. When the communes collapsed, so did their provision of public goods, including health care. Today rural residents pay more out of pocket for health care than urban residents.

THE NEW SOCIALIST COUNTRYSIDE AND NEW AGRICULTURAL TOWNS

Two successive administrations launched policies to address the widening urban-rural divide. In 2002, Jiang Zemin called for coordinated urban-rural development; he saw the urban and the rural as a complete interdependent entity, not as two poles in a parasitic relationship. More notably, the New Socialist Countryside, an approach announced in the third plenary session of the 17th Central Committee of the CCP in April 2006, focused on rebalancing regional development between urban and rural, social and economic, human needs and nature, domestic and foreign. It abolished the agricultural tax, a tax that China had been collecting for 2,600 years. The most significant aspect of this movement as announced by Wen Jiabao was:

> We will implement a policy of getting industry to support agriculture and cities to support the countryside, strengthen support for agriculture, rural areas and farmers, continue making reforms in rural systems and innovations in rural institutions to bring about a rapid and significant change in the overall appearance of the countryside. This is a major fundamental step to be taken in the overall modernization drive.
>
> Building a new socialist countryside should focus on developing a modern agricultural operation and improving comprehensive agricultural capacity. In order to build a new socialist countryside, we must accelerate development of rural infrastructure. We need to resolutely work to reorient investment by shifting the government's priority in infrastructure investment to the countryside. This constitutes a major change.[15]

This announcement ushered in a new phase of development for villages and rural areas, a phase aimed at safeguarding agricultural land, making agricultural production more efficient, and returning to a market-friendly version of the Dazhai model in which villages were once again demolished and combined into new agricultural towns.

The strategic purpose of these new towns follows from the ambitions set out in the New Socialist Countryside. First, they safeguard agricultural land and make it more efficient by combining fragmented farming

13 Kam Wing Chan, "China, Internal Migration," in Immanuel Ness, ed., *The Encyclopedia of Global Human Migration* (London: Blackwell, 2013).

14 Barry J. Naughton, *The Chinese Economy: Transitions and Growth* (Cambridge, MA: MIT Press, 2007).

15 Wen Jiabao, "New Socialist Countryside: What Does It Mean?" *Beijing Review*, Apr. 6, 2006, updated Oct. 10, 2008, accessed Aug. 29, 2014, http://www.bjreview.com.cn/special/third_plenum_17thcpc/txt/2008-10/10/content_156190.htm.

Fig. 8 Zhengzhou Architectural Design Institute, Tushan New
Agricultural Town, Zhongmu County, 2013.

Fig. 9 Zhengzhou Architectural Design Institute, rendering of dwelling units, Tushan New Agricultural Town, 2013.

Fig. 10   Zhengzhou Architectural Design Institute, rendering of
landscape design between dwelling units, Tushan New Agricultural
Town, 2013.

Fig. 11   Zhengzhou Architectural Design Institute, rendering of shopping street, Tushan New Agricultural Town, 2013.

areas, entailing the demolition of villages deemed to be inefficiently located or laid out. Second, they aim to improve the living conditions in the villages by building new structures, doing away with the cumbersome process of inserting and upgrading existing villages with basic sanitation and energy, amenities, and housing stock. Third, they increase the GDP of the villages by making agriculture more efficient and mechanized and by promoting the introduction of small commercial streets with workshops, retail, restaurants, and small markets. Finally, with the increased GDP and the improved conditions, they make the villages viable again, stemming the flow of rural migrants to the cities.

Several examples of such new agricultural towns are found in Zhongmu County, Henan Province, approximately 20 kilometers southeast of Zhengzhou. Henan is the agricultural heartland of China, and Zhengzhou is the largest city in the province. Logistics and light manufacturing are fast becoming important economic generators in the region, due in part to Zhengzhou's location at the crossroads between north-south and east-west transportation routes. Tushan New Agricultural Town, now almost complete, was created from the demolition of four existing villages, Tushan, Nianluo, Tangjia, and Leijia, and will contain more than 5,500 residents (fig. 8).

The layout of Tushan New Agricultural Town is distinctly urban, with an efficient grid. Semidetached houses are laid out along east-west streets, with main living rooms facing south; the north-south grid is the main vehicular network. All amenities—market, school, entertainment halls, and so on—are located in a landscape strip in the central spine of the town. Individual housing units are landed on equally sized plots. The local government grants housing units to each household in exchange for half of the household's agricultural land. The local design institute has envisioned the new agricultural town as a wealthy suburban enclave. The courtyard, the quintessential component of the village house, has been replaced by a garage for luxury cars; the expanse of agricultural land that formed the pastoral landscape of the village has been substituted by a manicured artificial and ornamental landscape of rocks and water (figs. 9–11). Such a vision is obviously far removed from the way of life of the villagers; more insidiously, demolishing and reconstructing the edifices of a village by means of the same logic that has fueled the speculative urbanization of the developmental

city obliterates the essence and beauty of the Chinese countryside (figs. 12–15).

Evidence of the way in which these spaces will be used is found not too far away, in another newly constructed and occupied new agricultural town, Madu Shequ (fig. 16). Located just northeast of Zhengzhou, Madu Shequ has the same layout, housing types, and amenities. Residents in the town lament the dwellings' insular layout and the abandonment of a generations-long connection—not just a physical one—with the agricultural fields. In fact, villagers continue to grow vegetables and fruit trees in leftover common spaces to regain the association with the land. Access roads that were designed to guarantee a smooth ride for luxury cars have been turned into drying areas for corn and other produce. These streets thus become an extension of the town squares, common spaces for the villagers to sort and dry their harvests. Close by stands the newly designed communal hall, empty, its glass doors shattered (figs. 17–21). The residents of Madu Shequ, grandparents and elderly parents, do not farm for economic necessity, since the town relies largely on remittances from adult children working in the cities. Rather, they tend the land for cultural and social reasons, born from millenniums of tradition and philosophy that see existence as a unified oneness between humans and nature.

NATURE, LANDSCAPE, VILLAGE

As recently as 1992, 80 percent of China's 1.13 billion people still lived in rural communities in the countryside. These ranged from small towns to isolated clusters of farmsteads.[16] The morphology and character of these villages varied greatly due to their economic function, which was tied inextricably to geography. Uses extended from traditional grain-based farming to herding, fishing, and forestry.

In principle, there are two main categories of villages in China, nucleated and dispersed, though dispersed villages are less common and usually the result of adaptation to topography. Nucleated villages are dense and lack open spaces. Dwellings butt against each other; all residences, and all rooms in residences, face south. This compact configuration allows for efficient sharing of amenities and communal buildings and results from the logical decision to free as much land as possible for agriculture. The

16   Jin Qiming and Li Wei, "China's Rural Settlement Patterns," in Knapp, *Chinese Landscapes*, 13, 19.

Fig. 12 Villagers playing mahjong in current Tushan Village, 2013.

Fig. 13 Weekly market in current Tushan Village, 2013.

Fig. 14 Agricultural fields surrounding current Tushan Village, 2013.

Fig. 15 Tushan New Agricultural Town under construction, 2014.

outlines of these villages approximate linear bars or rectangles to maximize the southern exposure.

Despite a century of calamities and great hopes, from war, revolution, and famine to an economic transformation that has caused steep social inequalities, the village has for more than two millenniums held a special place in the philosophical and cultural tradition of the Chinese. The village and its relationship to nature, vis-à-vis landscape, encapsulates the very essence of the Chinese worldview of the universe and existence itself. This belief—oneness, described in the concept of heaven and earth (*tiandi*)—is prevalent in the moral philosophy of Confucianism, the cosmology of Daoism, and the natural philosophy of yin and yang.

As a moral philosophy, oneness supports the view that natural phenomena and constructed institutions are a single, mutually related entity. If a good ruler, a representative of humankind, governs well, then natural phenomena such as weather, wind, and rain support his or her leadership. To a poor ruler, nature responds with calamities.[17] This understanding extends to conduct in or out of society, as evidenced in the saying "One is a

Confucian in one's home and in the city—formal, dutiful, and restrained—but a Daoist in the countryside—carefree, primitive, and romantic."[18] Yin-yang philosophy sees nature as a cosmos in perpetual transformation, oscillating between the opposing but complementary poles of yin and yang. Humanity and nature are inseparable in this cosmos, and it is the task of human beings to find the way or path (*dao*) and to align themselves and their actions with the direction of transformation between yin and yang (feminine/masculine, dark side of mountain/light side of mountain).

This Chinese worldview differs fundamentally from European philosophical traditions, where "we set up an ideal form (*eidos*), which we take to be a goal (*telos*), and we then act in such a way as to make it become fact."[19] Plato expresses this ideal as an abstract concept that resides in the realm of forms, beyond the physical grasp of humankind; the lived world is merely a pale reflection of a reality that can be accessed only by abstract philosophical thought. In Chinese thought, humanity and nature are interconnected; there is no "abstract space" separate from reality. Humans do not just occupy empty space but,

17 Li Xiaodong and Yeo Kang Shua, *Chinese Conception of Space* (Beijing: China Architecture Building Press, 1991), 19.

18 Fan Wei, "Village *Fengshui* Principles," in Knapp, *Chinese Landscapes*, 38.

19 François Jullien, *A Treatise on Efficacy: Between Western and Chinese Thinking*, trans. Janet Lloyd (Honolulu: University of Hawaii Press, 2004), 1.

Fig. 16   Madu Shequ, Zhengzhou, 2014.

through altering and residing in landscapes, manifest "certain properties which influence, even control, the fortunes of those who intrude upon the site."[20] The landscape is not inert and thus is moldable by humanity's will to achieve certain ideals. For the Chinese, nature is a realm of reality that exerts tangible consequences. Human beings are in the center, and the site of their dwellings is the place that gathers the simple oneness of existence.

All these thoughts are intrinsic to the formation of villages. From the dawn of civilization, peasants have based their existence on agriculture, therefore giving great and careful consideration to the physical landscape.[21] This deference to nature is guided by feng shui, the esoteric theories and principles of geomancy. Based on ancient philosophies and human experiences, feng shui offers an analytical and descriptive survey of sites to ensure appropriate human occupation. This practice has been documented as early as the Zhou dynasty (c. 1046–256 BC) in *Shijing* (*Book of Songs*) and *Shujing* (*Book of Documents*).

"Feng shui" means wind and water, the yin and yang that guide the flow of qi, or nature's life force. Sites are favorable for habitation when yin and yang are in equilibrium. In a description of landscape, yin expresses the female aspect—shade, south bank of river, north side of mountain—and is associated with burial. Yang expresses the male aspect—bright and active, north bank of river, south side of mountain—and is associated with human habitation. According to the principles of feng shui, auspicious sites are located at the confluences of rivers with mountains to the north. (Mountains on the north block invaders; those on the east, west, and south block the sun.) Most advantageous are long sites with mountain ridges that follow the silhouette of a dragon's back.

The mystical theories and poetics that bind human settlement and humankind's place in nature notwithstanding, the practical aspects of feng shui are eminently sensible. Villages sited according to feng shui are on a slightly higher plane, do not occupy farmland, have limited risk of floods and typhoons, and are in close proximity to waterways. This balanced way of siting and altering the landscape has contributed to the beauty of the placement in nature of constructed artifacts throughout the realm of Chinese culture, including farmhouses, manors, villages,

20   Ronald G. Knapp, *China's Traditional Rural Architecture: A Cultural Geography of the Common House* (Honolulu: University of Hawaii Press, 1986), 108–9.

21   Fan, "Village *Fengshui*," 37.

Fig. 17 Semidetached houses in front of high-rise residential blocks, Madu Shequ, 2014.

Fig. 18 Crops drying in the street, Madu Shequ, 2014.

and cities.[22] According to the poet Tao Yuanming (356–427), the Chinese aspired to a secluded village that fostered a peaceful lifestyle. A common motif in ancient Chinese landscape paintings is an idyllic village and farmstead nestled in a vast expanse of mountains and water. Small figures of a scholar and a disciple find solace and tranquility in nature, where humans and nature achieve oneness.

POLARISM: A COUNTRYSIDE CITY

Since the cultural value and the social history of the countryside endure in the collective imagination of villagers, it is irresponsible to transform these rural settlements into cheap versions of wealthy suburbs that are severed from the essence of the reciprocal relationship between nature and humans, landscape and dwelling. However, to reject the subjugation of the countryside to the logic of the developmental city and speculative urbanization is not a plea to re-create the sublime landscapes and tranquil villages of ancient Chinese landscape paintings. Economic and developmental realities must be addressed in the state's effort to alleviate the rural-urban divide, and it is possible to do so with nuanced and varied strategies.

A seemingly scientific and efficient planning strategy to regularize the villages—compacting them to increase the available land for farming—appears on the surface to be flawlessly logical.[23] But coupled with the agricultural land swap for new homes, this approach has disconnected the villagers from their role as farmers, a situation with both economic and cultural implications. First, the new homes they have received in return for their agricultural land are inferior investments. Houses in villages, considered as real estate, are unproductive and unlikely to rise in value significantly, especially compared to residential properties in cities. Second, villagers have lost the cultural connection to working the land and the social solidarity that comes from collective farming.

The alternative to this tactic is to compact these villages less and to incorporate the half of the farmland that the villagers still own into the layout of the new town. This method achieves the goal of increasing agricultural land for efficient and mechanized farming and sustains the existing livelihoods and occupations of the villagers. The strategy also promotes two types of farming: on the released and regularized farmland immediately outside the new town, land-intensive crops, like grains, can be planted and tended mechanically, increasing the overall

---

22 Fan, "Village *Fengshui*," 37.

23 This situation is not unique to Henan; see also David Bray, "Urban Planning Goes Rural: Conceptualising the 'New Village,'" *China Perspectives*, no. 3 (2013): 53–62.

yield. Higher-value cash crops can be planted on smaller pieces of redistributed farmland within the new towns, an approach that integrates smaller-scale organic vegetable gardens and fruit orchards into the villagers' new dwellings. Small processing plants on the periphery of larger new towns can transform the larger-scale produce into more valuable products, wheat into noodles, for instance. Likewise, villagers can establish weekend farmers' markets, attracting city dwellers, to increase the worth of their produce. Retaining the livelihood of the villagers with a less compact village strategy would increase the GDP of rural areas in a less concentrated manner (see pages 253–55).

When the development methodologies for these villages are considered as something more than the inevitable technocratic outcome of a "scientific" or "rational" planning endeavor, it is possible to rethink, recuperate, and recast the philosophical and cultural traditions of living and experiencing the countryside. The fundamental question is how to urbanize the rural without losing the countryside. There are three habitual tendencies that should be avoided. The first is the habit of urban designers to turn the core of any development, even in the countryside, into a dense urban center. The second is the reduction of design to the mere provision of basic sanitation and infrastructure. The third is the practice of treating every surviving brick as a piece of the Elgin Marbles. To retain the essence of the countryside, to capture its expansive beauty, and to sustain villagers' engagement with the land through work, leisure, and repose, it is necessary to acknowledge that the distinct separation, conceptual as well as literal, between rural and urban, nature and human-made, and landscape and architecture should be whittled away. In other words, dualism should be replaced with polarism in binary thinking.

The difference between dualism and polarism, alternate conceptions of the relationships of binaries, epitomizes the difference between Western and Chinese thinking. Binary thinking in Western or, to be more precise, Greek and European philosophy is underpinned by a worldview characterized by ex nihilo creation, in which "a fundamentally indeterminate and unconditioned power determines the meaning and order of the world."[24] This way of thinking leads to binary pairings of nature/culture and universal/particular. Thus, the ordering or alteration of nature rests firmly on a rational application, by humankind, of universal principles. This extends to Western architecture and landscape design, where rational and mathematically precise principles are imposed onto any site. Architecture imitates nature not in appearance but in principles deduced by the mind, qualities of symmetry and self-similarity, for instance.[25]

Chinese philosophical tradition rests on the foundations of the bipolarity of yin and yang. These two terms can be explained only in reference to the other, unlike those in dualistic oppositions. Each term in a bipolar relationship requires the other: yin has no meaning without yang. In Western binaries, dualistic terms are autonomous: nature can be understood independently from culture. This Chinese polarism is not dialectical, that is, it does not follow the Hegelian progression from contradiction to synthesis to sublation. In Chinese tradition, yin and yang are not dualistic extremes of dark and light, female and male; rather, they are points along a movement or flow. In this manner, each of the terms of a polarism is involved in the other, and at any given moment anything—reality, even the universe—is a shade, gradient, or intensity of its other.[26] An understanding of polarism allows a response to the problem of urbanizing the countryside that eliminates rural and urban, natural and built, farmland and structure, landscape and architecture. The relationship between terms is one of degrees and intensities, of mutuality, not one of opposites. It is important to note that this theory does not lead to a single indisputable design solution. Instead, polarism informs in various ways how a more thoughtful and relevant alternative to the current treatment of the countryside may be conceived: the countryside city.

Considered as a space of mutuality, this entity is in constant oscillation between binary opposites. It is composed as a total environment, one made up of the countryside and the city, the rural and the urban, landscape and architecture, field and farmstead. The irreducible element of the countryside city is the dominant type of the village, the three-sided courtyard house. This courtyard house and its urban counterpart, the *siheyuan*, retain the essence of the traditional Chinese courtyard house. They are made up of several independent pavilions bound together by a wall, and space within is experienced in an alternating sequence of closed and open, light and dark, indoor and outdoor—an outstanding example of a bipolar type. The main living pavilion faces directly south, overlooking the courtyard. The principal difference between city and country courtyard houses is

24   See Stanislaus Fung, "Mutuality and the Cultures of Landscape Architecture," in *Recovering Landscape: Essays in Contemporary Landscape Architecture*, ed. James Corner (New York: Princeton Architectural Press, 1999).

25   See Plato's theory of art and its latter incarnation in Antoine Quatremère de Quincy, "Imitation," in *The True, the Fictive, and the Real: The Historical Dictionary of Architecture of Quatremère De Quincy*, ed. Younés Samir (London: Papadakis Publisher, 2000).

26   This mutuality also refers to the concept of propensity as described by François Jullien in *The Propensity of Things: Toward a History of Efficacy in China*, trans. Janet Lloyd (New York: Zone Books, 1999), 25–71, and in *Treatise on Efficacy*, 1–31.

the absence, in the countryside, of the south, or front, pavilion (see pages 264–65). Without this structure, farming tools and carts can pass easily through the front gate and into storage pavilions to the west or east.

There are three principal versions of the countryside city—the frame, the mat, and the punctuated field—along with their various combinations. All three versions are spaces of plural coexistence, like any city; the delineation marks the land indelibly, declaring its very existence. Defining a new agricultural town with a clear figure owes not only to the tradition of city making in China since ancient times but also arises naturally from the plow lines of tended farmland. Yet this delineated artifact should not be a wall or an unbroken, impenetrable structure, as it is in Chinese imperial cities.

The frame as a definable figure is articulated by thickened borders formed by the accumulation of self-similar elements. In Carly Augustine and Nicolas Lee's "Within the Frame" (pages 274–79), the figure occurs at several scales. A large outer frame circumscribes the reconstituted village. A smaller inner frame contains the fields for communal farming and a forest. This central area is deliberately empty of buildings to contain and capture the beauty of the expansive field. The space between the two frames is divided into an alternating sequence of agricultural fields and dwellings. Some of the agricultural fields are shared; others are an amalgamation of private garden strips. The dwellings comprise alternating pavilions with small courtyards, breaking down the courtyard house to an even finer grain and drawing nature closer to individual rooms. The organizing element of the frame is repeated and varied, with forms large and small, open and closed, composed of pavilions and courtyards, striated by intimate gardens and expansive agricultural fields. The experience of moving through these spaces is an experience imbued with the bipolarity of the countryside and the city.

The second type, the mat, uses closely spaced dwellings as the typical component of the agricultural town. Feng Shen and Zhenhuan Xu's "Common Fields" (pages 280–85) clearly defines the limits of the agricultural town, using not a frame but a clear edge. The typical dwelling unit is a transformation of the three-sided courtyard house. The outer walls have been removed, and the house is configured to allow the courtyard to extend as a garden for small-scale farming. Gardens separate the dwelling units, a departure from overly compacted new agricultural towns. The mat is less compact than the frame because it disperses open spaces evenly and because the rooms of the two-story dwellings are convertible throughout the seasons, supporting both dwelling and harvesting. Buildings for shared amenities follow the same typological grain and rhythm of open spaces; they are differentiated only by height. The mat also subjugates roads: as they enter the new agricultural town, they dissolve into the landscape, encouraging traffic to slow as demarcations between street, pavement, and landscape become less pronounced. The same is true of the forest. As woodland permeates the mat, dwellings are thinned so that they gradually give way to the wilderness. Movement through the town, from room to courtyard, house to garden, garden to forest, town to farmland, from one polar opposite to another, is subtly evident—a silent transformation of the propensity of things.

The punctuated field is perhaps the most radical of the three types, though only when it is compared to the current model for new agricultural towns. Bicen Yue and Siwei Gou's "The City as a Field" (pages 304–9) completely negates the strategy of consolidation and compaction, instead exacerbating the expanse of the countryside and recognizing the sublime beauty of the distant horizon. The punctuated field is organized in nested bands of varying scales. At the smallest scale, dwellings consist of alternating rooms placed within a band, which extends to a private garden, which extends farther to collectivized bands of farmland. This structure allows each villager to control the amount of land allocated to private and collectivized farming. At a larger scale, east-west groups of dwellings form another band, this one demarcating an alternation between architecture and landscape. Multiplication of this east-west band creates the field. Amenities are conceived as small pavilions within the field; they are spaced at a deliberate distance from the dwellings so that the act of moving from one to another requires effort and hence awareness of the essence and the extent of the countryside. The intimate pavilions, which look out to the vast field, to the faint horizon, intensify the experience.

These propositions are not simply spatial illustrations of theory, nor should they be. Implicit in this conception is the betterment of the rural living environment by means of accentuating the beauty of the expansive agricultural field and the closeness to the distilled typical architecture of the villages. If the urbanization of the

Fig. 19 Vegetable plot in untiled area of road, Madu Shequ, 2014.

Fig. 20 Harvest drying outside new communal hall, Madu Shequ, 2014.

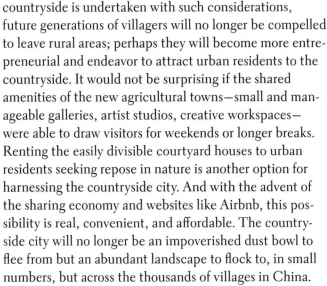

Fig. 21 New communal hall abandoned and strewn with rubbish, Madu Shequ, 2014.

countryside is undertaken with such considerations, future generations of villagers will no longer be compelled to leave rural areas; perhaps they will become more entrepreneurial and endeavor to attract urban residents to the countryside. It would not be surprising if the shared amenities of the new agricultural towns—small and manageable galleries, artist studios, creative workspaces—were able to draw visitors for weekends or longer breaks. Renting the easily divisible courtyard houses to urban residents seeking repose in nature is another option for harnessing the countryside city. And with the advent of the sharing economy and websites like Airbnb, this possibility is real, convenient, and affordable. The countryside city will no longer be an impoverished dust bowl to flee from but an abundant landscape to flock to, in small numbers, but across the thousands of villages in China.

Is this countryside city plausible? Indeed it is, more so now than it was just a few years ago, when the dominance of the developmental city and the hegemony of speculative urbanization were unquestioned. As China's growth has slowed, empty real estate and overpopulated and polluted cities have been left behind. The mantra of "build it and they'll come" or "design it and they'll buy" is bankrupt. A consensus for balanced developments, equitable cities, and in this instance, rural areas is emerging. Rethinking the urbanization of rural China through the lens of its own cultural and social history, culminating in the countryside city, is one small step in that direction.

Designing China's Rural Transformation

Dingliang Yang

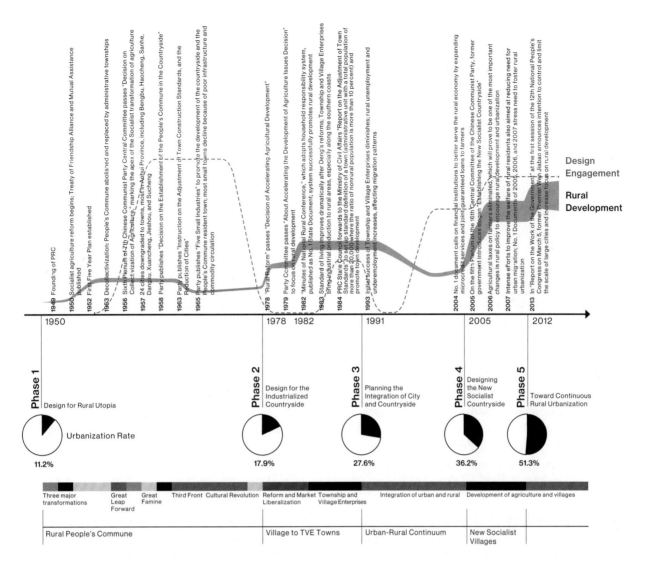

Fig. 1 Five phases of design engagement and rural development.

Since 1949, five different phases of architecture and urban planning have brought about an evolution and identity shift within the Chinese countryside. The context and design strategies underlying this rural development, which are manifested in planning and design proposals, give specific meaning to the Chinese rural transformation. A knowledge of the political and historical background of the period is necessary to comprehend the importance of the design and intellectual forces that contributed to this rural configuration and development, notably the historical and political context of rural regions; planning decisions regarding rural development; urban and architectural design strategies; and the significance of design engagement in the period (fig. 1). Different phases were characterized by different degrees of involvement by the design professions, some remaining at the planning level and others going deeper to room layout and the decorations of buildings; overall, however, the design for rural China is largely utilitarian, monotonous, and without cultural nuance. There are two reasons for this outcome. First, most of the design solutions provided for the countryside were out of context, that is, they were developed by city-based designers who superimposed urban-centered design concepts on the rural context. Second, the various design disciplines were segregated, that is, urban planners, urban designers, and architects restricted their work to distinct and independent disciplinary spheres. To counteract these substandard designs, an altogether unique design activity is required—"commune design," that is, a holistic approach to design in rural China that combines the different design disciplines and, more important, is based on rural cultures.

1949–1978: DESIGN FOR RURAL UTOPIAS

After the establishment of the People's Republic of China, the central government, led by Mao Zedong, began in December 1951 to publish a series of land reform policies, known as the agricultural cooperative movement, for the Socialist transformation of rural areas and agriculture. After five years of reform, rural China was gradually converted from an economy of individual farmers to a collective Socialist economy. The agricultural production cooperative[1] became the major unit of the villages, comprising 96.3 percent of the rural population.

Because of the nationalistic notion in the late 1960s that genuine "Chineseness" existed in the countryside, Mao declared that certain privileged urban young people would be sent to mountainous areas or farming villages to learn from the farmers and countryside. The propagandistic "Up to the Mountains and Down to the Villages" movement resulted in hundreds of thousands of young people being sent to work in rural villages, later in different rural people's communes. This policy eventually created a period of anti-urbanization in China. Though this period is now known as a catastrophic failure, it unintentionally gave rise to an era of Chinese rural modernity.

In July 1958, toward the beginning of a time of over-romanticized rural construction, *Red Flag* magazine, the official publication of the central government, published an essay, "Brand-New Society and Brand-New People,"[2] that introduced the idea of agricultural collectivization, which would transform and combine existing agricultural production cooperatives into a new type of organizational unit that integrated agriculture, trade, and education in rural areas: the rural people's commune. Each commune combined smaller farm collectives and consisted of 4,000–5,000 households; larger communes could consist of up to 20,000 households. The people's commune was made official state policy in 1958 after Mao visited an unofficial commune, Ant Island People's Commune in Henan Province, and said, "The establishment of people's

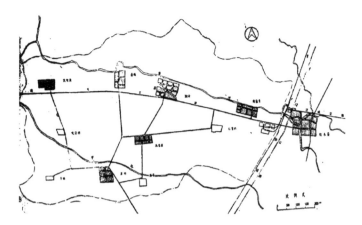

Fig. 2   Siting considerations for rural people's commune.

communes . . . is the fundamental policy to guide the peasants to accelerate socialist construction, complete the building of socialism ahead of time and carry out the gradual transition to communism."[3] From then on, planning and designing rural people's communes, and creating architectural prototypes suitable for this political and economic unit, which incorporated 90.4 percent of rural households, became the major "honorable task" for Chinese architects and urban planners. The central government ordered urban-based planners and architects to go "down to the villages" to work with local peasants to plan and build the communes' central clusters.

People's communes called for combining utopian and modern elements in a rural context, improving production forces with practical means, eliminating distinctions between the urban and the rural, and promoting collective living. The planning and design of a people's commune was based on a comprehensive cross-scale system. Similar to today's design process for master plans for new communities, the planning of a people's commune always started with the siting: within relatively close range of a city, to take advantage of the railway, but in a place with several existing villages or townships with populations normally between 21,000 and 61,000 and a large amount of arable land with agricultural resources (fig. 2).

1   Kang Jian, *Brilliant Failure: Lessons from the People's Commune* (Beijing: China Society Press, 1998), 12.

2   John Gittings, *The Changing Face of China: From Mao to Market* (New York: Oxford University Press, 2005), 27.

3   Henry J. Lethbridge, *The Peasant and the Communes* (Hong Kong: Dragonfly Books, 1963), 72.

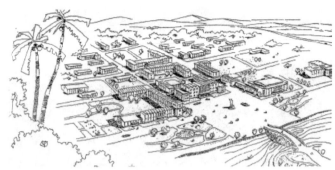

Fig. 4 South China University of Technology Design Institute, perspective, Suiping People's Commune, 1958.

Fig. 3 South China University of Technology Design Institute, site plan, Suiping People's Commune, 1958.

The difference from design programs today was the notion of utopia, which was inherent in planning and designing a commune. This organizational unit attempted to address multiple social and economic issues, including two political ones—raising the political consciousness of peasants and increasing agricultural production—by experimenting with modernist planning and architectural strategies based on unrealistic mathematical calculations. In addition, the designers firmly believed that "traditional rural settlements should be revolutionized through a fundamental reorganization of physical settlements."[4]

The first step of the design was the rationalization of the agricultural fields. The fields were planned based on projected, not existing, natural conditions and agricultural requirements. The size was also calculated according to estimated numbers of residents and households. Thus, although the calculation process seemed to be precise, the specifications were speculative and subjective rather than objective. After the size and position of the agricultural fields were determined, the remaining land was selectively transformed into different clusters. The resulting allocation consisted of a new orthogonal formation with clear spatial hierarchies. The central cluster consisted of economic, civic, cultural, medical, and educational facilities; satellite residential clusters included

parks and other social facilities and were also closely linked to the fields. The two main components of each cluster, the neighborhood unit and the microdistrict, were also major design concepts.[5] These components were particularly emphasized in the making of new residential clusters, each of which was planned to accommodate 4,500 to 10,000 people within a 2.5-kilometer circle. The clusters were to reorder "scattered, small villages ... into concentrated, large residential clusters. In place of diverse vernacular dwellings, modernist structures were arranged in a rigidly stipulated order."[6] The modern characteristics most relevant to the design of people's communes were order and efficiency, not form. Within the neighborhood unit, freestanding buildings were ordered in rows on an orthogonal grid. Floor plans of individual living quarters abolished restrooms and kitchens; the collectivization of rural life meant that families would share common baths (on the same floor) and dining facilities (in a community center).

The plan for the people's commune in Suiping County, Henan Province, is representative of the numerous proposals generated in the late 1950s and early 1960s. A new gridded master plan was superimposed on an area of more than 100,000 hectares, which encompassed about 60,000 peasants and 19 villages. The commune

4   Lu Duanfang, "Third World Modernism: Utopia, Modernity, and the People's Commune in China," *Journal of Architectural Education* 60, no. 3 (Feb. 2007): 40.

5   Lu Duanfang, "Travelling Urban Form: The Neighbourhood Unit in China," *Planning Perspectives* 21, no. 4 (Oct. 2006): 374.

6   Pei Xuan and Shen Lanqian, "The Problems in Planning the People's Commune," *Jianzhu xuebao* [Architectural journal], Sept. 1958, 10.

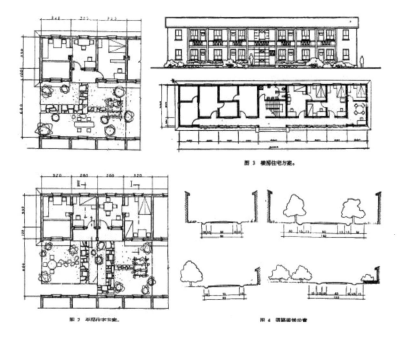

Fig. 5   South China University of Technology Design Institute, plans, elevation, and sections, residential buildings, Suiping People's Commune, 1958.

was organized into one central cluster and six satellite residential clusters. The central cluster, which replaced the existing town, provided major civic and economic activities; the residential ones each contained a park, community center, and production space and were located near a planned highway (figs. 3, 4). As was typical in the design of communes, the plan was "particularly revealing of the planners' 'quasi-religious faith in a visual sign or representation of order' . . . [T]he ground was dominated by the grand, symmetrical main building group, the central cluster; a spacious square was laid in front of the main building to strengthen its central status."[7] None of the existing rural villages were represented in the plan, although the footprints and spatial organization of their vernacular buildings and the allocation of production facilities were replicated. Efficient in economy and function, the new buildings in the central cluster were four to five floors high with no decoration. The residential buildings were two floors high; living units of about 15 square meters were arranged, four to a floor, along single-loaded corridors. All units had the same spatial hierarchy: one bedroom and one living room, no kitchen or restroom. Ground-floor units opened to outdoor common spaces, some of them neighborhood parks and some of

them specialized small production areas, such as orchards, associated with the wider agricultural production space (fig. 5).

This period of architecture and planning in China attempted to create, in the rural people's commune and by means of modernist planning and architectural principles, a Chinese utopia. Design in this era was thorough, incursive, and systematic. As first endeavors, designs contributing to rural redevelopment had certain positive attributes and to a certain degree changed the landscape of rural regions. On the other hand, these proposals commonly tended to proclaim the end of peasantry and its traditional lifestyle and architectural typologies. Further, there was no effort to acknowledge local customs. Plans were developed for efficiency and spatial order but ignored context, superimposing a rigid, centrally disposed grid pattern on the land; building allocation did not respect existing patterns of rural life, replacing cultural focal points, like temples, with utilitarian community centers, like canteens, schools, and clinics; architectural design proposed replacing existing vernacular settlements with modern residential buildings that did not reflect or relate to earlier motifs or forms; and landscape design was based solely on an aesthetic assumption that all trees are

7   South China University of Technology Design Institute, "Planning Proposal for the Basic Unit of the Commune, Suiping County, Henan Province," *Jianzhu xuebao* [Architectural journal], Nov. 1958, 11.

palms. Despite the energy and enthusiasm instilled in these rural utopias, the plans rarely progressed from paper to practice, not because of inadequate design but because of over-optimistic projections, the egalitarian distribution system of the commune, and natural disasters that reduced productivity and forced the government to suspend development of rural communes.

1978–1991: DESIGN FOR THE INDUSTRIALIZED COUNTRYSIDE

Two economic and social campaigns between 1958 and 1976—the Great Leap Forward and the Cultural Revolution—weakened China's productivity, especially its food productivity.[8] Mao's death in 1976 and Deng Xiaoping's ascension in 1978 prompted an extraordinary Chinese economic reform, marking the end of intensive collectivization and all-encompassing planning. As the leader of China, Deng publicly supported the Provincial Party Committee Six-Point Proposal and the secret self-generated experiment of the farmers in Xiaogang Village, Anhui Province. These measures broke with the state-planned production methods and egalitarian distribution system within the people's communes, allowing local households the freedom to grow crops at their own discretion once they had fulfilled their contracts. The additional produce could be used by the family or sold; in other words, households began to take responsibility for their own profits and losses. The new household responsibility system created within the rural experiment was advanced in No. 1 Central Document of the country—which put forward the policy of the highest priority—adopted for rural reform in the Central Rural Work Conference of 1982, and then published by the central government and applied, under the party's guidance, to rural China.[9] The new system allowed farm households to grow crops in their own way and gave them the right to lease farmland from the collective. Signed contracts with the state gave to the state a certain amount of crop production; additional production could be sold independently. In reality, the household responsibility system, which linked remuneration to output, created a new path for rural development both economically and spatially.

In 1983, the central government abolished the people's communes. Their political functions were taken on by reestablished towns, townships, or large administrative village governments; their workshops and other economic production units became independent "collective enterprises." In the process of decollectivization, the transformation from people's commune partly to household-collective organization offered the opportunity to develop collective enterprises under the jurisdiction of the recently established towns, townships, and villages, which later evolved into the well-known Township and Village Enterprises. Though the central government did not launch the TVEs, or in any way anticipate their emergence in large numbers, conditions at the time were ripe for their growth. Until 1984, most of the spatial transformation related to the household responsibility system, including the abolition of large public-works projects and large-scale collective farming, was more spontaneous than designed or planned.[10] Nevertheless, the transition of rural production factors from a static to a dynamic state prepared the countryside for the next round of rural reconfiguration: from villages to TVE towns. In 1984, the central government of China began to explicitly encourage the making and development of TVEs; in the following decade, 6.06 million TVEs, employing 105.8 million people, were founded.[11]

The emergence of TVEs unquestionably stimulated rural development, and because of them, the years between 1985 and 1991 are considered the second period of rapid rural development in China. Planners and designers, however, were seldom engaged in reconfiguring the countryside; at least, there is no evidence indicating that TVE buildings and town plans were created by urban-based architects and planners. Instead, local craftsmen acted as both architects and builders. In appearance, most TVE towns were a slightly chaotic collage of different, frequently odd buildings without a clear spatial order. Because the development and formation of TVE towns was largely an autonomous, bottom-up process—as opposed to the generation of a plan, generally a top-down operation—even in later years the involvement of designers was very limited and small in scale, for the most part restricted to wealthy villages and townships that caught the attention of upper-level government. For the limited number of TVE towns that did have a master plan to guide development, the main consideration was maximizing functional efficiency and minimizing construction expense. As a consequence, these towns were dominated by homogeneous building types, single-family houses or rectangular industrial warehouses, without any

8   Dennis Tao Yang, "China's Agricultural Crisis and Famine of 1959–1961: A Survey and Comparison to Soviet Famines," *Comparative Economic Studies* 50 (Mar. 2008): 1–29.

9   "China Seeks Better Rural-Urban Integration," *China Daily*, Feb. 3, 2011, updated Feb. 3, 2015, accessed June 6, 2015, http://usa.chinadaily.com.cn/china/2015-02/03/content_19477338.htm.

10   Ezra F. Vogel, *Deng Xiaoping and the Transformation of China* (Cambridge, MA: Harvard University Press, 2011), 442–43.

11   Richard J. R. Kirkby, *Urbanization in China: Town and Country in a Developing Economy 1949–2000 AD* (New York: Columbia University Press, 1985), 380.

distinguishing aesthetic. Thus, later TVE towns are characterized by uniform building typologies as well as by chaotic collage.

One good example of a TVE town that initially developed spontaneously and then was guided by a master plan is Huaxi Village, Jiangsu Province. Taking advantage of the flexibility to adapt to demand and the freedom to produce marketable goods, Huaxi started its rural transformation by developing industries beyond those required to meet production requirements. Well located near Shanghai, Wuxi, and Suzhou, the three hub cities of the Changjiang River Delta, it grew from a modest, agrarian, communally owned township into an enormously profitable town with a large number of manufacturing and industrial facilities. During the first period of its transition, Huaxi turned into "a messy and tasteless place… enormous superfluous construction projects footnoted by equally purposeless buildings in the shapes of bulls, chicken and turtles. Many other buildings evoke images of Western opulence"[12] (fig. 6). Touted until 1990 as China's richest village, and supporting businesses with an agricultural and industrial output totaling 516 million yuan, Huaxi was acknowledged, after a visit by Premier Li Peng in 1992, as setting a standard of economic and civil development for Chinese agrarian communities, villages, and townships.[13]

Wu Renbao, the chief village patriarch and architect of Huaxi's success, originated the "One Division, Five Unifications" planning tactics[14] in which governance of the TVEs and the village was independent (one division) while all other aspects—economic administration, employment administration, leadership appointment, welfare distribution, and village construction—were part of a top-down plan (five unifications). This strategy was manifested physically in the master plan, which consolidated 16 surrounding villages previously under the administration of Zhangjiagang City and Jiangyin County into larger Huaxi. Regardless of existing rural distribution, the plan replaced the crop fields with new settlements, which were divided into four districts based on program—industrial agricultural fields, town center (mainly for residential uses), cultural plaza, and industrial campus (fig. 8). Each district was dominated by a single building type. In the industrial area, similarly sized boxes—factories and warehouses—were organized in a rigid grid

superimposed on the existing agricultural land. In the residential area and town center, supposedly the most dynamic area in terms of lifestyle and building type, European-style gridded villas were widely duplicated (fig. 7). In all, the planning and design of Huaxi was oversimplified, brutal, and boring, lacking complexity, aesthetic value, and any consideration of the environment.

The sole purpose of planners and architects in TVE towns was to create an industrialized countryside with a simple, rigid, economical, and efficient pattern. Buildings were meant for economic purposes, not ecological or aesthetic considerations. And the design disciplines were isolated: urban planners developed master plans without any input from architects, and vice versa. It was industrialization rather than urbanization that was transforming rural areas. The majority of TVE towns, which were not equipped with tools for urban planning or architecture, grew into messy, disordered, and polluted areas. Because of the lack of a systematic master plan, TVE towns were consuming raw materials and resources inefficiently; since the locations of the TVE towns were not carefully selected, they developed in places that offered good transportation but in the end caused environmental problems far more severe than those created by the urban state industries.[15] Therefore, the central government was eventually required to substantially restructure the TVEs. With increased market integration and competition, official discrimination against TVEs, and an official preference for foreign-owned enterprises, TVEs lost their competitive position, and some estimates suggest that about 30 percent have gone bankrupt.[16] As the success of the TVEs receded, the rural development of China again declined.

1991–2005: PLANNING THE INTEGRATION OF CITY AND COUNTRYSIDE

As the initial success of the Township and Village Enterprises faded, leaving rural areas to search for a way to stimulate development, cities were about to embark on their most rapid urbanization period with the adoption of the Socialist market economy model at the 14th National Party Congress.[17] With the nation's focus on expansive urbanization, rural development was set aside: "The

12   Nathaniel Rickert Flagg, "Branding Heaven: Commodity, Fantasy, and Conceptual Architecture in the Chinese Countryside" (PhD diss., Reed College, 2011), 20.

13   Han-Sun Yang, "Celebration of Wealth and Emulation of Modernity: The Politics of Model Tourism in China's Richest Village" (PhD diss., University of Illinois at Urbana-Champaign, 2006), 4.

14   Weifeng Peng, "Huaxi Village 'One Division Five Unification' Practical Experience Study," *Journal of Central Agricultural Management Institute of Ministry of Agriculture* 2012, no. 1, 17–21.

15   Saehoon Kim and Peter G. Rowe, "Does Large-Sized Cities' Urbanisation Predominantly Degrade Environmental Resources in China? Relationships between Urbanisation and Resources in the Changjiang

Delta Region," *International Journal of Sustainable Development and World Ecology* 19, no. 4 (2012): 321–29.

16   Tony Saich, *Governance and Politics of China* (New York: Palgrave, 2001).

17   A. Doak Barnett and Ralph N. Clough, eds., *Modernizing China: Post-Mao Reform and Development* (Boulder, CO: Westview Press, 1986).

Fig. 6   Aerial view of Huaxi Village.

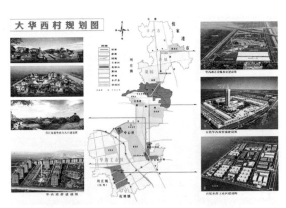

Fig. 8   Master plan, Huaxi Village.

Fig. 7   Central district (residential area), Huaxi Village.

Open-up Policy prompted extraordinary economic reform, but didn't sever the Party's deep ideological roots in rural China's native soil opposed to its soiled urban environments."[18] Even after 1978, the government continued to draw a distinction between city and countryside.

The relationship between the urban and the rural that prevailed until the late 1990s was the dual-sector model. In this system, the urban economy was based on modern large-scale industrial production while the rural economy was still characterized by typical peasant production. In addition, urban infrastructure, both hard and soft, was far in advance of infrastructure in rural areas. Income and consumption levels were much higher for the urban population than for the rural population, and because the latter was larger than the former, there was more unproductive labor in agricultural areas. Finally, the urban area relied for its development on exploiting the rural area. The dual-sector model explains why planned urbanization and a market economy drastically altered urban China but left rural China struggling in a dark period, creating an unprecedented and immense disparity

between urban centers and rural villages. In reality, Chinese cities have never been completely separate from the rural areas that support and surround them, nor has the countryside truly prospered without urban patronage. However, in the 1990s, in order to implement the Socialist market economy, China's urban and industrial centers required a cheap labor force. These workers, rural inhabitants who migrated from the countryside, altered the dynamics of the urban-rural exchange: "Migrations of millions from rural to urban areas can dramatically increase tension and even conflict between the priorities and psyches of urban and rural communities, putting strains on urban services and capacities while marginalizing rural communities and pushing them further apart while they still remain so interdependent."[19] An additional important element, the household registration, or *hukou*, system, protected the benefits of urban residents, further widening the disparity between the urban and the rural.

This misaligned situation provoked the country to reexamine the relationship between urban, peri-urban, and rural systems and to come up with a new solution to

18   Cole Roskam, "Back to the Village," in *Homecoming: Contextualizing, Materializing and Practicing the Rural in China*, ed. Christiane Lange, Joshua Bolchover, and John Lin (Berlin: Gestalten, 2013), 29–31.

19   Thomas Forster, "Reimagining the Urban and Rural as Integrated City Region Landscapes," *Foodtank*, Mar. 8, 2014, accessed June 6, 2015, http://foodtank.com/news/2014/03/reimagining-the-urban-and-rural-as-integrated-city-region-landscapes.

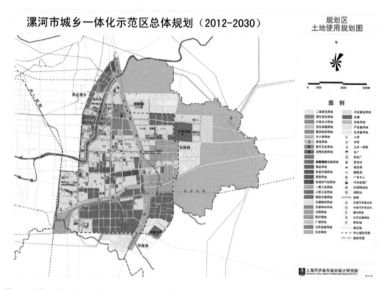

Fig. 9 Shanghai Tongji Urban Planning and Design Institute, plan for integration of Luohe and the surrounding rural area, 2005.

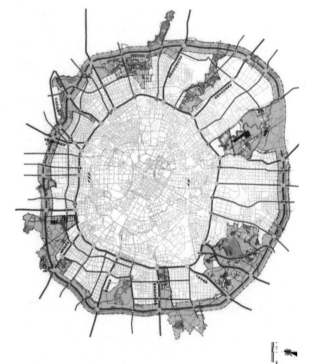

Fig. 10 Chengdu Institute of Planning and Design, master plan for fringe zone of Chongqing-Chengdu District, 2007.

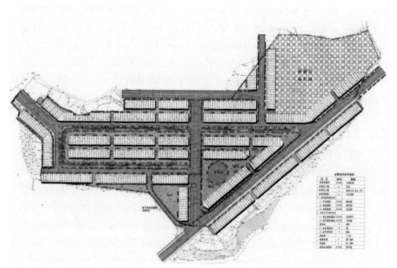

Fig. 11 Master plan for affordable housing, Chongqing.

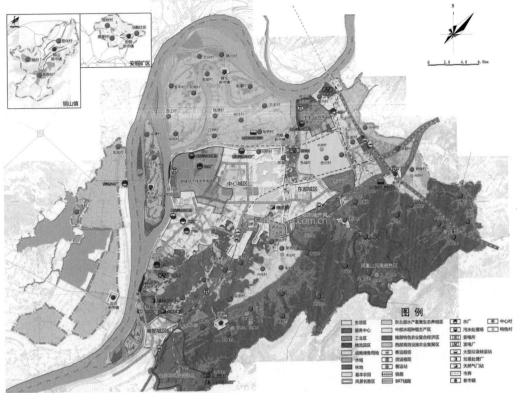

Fig. 12   Tongling Urban Planning and Reconnaissance and Surveying Design Institute with Lay-Out Planning Consultants Ltd., plan for integration of Tongling and the surrounding rural area, 2005.

develop rural areas. In 1992, the strategy of integrating city and countryside was taken up in both urban planning and politics. The aim of urban-rural integration was to unite industry and agriculture, urban residents and rural villagers, through policy reform and space making. At the 16th National Party Congress, in 2002, Jiang Zemin, then president of China, stated that a widening urban-rural gap impeded China's efforts to build a moderately prosperous (*xiaokang*) society. To reverse this trend, the report of the congress set out coordinated urban-rural development (*chengxiang tongchou*) as a major national policy.[20] Coordinated urban-rural development emphasized that future resilience and sustainability in both urban and rural areas of China would require a stronger urban-rural continuum as well as the resource base of food, energy, water, soil, and the built environment. The model covered multiple disciplines, including sociology, economy, ecology, and urban planning and design. Design activity in this period was focused on urban planning, and planning strategies for rural development were intertwined with those for urban development. The tendency for

urban-rural integration is evident in most master plans of this period (figs. 9, 12).

Chongqing-Chengdu District, a so-called Comprehensive Experimental Zone of coordinated urban-rural development, pioneered the notion of using urban-rural integration to stimulate rural development. The master plan for the district listed three concentrations, or more detailed planning tactics: consolidating industrial compounds into larger industry campuses; building residential districts for rural migrants close to the city; and reorganizing agricultural fields into corporate-run industrialized farms[21] (fig. 10). The focus of the master plan was the urban-rural fringe. The planners intended to create architectural prototypes within these buffer zones. These would bridge city and countryside and also offer adequate living space and amenities for rural-urban migrant workers. Three reforms were executed in order to realize this plan. The *hukou* system was reformed to allow rural residents to be converted into urban residents; in this way migrants could enjoy urban services. Land reforms were enacted that permitted the

20   Zhong Sheng, "Towards China's Urban-Rural Integration: Issues and Options," *International Journal of China Studies* 2, no. 2 (Aug./Sept. 2011): 346.

21   Ye Yumin and Richard LeGates, *Coordinating Urban and Rural Development in China: Learning from Chengdu* (Cheltenham, UK: Edward Elgar Publishing, 2013), 69.

exchange of rural land for urban development. And affordable housing programs in the fringe accommodated
migrant workers. Architects took on the task of urban and
architectural design for the affordable housing and its
environs. The fringe districts consisted of rows of slab
buildings oriented north to south. These structures filled
the site and satisfied requirements for solar orientation.
But they did not reflect local culture in terms of building
shape, decoration, and layouts, nor did they promote a
blend of urban and rural lifestyles, instead trying to
replace rural customs with urban ones (fig. 11). Within the
slab buildings, the one-bedroom units were efficient and
well appointed.

In this stage of architecture and planning in China,
design engagement was directed at the planning level.
Urban planners contributed to the integration of city and
countryside by carefully plugging industrial campuses,
ecological zones, and affordable housing into new infrastructure and landscapes that spatially connected the
urban and the rural. Almost all cities in China at this time
had integration master plans produced by various urban
planning institutions in China. The main purpose of
these master plans was to consolidate city and countryside on the scale of a district and then allow smaller
interventions to further improve the rural situation and, in
general, decrease the urban-rural disparity. Architectural
efforts were mostly limited to designing neighborhoods
and housing for rural migrant workers on the edge
between city and countryside. Without a doubt, architecture and urban planning improved or even reconfigured
the urban-rural fringe, at the same time providing a
decent standard of living. But no designers participated at
an intermediate scale of urban design. Without a bridge
between planners and architects, the planning strategies
and architectural strategies were somehow at odds: the
master plan emphasized integration while the buildings
and neighborhoods in the fringe turned out to be another
form of urban expansion.

2005–2012: DESIGNING THE NEW SOCIALIST COUNTRYSIDE

The integration of city and countryside was originally
aimed at improving the built environment of rural areas.
However, 10 years into the implementation of this idea, it
became clear that this policy was yet another instance of
the urban exploiting the rural. In the years 1991 to 2005,
which saw the most rapid city-based urbanization, the
disparity between urban and rural increased steeply and
continuously, the opposite of what had been intended.
This state of affairs encouraged the new leadership group,
headed by Hu Jintao and Wen Jiabao, to address rural
development. Three topics—the rural area, the farmer,
and agriculture—were raised as the major concerns of the
central government three years in a row, in 2005, 2006,
and 2007.[22] In those three years, the Hu-Wen administration tried to foster rural urbanization by eliminating
agricultural taxes on farmers ($12.3 billion in 2006),
improving basic infrastructure for the rural population,
increasing the subsidies to farmers for village infrastructure, promoting small businesses in rural areas by means
of microcredits, and improving welfare, health care, and
education for rural residents. The intense efforts to
improve the circumstances of rural residents can be seen
as a strategy to reduce urban migration. At the 2006
National People's Congress, rural issues were emphasized
throughout Wen Jiabao's speech on the activities of 2005
and the direction for 2006.[23] This speech advanced a significant policy change, redirecting the national focus
from extensive urban development to sustainable rural
development, and set out a new, historically significant
task for China—constructing the New Socialist
Countryside—within the 11th Five Year Plan (2006–
2010).[24] Later, a publication of the Central Committee
of the CCP and the State Council promoting the construction of the New Socialist Countryside indicated a
new development methodology—new Socialist village
making—to achieve the goal of balancing regional development, urban and rural development, social and
economic development, human needs and nature, and
domestic development and opening up of the country.

The Five Year Plan stated:

The target and requirement for building socialist
new villages can be summed up as follows:
Developed production, well-off life, civilized rural
customs, a neat and tidy appearance of village
and democratic management . . . Building socialist
new villages requires upholding the principles of
"giving more to villages, taking less from them
and breathing new life to them," and "industry
nurturing agriculture and cities supporting villages," improving farmers' living quality, bringing
about a relatively big change in the outlook of

22   Niu Ruofeng and Li Chenggui, *Three Rural Issues of China: Retrospect and Perspect* (Beijing: China Social Sciences Press, 2004), 22.

23   Wen Jiabao, "Report of the Work of the Govern-ment," press release, Xinhua News Agency, 2006, 2.

24   Jessica Wade, "China's Good Earth: From Urbanization to Rural Development under Hu Jintao's Administration," Paper 1, *Global Asia Journal* (2007).

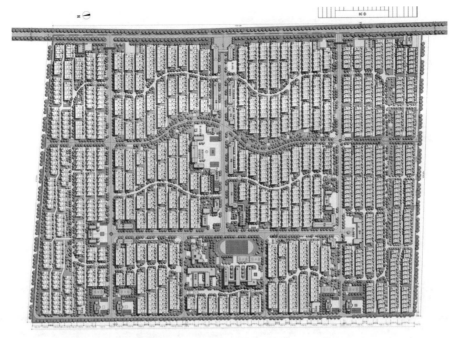

Fig. 13 Zhengzhou Architectural Design Institute, master plan, Liuzhuang New Socialist Village, 2013.

rural areas as a whole. Emphasis is placed on strengthening plans for the construction of villages and towns and improving the environment, and on the construction of new villages and towns; developing various social undertakings in rural areas, fostering new farmers; strengthening construction of rural democracy and legal system and construction of spiritual civilization and encouraging new social practices.[25] The document demonstrated two courses for rural urbanization though urban planning and architecture. The first called for improving and upgrading the existing natural landscape and built environment by renovating and adding amenities and services; separate villages would form single entities, which would raise living standards for the area. The second proposed the wholesale demolition of several villages and their re-creation as a new, larger "new agricultural town." This practice would enable the sharing of new communal amenities and the efficient introduction of improved services and infrastructure into the countryside, again raising living standards to those of the city. In the end, however, few or no master plans followed the first alternative; almost all began with the idea of

demolition and therefore worked from a tabula rasa, that is, an empty agricultural field located in the center of a group of villages.

Hence, the idea of constructing the New Socialist Countryside manifested unilaterally in the demolition of existing villages with vernacular buildings and the reconstruction from the resulting tabula rasa of substandard housing with shared communal amenities in the merged new village or new town. And so the new Socialist village came to be understood, wrongly, in the planning realm as a brand-new village built on agricultural fields. Another misunderstanding on the part of the planners was the concept that in order to bring the living standards of the rural population up to those of life in the city, village plans should follow the modes and manners of urban construction. For this reason, the master plans of the new Socialist villages blindly aimed at constructing small new cities.

The sites of the new Socialist villages were always rectangular, for efficiency's sake, and situated at a crossroads or along a newly constructed highway.[26] The master plans were symmetrical and located public facilities and community amenities along a central axis with a linear communal park. On either side were three-story

25 "Building Socialist New Villages," 17th National Congress of the CCP, Sept. 30, 2007, accessed June 6, 2015, http://en.people.cn/90002/92169/92211/6275027.html.

26 Zhang Jianming and Wang Ning, "Discussion on Site Layout Planning for Villages in County Region," *Planners* 21, no. 3 (2005): 23–25.

Fig. 14   Hainan Highway Reconnaissance Design Institute, Hainan Lingshui New Socialist Village, 2010.

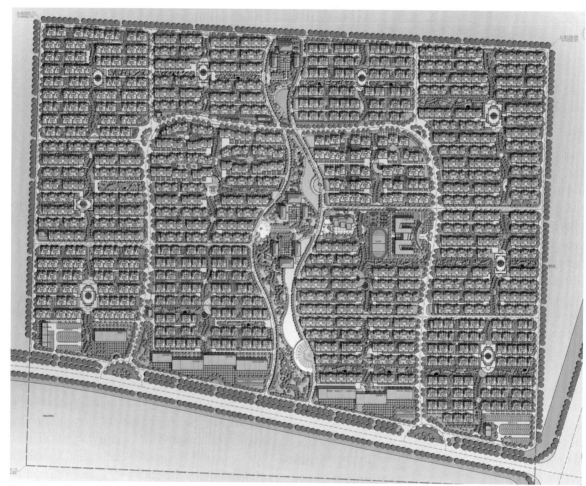

Fig. 15   Zhengzhou Architectural Design Institute, master plan, Tushan New Agricultural Town, 2013.

single-family houses densely distributed on an orthogonal grid (fig. 13). The floor area ratio of the new village was generally about 1 to 1.5. The massive number of identical houses, aligned in dozens of rows for kilometers at a time, was as problematic as the planned TVE towns in the 1990s. Designed by local architecture institutes, the houses were affordable and efficient, with living and dining areas and a semi-outdoor parking space on the first floor and two bedrooms and a terrace on each of the second and third floors. But their appearance was banal, unsuccessfully imitating, and oversimplifying, features of the traditional Chinese vernacular rural house, such as the flat red-brick wall and 30-degree sloped roof. The new houses actually contributed to the loss of traditional architectural attributes and regional architectural cultures[27] (fig. 14). The official architecture press published a series of manuals for constructing the new Socialist village. Two in particular fostered the rigid copy-and-paste aesthetic that characterized new Socialist village design all over vast rural China: "Manual for Master Plan of New Socialist Village" and "Manual for Building Design of New Socialist Village."

Tushan New Agricultural Town is a new Socialist village in Henan Province in central China, one of the largest rural areas of China. The site of the new town is a 942,000-square-meter former agricultural field in the center of Zhongmu County. The site, next to the S223 provincial-level highway, is surrounded by four existing villages with about 1,515 households in total. The master plan conforms to the template provided by the planning manual. A central axis with park and amenities follows the spine of a major road. The symmetrical rectangular site is divided into four subprecincts. All houses are disposed according to the same spatial hierarchy, showing the notion of equality that characterizes rural communities (fig. 15). The master plan of Tushan New Agricultural Town is efficient and meets the requirements set out in the manual, but it neglects rural production methods and services, farmers' lifestyles, social groupings, and ecological and aesthetic considerations. The master plan centralizes the population and residential areas, adds new amenities, and improves environmental conditions, but it separates the residents from the land and destroys the previous rural landscape.

There are two categories of architecture in Tushan: public/communal buildings and houses for farmers. The buildings for the community, including commercial, educational, civic, and waste-sewage buildings, balance functional, economic, and aesthetic requirements appropriately.[28] For instance, one of the new schools, as seen in a rendering, is simple and modest, offering a comfortable environment for study (figs. 16, 17). The houses, on the other hand, lack diversity or local cultural distinction. All of three stories, they range from 180 to 280 square meters in size. Houses are assigned based on the floor area of the owners' previous houses. Their design is again simply iterative and falls into a clichéd typology of sloped roof and brick facade. On one hand, erecting similar or identical houses simplifies building methods and accelerates construction;[29] on the other hand, it creates a conventional and undifferentiated townscape. It is worth noting that new construction requires the demolition of existing vernacular buildings, an irreparable loss when viewed from the perspective of historic preservation. Indeed, many of the demolished villages contain significant and distinctive traditional architecture: "They can reveal the existence of different environments in construction and development of laws, reflecting the philosophy, aesthetics, ethics, customs, religions, spiritual beliefs, cultural value of different times, the harmonious relationship between human and nature, and the harmonious relationship between neighborhoods."[30]

The principal goal of the new Socialist village is to offer a higher standard of living, creating an acceptable residential and infrastructural estate. In general, the contributions to this goal of planners, urban designers, and architects are banal and unreasonably homogeneous master plans and architecture. In other words, building the new villages is considered a project of engineering and systems; function is privileged above all other aspects, including culture, crop-field context, and ecology. In the period of the new Socialist village, all of China has feverishly remade the countryside, but with a clichéd vision: tearing down existing villages, replacing the countryside with extensive geometrically patterned plans, superimposing new infrastructure, and switching centuries-old agricultural lands into concrete platforms. A study of a new town in Guangdong Province notes: "The new socialist countryside movement in China has overtaken hundreds of thousands of native rural habitats . . . destroying hundreds and thousands of years of history among vernacular landscapes and villages."[31] In planning and

27 Bai Xianchen, He Ziqi, and Zhang Yizhong, "Resources in Construction of New Socialism Countryside: A Case Study on the Yuxi Areas, Henan Province," *Resources Science* 32, no. 9 (2010): 1,792–98.

28 Bin Zheng, Qi Gong, Xiaofang Zhang, Lu Gan, and Ying Zhu, "Experience in New Socialist Countryside Planning and Construction and Recommendations: A

Case Study of Haotang Village in Xinyang City of Henan Province," *Asian Agricultural Research* 11, no. 6 (Nov. 2014): 87–90.

29 Yongjun Zhou, "Study on Construction of Socialist New Rural Houses," *Shanxi Architecture*, no. 4 (2007): 33–34.

30 Zheng et al., "Experience in New Socialist Countryside," 87–90.

31 Kongjian Yu, Dihua Li, Xili Han, and Bo Luan, "Rescuing a Village: The Approach of Landscape Security Patterns, with the Case of Magang, Shunde, Guangdong Province," *Urban Planning Forum*, no. 5 (2006): 38–45.

Fig. 16 Zhengzhou Architectural Design Institute, exterior rendering of school, Tushan New Agricultural Town, 2013.

Fig. 17 Zhengzhou Architectural Design Institute, interior rendering of school, Tushan New Agricultural Town, 2013.

building the New Socialist Countryside, designers have completed their jobs within their own disciplines but without fully understanding the historic and cultural value of traditional village and architectural resources or developing innovative and cross-scale design strategies that rendered local cultures and construction features into modern construction technology. Besides designing new buildings and facilities, designers for new Socialist villages should also adhere to the principle of protection and utilization, thoughtfully preserving traditional architecture and physically connecting the new with the old. In addition, sustainability is just one subject that should be more emphasized during the planning and construction phases.

2012–PRESENT: TOWARD CONTINUOUS RURAL URBANIZATION

It is a simple yet utterly unsettling statement: after three decades of economic development encouraged farmers to seek better living standards in towns and cities, for the first time in the more-than-2,000-year history of China, the majority of the population lives in urban areas. The National Bureau of Statistics of China, in noting this epochal moment, stated that as of 2012, 51 percent of

Chinese people are living in cities. This great achievement of Chinese urbanization, which has accelerated since Deng Xiaoping introduced capitalist reforms in the late 1970s, has lifted more than 200 million people, mostly rural residents, out of poverty and has transformed the nation into the world's second-largest economy.

The urbanization of rural areas is set to come to the fore once again in China's economic and social development. In the report on government activity presented at the first session of the 12th National People's Congress on March 5, 2013, Wen Jiabao for the first time announced the intention to control and limit the scale of megacities and to focus on third-tier and town/township development. The new Chinese government's slogan, "Chinese Townization," conforms to the idea of the New Socialist Countryside, emphasizing the development and urbanization of rural and less developed areas in China and also continuing to increase the rate of urbanization. Li Keqiang's plan, announced in 2014, for "promoting the healthy development of national urbanization (2011–2020)" set forth a target of urbanizing another 20 percent of China's population by means of local efforts. The National Health and Family Planning Commission of China estimates that this target will affect about 300 million people, close to the entire population of the United States, subsuming them into China's urban population by

2025. Clearly, one of the most important national tasks will be the growth of rural towns and small cities, not the further expansion of large cities.

However, there is currently no clear definition or process of implementation for "rural urbanization" or "townization"; it is still a vague, conceptual model. Given the significant policy reorientation and the gap between the policy and its implementation, I believe there are four questions that deserve consideration by urban planners and architects: How will the new policy, with its stress on rural urbanization and development, shape the rural landscape and deal with the relationship between the countryside and the city? During this emergent rural urbanization, what are possible planning models—other than the urban-based extensive urbanization model on agricultural land, such as was used in constructing the New Socialist Countryside—for creating a different rural image or rural landscape? How can urban designers and architects redevelop villages into higher-density areas and improve the infrastructure while also protecting rural traditions and cultures, as opposed to the wholesale demolition of villages or the amalgamation and rebuilding of villages into new towns? How can cross-disciplinary design communication and collaboration, with a goal of creating proposals that can significantly and sustainably improve the rural built environment and at the same time reduce environmental pollution, protect agricultural land and natural resources in order to achieve a better quality of rural life?

CONCLUSION

Since 1949, the Chinese countryside has undergone drastic transformation. At the same time, the question of design for rural China is a familiar theme that has reappeared almost every decade and has always been a factor in rural reconfiguration. In each different political, economic, and social period, design for rural China has had a specific meaning and mission with a corresponding level of engagement on the part of designers. From 1949 to 1978, planners and architects used modernist planning principles, regardless of rural traditions and cultures, and provided thorough, incursive, and systematic design strategies and tactics to create a Chinese utopia, the rural people's commune. However, despite the energy and enthusiasm instilled in plans for thousands of communes, the designs rarely progressed from paper to practice for political reasons and also due to natural disasters. From 1978 to 1991, the rural transformation was mostly a bottom-up autonomous industrialization process; the involvement of design practices came quite late and was on a very limited scale. Although the designs were simple, rigid, and economical, aimed at increasing economic benefits without consideration of ecological and aesthetic issues (primarily because of the segregation of urban planning and architecture), they still served the countryside better than areas without urban planning and architecture, which turned out to be messy, disordered, and contaminated. From 1991 to 2005, design engagement was seen mainly in urban planning, addressing the increasing urban-rural disparity by creating urban-rural continuums. Though planning interventions did not markedly control the disparity, they did help to some degree to reconfigure the urban-rural fringe and provided an improved standard of living. From 2005 to 2012, the principal development goal was construction of the new Socialist village to offer a better standard of living, upgrading basic infrastructure and sanitation and building satisfactory residential housing for rural China. Planners, urban designers, and architects largely helped achieve the goal with banal and homogeneous master plans and buildings on a tabula rasa; efficiency and basic infrastructural provisions were valued above cultural, agricultural, and ecological concerns. While the role of the design professions is evident within the upgrading and ameliorating of rural areas, the specific design solutions leave a lot to be desired.

The shortcomings in the designs were twofold. First, design that was not based on the existing rural context tended to eliminate the traditional rural lifestyle and local customs. Second, segregation of the design disciplines did not allow planners, urban designers, and architects to work in a coordinated manner, which degraded design quality. Hence, when China embarks on its new strategy, continuous rural urbanization, urban planners, designers, and architects must communicate and collaborate across disciplines, generating projects for the reconfiguration of the countryside that besides functional requirements also address issues related to rural lifestyle, agricultural production, ecology, and local cultural traditions.

China's Townization Plan and Its Implications

Peter G. Rowe, Har Ye Kan

China's National New Townization Plan, enacted in 2014, aims to chart a new way forward for the nation's urbanization. At this point in its development, China finds itself becoming a *xiaokang*, or a moderately prosperous society, amid a restructuring of its economy. This restructuring emphasizes domestic consumption and growth in the service sector in contrast to the prior focus on export-oriented and energy-intensive production. Indeed, as the preamble to the plan makes obvious, domestic demand is the key to the nation's future economic development, and the best chance of success lies with an urbanization strategy that promotes socioeconomic development through townization.

In setting out this course, the national leadership and central authorities have essentially reframed *chengshihua*, or urbanization, as *chengzhenhua*, or townization, shifting the emphasis from large and medium centers to smaller cities, towns, and villages. In addition, they are actively seeking to create complex conurbations that balance development between large, medium, and small cities, as well as towns. The plan is part of the pursuit of the "Chinese Dream" articulated by China's president, Xi Jinping, when he took leadership of the country in November 2012.[1] With this phrase, Xi seems to mean the integration of the fulfillment of national and personal aspirations with the goals of recovering national pride and achieving personal well-being. Consequently, the guiding philosophy of the townization plan is that it should be people-oriented, should enable an ecological society, should ensure continuities with traditions and cultures of the past, and should promote harmonious economic and social development.[2] In short, it represents a distinct pivot toward the majority of Chinese citizens who still live in smaller communities in rural and urban areas and also toward the promise of a better life. Needless to say, progress in these directions will need to attain certain objectives, all also pointed out in the plan. Among them are more complete integration of rural migrants into urban society, more efficient use of urban lands, better conformance with regard to environmental carrying capacities, more sufficient concentration of populations to overcome weak services, greater protection and conservation of natural and historic heritage, and substantially improved mechanisms of social security provision.[3] While it is not yet possible to assess the plan's success, it is worthwhile to review its broader contextual circumstances, particularly concerning patterns, scales, and relationships in urbanization.

TOWNS AND CHINA'S SPATIAL FORMATION

An important aspect of China's urbanization, which underlies and reinforces the townization plan, is the distinctly binary distribution of settlement according to scale. In the larger size are about 658 statutory cities. These fall into seven class sizes, based on the 2010 census, with Shanghai and Beijing above 15 million residents in the first category. Indeed, Shanghai's resident population has been put as high as 26.1 million, depending on criteria including the elapsed time of migrant workers' stays, and Beijing's at around 20 million.[4] Shenzhen and Chongqing, with between 10 and 15 million inhabitants each, are in the second category. The third, 5 to 10 million, includes only 10 cities, and the fourth, 1 to 5 million, 67 cities. That being the case, the vast majority of statutory cities—more than 550—comprise 1 million or fewer inhabitants; however, it is expected that many will increase in population and that China will have 120 cities above 1 million in population by 2020.[5] In comparison, the United States, with less than a quarter of China's inhabitants, has about 50 metropolitan populations of comparable size. This last observation implies that China is probably underurbanized, despite recent rapid growth, and may remain so until 2025 to 2035 or thereabouts, when the total population will begin to decline fairly rapidly.[6] Put another way, although the number of people living in cities of 1 million or more (also called metropolitan-level populations) is high in absolute terms—311.5 million people in 2010—this number represents only 23 percent of China's total population. In 2000, the number was 19 percent.[7]

On the other side of the twofold distribution of settlement are some 20,113 designated towns. These are defined as areas with nonagricultural populations above a minimum threshold, appropriate densities, and other urban characteristics. This number represents a rise from a mere 2,173 towns in 1978, at the beginning of China's historic opening to the outside world, and part of the nation's average annual urbanization growth rate, from 1978 to 2010, of just 1.02 percent.[8] In absolute terms, about 368

1   Coverage of Chinese Dream, *China Daily*, accessed Apr. 9, 2015, http://www.chinadaily.com.cn/china/Chinese-dream.html.

2   Central Government of the People's Republic of China, "National New Townization Plan (2014–2020)," 14–18.

3   Central Government of the PRC, "National New Townization Plan," 8.

4   The Economist, *Pocket World in Figures 2015* (London: Profile Books, 2014), 19.

5   Chreod Ltd., "China Regional Urbanization Trends," vol. 1 (Toronto, 2013), 20.

6   "World Population Prospects: The 2012 Revision," Population Division, Department of Economic and Social Affairs, United Nations, accessed Apr. 9, 2015, http://esa.un.org/unpd/wpp/index.htm.

7   Chreod Ltd., "China Regional Urbanization Trends," 21.

8   Between 1978 and 2013, the urban resident population in cities and towns increased from 170 million to 730 million, and the level of urbanization based on the urban resident population increased from 17.9 percent to 53.7 percent, equivalent to a 1.02 percent average annual growth rate; Central Government of the PRC, "National New Townization Plan," 8.

million people live in 12,000 towns and counties and a further 260 million in townships comprised of villages and hamlets.[9] Again, the criteria used to establish population do not always culminate in the same number, but the level of urbanization based on resident population stands at 53.7 percent, whereas the registered population is only 36 percent of the total population. Also, the size of towns varies considerably, from upward of 125,000 inhabitants to 25,000 and fewer, with an overall average of about 35,000.[10] Although cities have surged in number and scale, town-based urbanization has also grown markedly between 2002 and 2010. Such growth has occurred by way of accretion and merger of smaller urban areas, consolidation of scattered villages, administrative conversion of rural residents in towns to urban residents, and both short- and long-term migration of residents into towns.

The bifurcated distribution of urban settlement in both statistical and morphological terms, alongside population movement up and down in the divide between cities and towns, is markedly if not uniquely Chinese. Furthermore, and particularly on the small scale of urban settlements in fertile delta regions like the Changjiang and Pearl River Deltas, it is historically long-lived. Shanghai Xian (County), for instance, consisted of dense small settlements, amounting to more than half a million people, during the Ming and Qing dynasties from the late 14th to the early 20th century. Similarly, nearby Suzhou was the center of an even larger population—2 million people—over roughly the same period, all located in small towns, villages, and hamlets.[11] Although since about 1990, with Township and Village Enterprises suffering a sharp decline, many of these smaller areas have diminished significantly, as migrants sought a better life in cities and larger towns, a relatively steady unfolding of a conurbated arrangement among small, medium, and large urban settlements appears to be a prudent strategy. In most if not all parts of the world, as a nation reaches an asymptotic urbanization rate, often around 75 percent of the total population, it takes time for the gains of urbanization and the gains of economic development to balance out. If, for instance, urbanization runs too far ahead of economic growth and development, poor and dysfunctional city development may ensue. If, on the other hand, economic growth exceeds urbanization significantly, labor and other shortages will likely ensue along with higher costs of

doing business, declining competitiveness, and decelerating growth that threatens citizens' livelihoods.[12] By building on the binary distribution of big and little settlements, along with what is emerging in between—the lower end of the statutory cities and the upper end of the designated towns—China may well achieve a gradual enough and virtuous convergence of urbanization with environmentally sustainable and market-led economic growth.

TOWNS, COUNTRYSIDE, AND MODERN CIVILIZATION

The merger of cities and countryside and the erasure of an urban distinction have been at the heart of modern Chinese sociopolitical discourse for some time. In fact, the relative absence of markedly compact citylike places in China amid the domains of landed gentry and market towns of antiquity underlined a bias in national character, a bias toward the goodness, healthfulness, and moral righteousness of the countryside. To be sure, the people's communes of the Maoist period in both urban and rural areas follow from earlier urbanist and disurbanist debates in the Soviet Union, as well as from the sheer deployment of a potentially productive population that hovered around the eradication of the same distinction.[13] In more recent times, Hu Jintao and Wen Jiabao's program of urban-rural coordination, promulgated in 2003, also sought a productive rapprochement between urban settlements and rural collectives, with the former leading the latter. Today's townization planning seems to aim for a more complete urban-rural integration, one that will eventually efface any distinction between the rights, opportunities, and aspirations of citizens from either domain. At root, it is a policy about one people and a largely modern urban outcome.

Another term that arises in a consideration of the urban-rural distinction is *shiminhua*, or the idea of easy integration of rural migrants, through a step-by-step process, into towns and smaller cities.[14] Clearly, what is implied is that townization and, by extension, urbanization are civilizing influences on the populace. The notion of *shiminhua* also lies conceptually behind the people-oriented approach, as distinct from a purely physical

9   Chreod Ltd., "China Regional Urbanization Trends," 13.

10   Chreod Ltd., "China Regional Urbanization Trends," 13.

11   Linda Cooke Johnson, *Shanghai: From Market Town to Treaty Port, 1074–1858* (Stanford: Stanford University Press, 1995), 50–56.

12   Chreod Ltd., "China Regional Urbanization Trends," 2–3; James K. Galbraith, "Global Inequality and Global Macroeconomics," *Journal of Policy Modeling* 29, no. 4 (July/Aug. 2007): 587–607.

13   The "urbanists," led largely by Leonid Sabsovich, promulgated compact urbanization in the form of the *sotsgorod* (Socialist city). The "disurbanists," such as Mikhail Okhitovich, Moisei Ginzburg, and Alexander Pasternak, rejected the idea of the city and argued for a dispersed distribution of individual homes in the countryside. For an in-depth discussion, see Selim O. Khan-Magomedov, *Pioneers of Soviet Architecture* (New York: Rizzoli, 1987), 271–340.

14   Central Government of the PRC, "National New Townization Plan," 10.

strategy, being advanced in the townization plan. Indeed, it is the cultivation of a particular set of urban attitudes and orientations that is being touted in the plan, not matters of building. In addition, the core issue indicated in the need for integration is *hukou* status, or household registration; without such registration, migrants are deprived of basic public services, including access to education, health care, and affordable housing. Again the problem of unequal access to social services suggests that decisions and remedies, administrative and otherwise, well beyond matters of physical development, are necessary.

In reference to the dilemma of striking an appropriate balance between rates of urbanization and economic development, a disquieting aspect of the relatively rapid recent town-based urbanization is that nonagricultural employment has not kept pace. This was the case in about 60 percent of all local administrative units in China. To put it another way, in 67 percent of China's counties, most towns did not create enough significant nonagricultural employment to enable the majority of new urban residents to cut ties to farming.[15] In some places, this disparity appears to be more a matter of economic opportunity than of wealth. Numerous towns in Zhejiang Province, for example, have ratios of disposable income to expenditures of 1.5 or even 2 to 1, indicating a pent-up demand for, among other things, commercial, community, and lifestyle services.[16] This is hardly surprising given the rather crude array of stores and other local enterprises in certain areas, as well as the relative isolation of townships from markets and larger urban areas. The larger point, though, is that there is a need to stimulate domestic consumption in these places in order to move the economy of China in a sustainable direction, that is, away from energy-intensive and export-oriented manufacturing. Failure to encourage this type of economic development may well result in the nation falling again into a "middle-income trap," as noted in the narrative of the townization plan.[17] Beyond the development of a *xiaokang*—or a moderately prosperous society—progress to higher levels of economic well-being is also necessary.

In many of these regards, the demographic profile of the nation is less than advantageous. The economic benefits of an expanding, economically active population peaked in 2010 and have begun to decline quite rapidly. Furthermore, most projections show that China's total population is also likely to decline by around 2025 to 2035. Unless substantial productivity gains can be mustered by about 2025, including considerable shifts to the service or tertiary industrial sector, it will be ever more difficult to move beyond the attainment of *xiaokang*. In short, China is in something of a race with time, one in which success in reaching productive measures of urbanization and especially townization is pitted against failure in reaching sustainable levels of economic production and environmental well-being. The crucial period of transition—between 2015 and 2025—will be accompanied by an increasing risk to the future existence of villages, resulting in a continuous decline in the number of villages at the lower end of the urban-rural spectrum. Blandishments in the townization plan—rural residents increasing income by moving to towns and small cities, improvement of policies as incentives for those who decide to relocate, and plans for upgrading the urban employment of laborers—clearly minimize support for villages.[18] Of course, increasing levels of townization involving many more residents may well enable these residents to increase their incomes through resettlement and employment in urban areas. Moreover, if townization is done appropriately, domestic demand—a foundational force in China's economic development—will expand.[19]

TOWNS, CITIES, LOCATIONS, AND MATTERS OF SCALE

For the townization plan to achieve its objectives and have a meaningful impact on China's urban development, it is important to take into consideration the relationship between towns, cities, and the broader conurbations in which they are located. Among the points at issue are why having settlements of varying scales matters and how towns can be developed in a sustainable manner that leverages their intrinsic assets. As even a cursory study of China's small cities and towns makes obvious, these areas cannot be regarded as anywhere near equal with respect to location, relationships to larger cities, or scale. Townships that are within the halo of larger metropolitan areas quite often offer better lifestyle and economic opportunities; those that are more isolated do not. In China, coastal regions are more developed in comparison to central and western inland regions; likewise, areas within provinces that are closer to larger cities, even in coastal areas, are more developed than those within more rugged countryside.

15   Chreod Ltd., "China Regional Urbanization Trends," 16.

16   SURBA, "Study of 43 Townships in Zhejiang Province for Commercial, Community and Lifestyle Services" (Hangzhou: Township Development and Data Research Institute, 2015).

17   Central Government of the PRC, "National New Townization Plan," 12.

18   Central Government of the PRC, "National New Townization Plan," 6, 7, 19, 21.

19   Central Government of the PRC, "National New Townization Plan," 6.

It is worth appraising this trend in China in relation to a noteworthy tendency in different parts of the world. Although larger cities in Italy have lost population in recent decades, a crown, or corona, of some 38 small municipal communities has grown around Rome; these have developed faster than the central city.[20] Residents of Rome have been moving toward and into the countryside in search of different, better lifestyles; some have retained jobs in the city, often on its periphery, while others have taken new jobs within the peripheral areas. A similar trend can be seen in the Boston metropolitan region. The population growth in surrounding towns, of which there are dozens, has been more significant than that within the city itself, which has also continued to grow.[21] Much the same thing appears to be happening to towns in the orbit of larger cities in China, for instance Hangzhou in the prosperous Zhejiang Province.

In terms of relationships of towns and small cities to broader urbanizing contexts, these observations from different parts of the world have several consequences. First, towns are not big cities and should not be regarded in the same or similar ways. Second, towns and cities in regional urban contexts can and should enjoy complementary relationships. Third, lifestyle diversity increases in a region comprised of a variety of settlement scales, an advantage of well-balanced conurbations. Indeed, all other things being equal, such diversity probably makes regions more attractive to potential inhabitants and more environmentally sustainable.

Towns and small cities have intrinsic assets to offer in an analysis of the scope of conurbated arrangements. Sociological investigations of big and small towns and cities seem to suggest that such entities are more cohesive and less prone to conditions of alienation and pathology than their larger counterparts.[22] Social capital accumulation—strong personal networks that share norms, values, and understandings, facilitating cooperation within and among groups—is also likely to be higher in small towns and cities. This accumulation—a degree of trust to "pull together"—can have profound effects on the quality of life and, by extension, on the attractiveness and vibrancy of urban regions. Another strength that towns and small cities seem to routinely offer is a more desirable environment: cleaner air, better water quality, more open space.

Provided that the scale allows towns to be maintained, such qualities have the potential to make them more environmentally sustainable. The cost of living in towns and small cities tends to be relatively lower than in their larger counterparts. In certain parts of China, where temperature-regulated transport of food is limited, it is the small communities close to rural areas that commonly have access to healthy and fresh food. In addition, basic household goods are often less expensive, with a lower price markup. Such advantages, however, are typically accompanied by less choice in the products and services on offer, though near metropolitan regions these drawbacks can be offset by ready access to city markets.

Excessive smallness in population size or scale brings with it a specific set of inconveniences, such as inadequate provision of basic infrastructure and the lack of diverse commercial, community, and lifestyle services. Various studies have attempted to establish guidelines for a practical population threshold. A recent survey of towns in Jiangsu Province showed that communities with fewer than 50,000 inhabitants witnessed significant drops in basic services as compared to larger, more populated towns.[23] A similar threshold was revealed in a study of townships in neighboring Zhejiang Province, which investigated levels of income, GDP per capita, and access to services.[24] Intended to compensate for concerns of scale are the mergers of small urban areas; pooling and combining resources, without actually combining communities, is another way to counterbalance small size or population. In Italy, it has become relatively common practice for towns to share fire protection, health care, and other municipal services, thereby broadening service boundaries.[25]

Planning of new towns and conurbations requires that new development be balanced with old and that redevelopment be balanced with an improved environment for all. The first among many aspects that must be considered in this equation are the advantages and disadvantages of the side-by-side development common in China. Often this type of planning involves placing new districts next to relatively untouched old ones. One benefit is the facilitation of building on new sites in more flexible, modern ways, unencumbered by existing structures and roads. Side-by-side development is also invariably less costly with regard to social displacement and payment of

20   Giancarlo Storto, ed., *Rapporto sulla condizione abitativa in Italia* (Rome, 1996), 45–52.

21   UMass Donahue Institute Population Estimates Program, "Massachusetts Total Population by Minor Civil Divisions, 2010," Mar. 22, 2011, accessed Apr. 9, 2015, http://www.massbenchmarks.org/statedata/data/census_2010_redistricting_data/pop_2010_mcd.jpg.

22   Pierre Bourdieu, "The Forms of Capital," in *Handbook of Theory and Research for the Sociology of Education*, ed. John G. Richardson (New York: Greenwood, 1986), 241–58; James S. Coleman, *Foundations of Social Theory* (Cambridge, MA: Harvard University Press, 1990).

23   Bing Zhu, "Urbanization, Spatial Configuration and Regional Management: The Case of the Changjiang

Delta Region, China" (PhD diss., Harvard Graduate School of Design, 2006), 163.

24   SURBA, "Study of 43 Townships," 33.

25   Peter G. Rowe and Roberto Pasini, eds., *Urban Territorialization in Areas of Romagna, Italy* (Cambridge, MA: Harvard Graduate School of Design, 2004), 86–89.

relocation fees. However, if done without consideration and redress of issues in the older adjacent areas, these practices can result in fragmentation and the removal of life from older centers, creating poverty where once there were simply older buildings. In fact, in the current conurbated state of the lower Changjiang Delta, it is the smaller communities and not their larger counterparts that appear to be causing the most environmental and land cover–related damages, such as loss of forests, wetlands, fresh water, and fields for cash crops.[26] It is likely that continued expansive side-by-side development will deteriorate environmental and productive performance still further. Other factors that should be considered in the balancing act of town development are whether full use is made of opportunities for adaptive reuse and whether specialized districts have the capacity to be made less so over time. Such practices are as applicable to lots and blocks as to buildings. In the development of new districts in towns, the use of megaplots, also very common in China, may be cheap with regard to first costs of basic roadways and infrastructure. But this common practice is demonstrably harmful to the prospects of eventual despecialization of uses that can be so invigorating and sustaining over time.

A last key component in developing desirable towns is China's careful attention to, on the one hand, deindustrialization of sunset or nonsustainable industries and, on the other, reindustrialization in sustainable or at least long-lasting ways. One way to make decisions about industrialization is to take an asset-building approach. This method, made popular by sociologists in the 1990s, harnesses comparative advantages, associated institutional arrangements, specific skills, individual gifts, and so on, alongside provision for residents of a sense of place, ownership, and opportunity.[27] In several New England communities, asset building has successfully converted a reliance on textile and other outmoded manufacturing into an economy of tourism, biotech, educational development, and medical research.

In conclusion, towns and small cities in China have important roles to play, particularly in urbanizing regions in conjunction with larger cities. They offer or can be made to offer unique qualities of life not found in larger urban areas. In combination with medium-sized and larger cities, they can enhance the attractiveness and appeal of particular regions. However, China suffers from overpopulation in rural regions, not least because of a

pressing need to scale up agricultural production and mechanization. An effective implementation of the new townization plan will require a further culling of under-scaled towns and villages, though the risk is that certain forms of Chineseness, particularly with regard to family relationships, native places, and related rituals of life, will be lost.

26 Saehoon Kim and Peter G. Rowe, "Does Large-Sized Cities' Urbanisation Predominantly Degrade Environmental Resources in China? Relationships between Urbanisation and Resources in the Changjiang Delta Region," *International Journal of Sustainable Development and World Ecology* 19, no. 4 (2012): 321–29.

27 John P. Kretzmann and John L. McKnight, *Building Communities from the Inside Out: A Path Toward Finding and Mobilizing a Community's Assets* (Evanston, IL: Northwestern University Center for Urban Affairs and Policy Research, 1993), 25.

Analysis: Taiqian

Structure of the Countryside

Radhya Adityavarman, Carly Augustine, Jyri Eskola,
Siwei Gou, Shaoliang Hua, Nicolas Lee, Wilfred
Leung, Alexandro Medina, Feng Shen, PG Smit,
Dimitris Venizelos, Zhenhuan Xu, Bicen Yue

MD: 4 cities
Municipalities directly under central government

SPC: 15 cities
Subprovincial cities

OPCC: 17 cities
Other provincial capital cities

PLC: 250 cities
Prefecture-level cities

CLC: 368 cities
County-level cities

Counties

Fig. 1 Urban administrative areas, China, 2011; anything not categorized as an urban area is considered countryside.

Despite its long urban history, China was largely an agrarian society until the second half of the 20th century. Since the founding of the People's Republic of China in 1949, the relationship between the urban and the rural has been continuously transformed by successive political regimes. Each administration has used policies directed at urban and rural areas to further their political and economic aims. The past and present of Taiqian New Agricultural Town record in a specific place the evolution of these national policies.

In China, all land is divided into two kinds of administrative areas: urban and rural (figs. 1, 2). It is important to note that China's administrative system intertwines urban and rural areas: rural areas are in fact embedded in the urban administration (fig. 3). Administrative divisions have profound implications for development policy, in particular because the Chinese central government uses this system to focus on urban or rural development—or both—in accordance with the agenda of the time.

Since China's efforts toward market reforms commenced in the 1980s, the state has taken numerous measures to boost economic development, many of which are based on exploiting rural areas to subsidize urban areas. Indeed, there is a long history of preferential policies toward nonrural residents. Even after three decades of reform, urban residents continue to enjoy a higher standard of living due to support from the state. Policies that promote the urban at the expense of the rural can be divided into three types. The first is capital incentives, in which state-owned banks provide low-interest loans for urban factories and infrastructure construction. The second is labor, where the government restricts free migration to urban areas through the household registration, or *hukou*, system. This system divides Chinese citizens into rural residents and urban residents and thereby restricts migration to urban areas; urban residents enjoy higher-quality social welfare, retirement, labor protection, and health care than do rural residents. The third is land. In China, urban land belongs to the state and rural land belongs to the collective. Land use is controlled by the state land administration, and the two kinds of land have different implications for development, which makes the transferring and mortgaging of rural land almost impossible.

Built land

Urban centers

Borders of Zhongmu County
and Henan Province

Fig. 2   Patterns of urban development in China, 2011.

Since 1949, the overall percentage of the population living in urban areas in China has grown from 10 percent to more than 50 percent (fig. 4). This precipitous rise has its origin in the reforms of 1978, when laborers started migrating to the city to live and work. Because of the *hukou* system, however, not all rural migrants can lawfully reside in urban areas. In 2014, only 37.6 percent of people were registered as urban residents, even though the urbanized population reached 52.6 percent. The 15 percent of people who live in cities but are registered in rural areas therefore do not have equal welfare. At the same time, the ever increasing income gap between cities and rural areas continues to draw migrants from the countryside, resulting in high vacancy rates in rural villages. It is in this context, and fearing that the imbalance will bring about wide social instability, that the Chinese government has promulgated a policy of rural urbanization, aiming to reverse the population flow by creating economic drivers and jobs at the town level.

AGRICULTURAL POLICY AND ISSUES

The character of the Chinese countryside cannot be separated from agricultural production and successive attempts by the central government to modernize it. China's economy is traditionally an agrarian one. Crop production, including rice production, is labor-intensive. The workforce on a single farm would typically be provided by a large family, leading to a close correlation between population and traditional agricultural production. Allocation of land, in many places, is still based on how many sons a family has, a system of distribution based on potential production that has been in place for generations. Because population and output remained in equilibrium, there was little incentive for modernization and little surplus for the state.

The overall trend toward modernization can be broken down into three periods of reform. In the first period, Mao Zedong envisioned a large-scale governmental takeover of agriculture. His Treaty of Friendship Alliance and Mutual Assistance of 1950 was a means of generating

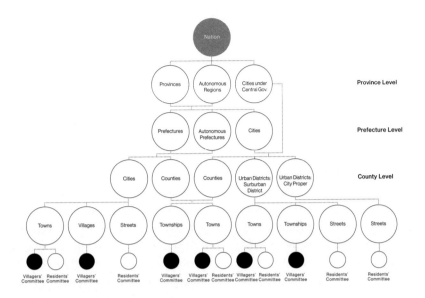

Fig. 3   Administration hierarchy diagram.

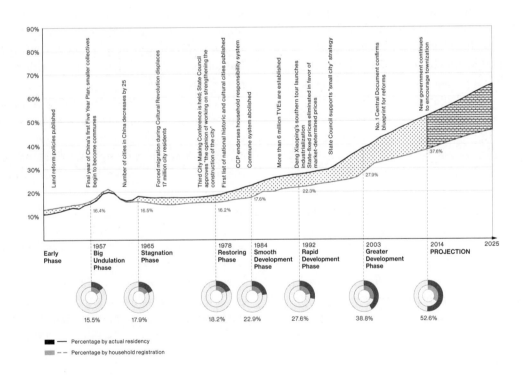

Fig. 4   Percentage of urbanized population, 1949–2025.

agricultural surplus to be used to support industrial development in urban areas. Half a decade later, the Mao government adopted a series of policies for the collectivization of agriculture that would culminate in the Great Leap Forward, which marked the apex of the Socialist transformation of agriculture and led to the collectivization of nearly all farmland by 1962. In this commune system, somewhat similar to the *kolkhoz* arrangement in Soviet Russia, production entities consisted of thousands of workers assigned to production brigades. But this was not a satisfactory solution: village communes were poorly run by inefficient and corrupt top-down management, and the fixed prices and quotas set by the state led to reduced land utilization, since the farmers could not gain any competitive advantage. In the years after the policy was implemented, agricultural production fell by 30 percent. Communal farming was a failed experiment, underscored by the famine of 1959–1961, in which 30 million Chinese lost their lives.

In 1978, the policies of decollectivization, such as the household responsibility system, accelerated agricultural development by abolishing the commune system and returned agriculture to a family-oriented management structure. This second reform gave households small plots along with production quotas. Profit incentives were tied to production and market-determined prices. The land was still owned and allocated by a collective—in the form of the village administration—and farming rights contracts were granted for 15-year periods, but the responsibility belonged to the households, and higher pricing was allowed. This period alleviated some rural poverty, accelerated agricultural production, and also led to the creation of Township and Village Enterprises, which brought some industrial production to the countryside. By the beginning of the 1980s, the standard of living had improved dramatically.

Yet the second reform brought about its own set of negative consequences. The return to family farming worked against the state's policy of population control; since families lost land if they were unable to farm it effectively, family size was closely related to economic standing in the village. By 1993, the initial success of the TVEs had diminished, and the negative changes in rural employment began to affect migration patterns of young villagers to cities. The astounding economic development of contemporary China, rooted in the reforms of the agricultural sector, transformed a top-down planned economy to a market economy. But the rapid urbanization that was a key outcome of this economic liberalization prompted migration from rural to urban areas in one of the largest movements of people ever seen. Thus, by the 21st century, the discrepancy in welfare between the urban and the rural had grown more significant. In addition, land ownership, or the lack thereof, was a complicating factor. China's farmers cannot buy or sell their land, which discourages investment and consolidation into larger and more efficient farms. And because land-use rights are still attached to village residency, an incentive to leave agriculture is inherent in the system, which keeps farm incomes low and gradually withers the countryside.

The third period of reform developed against the growing discontent within rural areas, the urgent need to secure food production, and the aim of reversing countryside-to-city migration. Almost three decades after China abandoned commune-based farming policies, the administration introduced the New Socialist Countryside program of 2006. In his speech to the National People's Congress in March 2006, Wen Jiabao referred to the project as a "major historic task"; he has increased governmental focus on problems related to agriculture, farmers, and rural development and society. New Socialist villages were devised in order to increase production, raise living standards, create a cultured environment, ensure tidy and clean villages, and institute democratic management. In most areas, this initiative culminated in a total reorganization of rural areas, forcefully combining existing villages into entirely new village-town constructions. Denser and more efficient, these entities were meant to liberate land for farming.

A renewed emphasis on rural development is certainly long overdue. The urban-rural income gap has grown since the mid-1990s, and urban income per capita now stands at more than three times rural income, a disparity that is among the largest in the world. Moreover, under China's decentralized fiscal system, the provision of public services has also increasingly favored urban, prosperous areas, disadvantaging rural areas. Rural areas were asked to provide their own basic services—infrastructure, health care, and education—although in many places, rural governments were unable to finance these services.

Despite the radical attempts to reorganize the countryside since the implementation of New Socialist Countryside policies, it seems that little attention has been paid to the efficiency of farming methods.

Fig. 5   Aerial view of Zhengzhou, 2014.

Present-day rural land structures raise numerous questions with respect to transitioning China's agricultural sector toward a more modern industry. Still today, because of the land-ownership rules, China's farms are for the most part very small, about an acre, and the work remains labor-intensive and difficult. If China wishes for its economic growth to continue to be propelled by the migration of labor from the countryside, output per farmer needs to more than double between now and the mid-2040s, and farms must be mechanized. The central government must rethink the current system of creating value through construction. Despite its good intentions, the development process has stagnated, as seen in the production of homogenized social housing, the failure to identify local problems, and the lack of any economically feasible drivers to promote village life in these new communities. To move forward, China must address the problems of rural social structures, demographics, and proprietary rights and adapt a more comprehensive and wholesome approach to delivering value to the countryside.

ECONOMY IN ZHENGZHOU AND ZHONGMU COUNTY

Zhengzhou is the capital of Henan Province, the bread-basket of China (fig. 5). It is located at the crossing point of the country's main north-south and east-west rail lines. Naturally, Zhengzhou is a hub for distribution, manufacturing, and food processing. Since the mid-1990s, the economy has shifted away from raw agricultural production and toward more profitable processed-food factories. Zhengzhou produces a third of the instant noodles and a fifth of the frozen dumplings in China. One of China's three agricultural futures markets is located there, making it one of the most important agricultural trading centers in China. As the GDP of Zhengzhou has been growing, the portion that is basic agriculture has been falling, from 22.6 percent in 2000 to 17.9 percent in 2013 (fig. 6). Compared to the rapid development of manufacturing and merchandise trading, the development of agriculture is slow. Future growth in Zhengzhou will come from advanced industry, with electronics manufacturer

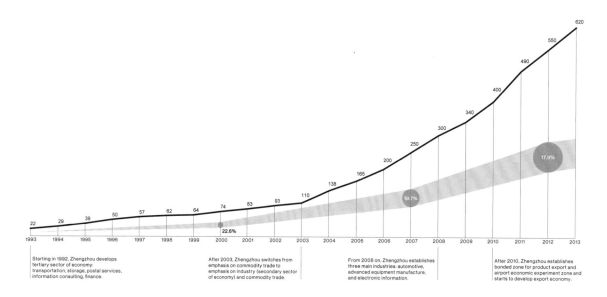

22   29   39   50   57   62   64   74   83   93   110   138   165   200   250   300   340   400   490   550   620

Fig. 6   Economic growth in Zhengzhou (in billions of RMB), 1993–2013.

Foxconn and various car manufacturers setting up sizable factories in the region.

Just beyond the edge of the city, in the eastern part of Zhengzhou, lies Zhongmu County. The city of Zhongmu is the only large urban area in the county. Agriculture and small-scale manufacturing form the basis of the economy, with most of this activity situated in small villages consisting mainly of family-scale farms and light industry. The economic development of Zhengzhou has created an incentive for the younger population to move to and work in the city and send part of their wages home to support their families. Much of the advanced industry and agriculture being developed in Zhengzhou will be located in Zhongmu County.

The incomes of people with different employment and social identities (fig. 7) give a snapshot of the economic structure of the area:

— A disabled person with no income receives from the government a stipend of $18–54 per month.
— A farmer who plants corn on a plot of two to five

mou (a *mou* is about one-sixth of an acre) earns $28–70 per month.
— A farmer who leases a plot of two to five *mou* to a modern farming company earns $39–91 per month, more than by farming the land him- or herself.
— A recent graduate of an agricultural university who works for a modern farming company, such as Chenming Modern Agriculture Group, earns $267–333 per month.
— A villager who assembles iPhones at Foxconn earns $417–583 per month.
— A villager who sells produce in the town food market earns $583–833 per month.
— A contractor with good connections to the local government earns $1,667–3,000 per month.

For comparison, the Chenming Modern Agriculture Group, which rents 10,000 *mou* of land for 40 years (at a cost of $560 million) and invests $50 million in construction, earns $600,000 per month in this single village. The company will recoup its investment in five years.

Disabled villager.

Villager who assembles iPhones at Foxconn.

Farmer who plants corn.

Villager who sells produce in town food market.

Farmer who leases plot to farming company.

Contractor with good connections to local government.

Recent graduate of agricultural university.

Executive at Chenming Modern Agriculture Group.

Fig. 7   Employment of Zhongmu villagers, 2014.

Fig. 8   Zhongmu County Development Plan for 2030.

LOCAL GEOGRAPHY AND REGIONAL DEVELOPMENT PLANS

The policy of consolidating villages into larger agricultural towns, or "townization," is a key aspect of the New Socialist Countryside. This is a policy that is set to be implemented across the county. In Zhongmu County, the four villages of Taiqian, Dongzhao, Yantai, and Heiniuzhang are in the process of being consolidated into Taiqian New Agricultural Town. The land released through this consolidation, which will be converted from traditional small-scale farms to industrial large-scale agriculture, will form part of an ecological demonstration area of 450 square kilometers. The central government's townization policy is intended to foster economic development; the original villages are converted to farmland or other functions. The villagers give half their land to the local government in order to offset infrastructure construction costs for the new town; in return, they receive a plot of land with basic utilities in the new town, where they are required to build a new house following the plans of a government design institute.

Currently, the villages of Zhongmu are spread evenly over the county, since each settlement farms the land in its immediate vicinity (fig. 9). The development plan is distinguished by the new axes and connections that will be formed as infrastructure is expanded and villages consolidated (fig. 10). A band of urban development to the north of Zhongmu is planned to connect Kaifeng to Zhengzhou (fig. 8). To the west is an area for expansion of locales currently devoted to aircraft logistics and distribution, one of the industries singled out by the county.

The area is reasonably well connected to rail and airport infrastructure, with a train station in Zhongmu and a new airport in Zhengzhou. The railway is part of the east-west train network, while the airport aims to be an international distribution center for goods produced in Zhengzhou.

Urban areas

Towns

Villages

Fig. 9 Existing towns and villages in Zhongmu County, 2010.

Urban areas

Planned communities, 2010

Planned towns, 2020

Fig. 10 Planned towns and rural communities in Zhongmu County, 2010.

5km

10km

Zhengzhou-Taiqian

1h 6min

Zhengzhou-Airport

47min

Taiqian-Airport

33min

Fig. 11 Distribution of villages in Zhongmu County, indicating distances from
Taiqian New Agricultural Town to center of Zhengzhou City and airport, 2014.

Village DZ (东赵村)
Population: 1,896
Households: 426 (4.45 ppl/fam)
Agr. Land: 1982亩 (1.32 sq km)
Area: 210,000 sq m
Avg. Income: 6500¥

Village HNZ (黑牛张村)
Population: 1,144
Households: 308 (3.71 ppl/fam)
Agr. Land: 2150亩 (1.43 sq km)
Area: 210,100 sq m
Avg. Income: 3600¥

Village YTS (砚台寺村)
Population: 1,187
Households: 278 (4.26ppl/fam)
Agr. Land: 1855亩 (1.24 sq km)
Area: 172,620 sq m
Avg. Income: 4300¥

Village TQ (台前村)
Population: 1,962
Households: 450 (4.35ppl/fam)
Agr. Land: 2970亩 (1.98 sq km)
Area: 336,000 sq m
Avg. Income: 8000¥

0KM   0.5KM   1.00KM   1.5KM

Fig. 12   Agricultural parcelization for Taiqian, Dongzhao, Yantai, and Heiniuzhang villages, 2014.

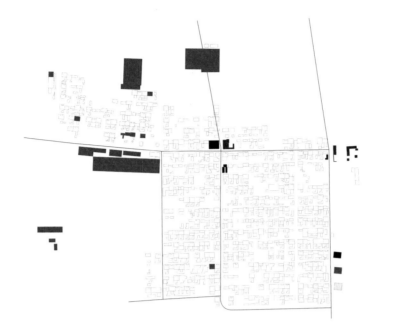

Town Hall
School
Market
Industry/Warehouse
Restaurant
Recycling/Trash

Fig. 13   Programmatic distribution of Taiqian Village, 2014.

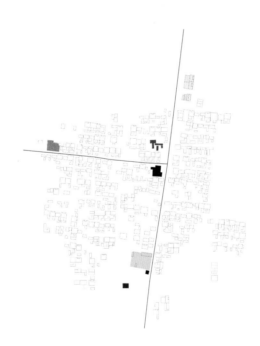

Town Hall
School
Market
Industry/Warehouse
Restaurant
Recycling/Trash

Fig. 14   Programmatic distribution of Dongzhao Village, 2014.

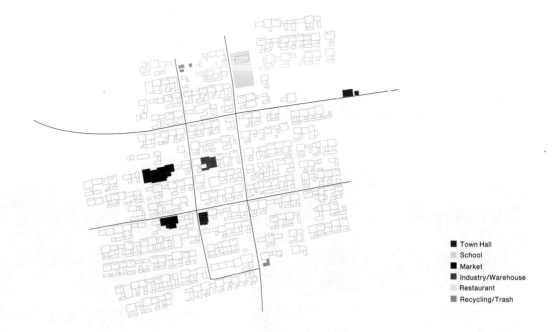

Legend:
■ Town Hall
  School
■ Market
■ Industry/Warehouse
  Restaurant
  Recycling/Trash

Fig. 15 Programmatic distribution of Yantai Village, 2014.

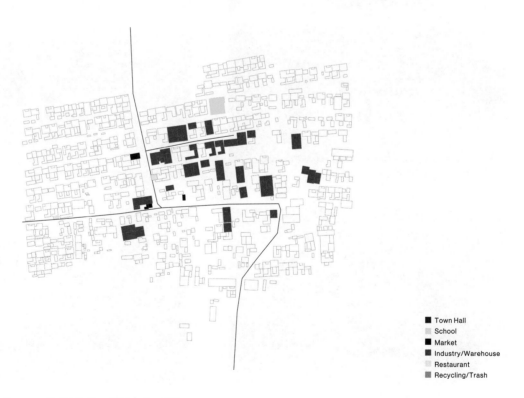

Legend:
■ Town Hall
  School
■ Market
■ Industry/Warehouse
  Restaurant
  Recycling/Trash

Fig. 16 Programmatic distribution of Heiniuzhang Village, 2014.

Residence converted into a warehouse.

Crops drying in the streets.

Farmland and water tank within residential courtyard.

Livestock in residential courtyard.

Facade of traditional courtyard house.

Ceremonial building.

Harvest stored in courtyard.

Leisure farming in courtyard.

Fig. 17   Dwellings, industry, and agriculture in Taiqian, Dongzhao, Yantai, and Heiniuzhang villages.

Harvesting activity on main street.

Water pump facility and community gathering area.

Recycling.

Irrigation well.

Warehouse.

Warehouse.

Old village dwelling for small, disabled family.

Primary school shared between four villages.

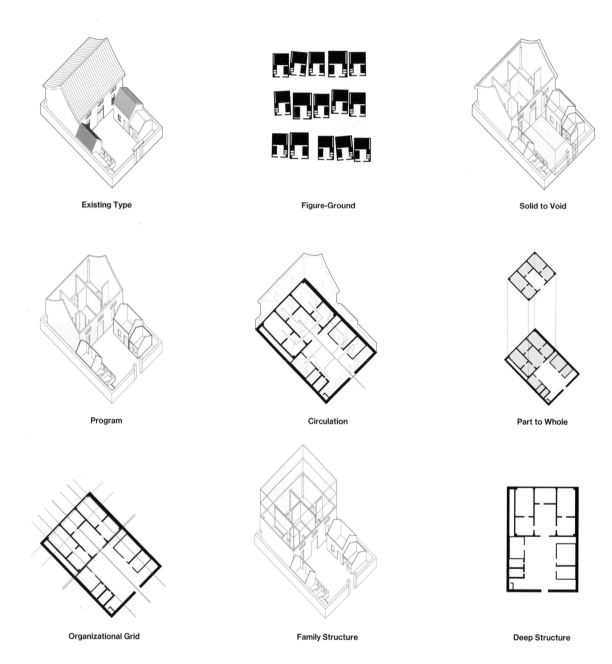

Existing Type

Figure-Ground

Solid to Void

Program

Circulation

Part to Whole

Organizational Grid

Family Structure

Deep Structure

Fig. 18   Analytical study of 1960s courtyard house.

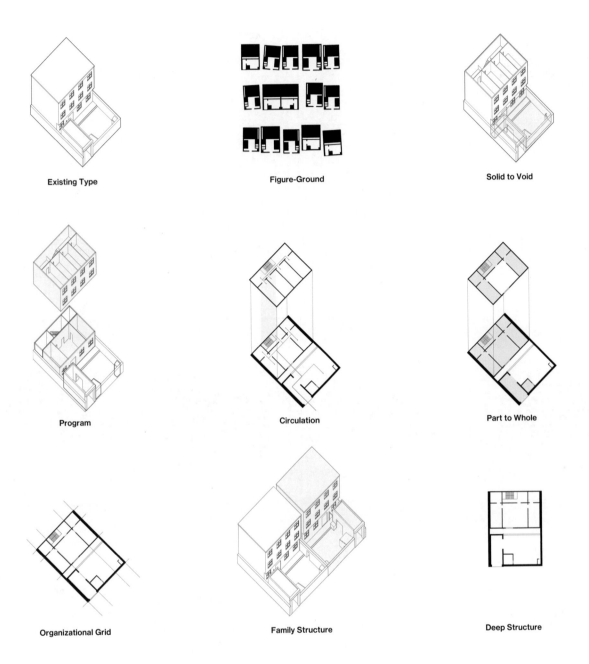

Existing Type

Figure-Ground

Solid to Void

Program

Circulation

Part to Whole

Organizational Grid

Family Structure

Deep Structure

Fig. 19 Analytical study of modern courtyard house.

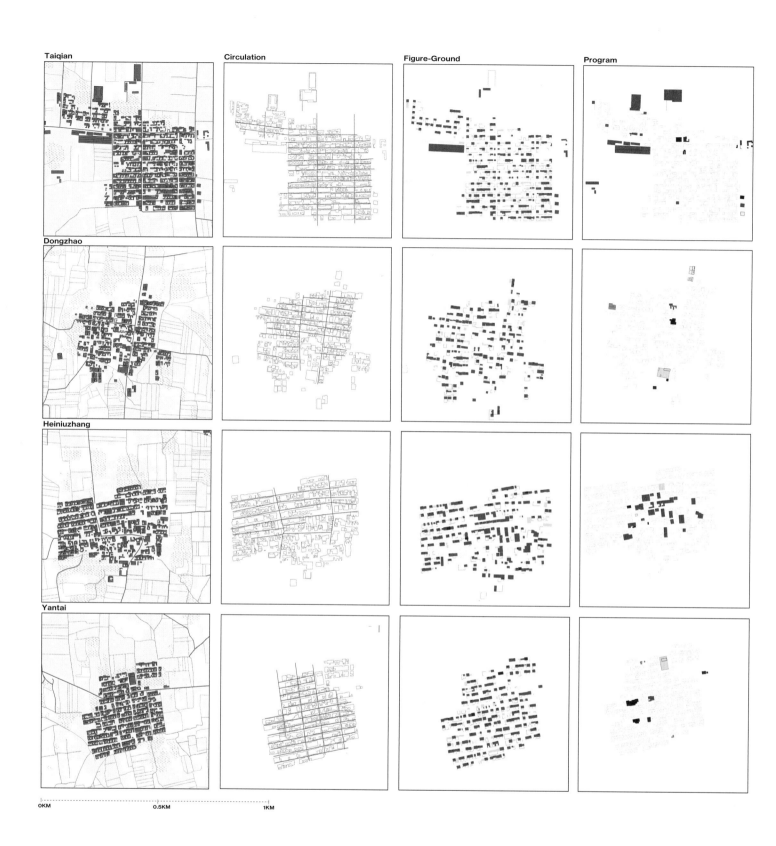

Taiqian Circulation Figure-Ground Program

Dongzhao

Heiniuzhang

Yantai

0KM 0.5KM 1KM

Fig. 20 Circulation, figure-ground, and program in Taiqian, Dongzhao, Heiniuzhang, and Yantai villages.

The villages of Taiqian, Dongzhao, Yantai, and Heiniuzhang own agricultural land that is about six times larger than their built areas (figs. 11, 12). A comparison of the four villages reveals variations in land use and urban structure (fig. 20). The wealthiest village, Taiqian, has the most regular street structure. Most communal programs in Taiqian are situated along the main street; industries are located around the outer edges of the village. In the poorer villages, the street structure is often disturbed by earth dunes and trash piles. Basic infrastructure for water supply and vehicular access is not reliable, especially during the rainy season.

Corn and peanuts are the primary crops grown for market. A close relationship exists between agriculture and living, and spaces are both appropriated and purpose-built for farming (figs. 13–17). During harvest times, crops fill every corner of the villages, from the streets to the interiors of the living quarters (figs. 21, 22).

The dominant type of housing in all four villages is the courtyard house. An older, smaller iteration of this typology generally consists of three buildings with pitched tiled roofs surrounded by a wall. Dwellings of this type can be a hundred years old. Since the mid-2000s, many families have replaced older houses with larger, more modern versions (fig. 23).

In general, the older courtyard houses have a taller, multistory building to the north (fig. 18). This structure and two flanking buildings frame a courtyard. The main building is typically used for living room and bedrooms; the flanking buildings are more flexible and can be used as additional rooms or working spaces. All three structures are enclosed by a wall along the property line with a south-facing gate; the wall defines and separates each individual house. The courtyard is the nucleus of the building, connecting all programs. Family members use the central courtyard for daily activities; more important, it is a productive space for farmers, where produce can be dried, products made, and animals raised. The three buildings are arranged according to a tripartite division known as *jian*, which emphasizes the central room.

A nested relationship of spaces is evident in these courtyard houses. The central courtyard is the dominant space within the house. Within the supporting structures, the central room is the dominant space. Functionally, the central courtyard plays the same role outside the building as the living room inside the building.

The second iteration of the courtyard house, though more recently built, shares the same deep structure, though with two key differences (fig. 19). First, entrance is from one of the side gates rather than from the center of the courtyard. Second, the main building is triple the size of that in the older houses, with kitchen, living room, bedrooms, and utilities on the ground floor, and more bedrooms above. It is typically two to three stories and provides room for up to three generations. However, since rural laborers are moving to bigger cities, only the older generation and the younger generation are living in such houses. As in the older version of the courtyard house, the central open area is a vital social and productive space. Another similarity is the perimeter wall that delineates the property.

The ground floor of the main building follows the *jian* system, with two service rooms flanking the central living room. On the upper floors, however, rooms are disposed along a corridor. Some larger families own several buildings that are connected by means of openings in the exterior wall, allowing the separate courtyard spaces to be connected.

NEW AGRICULTURAL TOWNS

Tushan New Agricultural Town, one of five village consolidation projects underway within the Yaojia Town area in Zhongmu County, is currently nearing the end of construction and offers insight into the design of new agricultural towns. Like Taiqian New Agricultural Town, Tushan New Agricultural Town combines four administrative villages, Tushan, Nianluo, Tangjia, and Leijia (figs. 25, 26). The project as a whole involves 5,500 rural inhabitants. Mechanized agriculture, made possible by a more efficient distribution of land, is foreseen as the new economic driver of the area.

New towns, as planned by the government and designed by local design institutes, are similar in many ways to the megaplot developments typical of China's large cities and suburbs. Semidetached housing units, always oriented in a consistent direction, follow parallel streets to form a distinct rectangular town (fig. 27). Amenities are located in the center of the town as well as in the center of each of the neighborhood quadrants.

Fig. 21   Street in Taiqian Village during harvest, with produce stacked along roadways, 2014.

The town is sited to align with a major road or roads; these routes abut the edge of the community. Within the town, main streets lead off the major roads; a secondary network connects the centers of the town's four quadrants. A ring road defines the boundary of the new town. Green space is located along the secondary roads inside each quadrant, and an artificial lake with parkland sits in the middle of the village.

The amenities in the newly constructed towns include markets, schools, entertainment venues, ancestral halls, clinics, senior homes, libraries, and other services; these are located near green areas and infrastructure. The landscaped areas within the quadrants are accessible only to pedestrians. Informal farming and the drying of produce from surrounding fields often take over the landscaped areas.

The housing units in Tushan New Agricultural Town come in three sizes: 180, 240, and 280 square meters (figs. 28, 29). Unlike the older village residences, these have a yard for parking, drying harvested crops, or growing salable vegetables and fruit. The villagers choose the size, construction team, and building materials. But for the most part, almost all families choose the largest model and relatively low-quality materials.

The new towns as built vary significantly in construction standards and appearance from the depictions offered by their designers. Due to the way in which economic and political policies are enacted in China, the planning and design of the countryside was implemented through a top-down process, while construction is accomplished from the bottom up. This is a common state of affairs in the countryside, by which the local government profits enormously from land transformation but does not take into consideration how the daily life of the villagers is changed.

Residents from the former villages have moved into Tushan New Agricultural Town, but they have retained their previous way of life, adapting newly built spaces to traditional functions, much as residents do in another recent new agricultural town, Madu Shequ (fig. 24). Hedgerows and public gardens have been turned into farmland. Large, formal plazas, not characteristic of agricultural villages, stand empty; they might be used for drying peanuts. But in the end, social and cultural continuity mitigate and absorb spatial discontinuity. Despite the upheavals and massive social change experienced by the villagers, the traditions, practices, and activities rooted in the countryside endure, finding a place in the new urbanized environments.

Fig. 22   Crops drying in entrance gate of modern courtyard house in Dongzhao Village, 2014.

Fig. 23   Typical courtyard house in Dongzhao Village with three pavilions opening to the south, 2014.

Fig. 24   Main square of Madu Shequ, 2014.

Fig. 25 Areas of consolidation for Taiqian New Agricultural Town (left) and Tushan New Agricultural Town (right), 2014.

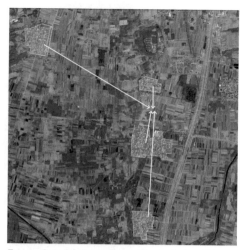

Fig. 26 Consolidation for Tushan New Agricultural Town, 2014.

Fig. 27 Zhengzhou Architectural Design Institute, master plan, Tushan New Agricultural Town, 2013.

Fig. 28   Tushan New Agricultural Town under construction, 2014.

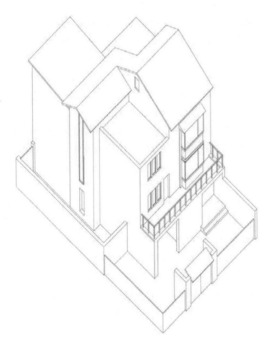

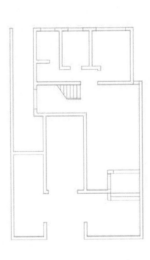

Fig. 29   Zhengzhou Architectural Design Institute, new housing unit of
280 square meters for Tushan New Agricultural Town, 2013.

The Taiqian Studio: An Introduction

These studio projects are based on a typological approach to the problem of the city. An investigation into and redefinition of the city reveals its persistent architectures, or dominant types. Any attempt to define type is an attempt to define what is typical; what is most typical is common to all. Thus type is an effective heuristic device through which to locate commonalities. The goal of a search for what is common in architecture is not formal or tectonic similitude but a commonly held idea that invests architecture with a social and political role.

URBANIZING THE COUNTRYSIDE

After more than three decades of urban-centric developments, which entrenched China's unique rural-urban divide, Li Keqiang announced in 2014 a state urbanization target of 70 percent by 2025 (as compared to 2011's 50 percent), an effort that will affect 300 million people. The increase will not come from the further expansion of large cities but will instead be focused on the growth of rural towns and small cities. This effort to address the unbalanced development of China is a continuation of the Building a New Socialist Countryside program of 2006, set in motion to preempt rural unrest and to secure China's food production by safeguarding farmland from speculative urban developments. The policy also seeks to improve the living conditions and livelihood of the rural populace and, by doing so, to reverse or at least stem rural-to-urban migration.

In the counties surrounding Zhengzhou, in Henan Province, this form of urbanization can be divided into three categories: the redevelopment of villages stranded in the city into higher-density developments; the demolition of villages to make way for urban developments at the edges of the city; and the wholesale demolition, amalgamation, and rebuilding of villages into new agricultural towns. China's rural urbanization should not be confused with the creation of picturesque garden cities in Britain or the suburbanization of the United States that was made possible by private land ownership and the automobile. It is likewise key to avoid the assumption that any form of development must be anchored by a dense urban center, wherever that may be. On the other hand, rural urbanization should also shy away from the uncritical position of preserving every surviving fragment of a village, reducing design action to the mere provision and upgrading of infrastructure and sanitation. The challenge for the studio was to imagine a self-sufficient place able to support a dynamic economy in the countryside, providing cultural and intellectual stimulation and offering a respite from the inequalities and divisions that plague the developmental city; in other words, to imagine the city as a space of equal and plural coexistence.

THE COUNTRYSIDE AS A CITY

The studio focused on the version of rural urbanization that promotes the demolition of several villages and the attendant construction of a larger new agricultural town. The amalgamation of villages enables the sharing of new communal amenities and the efficient introduction of improved services and infrastructure into the countryside, raising living standards to those of urban areas. Yet this strategy also uproots the villagers from their farmland and fails to take into account the millenniums-long cultural and social connection between the two, a bond that is both economic sustenance and spiritual nourishment.

The studio proposed two design responses, one that rejects erasure as a precondition for transformation and one that accepts the demolition and therefore works from a tabula rasa. The first involves the renovation and strategic insertion of the amenities and services that have cohered disparate villages into a single entity, while the second addresses the design of complete new agricultural towns.

The design site is in Zhongmu County, on the outskirts of Zhengzhou. Current rural urbanization plans call for the demolition of four villages—Taiqian, Dongzhao, Yantai, and Heiniuzhang—to form a new community, Taiqian New Agricultural Town. Housing a combined population of 4,400, the new town will include 1,200 dwellings, two schools, a community center, a cultural center, and commercial spaces.

The design task for the studio was to conceive of the restructured villages as a common framework that would allow housing, cultural and communal facilities, and work spaces to cultivate an economy alongside the existing

agricultural base. These proposals were supported by empirical research as well as by a historical and theoretical argument. Indeed, the title "The Countryside as a City" is a provocation that leads to the rethinking of the age-old division between rural and urban, between countryside and city. In order for these new towns to exist as small cities and to reify the idea of the city as a plural and diverse space of coexistence, it must offer a sense of familiarity and community as well as the possibility for surprise and anonymity. It can be compact yet expansive on the horizon, vibrant yet contemplative when required. Perhaps a city envisioned through the countryside offers an alternative to the culture of hyperdensity and congestion of the recent past.

This idea of the city and the challenges of urbanization have corresponding architectural, landscape, and infrastructural problems and responses. In considering the city as a common framework, the studio produced three principal versions of the countryside city—frame, mat, and punctuated field. It is critical to note that these proposals do not react solely to the practical problems of rural urbanization but speculate on whether the concept of polarism in Chinese thought might provide a basis with which to reinvent a cohesive whole—a common framework that brings together architecture and landscape, rural and urban, and city and countryside.

Christopher C. M. Lee

Within the Frame

Carly Augustine, Nicolas Lee

With its rapid urbanization rates and increasing social and economic disparity between urban and rural populations, China is searching for means to bridge the gap between urban residents and rural villagers. The government's goals in urbanizing rural areas include upgrading and consolidating villages to provide better amenities and services, making the land more efficient to improve food security, and developing attractive towns to prevent rural-to-urban migration. This project challenges the government's understanding of rural urbanization with a master plan that harmoniously brings together rural and urban living.

Agricultural production is a part of a villager's cultural identity, defining the activities of everyday life. Village residents are allowed to own land as part of a collective, enabling them to live off this territory. However, state-sponsored rural urbanization strips the land away, eliminating jobs and a way of life in the process. This shift toward rural urbanization is spatially unbalanced and is therefore disconnected from all that is rural. Villagers are forced to change their customs to adapt to suburban life; migration to cities for jobs and new opportunities causes a consistent decline in rural populations; labor-intensive and inefficient agricultural production is a dying industry. The transition has diminished the collective and social dynamics of the old villages and generated a homogeneous living environment.

In the old villages, proximity of dwelling unit to land facilitated daily agricultural activities. This link foments a feeling of ownership over the space, providing identity and order. However, new agricultural towns ignore farming as a cultural act. There is no porosity between landscape and town; instead, leftover space is appropriated to fill the needs of the users. The prevalence of farming over modern luxuries is evident in the new agricultural towns: garages are taken over for crop storage, driveways for gardens, and roads for sorting areas. In both old and new villages,

agricultural activity is integral to social life. Social interaction occurs among heaps of corn, peanuts, and garlic as villagers come together to complete tasks of sorting and peeling. In other words, agricultural production is not seen only as a tool to generate income; it is also a cultural practice, a part of the collective memory of the community.

The project counteracts the vanishing of the collective and social dynamics of the old villages and the creation of homogeneous environments for living. Drawing from the dominant type of the traditional Chinese city, the scalable deep structure of the courtyard house inspires new ways of understanding development within the new agricultural towns. These strategies embrace and preserve tradition while still accommodating the needs of modern urbanization. The concept of the frame, as evidenced in the courtyard house, can be utilized within the countryside as an organizational tool. It separates, contains, and captures images of the landscape that are perceived and can be appropriated by each resident. The frame defines a duality of living, whether ornamental or productive, for a range of demographics by a spatial layering of the landscape at various scales. The frame helps to centralize the ideas of collectivity of the rural villages. In delineating four edges, the frame does not promote a dense urban core but rather creates, with a strong, simple, and clear architectural artifact, an aesthetic and productive object through the use of landscape. Agriculture is a conscious and deliberate way of production as well as a source of beauty. The study of history, philosophy, and urbanism offers a way to reimagine the advent of rural urbanization, providing a basis for new solutions and for alternatives to the conventional way of viewing the countryside as a city.

Satellite view. Villages are consolidated in a single structure that frames different landscapes.

Bands of housing, industry, and commercial buildings form a square.

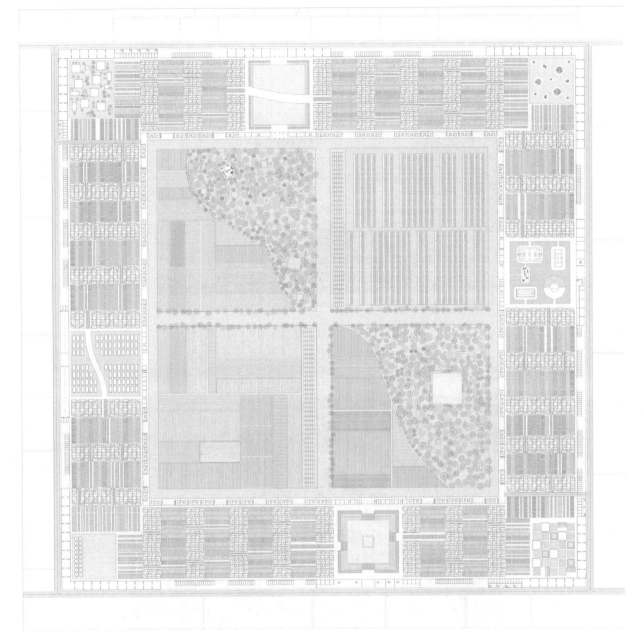

Ground-floor plan. Dwellings consist of solid-void spaces moving from private to public areas.

Each room within the house looks onto the landscape.

Model. Housing forms a field of individual pavilions that almost touch.

Axonometric. Frame consists of bands of housing. Denser apartments combine in the border. Industry occupies the corners.

Common Fields:
Frameworks for Rural Life

Feng Shen, Zhenhuan Xu

In light of the urgent need to mitigate the income disparity between urban and rural residents, in 2006 the Chinese government initiated a set of policies to confront the issue of developing the countryside, constructing new rural towns with the intention of ensuring social stability, providing a strong economic base for the adjacent urban areas, and stemming rural-to-urban migration. However, most of the current rural developments take no advantage of the picturesque landscape or the cultural richness of traditional Chinese villages. Moreover, these new rural communities lack economic drivers to support their vibrancy and future prosperity.

This project returns to the fundamental idea of the city in China. In traditional Chinese cities like Beijing, the urban fabric has a common structure across the whole of the city. The same structure can accommodate a wide range of programs, from the emperor's palace to the common dwelling to the shops, schools, and ceremonial spaces. Similar principles of urban form were prevalent in the countryside, but with an added cultural dimension. If the city was the embodiment of politics and power, the countryside was the reification of the relationship between human and nature.

Under agrarian traditions, the owners of large properties situated themselves politically as highly educated gentlemen farmers. "Cultivation" is not just an alternative source of income for the rural household; it also has the potential to create a meaningful and distinctive built environment. The project also takes note of the collective living of the people's commune period. Even though this policy is no longer in effect, life in rural areas still retains a degree of collectivity.

This project attempts to tackle these socio-economic issues in a holistic manner, starting with the reinvention of the dominant type—courtyard housing. The existing courtyard typology consists of three houses: at the north (the most important), west, and east. The new housing units adopt a two-part modular system.

The house at the north is fixed, while the rest vary to meet the spatial requirements of each family. The courtyard is open, adaptable, and has the potential to become a place for serendipitous social interactions. The ground floor is mainly used for leisure, gardening, and production; living activities are on the second floor. These residences can be built over time without abandoning the underlying typology.

As the housing units are assembled into clusters, they form collective gardens that run north-south. During harvesting, neighbors can work together in all the gardens in a single area. The collective realm comprises the village as a whole. The ground floor becomes a pervasive field that accepts both landscape and social interactions. The courtyard is a plural space, serving for productive collaboration, social interactions, and appreciating the landscape. The cluster also achieves a higher density and reduces land use without undermining living conditions.

Amenities such as primary and secondary schools, clinics, town hall, and so on punctuate the even field of housing. Each facility consists of two parts: a series of scattered boxes that are indifferent to program and a table structure lifted 10 to 20 meters above the ground. This table functions both as a supplemental playground and as a roof for the in-between spaces. The verticality of the table structure maintains the permeability of the ground floor. A series of houses supports agricultural tourism, which in conjunction with the preservation of the existing ecological system forms a linear grove that runs through the site.

The very light built structures and the multiple layers of activities coexist with the current landscape of the site. Most of the existing farmland is maintained as family gardens. The new programs serve as economic drivers, creating functional synergies to help the villages to thrive and develop into self-sufficient communities.

Satellite view. The new village is a delicate field laid over the countryside.

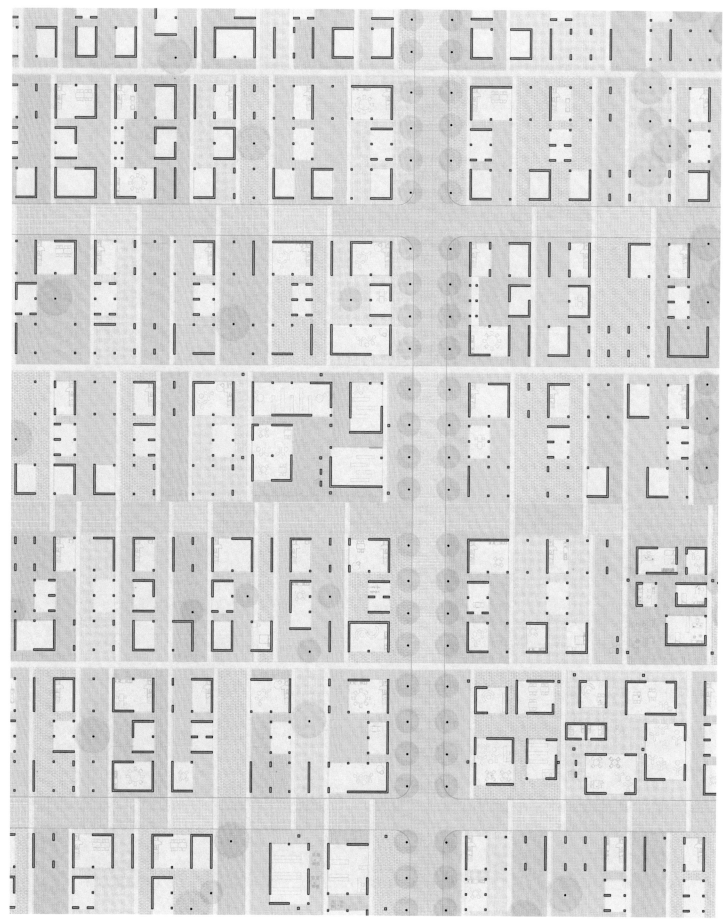

Plan detail. An even grid of structure is adapted to form a variety of building types.

Model. Public buildings and amenities are placed under table structures.

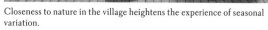
Closeness to nature in the village heightens the experience of seasonal variation.

Non-Urban Apparatus

Shaoliang Hua, Jyri Eskola, Radhya Adityavarman

Starting in 2006, the Chinese government implemented a development policy known as the New Socialist Countryside. This effort was aimed at maintaining the rural population and improving the quality of life in the countryside. But development stemming from this policy stagnated, evident especially in the production of homogenized social housing, failed to identify local problems, and did not create economically feasible drivers for successful village life.

Under newer methodologies, new villages being constructed in Chinese rural areas situate farmers' houses at some distance from their allocated agricultural land. As a result, the current state of the countryside, and construction there, is not linked meaningfully to the traditional rural culture and the landscape. This project proposes an alternative to the current trends and works toward regaining the agency, productivity, and economic independence of the rural.

The institutional framework and its related architectural typology advocate a new live-work mode based on the acknowledgment that a contemporary rural village must accommodate a variety of lifestyles and economic solutions, not just agriculture. The structure of the dwelling as a communal, productive, and spiritual archetype is at the core of this argument, while the new village typology reiterates the condition of the street within its design. This simple architectural foundation provides a familiar and adaptable framework for the emergence of a heterogeneous village life while furnishing a solid and functional background for the contemporary Chinese countryside. The street, where life takes place, is the stage of the everyday. In the project a street connecting two villages forms the spine of the architecture, suggesting a linear reading of urban life. Cross sections support communal spaces, while the central space functions as the heart of the urban apparatus.

A series of parallel walls forms an array of layers perpendicular to the street. This allows for a great degree of visual connectivity and creates a permeability that defines the architectural language of the project. The housing of the old villages is condensed into bands, preserving villagers' property rights yet releasing land that once maintained housing for agricultural uses.

A reinterpretation of the traditional courtyard house, in particular regarding the relationship of the wall to the courtyard, underlies the development of the residential typology. An archetypal wall is proposed as a space in which to restructure domestic inhabitation. Unlike the autonomous unit of the home, the linear archetype is instead a homogeneous bar with a flexible arrangement that borders an open linear courtyard. The inhabited wall becomes a cabinet for the body. The necessary infrastructure—bedrooms, bathrooms, kitchens, laundry, storage—is embedded within the wall. The remainder of the space, the linear courtyard, is freed of any visual or programmatic subdivision and may be occupied and reprogrammed as necessary. When populated with delicate glass pavilions that alternate with small exterior gardens, the courtyard generates a new social interior. Freed from any domestic requirements, the open spaces become clearings that frame and connect to the outdoor landscape, blurring the border between interior and exterior. A second typology, a communal dormitory, features a highly flexible interior for communal production and resting defined by two bordering functional walls. Both single-family and dormitory residences reinterpret traditional communal housing.

Public ensembles are created as residences are multiplied along the street. The single line of interconnected city rooms rethinks urban flexibility. In addition, the concentration of the construction into narrow bars has a double agenda: on one hand, the built band protects the landscape from urban sprawl and forces a consideration of housing typologies; on the other, it provides the community with an architecture that in its flexibility furnishes the capacity for further economic activity.

Satellite view. Cores of existing villages are linked to form two linear towns.

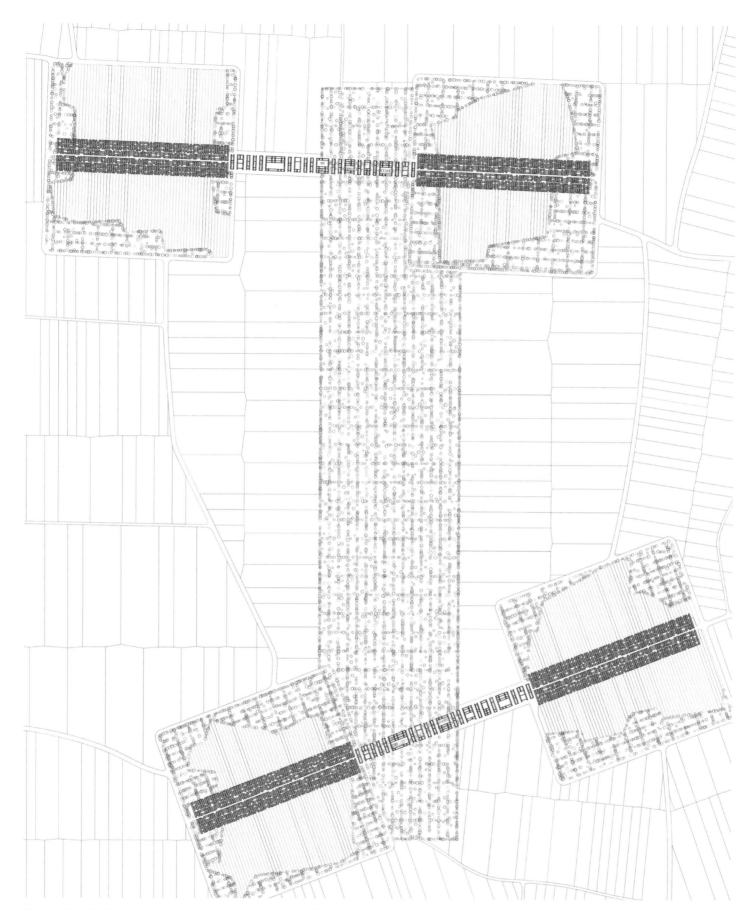

Site plan. The land of the existing village is rehabilitated into agricultural land by the houses/farms. Only traces remain in the landscape.

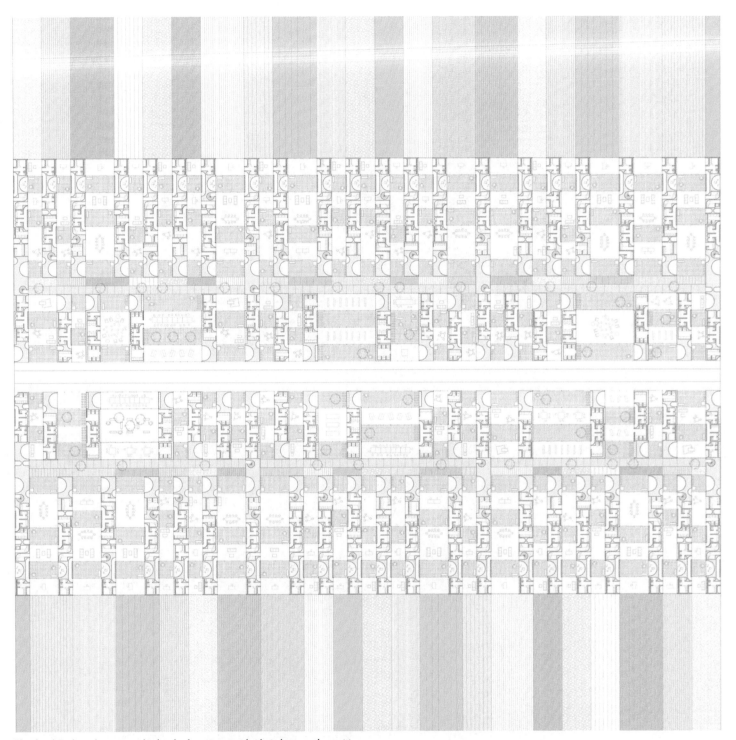

Plan detail. Linking elements are thin bands of apartments, schools, industry, and amenities.

The interior spaces of the house open onto the landscape.

The apartment interior embeds all service elements in the wall.

The Countryside as a City

The new town forms a line in the landscape.

Village

Dimitris Venizelos, PG Smit

The Chinese countryside is rapidly changing due to rampant industrialization and urban migration. The shift from agriculture to migrant working has eroded living conditions and strained family structure in rural villages. The central government has sought to alleviate this situation by combining villages into new agricultural towns. Yet these new areas offer little in terms of the real economic opportunity that is crucial to the long-term sustainability of the village. The raw ingredients of physical, mental, and social well-being are embedded in the small scale of the existing villages and the close relationship to nature and tradition.

This project questions the wholesale demolition and relocation of the villages, proposing instead to maintain their dispersed nature by augmenting the existing communities through a process of selective erasure and strategic insertion. Rural villages weave together agricultural tradition and social life in common spaces. This condition manifests spatially through the employment of every available surface as part of a band of agricultural production and processing. These activities penetrate all strata of privacy, from residential interior to public street. The streets are spaces of social activity and constitute the primary form of public space in the villages.

Large parts of the villages are abandoned and underutilized and need to be cleared or renovated, repurposed, and restructured. The existing fabric is comprised of an orthogonal grid that delineates strips of housing. The blocks are elongated to such an extent that they read as bands of fabric. Based on this ribbon structure, the project proposes a selective erasure of buildings along a single street to free land for development. The strips of liberated land are restructured through the insertion of new program; on the edges of the bands are buildings with a reduced footprint, and to the center are strips of agricultural land.

The plan consists of two primary elements, the bands forming horizontal strips and staggered perforations that create a secondary circulation system. The bands layer three components: new rental housing; productive and recreational landscapes (fields, community gardens, gathering spaces, and large surfaces for drying and processing); and new small-scale artisanal spaces. The bands not only create much-needed production and social spaces for the villages but also offer a platform for visitors to engage with agriculture and production first hand. New infrastructure, housing, amenities, and production spaces become the foundation for diversified economic activity centered around ecotourism. An overlay of light manufacturing works in tandem with organic show gardens for passive recreation.

The bands suggest an alternative reading of the village. Horizontally, the bands draw landscape in and frame the villages through the lens of landscape. Vertically, the village is perceived as an alternating sequence of old and new, with the new buildings serving as filters for this transition. In order to increase permeability of the fabric, as well as access to the bands, the existing village blocks are perforated by passages that use vacant or underutilized lots.

Within the bands, the new housing units are arranged in a sawtooth structure. Pockets of open space on alternate sides are shaped by the buildings' geometry, forming an elongated version of the traditional courtyard house. These are either private courtyards facing the agricultural land or small, public open spaces that serve as extensions of the street.

Infrastructure, services, and amenities are inserted strategically and surgically, at once restructuring the villages and projecting them forward. Specialized but diverse economic activities optimize land use and also create a range of employment opportunities; a more robust base of revenue; and enriching experiences, products, and services for the surrounding urban areas. In sum, the project offers an alternate vision for the countryside that extends into China's future a past that has not been forgotten.

Satellite view. Existing villages are preserved though selectively erased and reconstructed.

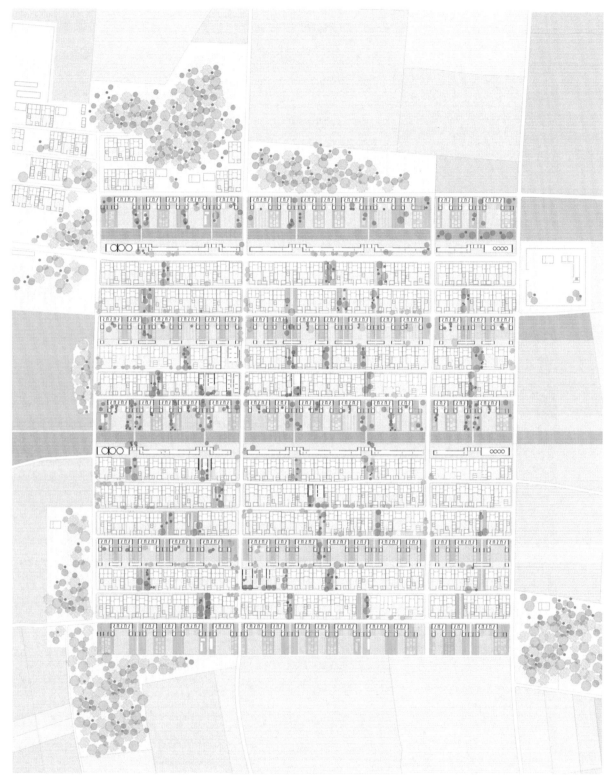

Site plan. East-west bands and north-south routes make the village a cohesive whole.

Strips of housing form gates between farmland and village territory.

Streetfronts alternate with courtyards.

Fragment axonometric. Workshops and housing flank farmland.

Model. New amenity buildings fill voids in the existing village fabric.

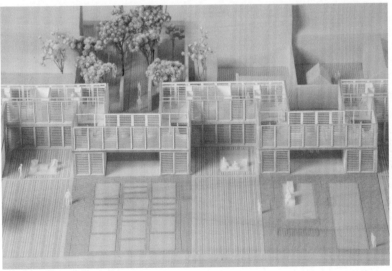

Model. Apartments overlook gardens and fields.

The Collective Frame

Alexandro Medina, Wilfred Leung

The countryside as cultural origin has long been embedded in the Chinese mindset. It exemplifies a life immersed in the landscape. Rural villages are characterized by an intricate relationship between dwelling and place of work, with houses opening up to receive harvests brought in from the fields. A community of individuals comes together to participate in the harvest.

But the current model of rural urbanization in Zhongmu County severely disrupts rural culture. The attempt to urbanize villages severs the close connection between dwelling and place of work, and immersion in the landscape is basically nonexistent. The new model is one of urbanization through the collapse of the traditional rural village structure.

This project seeks to plan villages as authentic places derived from the relationship to the natural environment, places that achieve social cohesion around agricultural ideals. The project highlights celebratory moments of communal life to reassert the value of agriculture in the rural context. It returns to the villagers the innate desire to be connected with the land that feeds and nourishes them; it brings back to the village its relationship to nature by preserving and enhancing existing connections to the landscape; and it offers an alternative to the villages' increasing dependency on outside resources.

The notion of framing activities offers a way to establish spaces for communal acts at various scales. The courtyard house, long the dominant type in rural areas, reduces privatization and encourages collective living. Ties between family members, partners, and neighbors promote a collective lifestyle within these enclosed units. The spatial order and social ties of the basic courtyard house, when aggregated, also generate a common framework for collective life. The dispersion of one basic unit, with a clear organization, can accommodate a wide variety of events and retain a high level of independence while fostering a deep structure through which the village can be understood, designed, and reconstructed.

The design follows a model of dispersion similar to that of the courtyard house. Four pavilions frame a central courtyard that is shared between members of the family. The design declares that the courtyard is a fundamental component of rural livelihood. Four family units then frame a dining space in the central communal area. The dwelling pavilions thus define both an interior private sector and a communal public platform. Demarcated on the street side are harvest courtyards that provide a space for showcasing the season's hard work as well as for gathering in collective production.

This framework leaves no leftover spaces. Gardens form a productive carpet that coheres dwelling pavilions, allowing room for villagers to retain their intimacy with the land and also exercise greater control over their livelihood. The consolidation and transformation of rooms that serve single functions into celebrated communal areas both reinforce social cohesion and increase densification.

A main canal that passes through the four village centers, a shared infrastructure forming another frame, unites the villages. Within this figure are all agricultural fields owned by the villages. The canal is also an economic driver, bringing with it shops and retail. In addition, the shops frame the open rooms, with the line of the canal cutting through to provide parcels of agricultural land for tourists to visit.

This model of urbanization respects the ideal of the collective and proximity to the landscape at the scale of the family, the neighborhood, the community, and the village. Life within the new rural model is the result of the collective efforts of villagers and tourists. The remaking of the rural is thus itself a communal act. It allows architecture and urban space to be first and foremost social and political constructs defined by the inhabitants.

Satellite view. Common area of mechanized agriculture links the four villages.

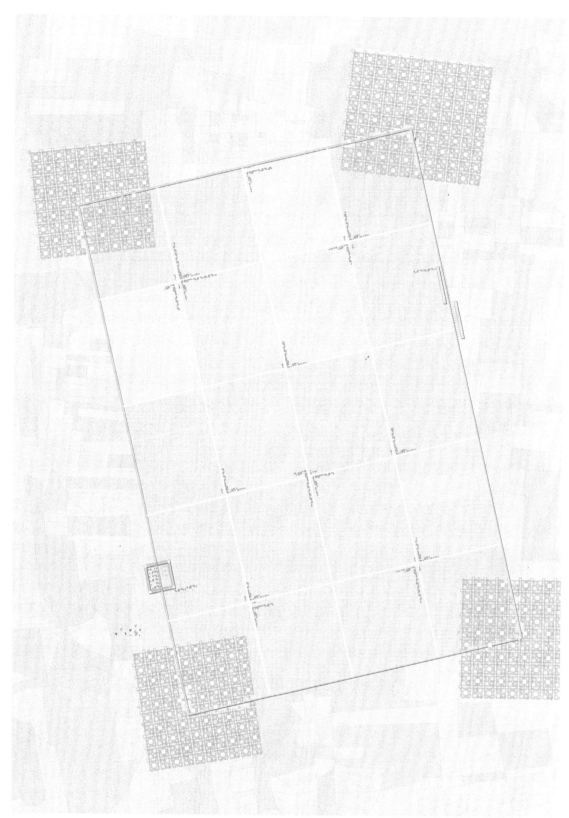

Site plan. The central area is delineated by an aqueduct, which connects
the centers of each village.

Plan detail. Canals cut through the villages.
Hydrology manifests physically in the countryside.

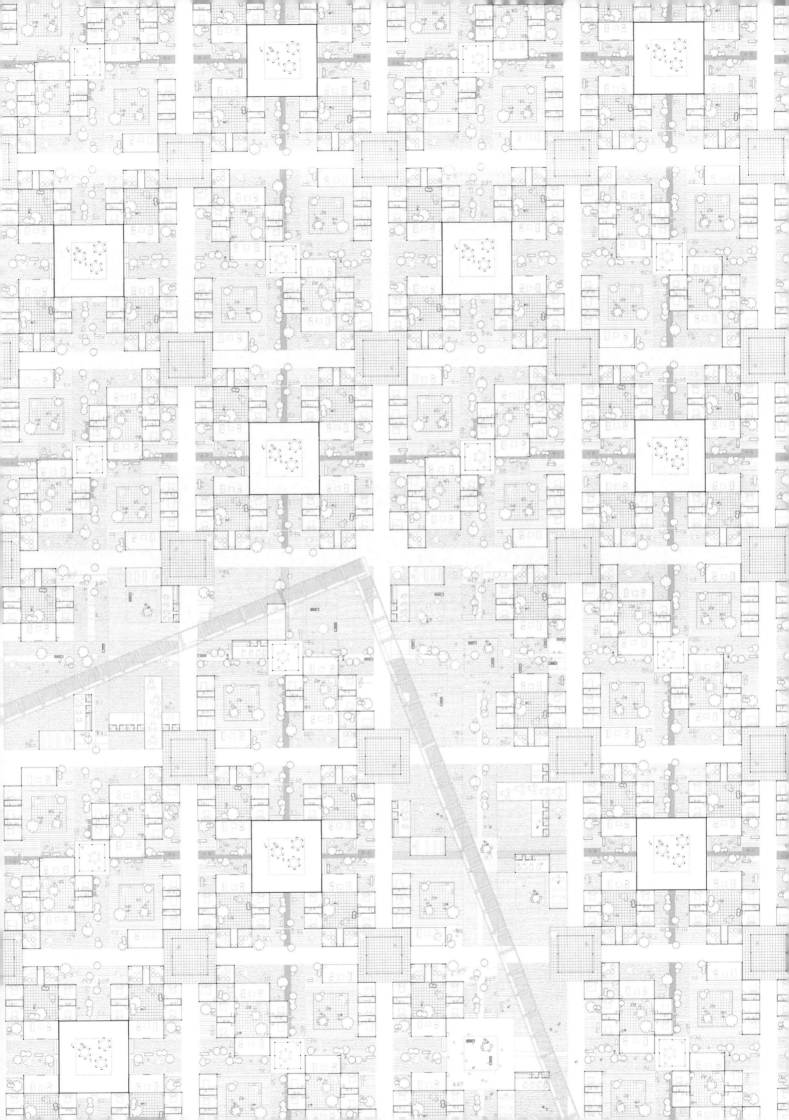

Model. Cluster of four dwellings and common area signals an extended family or neighborhood area.

Enclosed courtyards mark more intimate domestic space.

Taller structures indicate common dining areas.

The City as a Field

Bicen Yue, Siwei Gou

China has taken two approaches to rural urbanization: consolidation of multiple villages into a single town and preservation and improvement of natural villages. This project takes another tack: it attempts to harness the potential of the agricultural field. One of the most important ideas in Confucian ideology is the concept of an all-inclusive oneness. It is a bioethical and familial oneness, from nature to society and from society to statehood, that is embedded back into a self-generated nature as a self-justified whole. Humankind is included and embedded within the universe, leading to an intimate relationship between nature, human, and household. Chinese villagers prioritize the relationship between humankind and nature over relationships between people. Thus, the countryside has become a place where a household has its own farmland interspersed among other families' plots. Confucian philosophy is manifested in the design of human habitat.

The city is often associated with density, compactness, and centrality, while the agricultural field is identified with sparseness, fragments, and flatness. In the project, the seeming disadvantages of the field provide what is needed to construct a city of largeness and multiplicity. Limited density offers the possibility to prioritize relationships between humanity and nature. Voids and fragments become productive surfaces and islands of discovery. Large distances amplify the prominent role of the landscape over that of infrastructure and architecture. Fluidity and flatness encourage physical movement.

The starting point is the economic strategy implemented by local governments, which presents a threefold challenge. First, the strong relationship between villager and land must be regained. Second, the land taken from the villagers for agriculture-related economic development must be agglomerated to achieve more efficiency. Third, a structure that is highly adaptable to the rapid transformation of China's political and economic development yet prevents further speculative development must be imagined. The spatial structure of the project allows rapid transformation between the private and the collective to occur without altering the basic configuration. As family groupings, sources of income, and political-economic structures shift over time, the private-collective relationship changes accordingly, modifying the overall form. Regardless of how much reordering the land undergoes, privately farmed land remains associated with its homestead and collectively farmed land can be consolidated as a single entity.

In the traditional Chinese courtyard house, the spatial alternation between house and yard both strengthens the relationship between humanity and nature and also creates social and familial hierarchies. Passages between homesteads give freedom to use the yard privately or openly and publicly, promoting the development of joint household businesses. In this way the project validates the reciprocal relationship between the courtyard house and agriculture.

Amenities share a common grammar and a recognizable structure. Public activities take place on floating slabs in the center of the agricultural fields. The amenities are not defined by precise functions but respond to changing necessities. The small punctuators of the amenity platforms have determined serving radii: no one needs to walk more than 12 minutes or bike more than 3 minutes to access any of the programs. As landscape changes over time and season, the amenities remain, suggesting a contrast between landscapes and structures, changing and still.

The innate characteristics of the field offer an opportunity to create an enjoyable landscape with dispersed communal services. The project provokes an alternative way of life—a nonstop lifestyle of programs more attuned to daily and seasonal rhythms. The properties of the field give birth to a new understanding of the city, an understanding in which the city is a space of coexistence that eschews hyperdensity, that uses landscape and agriculture as the dominant agents in an alternative economic and spiritual life.

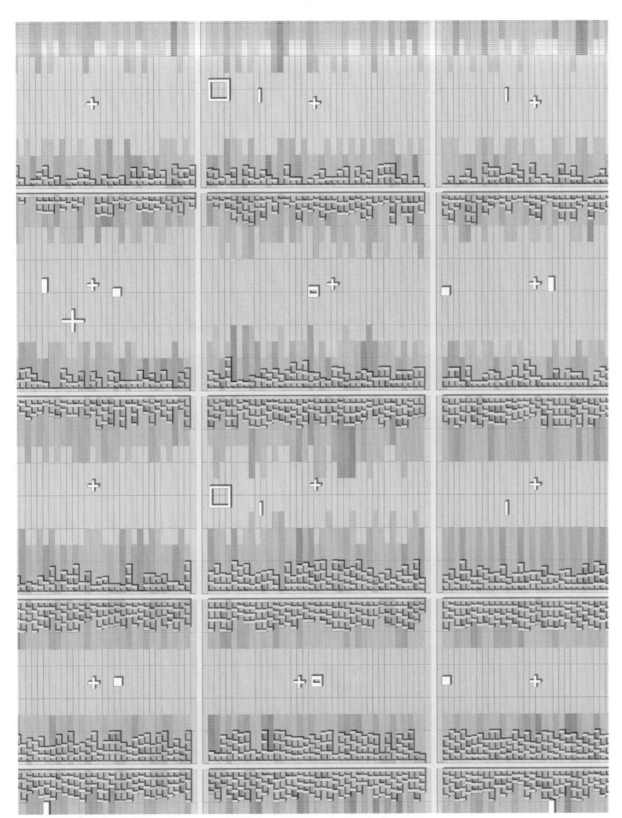

Plan. The project neither consolidates nor preserves the existing villages but proposes the model of the field.

Axonometrics. Cinema and market hall are among the public amenities that punctuate the agricultural fields.

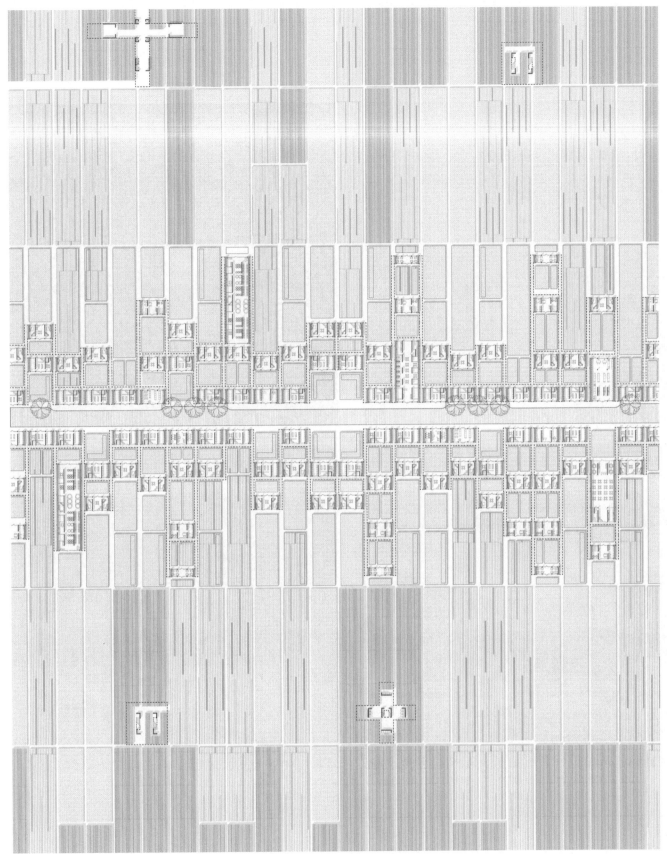

Fragment plan. The boundary between collective and private land fluctuates, thereby indexing economic change.

Funeral home, cinema, and other public amenities share a grammar and a structure.

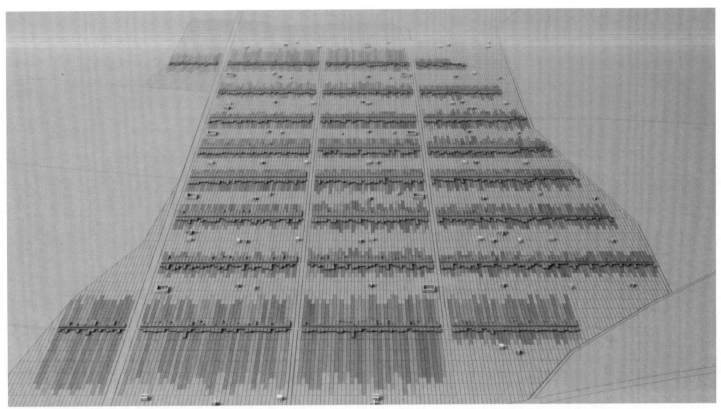

Model. Development is spread evenly across the entire territory of Taiqian.

Image and an Idea of Place

Simon Whittle

A short walk through a contemporary city can leave many different impressions. A harborside view of grand cargo ships and glossy magazines can speak of global economic flows and the city as a place of trade and industry; a glimpse up a building to a set of gables and down to the setback between facade and street can speak of the shared and negotiated resources of light and air and the political associations that divide them equitably; the various markets, apartment towers, and shops can speak of a shifting cultural and economic history. How is one of these ideas of a city to be captured and defined, the relationships forming these ideas depicted in a way that illustrates and reveals? Of equal importance, how is a viewer to depict an idea of the city when confronted with its polyphony? Perhaps it is within the image that he or she may find a way forward for both of these questions. Within the confines of the frame and the singularity of the view lies the potential of the fragment to capture an idea of place, a fragment that might illuminate a wider whole without diminishing its richness or complexity. Much of the studio work of the Harvard GSD AECOM Project on China was focused on how to achieve this type of depiction of place.

It was during the course of the artistic experiments of the 19th century that the city ceased to be represented as a singular image or idea and became a complex, multivalent composite of discrete stories, traces, and artifacts. Both the painting and the novel offered forms capable of conveying the disparate characters and views created by tectonic shifts in technology and society. In the 20th century, photography, collage/montage, and literature were the mediums used to explore and dissect the relationships present in the modern metropolis.

A brief paragraph in Robert Walser's short story *The Street (1)*, written in 1919, describes the author in the midst of a crowd:

> I wanted to speak with someone, but found no time; sought some fixed point, but found none. In the midst of the unrelenting forward thrust I felt the wish to stand still. The muchness and the motion were too much and too fast. Everyone withdrew from everyone. There was a running, as of something liquefied, a constant going forth, as of evaporation. Everything was schematic, ghostlike, even myself.[1]

Walser's writing illuminates a type of estrangement felt within the city, that of separation from the crowd into an internal consciousness. It is a definitive and universal experience of modernity and its changing cities, found as much in the new conurbations of Asia as in the urban areas of Europe at the turn of the 20th century. Walser does not present the experience as a negative one, a peaceful interiority disturbed, but as a different manner of interiority, one that is found amid the bright sights and sensations of the metropolis. It is a new world full of radically altered relationships, all presenting themselves to be seen and to be described. The lasting impression Walser leaves is a coupling of the act of withdrawing from a crowd, retreating internally, with the act of seeing through things, as if all is transparent. Estrangement enables the act of looking: it sets up a distance, a glass pane, that whether artificial or not enables the observer to observe differently.

Estrangement is not just one of the defining experiences of the contemporary city, it is also a distinct exponent of its representation. Artists have used estrangement, or the creation of distance between art and viewer, to create a space of reflection, a critical space, where the nature of the subject matter may be questioned. This is not so much a simulation of the experience of estrangement as a way of allowing the viewer to enter into an understanding of the conditions that bring it about. A close reading of five works of art—from the 17th century to the present, in Western and Eastern traditions, using various media—shows how this effect may be intentionally constructed and used to present the ideas contained within the work. Each does it in a different manner and with a different element of the image. Manet's *Un bar aux Folies-Bergère* uses surfaces to dissolve depth and set up inconsistent relationships for the viewer; Stephen Shore's *U.S. 97, South of Klamath Falls, Oregon* uses the frame of the photograph to betray the constructed nature of the composition, especially with the resulting adjacency of an image inside an image; Jeff Wall's *A view from an apartment* controls setting to a minute degree, raising questions of artificiality; Mies van der Rohe's perspective, drawn for the Friedrichstrasse Skyscraper competition, uses montage—and in particular the choice of composite image—to initiate an estrangement from the object that is concluded by his architecture. Offering a contrast is Shi Tao's landscape painting. This work does not aim to introduce distance between the piece and its viewer; rather, it offers a simulacra between experience and inscription that results in an understanding of the conceptual underpinnings of the place depicted.

---

1   Robert Walser, *Selected Stories* (New York: New York Review Books, 2012), 124.

The establishment of distance or, in the case of Shi Tao, experience is an initial step that allows for a deeper expression of an idea of place. It is a way of allowing, even directing, the viewer to see. It provides a focus on the relationships and conditions that structure a place rather than on the ensuing forms. It filters sensations by organizing them visually, giving them a coherence through composition, emphasizing what might be overlooked. The five works presented here engage their subject matter with a particular acuteness of vision. The contemporary urban condition is revealed; issues of social change, global flows of capital, alienation, peripheral landscapes, media-saturated environments, and discontinuity are depicted. What can be found in these works is insight, or insights, not just into the contemporary city but into the nature and role of the image within a design project, that is, where its projective qualities are required.

The pursuit of insights beyond immediate surface impressions is analogous both to an idea of place and to an idea of the city that has been a touchstone throughout the three briefs that make up the Project on China. To generate an idea of place is to develop a conceptual definition of a physical environment. This idea is produced by means of reading the material, cultural, historical, and social layers that constitute a place. It is propositional in nature and must be argued for. Images are particularly suited to the articulation of an idea of place and capture the relationships and conditions found within the contemporary city. The five works here have the potential to be both spatial and social; although they are fragments, or moments, they can explicate a whole truth. Critically, they allow for an awareness of the viewer's own subjectivity by making conscious the act of looking. Its capacity for interpretation is as much an asset in the process of viewing as its immediacy.

It would be futile to focus too much on the techniques of how this is accomplished. Our visual language changes far more quickly than our verbal one, and it is patience and dedication and searching—rather than a repetition of formula—that can lead to a new way of looking and making. The artworks presented are exemplars more than lessons. They offer particular approaches that are specific to certain historical contexts, and so it is not so much the way of doing that is to be emulated as the way of thinking and seeing. Reading each image through a single constituent element—surface, frame, background, texture, montage—brings a greater clarity to the mechanics of that image and the reasons for its efficacy.

To express an idea of place is to ascertain an essence of its nature. This act is both analytical and projective. A larger motive, therefore, in the context of the Project on China, was to explore the idea of place—three distinct places—within the images of the projects. By means of various approaches, the student projects were represented in a way that established a reading of their context, conveyed the idea of the city, and offered a depiction of the design itself. In this way, the students presented conceptual arguments alongside their subjects, often framing them. The use of estrangement within the image was key in this regard: establishing a certain distance established at the same time a critical space of the project. This distance manifested itself even in the studio's approach to drawing, which pursued a certain precision and objectivity as a buffer or foil to the nuances of the image within the project. The orthogonal line drawings resolutely show structure and its potential for acting as a framework.

SURFACE:
UN BAR AUX FOLIES-BERGÈRE, 1882

A well-trodden narrative in Western art charts the trajectory from figuration to abstraction. The materiality of a painting's surface is no longer solely that which defines form and color; it is a thing in itself, detached from a pictorial unity created by laws of perspective and the imitation of the real. To put it another way, no longer are viewers looking *through* the surface of a painting into a scene. Instead, the gaze stops *on* the surface, where color, form, and texture operate in a different realm and under different rules. The breaking of pictorial unity creates a conceptual space where objects or forms on the surface are juxtaposed with, enrich, or plainly ignore the surrounding pictorial space, giving the artist a new expressive language.

Edouard Manet's *Un bar aux Folies-Bergère* marks a transition along this trajectory (fig. 1). On the one hand, it presents legible pictorial space; on the other, objects and surfaces in that space actively rebel against it, forming a counternarrative that leads to a critical idea of place. The tension between surface and depth (or traditional pictorial space) creates a profound sense of unease in the viewer. Observers are not allowed to enter the scene; forced on them is a remoteness in which the relationship between subject, context, and viewer is openly questioned. It is by means of this questioning that the image forms a critique

Fig. 1 Edouard Manet, *Un bar aux Folies-Bergère*, 1882, oil on canvas, 96.0 × 130.0 cm.

of the city, in this case late 19th-century Paris, and constructs an alternate idea of place. *Un bar aux Folies-Bergère* is a fragment of modern life, distilling into a single image a set of relationships that reveal a certain truth about the nature of the contemporary metropolis.

This alternate idea of place is that of Paris as a city of surfaces. It is no longer a conventionally perspectival city with depth of space but rather an overlay of shimmering surfaces, juxtaposed and illuminated under the evenness of the gaslights that starkly adorn the columns of the theater. The prominence of the surface is achieved in three different ways. The first is flatness, which collapses depth into layered surfaces. There is very little shading on the objects, just a hint of volume, giving each the quality of a cutout. The foil on the champagne bottle has the same presence as the gold bracelet, the girl's necklace, the frame of the mirror: no hierarchy of importance is betrayed. The room is not defined as a space but as a series of backdrops placed one after the other: bar, barmaid, mirror, reflection of barmaid, reflection of man, reflection of audience. The second method is the materiality of the paint itself. Manet labors to make manifest the presence of the paint: it is scraped and smudged onto the canvas thickly, insisting that the viewer acknowledge that the impression of the scene is also just paint applied to a flat surface. The third technique to draw attention to the surface is the fact that the majority of the painting is of a mirror, a single plane. The dirt and clouds on the mirror, which indiscriminately obscure the reflection, help to bind the many layers together and reveal to the viewer that the entirety of the events portrayed is witnessed in the reflection of a single mirror behind a lone girl standing at a bar.

The prominence of the surface in the picture eradicates the possibility of reading its structure in conventional terms. A new way of ordering pictorial space must be established, one that relates more to a two-dimensional plane of relationships. Manet structures the image with a series of horizontal and vertical bands. The strict horizontal parallel lines assure, as T. J. Clark describes, "the orderly unfolding of the real world to the eye, band after band—counter, frame, counter, balcony, pillars—until the picture stops."[2] This ordering of space, however, creates an impossibility that makes the viewer question the relationships in the scene again and again: who is the man at the bar, is it a reflection of ourselves, the viewer, it cannot be, the man is in the scene, but who is he?

This questioning is found in the relationships between surfaces, in particular between the people standing in front of the mirror and their reflections within the mirror. Both the look of detachment on the face of the barmaid and her centrality in the composition are distorted in the mirror's reflection. Although it hangs straight on the wall, the mirror reflects everything askew. It appears to be a window onto a parallel world, one in which the barmaid leans slightly forward, as if talking to the customer. In the non-reflected scene, she is impassively upright, facing the viewer. The diagonal world, then, presents the viewer with a version of him- or herself. For is not the viewer the man in the hat talking to the barmaid? T. J. Clark writes that this moment is "a texture of uncertainties" that suggests

> how easily doubts about looking accumulate in front of *Un Bar aux Folies-Bergère*, doubts of various kinds, all reinforcing one another. What begins as a series of limited questions about relationships in space is likely to end as scepticism about relationship in general.[3]

"Doubts about looking" is the essence of estrangement in the image. These doubts work to distance the viewer from the picture, allowing a critical inspection of the general set of relationships portrayed.

What are the general relationships in the painting, and what is the milieu under observation? Late 19th-century Paris was a rapidly modernizing city with an emerging middle class. The bright lights that illuminate the Folies-Bergère also shine on a clash of classes and genders, as women of a lower class serve customers, typically men, of a higher class. Manet taps into this awareness of class by making the subject of the painting someone who is typically invisible to those viewing it. In the painting, unlike in real life, the viewer cannot *not* notice the girl behind the bar. But the painting goes further. In its creation of doubt, it prompts the viewer to question his or her role in this set of relationships. The man reflected in the mirror—the viewer of the painting—receives the girl's gaze. Even in this gaze, however, doubt persists. Perhaps she is not looking at anything at all. She seems absent and detached from her surroundings, purposely disengaged from her work. This separation from the core of the painting speaks directly to the nature of service work in the modern city.

Manet's complex composition of surfaces reflects not the Folies-Bergère but a version of modern Paris in which

---

2   T. J. Clark, *The Painting of Modern Life: Paris in the Art of Manet and His Followers*, rev. ed. (1984; repr. Princeton, NJ: Princeton University Press, 1999), 253.

3   Clark, *Painting of Modern Life*, 251.

Fig. 2   Stephen Shore, *U.S. 97, South of Klamath Falls, Oregon*, July 21, 1973, chromogenic color print, printed 2002, 45.1 × 55.7 cm.

social order is displayed and the condition of life in the modern city is made visible. The impression of this parallel world is heightened by the disinterest and detachment of the barmaid. This bearing was characteristic of the modern city, with its overstimulation, noise, and feeling of alienation. The final surface, or backdrop, is the crowd, a multitudinous sea of black hats bored at the trapeze act offered in front of them.

FRAME:
U.S. 97, SOUTH OF KLAMATH FALLS, OREGON, 1973

What does a photographer leave out when taking a photograph? How does that uncompromising cutting point, the frame, alter the viewer's understanding of what remains within? Stephen Shore's *U.S. 97, South of Klamath Falls, Oregon*, from his series *Uncommon Places*, demonstrates the power of this decision in image making (fig. 2). The fixing of the view can be used to create an obvious artificiality that leads to a distancing from the subject

matter and sets up a critical space of the image.

Two dominant and contradictory compositional forces are at work within this image. A centralized perspective draws the viewer's eye ever deeper into the photograph; simultaneously, the outer frames, first of the image edge and next of the billboard, with their wider view stop the gaze from narrowing. The seamless ease of the unfolding landscape—a form of representation with traditions in the picturesque—is jarringly juxtaposed to the artificiality of the construction of the image. The contrast, and consequently the expanded idea of place, lead to a wider critique, a counternarrative to the myths of the American landscape in the West. Determining the special within the generic is a project of Shore's photography as well as of those close to him within the discipline, notably Lewis Baltz, Thomas Struth, and members of the Düsseldorf School. The title of the series, *Uncommon Places*, speaks directly to the distinct sameness found in the rural and suburban landscapes of cities in the remote United States.

Photography achieves framing in two different dimensions. The first is space—only what is contained in the viewing angle of the lens is captured in the photograph—and the second is time—only the moment of exposure is captured, with the level of detail dependent on that length of exposure. Both of these aspects result from decisions made by the photographer: where the camera is situated and pointed, when the shutter release is triggered. The act of taking a photograph separates the image from its existence in space and time, hence its nomenclature: we *take* a photo. However, the decision to separate a view and a moment from the continuum of reality is not a simple act of editing; it allows for a new set of visual relationships to be made.[4] Reality is translated into surface, which in turn changes the understanding of that reality—a process that is not so different from Manet's mirror. While not every photograph calls attention to its artificiality, Shore's image makes the viewer aware of its own construction through an overt manipulation of the framing of space and time. It is a lesson in the process of seeing and a demonstration of the patience and practice that it demands. The revelatory in a photograph happens precisely because eyes are borrowed.

Along the highway and amid the vast landscape of Shore's image is a painted billboard that displays an idyllic if disheveled painting of a mountain, an explicit contrast to the dry flatlands of southern Oregon. The starkly different landscapes, one real, one fictive, each illuminate the other. And the apparent care with which Shore emphasizes the relationship is immediately obvious. He includes details that define the real landscape as unkempt and indistinct, heightening the comparison with the fictive one. The power lines extending from the horizon bisect the billboard, which in its stubborn flatness resists the receding pictorial space and the strong diagonals around it. A nip of asphalt in the bottom left corner of the frame refers to the American highway, while most of the foreground consists of a gravel driveway, tall weeds, and a timber and barbed-wire fence. Even the sky is well-chosen for its ordinariness, a messy mix of cumulus and high-strata clouds, which allows the clear blue sky of the billboard an additional prominence. If the juxtaposition of two qualitatively different types of landscapes does not make a comparison obvious, the dual frame does. The edge of the centered billboard duplicates that of the photo, immediately establishing the artificiality of its construction. It ceases to be just another billboard along Route 97 and becomes a picture with meaning, one that offers a critique of the American landscape and the nature of image making.

By placing a painted landscape in a photographed "real" landscape, the picture challenges the established cultural narratives each represents. The billboard portrays the great American landscape in all its optimism: cloud-free sky, sparkling lake, conifer forest, and towering yet graceful snowcapped mountain. Although the slogan has been painted over and part of the sign has fallen off, the image remains as an idealized portrait of nature and domesticated wilderness. While this version stands out against the ordinariness of the Oregon plains, that landscape too speaks of a narrative. The wide western plains were slowly traversed by settlers, who gained a tenuous hold on the wild land. Doesn't that landscape also have traces of the heroic, perhaps codified by the Western and other filmed vistas?

Few travelers along Route 97 would have these ideas. It is the photographic act that provokes them. They are in the nature of the photograph, in particular in the dualism between the instant the shutter is pressed and the enduring status of the image, in the tension between the material surface of the paper and the accurate reproduction of depth, and in the intentional, uncompromising exclusion of the rest of the world. They are also in the composition, in particular in the pause created by having one image of an artificial nature inside a larger image of a real nature, an almost effortless gaze across one landscape and into the space of another.

There is a stillness in the work of Stephen Shore, seen particularly well in this image, that is created by a calm precision of composition, a remarkable clarity of detail, and the absence of human life. This stillness provokes the viewer to look into the image for an extended time, but it also gives a sense of unease and distance. It is this feeling that provides an estrangement from the subject matter, that allows the viewer to grasp the relationships present and to question them.

BACKGROUND:
A VIEW FROM AN APARTMENT, 2004–2005

Jeff Wall's photograph *A view from an apartment* is also a picture within a picture, an urban exterior framed by a domestic interior (fig. 3). As in Shore's Oregon view, the relationship between the two landscapes elucidates the larger idea of the photograph. Wall, however, does not use overt compositional devices. Rather, he develops an unease and strangeness through a painstaking creation

4   For a discussion on the process of selection and the creation of new order within a photograph, see Stephen Shore, *The Nature of Photographs*, 2nd ed. (London: Phaidon, 2007), 37–95.

Fig. 3 Jeff Wall, *A view from an apartment*, 2004–2005, transparency in lightbox, 167.0 × 244.0 cm.

and enactment of the scene in front of the camera, enabling a close, precise control over the setting.

Wall's work blurs two photographic traditions: film and reportage. His images have a strong narrative, yet there is also the naturalness and immediacy of encountering a real event. Wall exploits the ease with which viewers ascribe truth to a photograph but also qualifies and challenges that ease. Much of Wall's work depicts scenes he witnesses that relate to a particular idea he is following, which he then reenacts or stages for the camera. Each is constructed in minute detail. Part of the strangeness sensed by viewers is the uncomfortableness of the ambiguity between reality and artifice. Is the scene real or invented, by actors or subjects, in one photo or many?

Wall's process reinforces this ambiguity. For *A view from an apartment* he wanted to photograph Vancouver Harbor from an interior. He searched for months for an apartment with the right view. Then he held auditions to find the young woman he envisioned, selecting the young art student at the left of the photograph. Wall explained to her the nature of the collaboration and his ideas for the piece, then left her to furnish and inhabit the apartment

for several months. A video camera recorded her actions. Finally, she and Wall looked for an event to re-create for the photograph. In all, the process was an elaborate orchestration aimed at finding a complete ordinariness.

Wall and his subject chose to focus on the act of ironing napkins, perhaps a trivial domestic event but one that shows care and basic maintenance of a common world. The art student asked a friend to join her: the woman reading on the sofa, absorbed in a magazine. In addition to creating the setting, Wall manipulated the photograph itself, which is a composite of many different shots. One exposure was used for the exterior, another for the interior. Wall altered the colors to make it what he called "pleasant and enjoyable to look at."[5]

For all the effort to emulate the real, the artificiality is striking. Both women appear staged, despite the casualness of their poses, especially the original subject as she turns to face the camera. The viewpoint, up high in the room, also gives a feeling of imposition. The presence of the camera, and therefore the viewers, in this intimate scene extends an immediate awareness of the act of looking, of a divide between actor and audience, of a

5   Jeff Wall, interview with Stedelijk Museum Amsterdam, "Artist Talk: Jeff Wall, Chapter 3: A View from an Apartment (2003–2005)," posted by Stedelijk Museum Amsterdam, April 2014, https://youtu.be/RNUqpyjOGVA.

self-conscious complicity in the image. Beyond this choreography of people, it is the management of clutter and the refined calibration of the relationships between objects that tell the story and give weight to the ideas behind the image.

One set of relationships—between interior and exterior—is established by the window as it divides and frames the scene. The window acts as a cutting line between inside and outside, a role marked particularly by a pair of scissors on the windowsill, and sets up a dialogue between the objects in the room and those in the landscape beyond. *ID* magazine links to the ship *Hanjin*; the yellow, pink, and purple flowers to the muted green conifers; the glass bottle of water to the wintry sea. Each pairing tells a story of global transport, artificial nature, and the heightened comfort that forms contemporary domesticity. The lights reflected in the window connect the two worlds, highlighting both their separateness and their interrelatedness: the apartment is reflected in the landscape; the landscape is made into the apartment.[6]

More stories become evident the longer a viewer looks at this photograph, additional comparisons are made between objects, and any lingering feeling of naturalness and normality is lost. It is this realization of artifice, present also in the works by Manet and Shore, that allows an observer to understand that he or she is looking not at a scene but at a set of relationships that relate to what Clark calls "doubts about looking." It is not just particular relationships but relationships in general that are questioned. With doubt comes distance and a separation from the initial subject and setting. The estrangement leaves the viewer in a different space, one that does not accept the relationships depicted but attempts to question them to gain a better understanding.

Wall's image, then, far from its banal beginnings as a view from an apartment, sets up a mirror to the human condition and insists on an awareness of subjectivity, distancing the viewer so that he or she may look back on the world with new eyes. In this sense, Wall's work follows from the approach of Bertolt Brecht: "'The situation is complicated by the fact that less than ever does the mere reflection of reality reveal anything about reality ... The reification of human relations—the factory, say—means that they are no longer explicit. So something must in fact be *built up*, something artificial, posed.'"[7]

TEXTURE: MUSIC OF MOUNTAINS AND WATERS (LANDSCAPE WITH PURE SOUND) (山水清音圖), 1707

François Jullien, in his book *The Great Image Has No Form*, quotes a critic from the Song Dynasty: "The mountains in rain or the mountains in fair weather are easy for a painter to figure ... but should fair weather tend towards rain, or should rain tend toward the return of fair weather, ... between there and there is not,—that is what is difficult to figure."[8] What most painters in the Western tradition would consider a technical challenge presents to those in the Eastern tradition a philosophical conundrum, where brushstrokes trace not only figure but the border between existence and non-existence. The subject matter consists of the precise moments of flux in which form is uncertain and the nature of reality most evident.

Unlike the works by Manet, Shore, and Wall, this early 18th-century painting by the artist Shi Tao of the early Qing dynasty does not provide a critical space from which to reflect on the nature of place; rather, it offers a close experience of landscape through which an understanding comes (fig. 4). The dialectical tradition that forms the bedrock of Western thought and therefore much of Western art is here an anathema. The process of estrangement that occurs in the works of the European and North American artists cited, which creates a distance between the viewer and the subject matter that allows for a questioning of relationships, happens here in a different way. The painter has suffused his brushstrokes with the experience of landscape to such an extent that the landscape, the painter, and the viewer are considered a single entity. In Western art, in the works of Claude Lorrain, for example, an experience of landscape might be conjured by an exquisite naturalness that entices the observer to enter the picture and take a stroll through the landscape. Shi Tao's work, by contrast, goes beyond the imitation of the landscape to reveal its essence through concept and sensation. This detachment from structure is a different form of estrangement: it is a removal from defined forms into sensation, impression, and texture; it is the stuff of raw experience unfiltered by cognition. These unprocessed sensations do not imply a lack of articulation; instead, an alternate vocabulary describes or rather emits a sense of place.

Of the unity he creates, Shi Tao wrote: "'Before I turned fifty, I had not yet given birth to myself in the

6   Michael Fried, *Why Photography Matters as Art as Never Before* (New Haven: Yale University Press, 2008), 59.

7   Bertolt Brecht, quoted in Walter Benjamin, "Little History of Photography," in *Walter Benjamin: Selected Writings*, ed. Michael W. Jennings, Howard Eiland, and

Gary Smith, trans. Rodney Livingstone et al., vol. 2, pt. 2, *1931–1934* (Cambridge, MA: Belknap Press of Harvard University Press, 2005), 526; italics original.

8   François Jullien, *The Great Image Has No Form, or On the Nonobject through Painting*, trans. Jane Marie Todd (Chicago: University of Chicago Press, 2009), 1.

landscape. Not that I treated the landscape as a mediocre thing, but I let the landscape exist independently and on its own.' But now 'the landscape calls upon me to speak in its place.'"[9] Landscape and image are therefore two different expressions of the same thing, and the painter is not an imitator but a translator and conduit between the two versions. *Music of Mountains and Waters* is not a view of a landscape but an experience of one, a cultural manifestation of landscape itself. (In this light, it is useful to acknowledge that in 17th- and early 18th-century China, painting, poetry, and garden design were considered a single discipline.)

The union of painter, landscape, and viewer, and what it reveals about the relationship between humanity and nature, is expressed most vividly in Shi Tao's painting through the totality of composition and the quality of texture. An immense range of topographies, weather patterns, rock formations, and flora is evident in the contours of the painting. The image offers not just a fragment of a landscape but a multitude of landscapes compressed in a single visual space. The negation of depth, and of definite form, leads to the impression of the infinite. Paths don't end but fade out imperceptibly or turn a corner, allowing the mind to continue even though the eye fails to see. Land is defined not by a line but by a shifting field of texture—trees fluttering, grass waving—giving rise to an ever changing, ever undefinable form. In Shi Tao's treatise on painting he wrote that the mountains, water, and trees are "'rendered up only in part,' 'amputated as they are at both ends.' 'So that, with every movement of the brush, and in every place of figuration, there is nothing that is not abruptly cut short.'"[10] Each form is unrooted, moving into absence, suggesting the possibility of further forms and landscapes. Sensation is also translated in a kind of totality: observers not only see each tree, each leaf blowing in the wind, but practically hear them too. The brushstrokes are almost audible, each flick suggesting a certain frequency. The sound of the landscape resonates in Shi Tao's brush to produce a startling effect of immanence. The sensation comes across most clearly in a reading of the painting as pure texture, that is, not tree but pattern. The rhythms of ink foster an aural patina that creates an overwhelming sensation of being in a landscape of constant movement.

With such intensity of texture and detail, the two figures in the pavilion on the side of the painting are almost lost. Although they seem inconsequential, it is their

Fig. 4 Shi Tao, *Music of Mountains and Water* (*Landscape with Pure Sound*), 1707, ink on paper, 102.6 × 42.5 cm.

9 Brecht, quoted in Jullien, *Great Image*, 133.

10 Brecht, quoted in Jullien, *Great Image*, 10.

presence that allows the viewer to enter into the painting and find a sense of scale and comprehension. It also situates humankind in harmony with nature; they are interrelated and part of the same system, a marked difference from Western traditions in which nature is often depicted as an antagonistic other. This harmony is not benign or pastoral, however; the vertiginous landscape approaches the sublime, and the heightened sensations, though frequently found in the image, are not always soothing. The consequential aspect of a unity between humankind and nature as regards the idea of landscape is the possibility that nature is molded by humanity as much as humanity is molded by nature. It is this reciprocity that Shi Tao referred to when he said he speaks "in its place." If an entire landscape can be captured in a painting, cannot a landscape be made to capture the qualities of a painting? Even with painting and horticulture held as the same act, the practice extends far beyond the garden walls. It represents a continuity between aesthetic production and production of landscape, a simulacra of painting in the landscape.

MONTAGE:
FRIEDRICHSTRASSE SKYSCRAPER PROJECT,
VIEWED FROM THE NORTH, 1921

Since the origins of photography montage has been used to portray illusory worlds. The camera even has a built-in capacity for montage: the double exposure. Images in which the background of one photo is placed behind the foreground of another to create visual puns, improved scenes, or fantastical environments can be found from the 1850s onward.[11] But it was the Dada movement of the 1920s that first explored photomontage for its artistic and expressive potential. A montage is a collection of heterogeneous elements from multiple sources arranged to form a unified image. The radical reuse of mechanically reproduced images that subverted all previous notions of art and the surreal became the focus of the Berlin Dada scene with Hannah Hoch, Raoul Hausmann, John Heartfield, Kurt Schwitters, and others as the principal protagonists. It was Mies van der Rohe's close friendship with Hannah Hoch and his attendance at the First International Dada Fair in 1920 that transformed his standard architectural montages into more considered works of representation that were closely aligned with the avant-garde principles of the day.[12]

In this light the photograph used in the montage for the northern view of the proposal for the Friedrichstrasse Skyscraper takes on increased significance (fig. 5). It is not just a neutral background depiction of the site, used to establish scale and context, but a visual element that plays an active role in constructing the message of the image and must be considered with respect to the Dada project of montage. The photograph is a Berlin *veduta* of the early Weimar-era city, empty, poor, and weary. It appears to be firmly rooted in the material culture of the 19th-century city, hardly a paragon for the 20th-century metropolis that it is to become. The montage as a whole is often read as a study in contrasts, a singular modern vision of crystalline glass rising from the tumbling dirty streets of a stone city. However, the photographic element acts in a further, more productive way. It actively provides a conceptual framework for the architecture and constructs a mental space entirely on its own through which the background—the object—is viewed. Moreover, the photograph sets out an idea of the city with which the project engages and forms a dialogue.

A horse pulling a laden cart, two men working in the road, hotel guests coming and going: the plainness of the scene goes a long way toward typifying it. It is not a monumental view of a street, nor does it possess an identifying object or accentuate one feature above another. It could be a street in many European cities of the time, a working thoroughfare with worn pavements and stone facades, water pumps and anachronistic, disheveled power lines cutting through. In the far distance, visible as a silhouette in the fog, stands the Kaiser-Friedrich-Museum (now called the Bode Museum), a temple of humanism partly blocked by a skewed utility pole. In short, the background photograph is not just an image of Friedrichstrasse, Berlin. Instead, it represents the European city of its day, the very fabric on the verge of rupture by undercurrents of modernity and technological advancement and also by the feelings of alienation, transience, and juxtaposition that occupied the mental space of the modern metropolis.

The haunting appearance of the figure in the foreground recalls another street photographer of the early 20th century: Eugène Atget. Atget too photographed the ordinary. His Paris scenes are of open doorways, old shopfronts, and empty streets; people are often obscured, glimpsed through glass, or seen as ghosts since the exposure was generally too long to allow for movement. Eschewing the recognizable and the picturesque, Atget's

11   Dawn Ades, *Photomontage* (London: Thames & Hudson, 1976), 19, 89–90.

12   Martino Stierli, "Mies Montage," *AA Files* 61 (2010): 66–67.

Fig. 5   Ludwig Mies van der Rohe, Friedrichstrasse Skyscraper
project, viewed from the north, 1921, photomontage.

work is a more casual, disarming, matter-of-fact study of
detail and place, content in only describing. There is a
silence in Atget's photographs, a silence of time past—his
scenes are of a Paris lost to modernization—but also a
silence of looking that creates a detachment and distance
from the thing itself. Walter Benjamin writes of Atget: "He
cleanses this atmosphere—indeed he dispels it altogether:
he initiates the emancipation of object from aura."[13]

If Atget initiated the emancipation, Mies can be said
to have completed it. The architecture of the Friedrichstrasse Skyscraper reduces the building-object to a
crystalline minimum, to horizontal floor slabs and vertical
plates of glass, to structure and space. He eradicates any
qualities that construct an architectural "aura"—materiality, craftsmanship, continuity of historical forms,
distinction of place. What remains is an architecture of
the generic, an archetypal expression of the mechanized
city. It is a distillation and negative critique of Grossstadt
architecture similar to Ludwig Hilberseimer's project for a
high-rise city, published in 1927.[14] Mies's skyscraper represents an apotheosis of reduction and abstraction within

architecture, an act equaled in art by Malevich's *Black
Square* of 1915, to which Mies's separate charcoal drawing
of the Friedrichstrasse project with its rectangular elevation expressed as a pure volume of black coal streaks bears
a striking resemblance.

But while Hilberseimer's drawings (and Malevich's
paintings) remain in a kind of paper space, Mies's use of
montage forces a comparison and contextualization with
the real. It is impossible to avoid asking questions and
defining distinctions in the relationship between the real
and the projected, and this way of looking creates an
active critical space within the image. Pier Vittorio Aureli
posits that the plinth as used by Mies in his later North
American projects sets up a space of exception within
the city and thereby allows the architecture to reify the
political and economic forces that shape urbanization
and at the same time establish distance from them, a
type of critical space.[15] Within Mies's montage, the distinction between light and dark works in a similar way.
The dark foreground frames the light building, setting up
a mute reflection of the idea of the city represented by the

13   Benjamin, "Little History," 518.

14   Ludwig Hilberseimer, *Metropolisarchitecture* (New
York: Columbia GSAPP Books on Architecture, 2012).

15   Pier Vittorio Aureli, *The Possibility of an Absolute
Architecture* (Cambridge, MA: MIT Press, 2011), 40–42.

photograph. It makes the electric wires stand out even more.

Montage, then, generates a kind of prefiguration in looking. It shades in subtle ways the other components of the image, creating a far richer dialogue of ideas than the constitutive parts would on their own. The differing characteristics of the parts create a secondary dimension to the image, one that recounts other narratives. André Breton, in the catalog to an early Paris exhibition of Dada montages, wrote of the power of using multiple source materials to create a heterogeneous whole: each component attains "two widely separated realities without departing from the realm of our experience, of bringing them together and drawing a spark from their contact."[16] Within the context of architectural visualization, montage offers the potential to do more than simply locate the project in a site: it allows for the advancement of a critical argument.

FROM ASPECT, IDEA

The five constituent elements of the works shown here—surface, frame, background, texture, and montage—represent five possible approaches to the construction of an idea of place in an image. Moreover, the way they have been used sets up a distance between the viewer and the subject matter that allows for a certain critical reflection on the idea of place put forth, an estrangement, but a productive one. The approaches are by no means purely didactic; they demonstrate the capacity of the image to encapsulate an essence of the contemporary city, to convey an immediacy of argument, and in architecture among other fields, to impart the intentions of a project in a realm other than standard modes of representation such as plans or models.

Working with surface allows the transcendence of a pictorial unity by means of the dissolution of depth, causing doubt in the viewer and fostering a questioning of the nature of spatial and social relationships within the modern metropolis. Working with frame emphasizes deliberate acts of inclusion in and exclusion from the image and the subsequent heightening of visual elements by repetition of that frame, thus controlling and parsing the understanding of the subject matter. Working with background permits a subtle illumination and manipulation of detail to establish a wider narrative that speaks directly to the nature of domesticity within the city and

creates a distance between the viewer and the picture through an oscillation between the artificial and the real. Working with texture brings about a confluence of mark and sensation that can speak of an underlying idea of landscape. Working with montage, one of the most widely used approaches to imagine an architectural or urban project in its context, both provides the environment and actively shades the reading of the architecture in the conceptual space of the work.

In architecture, there are two ways of going from the abstract to the real, from the working material—plans, sections, and other drawings—to something understandable as form and space. One way is built construction; the other is drawn projection. While it is the former that is generally the ultimate goal, it is the latter that consumes much of the practice of architecture and, within the academic studio, represents the final realization. Projection into perspectival space results in a static image that shares a language with the visual arts and applies various layers of visual culture. The potential this affords a project is coincident with the power of art itself. Emotions, thoughts, statements, atmospheres can be communicated in an image, lending a reading of a project that is often apart from its main pragmatic considerations. Projection also situates the project within a media space and forces it, at its inception, to confront the limits of the dominant form of representation—the image—that will be used to disseminate it.

The ability to successfully communicate is contingent on a familiarity with, even a literacy within, this language and the fundamental aspects of an image that give meaning. Within the Project on China studio, the elements used to construct an idea of place have formed the basis for students to think about image in their projects. Designs are projected into a pictorial space in order to represent the work both critically and spatially. The image has furnished a way to test the arguments of a project, to act as a laboratory for the architecture itself in which potential futures can be not just imagined but also reflected upon.

Investigations into image making within the Project on China have followed some of the themes set forth here. Carly Augustine and Nicolas Lee, with the project "Within the Frame," offer an interior image in which the process of flattening and providing an alternative organizational structure replaces traditional perspectival rules, as seen with Manet (page 278 top). The flat planes and overlaying of the objects construct multiple surfaces that

16   André Breton, preface to Max Ernst exhibition, Paris, May 1921, reprinted in Max Ernst, *Beyond Painting* (New York, 1948), 177.

play off one another. Framed portraits of the founding leaders of the Communist party, a colorful landscape bounded by an expanse of gray, sparsely arrayed domestic objects: these all identify the conceptual structure of the project as much as its spatial one.

The establishment of a point or line that detaches an image from the continuum of reality and makes new relationships within an image—the determination of view—is probably one of the most crucial decisions made during the creation or construction of a photograph or a rendering made within a three-dimensional modeling program. Stephen Shore's works demonstrate the productive possibilities of such a determination. As more architects become photographers, due to either the proliferation of cameras or the ubiquity of photographic processes within the creation of project imagery, and as more renderings leave the realm of the objective, attention to the choice of view is more important than ever. The process of establishing visual and therefore argumentative relationships by way of multiple frames has been used in many of the images of the studio, for instance in a dwelling interior from the project "Non-Urban Apparatus" by Shaoliang Hua, Jyri Eskola, and Radhya Adityavarman (page 290 top). Here, exterior frames interior (and vice versa) both spatially and in the image. Subsequent visual relationships are established between the objects inside and the landscape beyond, and the realm of labor is juxtaposed with the domain of the domestic. The use of figures from Millet's *Gleaners* in the distance, framed by the landscape and the window, underscores a connection to the figure from Taiqian in the foreground. Both subjects are living through a changing relationship between agriculture and everyday life, albeit in different contexts and eras.

The relentless display of seemingly unimportant items that ultimately convey the force of the message—as executed by Wall—is shown in the domestic interior of Bicen Yue and Siwei Guo's project, "The City as a Field" (page 308 lower right). The array of artifacts defines the subjectivity of the inhabitant of the dwelling both culturally and socially. The connection between, for instance, the fields outside and the produce inside, or the continuation of texture from the rows of corn plants to the floorboards, hints at the transitory nature of the architecture of the field. The control of the ambient is a key approach in architectural image making since it can portray the cycles and particularities of an envisioned occupancy.

A certain realness of texture that allows a viewer to be drawn into and experience a scene is apparent in the project "Common Fields: Frameworks for Rural Life" by Feng Shen and Zhenhuan Xu. In their views of the village throughout the four seasons, in particular autumn and winter (page 284), attention to the quality of textures and to the harmony between different parts of the image evidences the intertwined nature of landscape and village life. From ephemeral impressions of snow and wind to the perennial activities of harvesting and resting to the permanent structures of timber and concrete, a careful orchestration of textures, similar to that of Shi Tao, captures a spirit and idea of place. This is less a matter of medium and technique and more a demonstration of intent toward realizing sensations.

The distillation of the Dada practice of montage, with its avant-garde anarchy, into a controlled use of the technique by Mies offers an apt lesson on the origins of the approach and reclaims some of its potential for the polemical. In "A Few Sharp Lines," Ashley Takacs and Gabriel Tomasulo employ particular photographs of the Macau context in their exterior views (page 191). With an architecture that indexes local materiality and also represents a legible urban artifact, the montage establishes a language of taxonomy and a careful documentation of context that allows a specific reading of the project. The intervention always remains in the background, allowing the photograph to be read first and thereby enabling its qualities to influence the understanding of the architecture.

The idea of the city, by its nature, cannot be comprehended in a single form. It is in the qualities of a photograph, or in the arrangement of surfaces, or in the sensation of a texture, that an understanding may be grasped. The specificity of the fragment that can be captured in an image allows this to happen. The drawing works of the studio, by contrast, are a totalizing form of representation. Their orthogonality and omnipresence allow systems and frameworks to be exhibited in their entirety. The drawings have a didactic purpose: to illustrate, inform, explain. The standards that give a drawing clarity also flatten the qualities of the design that is represented. These conventions make a project comparable and thereby allow it to enter the discipline of architecture. Thus it is in the critical potential of an image, in its singularity of view, its multivalency, its specificity of place, that the viewer can start to understand, without the loss of layers and nuance, the built-up relationships of the contemporary city. A singular frame can provide a view—a moment's understanding—as the observer stands still in the crowd.

Studio Credits

COMMON FRAMEWORKS: RETHINKING THE
DEVELOPMENTAL CITY, OPTION STUDIO, FALL 2012,
FALL 2013, FALL 2014

Studio Instructor
    Christopher C. M. Lee
Teaching Associate
    Simon Whittle

COMMON FRAMEWORKS: RETHINKING THE
DEVELOPMENTAL CITY, FALL 2012

Students
    Sonja Cheng, Aanya Chugh, Lik Hang Gu, Waqas
    Jawaid, Michael Leef, Roy Yu-Ta Lin,
    Ryan Otterson, Ryley Poblete, Matthew Scarlett,
    John Martin Tubles, Jisoo Yang, Jonghyun Yi
Analysis
    Yuan Zhan, Roy Yu-Ta Lin, Dingliang Yang
Final Review Critics
    Sean Chiao, Felipe Correa, Eric Höweler, Hung-
    Chih Liu, Florian Idenburg, Nancy Lin, Rahul
    Mehrotra, Mohsen Mostafavi, Joan Ockman,
    Hashim Sarkis, Renata Sentkiewicz, Ben van Berkel,
    Charles Waldheim, Bing Wang, Zhao Yanjing

MACAU: CROSS-BORDER CITY, FALL 2013

Students
    Fabiana Alvear, Sung Joon Chae, Hao Chen, Yun Fu,
    Jing Guo, Navajeet KC, Yatian Li, Chen Hao Lin,
    Mina Nishio, Rae Pozdro, Josh Schecter, Ashley
    Takacs, Gabriel Tomasulo
Final Review Critics
    Iñaki Ábalos, Eve Blau, Sean Chiao, Felipe Correa,
    Piper Gaubatz, Florian Idenburg, Nancy Lin, Rahul
    Mehrotra, Mohsen Mostafavi, Albert Pope, Peter G.
    Rowe, Hashim Sarkis, Paola Viganò, Bing Wang

THE COUNTRYSIDE AS A CITY, FALL 2014

Students
    Radhya Adityavarman, Carly Augustine, Jyri Eskola,
    Siwei Gou, Shaoliang Hua, Nicolas Lee, Wilfred
    Leung, Alexandro Medina, Feng Shen, PG Smit,
    Dimitris Venizelos, Zhenhuan Xu, Bicen Yue
Final Review Critics
    Iñaki Ábalos, Leire Asensio-Villoria, Eve Blau,
    Sean Chiao, Felipe Correa, Linxue Li, Nancy Lin,
    Jing Liu, David Mah, Rahul Mehrotra, Mohsen
    Mostafavi, Guy Perry, Moshe Safdie, Nick R. Smith,
    Bing Wang

Contributor Biographies

LING FAN received his MArch from Princeton University and is a DDes candidate at the Harvard GSD. Based in Beijing, he practices spatial art and architectural design. He intervenes in issues of urbanism and architecture with design, writing, and teaching. He founded FANStudio in 2010 and has taught at the China Central Academy of Fine Arts.

PIPER GAUBATZ is Geography Program Head at the University of Massachusetts, Amherst. An urban geographer specializing in the study of urban change, development, and planning in East Asia and the United States, she is particularly interested in the processes that shape urban space, and especially in the historic and contemporary linkages between policy, practice, and physical and social urban forms. She is author and coauthor, respectively, of two books on Chinese cities: *Beyond the Great Wall: Urban Form and Transformation on the Chinese Frontiers* (1996) and *The Chinese City* (2013).

HAR YE KAN is a research associate and postdoctoral fellow at the Harvard GSD, where she completed her DDes degree. She received a BA from Cambridge University and an AM from Harvard Graduate School of Arts and Sciences. The author and coauthor of several articles, she focuses on East Asian architecture and urbanism and is the coauthor of *Urban Intensities: Contemporary Housing Types and Territories* (2014).

CHRISTOPHER C. M. LEE is the principal of Serie Architects. He is Associate Professor in Practice of Urban Design at the Harvard GSD. Lee graduated from the Architectural Association School of Architecture and received his PhD in architecture and urbanism from the Berlage Institute and the Delft University of Technology. He is the editor of *Common Frameworks: Rethinking the Developmental City in China, Part 1, Xiamen: The Megaplot* (2013), *Part 2, Macau: Cross-Border City* (2014), and *Part 3, Taiqian: The Countryside as a City* (2015); coauthor of *Working in Series* (2010); and coeditor of *Typological Formations: Renewable Building Types and the City* (2007) and a special issue of *Architectural Design, Typological Urbanism: Projective Cities* (2011).

MOHSEN MOSTAFAVI, an architect and educator, is Dean and Alexander and Victoria Wiley Professor of Design at the Harvard GSD. His recent publications include *Ecological Urbanism* (2010; recently translated into Chinese, Portuguese, and Spanish), *In the Life of Cities* (2012), *Nicholas Hawksmoor: London Churches* (2015), and *Ethics of the Urban: The City and the Spaces of the Political* (2016).

PETER G. ROWE is Raymond Garbe Professor of Architecture and Urban Design and Harvard University Distinguished Service Professor. He has taught at Harvard since 1985 and served as Dean of the Harvard GSD between 1992 and 2004. He is also the chairman and cofounder of the Studio for Urban Analysis (SURBA) in Brooklyn, New York. He is the author of numerous books and articles, including the recent publications *Emergent Architectural Territories in East Asian Cities* (2011) and, as coauthor, *Urban Intensities: Contemporary Housing Types and Territories* (2014).

SIMON WHITTLE is an architect and associate at Serie Architects, where he has led urban design and architecture projects in Asia, the Middle East, and Europe. He has been a teaching fellow at the Harvard GSD since 2011. Whittle graduated from the Architectural Association School of Architecture in London.

DINGLIANG YANG is a teaching fellow, research associate, and DDes candidate at the Harvard GSD. He received an MArch in urban design from the GSD and was awarded the Urban Planning and Design Thesis Prize and the Paul M. Heffernan International Travel Award.

JIANFEI ZHU is Associate Professor in Architecture at the University of Melbourne. He studied architecture at Tianjin University and University College London. He is the author of *Chinese Spatial Strategies: Imperial Beijing 1420-1911* (2004) and *Architecture of Modern China: A Historical Critique* (2009) and the editor of *Sixty Years of Chinese Architecture 1949-2009* (in Chinese, 2009). He has published numerous academic papers, including "Bentham, Foucault and Hanfei" (2003), "Criticality in between China and the West" (2005), and "Robin Evans in 1978" (2011). His research centers on politics, theory, and Chinese architecture, with a focus on statehood and its implications.

Illustration Credits

Fabiana Alvear: 147, 156 bottom

Architecture Institute of South China University of Technology: 229, 230

© 2015 Artists Rights Society (ARS), New York/VG Bild-Kunst, Bonn: 321

Joshua Bolchover and Peter Hasdell, "Opening the Frontier Closed Area: A Mutual Benefit Zone": 119

Peter Calthorpe, "Low Carbon Cities: Principles and Practices for China's Next Generation of Growth", © Calthorpe Associates: 21

Melinda Chan: 102, 105

K. Y. Cheng: 115

Chengdu Institute of Planning and Design: 234 middle, 234 bottom

http://china.huanqiu.com/photo/2013-01/2680666. html: 238 top

Construction Department, Guangdong Province; Development Bureau, Hong Kong SAR; and Secretariat for Transport and Public Works, Macau SAR, "Building Coordinated and Sustainable World-Class City-Region, Public Digest": 107

Wayne Cooper, from Colin Rowe and Fred Koetter Fred, *Collage City*: 20 right

Design Alliance Weihai China: 19 right

http://earthobservatory.nasa.gov: 47

http://www.eastartwork.com/new_page_ pmeiyijiaozptuo27.htm: 214 third from top

http://forum.xcitefun.net/richest-village-of-china-huaxi-village-t69204.html: 233 bottom

Piper Gaubatz, "Looking West Toward Mecca: Muslim Enclaves in Chinese Cities": 125 bottom

Google Earth: 214 top, 214 second from top, 221, 270 top

Siwei Gou: 269 bottom right

Walter Gropius, *The New Architecture and the Bauhaus*: 20 left top

Chaolin Gu, Xiaohui Yuan, and Jing Guo: 49 right, 50

ChengHe Guan: 144 bottom

Guisui quanzhi: 125 top

Hangzhou Municipal Planning Bureau: 19 left

Hengqin Land and Resource Bureau: 111 top right

HOK Group: 20 left bottom

Shaoliang Hua: 255

Yunsheng Huang, from Nancy Shatzman Steinhardt, *Chinese Imperial City Planning*: 28 left

Huaxi Village Government, http://xf.people.com.cn/ GB/42459/57445/57449/4022860.html: 233 right

Waqas Jawaid: 59, 62 left, 63 bottom, 66

User:Jérôme/Wikimedia Commons/CC-BY-SA-3.0: 124 left

Felipe Jorge: 113 left top

Spiro Kostof, *The City Shaped: Urban Patterns and Meanings throughout History*: 28 right

Leon Krier: 23 right

http://laboratoireurbanismeinsurrectionnel.blogspot. co.uk/2012/03/mao-zedong-dazhai-une-commune-populaire.html: 214 bottom

Lay-Out Planning Consultants, Ltd., Tongling Urban Planning and Reconnaissance and Surveying Design Institute: 235

Christopher C. M. Lee: 111 bottom, 213, 220, 222 left, 225 left bottom, 253

Nicolas Lee: 225 left top, 268, 269 top, 269 bottom left

Michael Leef/Ryan Otterson: 19 bottom

Jie Li, *Yingzao Fashi*; see *Liang Sicheng quanji*: 41 right

Chen Hao Lin: 153 bottom

Roy Yu-Ta Lin: 27 left, 63 top, 65, 67 bottom, 68 right

Dunzhen Liu, *Zhongguo gudai jianzhu shi*: 35, 42 top left, 42 top right, 42 bottom left

Duanfang Lu, "Third World Modernism: Utopia, Modernity and the People's Commune in China": 228

Edouard Manet/Wikimedia Commons/Public Domain: 313

photo by mikehedge.com: 17

Ryan Otterson: 14, 69 bottom

Palace Museum, Beijing, China: 40–41

Trevor Patt: 211

Aldo Rossi, *The Architecture of the City*: 30

Aldo Rossi, "Due Progetti": 31, 32, 33

Joseph Sakalak: 23 left

http://m.secretchina.com/node/490976: 233 top

Sebastiano Serlio, *The Five Books of Architecture*: 25

Shanghai Tongji Urban Planning and Design Institute: 234 top

Feng Shen: 225 right

Shi Tao/Shanghai Museum/Public Domain: 319

© Stephen Shore, courtesy 303 Gallery, New York/ Digital Image © The Museum of Modern Art/ Licensed by SCALA/Art Resource, NY: 315

Victor F. S. Sit, *Macau through 500 Years: Emergence and Development of an Untypical Chinese City*: 109

Kenny Teo: 111 top left

Gabriel Tomasulo: 152, 153 top, 163

Jiri Tondl: 27 right

US Signal Corps/CC-BY-SA-3.0: 127 top

Dimitris Venizelos: 262, 263

Virtual Beijing, http://beijing.virtualcities.fr/Asset/ Preview/vcMap_ID-811_No-1.jpeg: 29

Courtesy of Jeff Wall: 317

Wangcheng, from Nancy Shatzman Steinhardt, *Chinese Imperial City Planning*: 26

http://www.wdl.org/zh/item/3019/zoom/#group=1& page=3: 39

Simon Whittle: 1, 70 top, 70 middle, 208

http://en.wikipedia.org/wiki/Go_%28game%29: 38 left

http://zh.wikipedia.org/wiki/麻将: 38 right

World Development Report 2009: Reshaping Economic Geography: 129 right

Adapted from Weiping Wu and Piper Gaubatz, *The Chinese City*: 127 bottom

User:Xemenendura/Wikimedia Commons/ CC-BY-SA-3.0: 124 right

Xiamen Planning Bureau/HOK Group: 70 bottom

http://www.gd.xinhuanet.com/newscenter/ ztbd/2006-10/16/xin_21100316143300883657.jpg: 129 left

Fengxuan Xue, *Aomen wubainian: Yige teshu Zhongguo chengshi de xingqi yu fazhan*: 133, 136, 140, 142, 144 top

Bicen Yue: 222 right, 271 top

Zhengzou Architectural Design Institute: 212, 217, 218, 237, 238 bottom, 240

Jianfei Zhu, *Chinese Spatial Strategies*: 42 bottom right, 44

Common Frameworks:
Rethinking the Developmental City in China
Christopher C. M. Lee (ed.)

Project Manager
   Simon Whittle
Consulting Editor
   Andrea Monfried
Designer
   Sam de Groot
Typeface Customization
   Dinamo.us
Proofreader
   Rebecca McNamara
Printer
   Die Keure, Belgium
Distributor
   Harvard University Press

Harvard Design Studies is published by the Harvard University Graduate School of Design.

Dean and Alexander and Victoria Wiley Professor
   Mohsen Mostafavi
Editor in Chief
   Jennifer Sigler
Publications Coordinator
   Meghan Sandberg

Sponsored by the AECOM Fund for China Studios

Cover photograph: Shanghai, c. 2012; photo by mikehedge.com

Harvard University
Graduate School of Design
48 Quincy Street
Cambridge, MA 02138
gsd.harvard.edu

Library of Congress Cataloging-in-Publication Data
Christopher C. M. Lee, editor.
Common Frameworks: Rethinking the Developmental
   City in China / Christopher C. M. Lee (ed.).
Cambridge: Harvard University Graduate School of
   Design, 2016. Series: Harvard Design Studies
Includes bibliographical references.
   LCCN 2016013943
   ISBN 978-1-934510-53-7
   1. City planning—China. 2. Urbanization—China.
      3. Cities and towns—China—Growth.
LCC NA9265 C66 2016
DDC 307.1/2160951—dc23